CRIME AND FAMILY: SELECTED ESSAYS

'Tis education forms the common mind;
just as the twig is bent the tree's inclined.
—Alexander Pope

JOAN McCord (1930–2004)

Crime *and* Family

Selected Essays of Joan McCord

Edited and with a Foreword by
GEOFFREY SAYRE-MCCORD

With an Introduction by
DAVID P. FARRINGTON

TEMPLE UNIVERSITY PRESS
Philadelphia

JOAN McCORD (1930–2004) was Professor, Department of Criminology, Temple University and Senior Fellow in the Jerry Lee Center for Criminology at the University of Pennsylvania. She was the Past President of the American Society of Criminology and was awarded the Edwin H. Sutherland Award for Outstanding Contributions to Criminology and the Prix Emile Durkheim for her work in Criminology. Among her many books, she edited *Coercion and Punishment in Long-Term Perspectives*, *Facts, Frameworks, and Forecasts*, and *Beyond Empiricism* and coauthored *The Psychopath* and *Psychopathy and Delinquency*.

Temple University Press
1601 North Broad Street
Philadelphia, PA 19122
www.temple.edu/tempress

Text design by Lynne Frost

∞

The paper used in this publication meets the requirements
of the American National Standard for Information Sciences—
Permanence of Paper for Printed Library Materials,
ANSI Z39.48-1992

Library of Congress Cataloging-in-Publication Data

McCord, Joan, 1930–2004
Crime and family: selected essays of Joan McCord /
edited with a foreword by Geoffrey Sayre-McCord;
with an introduction by David P. Farrington.
p. cm.
Includes bibliographical references and index.

ISBN 13: 978-1-59213-557-8   ISBN 10: 1-59213-557-9 (cloth: alk. paper)
ISBN 13: 978-1-59213-558-5   ISBN 10: 1-59213-558-7 (pbk.: alk. paper)
1. Juvenile delinquency—United States—Prevention.
2. Crime—United States—Prevention.   3. Family—United States.
4. Family violence—United States—Prevention.   5. Child abuse—United States.
6. Socialization—United States.   7. Cambridge-Somerville Youth Study.
I. Sayre-McCord, Geoffrey, 1956– .   II. Title.

HV9104.M3284 2007
364.360973—dc22   20006050053

2 4 6 8 9 7 5 3 1

CONTENTS

FOREWORD

Geoffrey Sayre-McCord

THESE PAPERS were selected for this collection by my mother, Joan McCord, after she discovered she had only a short time to live. They reflect the breadth and depth of the work she did from the middle 1970s until her death.

Many of the papers use the Cambridge-Somerville Youth Study data. The details of that study are well laid out in the collection, but it is worth providing a brief overview. The study was begun in the 1930s by Dr. Richard Cabot. Cabot was hopeful that a big brother/big sister/mentoring program could significantly improve a child's prospects of leading a good life, and he put in place an extensive program that offered support of a sort that seemed especially likely to help. At the same time, though, he was concerned to study the effectiveness of the treatment scientifically and with an eye to collecting data that might usefully be relied on to study the long-term impact of the intervention.

Identifying slightly over 500 boys between the ages of 5 and 13, half thought to be at risk and half not, Cabot had them paired up (matching, as much as possible, for risk factors, age, personal history, family background, and third-party reports) and then randomly assigned one member of each pair to a control group and the other to a treatment group. The treatment and control groups thus each had an equal number of boys who were at risk and boys who were not, and for each boy randomly assigned to the treatment group, there was a boy in the control group with whom he had been matched.

The treatment group was then assigned a counselor who provided a broad range of services, including tutoring, medical and psychiatric support, time in the country at summer camp, and exposure to YMCA, the Boy Scouts, and other groups. In short, the program was largely indistinguishable from the sort of mentoring programs that are now widely thought to be an effective way of helping kids in need. On average, the counselors worked with the boys for five years. The control group, in contrast, was simply left alone (although the same initial information had been gathered about them as about the treatment group). Extensive

records were kept about the boys, about what was done for them by the counselors and others, and about what the counselors observed in their interactions
with the boys' families.

In 1975 and 1976, my mother, with the help of several dedicated researchers,
tracked down 95 percent of the boys, now men, who had been in the study (with
the treatment and the control groups more or less equally represented). Although
some had died, most were still alive and the majority were living in Massachusetts, near where they had grown up. In addition to gathering various objective
measures of these peoples' lives (from court records, mental hospital records,
records from alcoholic treatment centers, and the registry of vital records and statistics in Massachusetts), they were all sent questionnaires. A little over half of
the men filled out and returned the questionnaires.

I remember vividly when the data had been collected, and she began running
some analyses. The results shocked her. She had long been impressed by the care
and good sense behind the various treatments provided by the Cambridge-
Somerville Program. So she had been thinking that she would be discovering some
real benefits from the intervention, and had in any case assumed that, at worst,
no significant benefit would be provable. What she discovered was that the treatment group was statistically significantly *worse off* than the control group along
seven crucial dimensions: (1) the treatment group was more likely to have committed two or more crimes; (2) they were more likely to show signs of alcoholism;
(3) they were more likely to show signs of mental illness; (4) they were likely to
have died younger; (5) they were more likely to have health problems (specifically stress-related health problems); (6) they were more likely to have low-pres-
tige jobs; and (7) they were more likely to be dissatisfied with their jobs. I should
emphasize that the results were statistically significant along all seven dimensions, and the standard of relative harm is, in each case, set by a widely accepted
objective measure. The longer the treatment, the more likely the harm.

These results were all the more surprising in light of the subjective reports of
the treatment group, as revealed by the questionnaires. Those reports showed
that two-thirds of those who filled out the questionnaires thought, in retrospect,
that the program had helped them. Certainly, the fact that so many of the people who had counselors thought the program was helpful is important, and it
helps to explain why people who serve as mentors are convinced that they are
actually helping. But my mother regularly pointed out that the feeling of having
been helped, and the satisfaction of thinking one has helped, are severely under-
cut by the clear evidence that this sort of intervention is likely, in fact, to harm
the very people it is intended to help.

When the results of the Cambridge-Somerville Youth Study were published
(1978),[1] they were met with two responses that are both puzzling and disturbing:

1. On the one hand, many people (especially practitioners actively
involved in various mentoring programs) insisted that while the Cambridge-Somerville Program may have failed to help, and might actually
have hurt the boys in the program, they were sure that their own programs were in fact helping. Yet their insistence on this point was

rarely accompanied by any real evidence that might deserve credibility. In some cases, of course, there were surveys and subjective reports and personal stories testifying to some perceived effectiveness of one program or another. The Cambridge-Somerville Youth Study shows, however, that such reports might go hand in hand with the program manifestly causing serious harm to those in it, so such reports should be suspect, to say the least. Indeed, the fact that people so readily claim, without appropriate evidence, that their own program is better, in the relevant respects, than the Cambridge-Somerville Program is disconcerting. It is as if a doctor were to claim that his own experience with Thalidomide, which he knows from experience cures morning sickness, constitute grounds for continuing to prescribe it despite the overwhelming scientific evidence that it causes birth defects in many cases. No one honestly concerned with the welfare of others should be ignoring objective evidence that what they are doing is harmful, even if their own experience suggests that it is having a good effect.

2. On the other hand, many people (especially those opposed to social programs introduced to help those at risk) claimed that the results of the Cambridge-Somerville Study showed that social intervention was bound to be ineffective. The Cambridge-Somerville Study shows no such thing. On the contrary, it establishes, with compelling evidence, that interventions can and do have an impact on the lives of people in the programs. The problem is that the impact might be harmful rather than beneficial. Although the Cambridge-Somerville Study is rightly seen as a cause of concern and caution, it establishes that social interventions have a measurable impact and thus gives some hope that continued efforts to introduce new programs, *followed by careful study of their effects*, are likely to lead to the discovery of some good way to help improve the lives of others.

Why was the program damaging? There are a number of possible explanations. It might be that receiving the mentoring and other help served to label the boys in ways that account for the damage; or it might be that the boys came to depend on the support and suffered from a sense of abandonment when the program ended; or it might be that the counselors conveyed to the boys a set of (upper middle-class) values that were ill-suited to the boys' circumstances and prospects. Or, perhaps, there was something about the specific form of the mentoring that explains the damage. Unfortunately, the Cambridge-Somerville data does not provide a basis for choosing among these hypotheses. They each have some plausibility, but it would be worse than unwarranted to embrace one or the other, or all of them taken together, as if we knew why the treatment program damaged the very people it was designed to help. The evidence simply is not in.

The main lesson my mother drew from her research was that anyone concerned to help others—and she was deeply committed to doing that—ought to work hard to study, in a scientifically credible way, the effect of their efforts.

Specifically, she thought it was important to establish control groups, to collect data in a way that would allow the use of objective measures of success, and to provide for a longitudinal follow-up to study the long-term effects of the intervention. She argued that when it comes to intervening in peoples' lives, we should insist on respecting the very same standards of scientific investigation as we rely on when it comes to intervening on their bodies with drugs and medical treatments. Anything less is, in effect, an abdication of our responsibility to care for those we seek to help.

A good deal of my mother's research after 1978 mined the rich fields of the Cambridge-Somerville Study—to investigate the effects of child abuse, neglect, and parental absence, the impact of the family on crime, and the etiology of alcoholism. Some of this work is reported in papers collected here. At the same time, she concentrated on questions of theory and methodology in the social sciences, working tirelessly to identify useful scientific tools and to help others design studies that will generate results likely to be taken seriously.

Throughout her career, my mother was interested in figuring out how we might properly combine an understanding of the causes of behavior with an appreciation of agents as (often) responsible for what they do. She was convinced that criminology, and psychology more broadly, needs to explore why it is that people take the various considerations they do as reasons. To focus on the etiology of behavior, on the influence of genes or socialization or happenstance, without regard to the standing of those who engage in the behavior as agents acting for (what they take to be reasons) is to ignore the very feature of humans that make them responsible for what they do. Consequently, she began working on a theory of motivation—and of what it is to act for a reason—designed to explain how human beings become agents able to act on reasons. It is a theory that takes seriously the idea that people, in acting as they do, are acting not merely as a result of various causal influences but also as a result of what they (understandably, although not always correctly) take to be reasons. Sadly, this is a research program that she was unable to pursue as far as she hoped, but it did result in what she called *The Construct Theory of Motivation*, which she articulated and defended in her "He Did It Because He Wanted To . . . ,"[2] "A Theory of Motivation and Life Course,"[3] and "Toward a Theory of Criminal Responsibility."[4]

All who knew Joan McCord knew her as a person of phenomenal intelligence, imagination, energy, and integrity. A few of us had as well the opportunity to know her as the extraordinarily loving, and incomparably wonderful, mother she was.

Notes

1. McCord, J. A thirty-year follow-up of treatment effects. *American Psychologist* 33(3): 284–289.

2. In Motivation and delinquency. Nebraska Symposium on Motivation, edited by W. Osgood, 44: 1–43. Lincoln, NE: University of Nebraska Press, 1997.

3. In *Social Dynamics of Crime and Control: New Theories for a World in Transition*, edited by Susanne Karstedt & Kai-D Bussmann, 229–241. Portland, OR: Hart Publishing, 2000.

4. In *Beyond Empiricism: Institutions and Intentions in the Study of Crime. Advances in Criminological Theory*, edited by J. McCord, 13: 147–176. Picataway, NJ: Transaction Publishers, 2004.

INTRODUCTION

DAVID P. FARRINGTON

Institute of Criminology

Cambridge University

JOAN McCORD was a brilliant pioneer in criminology. Her best-known, most influential, and greatest contributions to knowledge arose from her pioneering work on the Cambridge-Somerville Youth Study, which was the first large-scale longitudinal-experimental study ever carried out in the history of criminology. Appropriately, most of the papers in this volume report results from that study.

As the name suggests, longitudinal-experimental studies combine two of the most important methods used in criminology, by conducting a randomized experiment within a prospective longitudinal survey (Farrington, 2006). Because they are prospective longitudinal surveys, these studies provide information about the natural history of development of offending and about the effects of early risk factors on later offending. Because they are randomized experiments, these studies provide information about the impact of interventions on offending.

The Effects of Intervention

In the Cambridge-Somerville Youth Study, schools, welfare agencies, churches, and police recommended both "difficult" and "average" boys to the program, in Cambridge and Somerville, Massachusetts (parts of the Greater Boston metropolitan area). Each boy was rated on his likelihood of becoming delinquent, and 325 pairs of boys were matched on this and on age, intelligence, family background, and home environment. By the toss of a coin, one member of each pair was randomly assigned to the treatment group, and the other was randomly assigned to the control group.

The treatment program began in 1939 when the boys were aged 10 on average. Except for those dropped from the program because of a counselor shortage in 1941, treatment continued for an average of 5 years, consisting mainly of individual counseling and frequent home visits. The counselors gave well-meaning, friendly advice to the boys and their families, took them on trips and to recreational activities, tutored them in reading and arithmetic, encouraged them to participate in the YMCA and summer camps, played games with them at the project's center, encouraged them to attend church, kept in close touch with the police, and generally gave support to the boys and their families.

The first paper in this collection, "A thirty-year follow-up of treatment effects" (McCord, 1978) was a landmark paper and is perhaps the most famous article that Joan McCord ever wrote. As the name suggests, it describes a thirty-year follow-up of the treated and control boys. In 1975 and 1976, attempts were made to trace the 253 experimental men who were still in the treatment program in 1942, together with their 253 matched controls. Criminal, mental hospital, and other records were searched, and questionnaires were mailed to the men.

The findings were shocking. While equal numbers of treated and control males were convicted as juveniles and as adults, slightly more treated men committed serious crimes, and significantly more treated men committed two or more crimes. The treated men were significantly more likely to die early, to be diagnosed as seriously mentally ill, to have stress-related diseases, and to show symptoms of alcoholism on a screening test. Significantly fewer treated men were in high-status jobs, and fewer of them (but not significantly so) were married.

This was one of the first criminological intervention projects to demonstrate harmful effects of a well-meaning prevention program. Why these effects were found is not entirely clear, but McCord (1978) speculated that the intervention might have created some dependency on outside assistance, which in turn led to resentment when the assistance was withdrawn. Alternatively, the treatment program might have generated high expectations that subsequently led to feelings of deprivation when these expectations were not met. Another possibility was that the treated group might have justified the treatment they received by perceiving themselves as being in need of welfare help. Whatever the true reason, Joan McCord's 1978 paper, published in the very widely distributed house journal of the American Psychological Association, was extremely influential in demonstrating that welfare-oriented counseling programs could end up damaging the clients.

The second paper, "Consideration of some effects of a counseling program" (McCord, 1981) was important because it was published by the very prestigious National Academy of Sciences panel on rehabilitation (Sechrest et al., 1979; Martin et al., 1981). In this 1981 paper, Joan McCord described the results of the intervention in more detail and tested various hypotheses about why it had damaging effects. She concluded that the treatment caused raised expectations which later led to disillusionment when the treatment was withdrawn.

The third paper, "The Cambridge-Somerville Study: A pioneering longitudinal-experimental study of delinquency prevention" (McCord, 1992) again described and discussed the results of the intervention. This paper concluded that significantly more of the treated men had an "undesirable" outcome: convicted for an Index crime, treated for psychosis or alcoholism, or died before age 35. It was published in a very influential book on the early developmental prevention of antisocial behavior that was jointly edited by Joan McCord (McCord and Tremblay, 1992). Interestingly, in her 1989 presidential address to the American Society of

Criminology, McCord (1990) reported that the boys who received more intensive treatment showed more adverse effects.

The most recent paper, "Cures that harm: Unanticipated outcomes of crime prevention programs" (McCord, 2003) described the harmful effects in some detail and placed them in the context of other well-meaning programs that had harmful effects. McCord (2003) reported that the adverse effects increased with intensity and duration of treatment, and that they occurred only among boys whose families had cooperated with the program. This paper was important because it was published in a showcase of papers presented by the Campbell Collaboration Crime and Justice Group, which aims to complete systematic reviews of evidence on the effectiveness of criminological interventions (Farrington and Petrosino, 2001).

The Effects of Child Rearing

As a longitudinal-experimental study, the Cambridge-Somerville Youth Study provided a great deal of information about the childhood antecedents of adult criminal behavior. The methods of measuring family factors, such as parental attitudes, discipline, and supervision, used by Joan and her first husband William McCord were very influential in our Cambridge Study in Delinquent Development (West and Farrington, 1973). Donald West told me that, when he was starting the study in 1960, he wrote to both the McCords and the Gluecks to ask them about their methods of measuring these family factors. Donald considered that the Gluecks' coding system was very subjective, but the McCords sent a very detailed coding system with numerous examples, and Donald carefully followed that in measuring family factors in the Cambridge Study in 1961–62 (see West, 1969, pp. 78–84). Hence, our original measures were very much inspired by those used by McCord et al. (1959), and we were able to replicate many of their findings on the ability of family factors to predict later delinquency and crime (see Farrington, 2002).

Undoubtedly Joan McCord's most influential and best-known paper on child-rearing and criminal behavior was "Some child-rearing antecedents of criminal behavior in adult men" (McCord, 1979). This reported on the subsequent criminal histories of the treated boys. McCord found that poor parental supervision and the mother's lack of confidence significantly predicted later property and violent crimes committed by the boys. In addition, low maternal affection and paternal deviance (criminality or alcoholism) predicted later property crimes, and parental conflict and parental aggression (including punitive discipline) predicted later violent crimes. This paper was crucial in demonstrating that early family and child-rearing factors predicted later offending by children.

"A longitudinal view of the relationship between paternal absence and crime" (McCord, 1982) was, if anything, even more interesting. This paper again investigated the later criminal histories of the treated boys, focusing on boys from homes broken by loss of the biological father. McCord found that the prevalence of serious offending was high for boys from broken homes without affectionate mothers (62%), and for boys from unbroken homes characterized by parental conflict (52%), irrespective of whether they had affectionate mothers. The prevalence of serious offending was low for boys from unbroken homes without conflict (26%) and—importantly—equally low for boys from broken homes with affectionate mothers (22%).

This paper challenged the prevailing wisdom that broken homes were criminogenic. It showed that the number of parents in a family was less important than features of family functioning such as parental conflict and maternal affection. It also suggested that a loving mother might be able to compensate for the loss of a father. Since Joan McCord spent many years as a single parent, at a time when single parents were stigmatized, she was very happy to report these results.

Joan McCord campaigned against the use of physical punishment on children and never used it on her own children. In "A forty year perspective on effects of child abuse and neglect" (McCord, 1983), she divided the treated boys into four categories: rejected, neglected, abused, or loved. The abused boys were those who received physical punishment on a regular basis. Interestingly, the rejected children (those who were repeatedly criticized) were the most likely to come from low social class families or broken families or to have alcoholic or criminal parents. Similarly, the rejected children were the most likely to be convicted (53%), followed by the abused children (39%), the neglected children (35%), and the loved children (23%).

In"Family relationships, juvenile delinquency, and adult criminality" (McCord, 1991b) investigated interactions between three composite features of family functioning, namely, maternal competence (including affection, self-confidence, and consistent nonpunitive discipline), paternal interaction (including affection, aggression, and conflict), and family expectations (mainly reflecting parental supervision). McCord concluded that maternal competence could act as a protective factor against other negative family influences.

Punishment and Discipline

One problem in interpreting the previous results was that physical punishment was sometimes given in the context of a warm parent-child relationship. Consequently, in "Questioning the value of punishment," McCord (1991c) divided the families who used physical punishment into those who also gave affection to the child and those who did not. She found that 28 percent of boys from punitive and affectionate families were convicted, compared with 44 percent of boys from punitive and nonaffectionate families. Hence, parental affection moderated the relationship between physical punishment and child offending.

In the next paper "Deterrence and the light touch of the law," McCord (1985) contrasted ideas of deterrence and labeling. She studied boys from the total sample who were picked up as juveniles for minor crimes. Contrary to labeling theory, those who were convicted had a lower probability of a subsequent conviction for a serious (index) crime than those who were merely warned (23% compared with 51%). However, among those who were convicted, those who received the most severe sanctions of incarceration had a higher probability of a subsequent conviction than those who received the less severe sanctions of probation, release, or fine. McCord concluded that neither deterrence nor labeling could explain her results.

In her later paper, "On discipline," McCord (1997a) studied physical punishment and warmth of fathers and mothers separately. She found that, among mothers who were not warm, physical punishment predicted the sons' convictions (51% convicted, compared with 33% of nonpunished boys). However, the percentage of those with warm punishing mothers who were convicted (21%) was similar to the percentage convicted of those with warm nonpunishing mothers (23%). This suggested that physical punishment did not have criminogenic effects if it was given in the context of a warm relationship, or alternatively that maternal warmth acted as a protective factor against the effects of physical punishment. However, different results were found for fathers. Physical punishment by fathers predicted sons' convictions whether or not the father was warm.

Finally, in "Discipline and the use of sanctions", McCord (1997b) summarized what she has had learned about the use of discipline, based on research by herself and others. She argued that parents should aim to establish habits consistent with the values that they hoped to teach, and that punishments were unnecessary and undesirable.

Crime in the Family

One of the great values of a longitudinal study is that it can investigate continuity in offending and antisocial behavior both within and between generations. In "Patterns of deviance," McCord (1980) reported that 79 percent of boys who were convicted as juveniles were also convicted as adults. She also showed that early onset predicted later serious offending. These analyses were based on both treated and control groups.

Few researchers have studied long criminal careers in two successive generations. In "The cycle of crime and socialization practices," McCord (1991d) studied criminal records of fathers up to age 52 on average, and criminal records of sons up to age 50 on average. She found that convicted fathers significantly tended to have convicted sons. McCord then investigated possible mediating factors accounting for intergenerational transmission, and identified the factors that criminal fathers tended to be alcoholic, aggressive, punitive, and absent.

McCord (1994) in "Family socialization and antisocial behavior: Searching for causal relationships in longitudinal research" investigated the continuity between childhood antisocial behavior (rated by teachers) and later life outcomes. She found that 42 percent of disruptive boys were later convicted for an Index crime, compared with 27 percent of the remainder, a significant difference. McCord also studied interactions between childhood disruptiveness and family factors. She discovered that good parental monitoring decreased the prevalence of convictions only among nondisruptive children, not among disruptive children.

Finally, in "Family as a crucible for violence: Comment on Gorman-smith et al.", McCord (1996) drew some conclusions about violence from the

Cambridge-Somerville Youth Study. She considered that violence was distinctive and should be investigated separately from associated types of antisocial behavior, and that family cohesiveness (warmth and affection), parenting practices (discipline and supervision), and antisocial parents contributed to the development of violence.

Alcoholism and Drunk Driving

Joan McCord was very interested in alcoholism, and she coauthored *Origins of Alcoholism* with her first husband William McCord (McCord and McCord, 1960). In "Drunken drivers in longitudinal perspective," McCord (1984) reported that drunk drivers disproportionately tended to show signs of alcoholism on the CAGE test and disproportionately tended to have received hospital treatment for alcoholism. Parental conflict, paternal rejection, and paternal alcoholism or criminality predicted later convictions for drunk driving. However, boys who were rated insecure or dependent were unlikely to drive after drinking.

As the title indicates, in "Alcoholism and crime across generations," McCord (1999) studied the intergenerational transmission of both alcoholism and criminality. She particularly focused on the mediating factors of paternal aggression (including punitive discipline and family conflict) and maternal competence (including affection and consistent nonpunitive discipline). She concluded that paternal aggression increased the risk of the intergenerational transmission of alcoholism or criminality, whereas maternal competence acted as a protective factor.

Like many other features, alcoholism tends to run in families. In "Identifying developmental paradigms leading to alcoholism," McCord (1988) found that 47 percent of men with alcoholic fathers tended to become alcoholics themselves, compared with 25 percent of men with non-alcoholic fathers. In a logistic regression analysis, the best predictor of a son's alcoholism was the father's alcoholism, followed by the mother's esteem for the father and maternal control. Sons were especially likely to become alcoholics if their father was an alcoholic, their mother had high esteem for their father, and their mother had little control.

In "Another time, another drug," McCord (1992a) studied the effect of Prohibition in the United States on alcohol problems of fathers. Fathers who were aged at least 21 when alcohol sales began to be restricted in 1917 were compared with fathers who were under 21 at that time. It might have been expected that the younger fathers would have been less likely to develop alcohol problems because of their presumed lesser exposure to alcohol as young men. However, McCord found that men who were exposed to Prohibition as adolescents had a significantly higher prevalence of alcohol problems than men who were already adults in 1917 (58% compared with 41%). She concluded that Prohibition increased rather than decreased alcohol use among young males, possibly because it was perceived as illegitimate and unfair by the lower-class males who were most affected by it. These results many have policy lessons for the present day.

Miscellany

Many of Joan McCord's papers provide information on negative or undesirable outcomes such as offending. However, in "Competence in long-term perspective," McCord (1991a) focused on the desirable adult outcomes of achievement (defined as a white-collar job) and adjustment (defined as not alcoholic, not criminal, not seriously mentally ill, did not die early). Both adult outcomes were predicted by teacher ratings of behavior at the beginning of the study (when the boys were age 8 on average). Attention seeking, fighting, restlessness, dullness, poor work habits, and being easily led predicted low achievement and poor adjustment in adulthood. However, family factors, especially maternal competence and low parental conflict, also predicted adult competence. McCord concluded that both types of adult competence were fostered by good family interactions in childhood.

Continuing the theme of desirable behavior, McCord (1992c) focused particularly on altruism in "Understanding motivations: Considering altruism and aggression." Her main argument was that all behavior is not selfish or egoistic. She also investigated whether altruism and aggression were opposite ends of a continuum or independent dimensions. In the Cambridge-Somerville Study, aggression (as measured by teacher ratings at the average age of 8) was not significantly predictive of altruism (as measured by the completion of questionnaires).

In "Ethnicity, acculturation, and opportunities: A study of two generations," McCord (1995) investigated whether immigrants tended to commit more crimes than native-born persons in the Cambridge-Somerville Study. She focused on the immigration status of the fathers and compared offending by fathers and sons. Perhaps surprisingly, immigrant fathers were (if anything) less likely to be convicted for violent or property crimes than native-born fathers. There was no evidence that immigrant fathers or their sons were disproportionately likely to commit crimes. Interestingly, native-born Catholic fathers had more convictions for violence and drunkenness than native-born Protestant fathers.

Joan McCord's Career

Joan McCord's career is summarized in her autobiographical essay "Learning to learn and its sequelae" (McCord, 2002) and in her curriculum vitae. These papers should be studied to obtain full details of her very rich life. However, I will conclude my introductory essay by mentioning some highlights.

Joan was born in 1930 and graduated in philosophy from Stanford University in 1952 with great distinction. She had a life-long enthusiasm for philosophy. She then worked as a teacher to support her first husband William ("Bud") McCord while he was studying for his Ph.D. at Harvard University. It is interesting to see the intellectual continuity at Harvard in the 1950s from the Gluecks to the McCords.

After Bud obtained his Ph.D., Joan worked as a researcher at Harvard and, in 1957, began analyzing the effects of the Cambridge-Somerville Youth Study on crime. This led to the landmark book on *Origins of Crime* (McCord et al., 1959) and also to their influence on the origins of the Cambridge Study in Delinquent Development in 1960.

However, the early 1960s were a very difficult time for Joan as she got divorced from Bud and lost financial support from the Stanford Philosophy department. Fortunately, she received an NIMH Fellowship and completed her Ph.D. in Sociology at Stanford in 1968. However, she then had problems in getting an academic position until she was appointed as an Assistant Professor at Drexel University in Philadelphia, which was a far cry from the likes of Harvard and Stanford. In 1970, she married her second husband Carl Silver, who was a psychologist.

Joan's career began to take off again in the 1970s, when she managed to obtain an NIMH grant to follow up the participants in the Cambridge-Somerville Youth Study. As mentioned above, her results showed that the treatment program had been harmful, and consequently she had difficulty getting them published. However, publication of the results in the *American Psychologist* in 1978 was a watershed event for Joan and she never looked back from then on.

I first met Joan at the American Society of Criminology meeting in Dallas in 1978 and had frequent contacts with her from then until her death in 2004. From the first time I met her, I was struck by her infectious enthusiasm for research questions, which was really inspiring, and which she retained throughout her life. Her intellectual curiosity appeared boundless. Coupled with her intellectual brilliance, this was a formidable combination.

In 1981, my family and I stayed at Joan's house outside Philadelphia. Joan and Carl were remarkably welcoming and tolerant of our three small children who rampaged around. Joan's house was an Aladdin's cave containing many books and journals on criminology and longitudinal studies. She kept a lot of Cambridge-Somerville data in her basement. Also in her basement was a ping-pong table, and she took great delight in thrashing me mercilessly at ping-pong. Joan was charming but also determined and competitive, and this is why she managed to overcome so many difficulties and have such a successful career. I was very proud to receive the Joan McCord Award of the Academy of Experimental Criminology in 2005, and paid fulsome praise to her work in my paper on key longitudinal-experimental studies in criminology (Farrington, 2006).

From 1978 onwards, Joan's fame increased, and she became a central figure in American—and world—criminology. She received many honors. It gave her particular pleasure to be the first woman president of the American Society of Criminology (1988–89), followed by her term as Chair of the American Sociological Association Section on Crime, Law, and Deviance (1989–90). She was always particularly keen to encourage the careers of women scholars. She received the prestigious Sutherland and Bloch awards of the ASC.

Joan contributed mightily to the International Society of Criminology, being a vice-president and member of the Board of Directors for nearly 15 years, and receiving the Durkheim Prize of the ISC. She also contributed enormously to the Campbell Collaboration Crime and Justice Group and was president of the Academy of Experimental Criminology at the time of her death. She also was vice-chair of the National Academy of Sciences Committee on Law and Justice and co-chair of the NAS panel on juvenile crime and juvenile justice (McCord et al., 2001).

Almost up to the time of her death, Joan retained her incredible energy and amazing enthusiasm. As proof of this, I have a photo of her dancing with me at the ASC Minority Scholarship Dance in Denver in November 2003. Her travel schedule would have exhausted most people. In Carl's final years, she traveled the world pushing Carl in a wheelchair. After Carl died in 1998, she traveled even more and seemed to be constantly criss-crossing the world.

It has been a great privilege for me to know Joan McCord. She was one of the most brilliant, inspiring, and enthusiastic researchers that criminology has ever seen.

References

Farrington, D. P. 2006. Key longitudinal-experimental studies in criminology. *Journal of Experimental Criminology* 2: 121–141.

Farrington, D. P. 2002. Families and crime. In *Crime: Public Policies for Crime Control*, 2nd ed., edited by J. Q. Wilson and J. Petersilia, 129–148. Oakland, CA: Institute for Contemporary Studies Press.

Farrington, D. P. and A. Petrosino. 2001. The Campbell Collaboration Crime and Justice Group. *Annals of the American Academy of Political and Social Science* 578: 35–49.

McCord, J. 2003. Cures that harm: Unanticipated outcomes of crime prevention programs. *Annals of the American Academy of Political and Social Science* 587: 16–30.

McCord, J. 2002. Learning how to learn and its sequelae. In *Lessons of Criminology*, edited by G. Geis and M. Dodge, 95–108. Cincinnati, OH: Anderson Publishing Co.

McCord, J. 1999. Alcoholism and crime across generations. In *Criminal Behaviour and Mental Health* 9: 107–117.

McCord, J. 1997a. On discipline. *Psychological Inquiry* 8 (3): 215–217.

McCord, J. 1997b. Discipline and the use of sanctions. In *Aggression and Violent Behavior* 2 (4): 313–319.

McCord, J. 1996. Family as crucible of violence. In *Journal of Family Psychology* 10 (2): 147–152.

McCord, J. 1995. Ethnicity, acculturation, and opportunities: A study of two generations. In *Ethnicity, Race and Crime: Perspectives Across Time and Place*, edited by D. F. Hawkins, 69–81. Albany, NY: SUNY Press.

McCord, J. 1994. Family socialization and antisocial behavior: Searching for causal relationships in longitudinal research. In *Cross-National Longitudinal Research on Human Development and Criminal Behavior*, edited by E. G. M. Weitekamp and H-J. Kerner, 177–188. Dordrecht, Netherlands: Kluwer.

McCord, J. 1992a. Another time, another drug. In *Vulnerability to Drug Abuse*, edited by M. Glantz and R. Pickens, 473–489. Washington, DC: American Psychological Association Press.

McCord, J. 1992b. The Cambridge-Somerville Study: A pioneering longitudinal-experimental study of delinquency prevention. In *Preventing Antisocial Behavior*, edited by J. McCord and R. E. Tremblay, 196–206. New York: Guilford.

McCord, J. 1992c. Understanding motivations: Considering altruism and aggression. In *Facts, Frameworks, and Forecasts: Advances in Criminological Theory*, edited by J. McCord, 3: 115–135. New Brunswick, NJ: Transaction.

McCord, J. 1991a. Competence in long-term perspective. *Psychiatry* 54 (3): 227–237.

McCord, J. 1991b. Family relationships, juvenile delinquency, and adult criminality. *Criminology* 29: 397–417.

McCord, J. 1991c. Questioning the value of punishment. *Social Problems* 38 (2): 167–179.

McCord, J. 1991d. The cycle of crime and socialization practices. *Journal of Criminal Law and Criminology* 82 (1): 211–228.

McCord, J. 1990. Crime in moral and social contexts — the American Society of Criminology 1989 Presidential Address. *Criminology* 28: 1–26.

McCord, J. 1988. Identifying developmental paradigms leading to alcoholism. *Journal of Studies on Alcohol* 49: 357–362.

McCord, J. 1985. Deterrence and the light touch of the law. In *Reactions to Crime: The Public, the Police, Courts and Prisons*, edited by D. P. Farrington and J. Gunn, 73–85. Chichester, England: Wiley.

McCord, J. 1984. Drunken drivers in longitudinal perspective. *Journal of Studies on Alcohol* 45 (4): 316–320.

McCord, J. 1983. A forty year perspective on effects of child abuse and neglect. *Child Abuse and Neglect* 7: 265–270.

McCord, J. 1982. A longitudinal view of the relationship between paternal absence and crime. In *Abnormal Offenders, Delinquency and the Criminal Justice System*, edited by J. Gunn and D. P. Farrington, 113–128. Chichester, England: Wiley.

McCord, J. 1981. Consideration of some effects of a counseling program. In *New Directions in the Rehabilitation of Criminal Offenders*, edited by S. E. Martin, L. Sechrest, and R. Redner, 394–405. Washington, DC: National Academy of Sciences.

McCord, J. 1980. Patterns of deviance. In *Human Functioning in Longitudinal Perspective: Studies of Normal and Psychopathological Populations*, edited by S. B. Sells, R. Crandall, M. Roff, J. Strauss, and W. Pollin, 157–167. Baltimore, MD: Williams and Wilkins.

McCord, J. 1978. A thirty-year follow-up of treatment effects. *American Psychologist* 33 (3): 284–289.

McCord, J. 1979. Some child-rearing antecedents of criminal behavior in adult men. *Journal of Personality and Social Psychology* 37 (9): 1477–1486.

McCord, J. and K. P. Conway. 2002. Patterns of juvenile delinquency and co-offending. In *Crime and Social Organization*, edited by E. Waring and D. Weisburd, 15–30. New Brunswick, NJ: Transaction.

McCord, J. and M. E. Ensminger. 1997. Multiple risks and comorbidity in an African-American population. *Criminal Behaviour and Mental Health* 7: 339–354.

McCord, J., C. S. Widom, and N. A. Crowell, eds. 2001. *Juvenile Crime, Juvenile Justice*. Washington, DC: National Academy Press.

McCord, J., R. E. Tremblay, F. Vitaro, and L. Desmarais-Gervais. 1994. Boys' disruptive behavior, school adjustment, and delinquency: The Montreal Prevention Experiment. *International Journal of Behavioral Development* 17: 739–752.

McCord, J. and R. E. Tremblay, eds. 1992. *Preventing Antisocial Behavior: Interventions from Birth Through Adolescence*. New York: Guilford.

Martin, S. E., L. Sechrest, and R. Redner, eds. 1981. *New Directions in the Rehabilitation of Criminal Offenders*. Washington, DC: National Academy of Sciences.

Sechrest, L., S. White, and E. Brown, eds. 1979. *The Rehabilitation of Criminal Offenders: Problems and Prospects*. Washington, DC: National Academy of Sciences.

West, D. J. and D. P. Farrington. 1973. *Who Becomes Delinquent?* London: Heinemann.

McCord, W. and J. McCord. 1960. *Origins of Alcoholism*. Stanford, CA: Stanford University Press.

West, D. J. 1969. *Present Conduct and Future Delinquency*. London: Heinemann.

McCord, W., J. McCord, and I. K. Zola. 1959. *Origins of Crime*. New York: Columbia University Press.

PART I

The Effects of Intervention

CHAPTER ONE

A Thirty-Year Follow-up of
Treatment Effects*

I N 1935, Richard Clark Cabot instigated one of the most imaginative and exciting programs ever designed in hopes of preventing delinquency. A social philosopher as well as physician, Dr. Cabot established a program that both avoided stigmatizing participants and permitted follow-up evaluation.

Several hundred boys from densely populated, factory-dominated areas of eastern Massachusetts were included in the project, known as the Cambridge-Somerville Youth Study. Schools, welfare agencies, churches, and the police recommended both "difficult" and "average" youngsters to the program. These boys and their families were given physical examinations and were interviewed by social workers who then rated each boy in such a way as to allow a selection committee to designate delinquency-prediction scores. In addition to giving delinquency-prediction scores, the selection committee studied each boy's records in order to identify pairs who were similar in age, delinquency-prone histories, family background, and home environments. By the toss of a coin, one member of each pair was assigned to the group that would receive treatment.[1]

The treatment program began in 1939, when the boys were between 5 and 13 years old. Their median age was 10½. Except for those dropped from the program because of a counselor shortage in 1941, treatment continued for an average of 5 years. Counselors assigned to each family visited, on the average, twice a month. They encouraged families to call on the program for assistance. Family problems became the focus of attention for approximately one third of the treatment group. Over half of the boys were tutored in academic subjects; over 100 received medical or psychiatric attention; one fourth were sent to summer camps; and most were brought into contact with the Boy Scouts, the YMCA, and other community programs. The control group, meanwhile, participated only through

*Reprinted from McCord, J. 1978. A thirty-year follow-up of treatment effects. In *American Psychologist* 33 (3): 284–289. Copyright © 1978 by the American Psychological Association; with permission.

providing information about themselves. Both groups, it should be remembered, contained boys referred as "average" and boys considered "difficult."

The present study compares the 253 men who had been in the treatment program after 1942 with the 253 "matched mates" assigned to the control group.

Method

Official records and personal contacts were used to obtain information about the long-term effects of the Cambridge-Somerville Youth Study.[2] In 1975 and 1976, the 506 former members of the program were traced through court records, mental hospital records, records from alcoholic treatment centers, and vital statistics in Massachusetts. Telephone calls, city directories, motor-vehicle registrations, marriage and death records, and lucky hunches were used to find the men themselves.

Four hundred eighty men (95%) were located; among these, 48 (9%) had died and 340 (79%) were living in Massachusetts.[3] Questionnaires were mailed to 208 men from the treatment group and 202 men from the control group. The questionnaire elicited information about marriage, children, occupations, drinking, health, and attitudes. Former members of the treatment group were asked how (if at all) the treatment program had been helpful to them.

Responses to the questionnaire were received from 113 men in the treatment group (54%) and 122 men in the control group (60%). These responses overrepresent men living outside of Massachusetts, $\chi^2(1)=10.97$, $p < .001$.[4] Official records, on the other hand, provide more complete information about those men living in Massachusetts.

Comparison of Criminal Behavior

The treatment and control groups were compared on a variety of measures for criminal behavior. With the exception of Crime Prevention Bureau records for unofficial crimes committed by juveniles, court convictions serve as the standard by which criminal behavior was assessed. Although official court records may be biased, there is no reason to believe that these biases would affect a comparison between the matched groups of control and treatment subjects.

Almost equal numbers in the treatment and control groups had committed crimes as juveniles—whether measured by official or by unofficial records (see Table 1.1).

TABLE 1.1   Juvenile Records

Record	Treatment group	Control group
No record for delinquency	136	140
Only unofficial crimes	45	46
Official crimes	72	67
TOTAL	253	253

TABLE 1.2   Juvenile Delinquency and Adult Criminal Records

Record	Treatment group	Control group
Official juvenile record		
No adult record	14	15
Only minor adult record	33	27
Serious crimes as adults	25	25
No official juvenile record		
No adult record	71	70
Only minor adult record	86	99
Serious crimes as adults	24	17
TOTAL	253	253

It seemed possible that the program might have benefited those referred as "difficult" while damaging those referred as "average." The evidence, however, failed to support this hypothesis. Among those referred as "difficult," 34 percent from the treatment group and 30 percent from the control group had official juvenile records; an additional 20 percent from the treatment group and 21 percent from the control group had unofficial records. Nor were there differences between the groups for those who had been referred as "average."[5]

As adults, equal numbers (168) had been convicted for some crime. Among men who had been in the treatment group, 119 committed only relatively minor crimes (against ordinances or order), but 49 had committed serious crimes against property (including burglary, larceny, and auto theft) or against persons (including assault, rape, and attempted homicide). Among men from the control group, 126 had committed only relatively minor crimes; 42 had committed serious property crimes or crimes against persons. Twenty-nine men from the treatment group and 25 men from the control group committed serious crimes after the age of 25.

Reasoning that the Youth Study project may have been differentially effective for those who did and did not have records as delinquents, it seemed advisable to compare adult criminal records while holding this background information constant. Again, there was no evidence that the treatment program had deflected people from committing crimes (see Table 1.2).

The treatment and control groups were compared to see whether there were differences (a) in the number of serious crimes committed, (b) in age when a first crime was committed, (c) in age when committing a first serious crime, and (d) in age after which no serious crime was committed. None of these measures showed reliable differences.

Benefits from the treatment program did not appear when delinquency-prediction scores were controlled or when seriousness of juvenile record and juvenile incarceration were controlled. Unexpectedly, however, a higher proportion of criminals from the treatment group than of criminals from the control group committed more than one crime, $\chi^2(1)=5.36$, $p < .05$. Among the 182 men with criminal records from the treatment group, 78 percent committed at least two crimes; among the 183 men with criminal records from the control group, 67 per-cent committed at least two crimes.

Comparison of Health

Signs of alcoholism, mental illness, stress-related diseases, and early death were used to evaluate possible impact of the treatment program on health.

A search through records from alcoholic treatment centers and mental hospi-tals in Massachusetts showed that almost equal numbers of men from the treatment and the control groups had been treated for alcoholism (7% and 8%, respectively).

The questionnaire asked respondents to note their drinking habits and to respond to four questions about drinking embedded in questions about smoking. The four questions, known as the CAGE test (Ewing & Rouse, Note 1), asked whether the respondent had ever taken a morning eye-opener, felt the need to cut down on drinking, felt annoyed by criticism of his drinking, or felt guilty about drinking.[6] The treatment group mentioned that they were alcoholic or responded yes more frequently, as do alcoholics, to at least three of the CAGE questions: 17 percent compared with 7 percent, $\chi^2(1)=4.98$, $p < .05$.

Twenty-one members of each group had received treatment in mental hospi-tals for disorders other than alcoholism.[7] A majority of those from the treatment group (71%) received diagnoses as manic-depressive or schizophrenic, whereas a majority of those from the control group (67%) received less serious diagnoses such as "personality disorder" or "psychoneurotic," $\chi^2(1)=4.68$, $p < .05$.

Twenty-four men from each group are known to have died. Although the groups were not distinguishable by causes of death, among those who died, men from the treatment group tended to die at younger ages, $t(94)=2.19$, $p < .05$.[8]

The questionnaire requested information about nine stress-related diseases: arthritis, gout, emphysema, depression, ulcers, asthma, allergies, high blood pres-sure, and heart trouble. Men from the treatment group were more likely to report having had at least one of these diseases, $\chi^2(1)=4.39$, $p < .05$.[9] In particular, symp-toms of stress in the circulatory system were more prevalent among men from the treatment group: 21 percent, as compared with 11 percent in the control group, reported having had high blood pressure or heart trouble, $\chi^2(1)=4.95$, $p < .05$.

Comparison of Family, Work, and Leisure Time

A majority of the men who responded to the questionnaire were married: 61 per-cent of the treatment group and 68 percent of the control group. An additional 15 percent of the treatment group and 10 percent of the control group noted that they were remarried. Fourteen percent of the treatment-group and 9 percent of the control-group respondents had never married. The remaining 10 percent of the treatment group and 13 percent of the control group were separated, divorced, or widowed. Among those ever married, 93 percent of each group had children. The median number of children for both sets of respondents was three.

About equal proportions of the treatment- and the control-group respondents were unskilled workers (29% and 27%, respectively). At the upper end of the socioeconomic scale, however, the control group had an advantage: 43 percent from the control group, compared with 29 percent from the treatment group, were white-collar workers or professionals, $\chi^2(2)=4.58$, $p < .05$. For those whose occupations could be classified according to National Opinion Research Center (NORC) ranks, comparison indicated that the control-group men were working in positions having higher prestige, $z=2.07$, $p < .05$ (Mann-Whitney U test).

The questionnaire inquired whether the men found their work, in general, to be satisfying. Almost all of the men who held white-collar or professional positions (97%) reported that their work was satisfying. Among blue-collar workers, those in the treatment group were less likely to report that their work was generally satisfying (80%, compared with 95% among the control group), $\chi^2(1)=6.60$, $p < .02$.

The men described how they used their spare time. These descriptions were grouped to compare the proportions who reported reading, traveling, doing things with their families, liking sports (as spectators or participants), working around the house, watching television, enjoying music or theater or photography, doing service work, enjoying crafts or tinkering, and participating in organized group activities. The treatment and control groups did not differ in their reported uses of leisure time.

Comparison of Beliefs and Attitudes

The men were asked to evaluate their satisfaction with how their lives were turning out, their chances for living the kinds of lives they'd like to have, and whether they were able to plan ahead.[10] Men from the treatment and the control groups did not differ in their responses to these questions.

A short form of the F scale (Adorno, Frenkel-Brunswik, Levinson, & Sanford, 1950) developed by Sanford and Older (Note 2) was included in the questionnaire. Men were asked whether they agreed or disagreed with the following statements: "Human nature being what it is, there must always be war and conflict. The most important thing a child should learn is obedience to his parents. A few strong leaders could make this country better than all the laws and talk. Most people who don't get ahead just don't have enough willpower. Women should stay out of politics. An insult to your honor should not be forgotten. In general, people can be trusted."

Despite diversity in opinions, neither answers to particular questions nor to the total scale suggested that treatment and control groups differed in authoritarianism. Both groups selected an average of 2.9 authoritarian answers; the standard deviation for each group was 1.7.

Each man was asked to describe his political orientation. About one fifth considered themselves liberals, two fifths considered themselves conservatives, and two fifths considered themselves as middle-of-the-road. No one considered himself a radical. Treatment and control groups did not differ reliably.

The men also identified the best periods of their lives, and, again, there was little difference between control and treatment groups.

Subjective Evaluation of the Program

Former members of the treatment group were asked, "In what ways (if any) was the Cambridge-Someville project helpful to you?"

Only 11 men failed to comment about this item. Thirteen noted that they could not remember the project. An additional 13 stated that the project had not been helpful—though several of these men amplified their judgments by mentioning that they had fond memories of their counselors or their activities in the project.

Two thirds of the men stated that the program had been helpful to them. Some wrote that, by providing interesting activities, the project kept them off the streets and out of trouble. Many believed that the project improved their lives through providing guidance or teaching them how to get along with others. The questionnaires were sprinkled with such comments as "helped me to have faith and trust in other people"; "I was put on the right road"; "helped prepare me for manhood"; "to overcome my prejudices"; "provided an initial grasp of our complex society outside of the ghetto"; and "better insight on life in general."

A few men believed that the project was responsible for their becoming law-abiding citizens. Such men wrote that, had it not been for their particular counselors, "I probably would be in jail"; "My life would have gone the other way"; or "I think I would have ended up in a life of crime."

More than a score requested information about their counselors and expressed the intention of communicating with them.

Summary and Discussion

This study of long-term effects of the Cambridge-Somerville Youth Study was based on the tracing of over 500 men, half of whom were randomly assigned to a treatment program. Those receiving treatment had (in varying degrees) been tutored, provided with medical assistance, and given friendly counsel for an extended period of time.

Thirty years after termination of the program, many of the men remembered their counselors—sometimes recalling particular acts of kindness and sometimes noting the general support they felt in having someone available with whom to discuss their problems. There seems to be little doubt that many of the men developed emotional ties to their counselors.

Were the Youth Study program to be assessed by the subjective judgment of its value as perceived by those who received its services, it would rate high marks. To the enormous credit of those who dedicated years of work to the project, it is possible to use objective criteria to evaluate the long-term impact of this program, which seems to have been successful in achieving the short-term goals of establishing rapport between social workers and teenage clients.

Despite the large number of comparisons between treatment and control groups, none of the objective measures confirmed hopes that treatment had improved the lives of those in the treatment group. Fifteen comparisons regarding criminal behavior were made; one was significant with alpha less than .05.

Fifteen comparisons for health indicated four—from three different record sources—favoring the control group. Thirteen comparisons of family, work, and leisure time yielded two that favored the control group. Fourteen comparisons of beliefs and attitudes failed to indicate reliable differences between the groups.

The objective evidence presents a disturbing picture. The program seems not only to have failed to prevent its clients from committing crimes—thus corroborating studies of other projects (see, e.g., Craig & Furst, 1965; Empey, 1972; Hackler, 1966; Miller, 1962; Robin, 1969)—but also to have produced negative side effects. As compared with the control group,

1. Men who had been in the treatment program were more likely to commit (at least) a second crime.
2. Men who had been in the treatment program were more likely to evidence signs of alcoholism.
3. Men from the treatment group more commonly manifested signs of serious mental illness.
4. Among men who had died, those from the treatment group died younger.
5. Men from the treatment group were more likely to report having had at least one stress-related disease; in particular, they were more likely to have experienced high blood pressure or heart trouble.
6. Men from the treatment group tended to have occupations with lower prestige.
7. Men from the treatment group tended more often to report their work as not satisfying.

It should be noted that the side effects that seem to have resulted from treatment were subtle. There is no reason to believe that treatment increased the probability of committing a first crime, although treatment may have increased the likelihood that those who committed a first crime would commit additional crimes. Although treatment may have increased the likelihood of alcoholism, the treatment group was not more likely to have appeared in clinics or hospitals. There was no difference between the groups in the number of men who had died before the age of 50, although men from the treatment group had been younger at the age of death. Almost equal proportions of the two groups of men had remained at the lowest rungs of the occupational structure, although men from the treatment group were less likely to be satisfied with their jobs and fewer men from the treatment group had become white-collar workers.

The probability of obtaining 7 reliably different comparisons among 57, with an alpha of .05, is less than 2 percent. The probability that, by chance, 7 of 57 comparisons would favor the control group is less than 1 in 10,000.[11]

At this juncture, it seems appropriate to suggest several possible interpretations of the subtle effects of treatment. Interaction with adults whose values are different from those of the family milieu may produce later internal conflicts that manifest themselves in disease and/or dissatisfaction.[12] Agency intervention may create dependency upon outside assistance. When this assistance is no longer available, the individual may experience symptoms of dependency and resentment. The treatment program may have generated such high expectations that subsequent experiences tended to produce symptoms of deprivation. Or finally, through receiving the services of a "welfare project," those in the treatment program may have justified the help they received by perceiving themselves as requiring help.

There were many variations to treatment. Some of these may have been beneficial. Overall, however, the message seems clear: Intervention programs risk damaging the individuals they are designed to assist. These findings may be taken by some as grounds for cessation of social-action programs. I believe that would be a mistake. In my opinion, new programs ought to be developed. We should, however, address the problems of potential damage through the use of pilot projects with mandatory evaluations.

Notes

This study was supported by U.S. Public Health Service Research Grant No. 5 R01 MH26779, National Institute of Mental Health (Center for Studies of Crime and Delinquency). It was conducted jointly with the Department of Probation of the Commonwealth of Massachusetts.

An earlier version of this paper was presented at the 28th annual meeting of the American Association of Psychiatric Services for Children, San Francisco, California, November 10–14, 1976.

1. An exception to assignment by chance was made if brothers were in the program; all brothers were assigned to that group which was the assignment of the first brother matched. See Powers and Witmer (1951) for details of the matching procedure.

2. A sample of 200 men had been retraced in 1948 (Powers & Witmer, 1951), and official records had been traced in 1956 (McCord & McCord, 1959a, 1959b).

3. Two hundred forty-one men from the treatment group and 239 men from the control group were found; 173 from the treatment group and 167 from the control group were living in Massachusetts.

4. Among those sent the questionnaire, the response rate for men living in Massachusetts was 53 percent; for men living outside Massachusetts, the response rate was 74 percent. A similar bias appeared for both groups.

5. For the treatment group, 18 percent had official records and an additional 13 percent had unofficial records. For the control-group "average" referrals, the figures were 19 percent and 13 percent, respectively.

6. This test was validated by comparing the responses of 58 acknowledged alcoholics in an alcoholism rehabilitation center with those of 68 nonalcoholic patients in a general hospital: 95 percent of the former and none of the latter answered yes to more than two of the four questions (Ewing & Rouse, Note 1). Additional information related to alcoholism is being gathered through interviews.

7. An additional five men from the treatment group and three men from the control group had been institutionalized as retarded.

8. The average age at death for the treatment group was 32 years ($SD=9.4$) and for the control group, 38 years ($SD=7.5$).

9. Thirty-six percent of those in the treatment group and 24 percent of those in the control group reported having had at least one of these diseases.

10. This set of questions was developed at the University of Michigan Survey Research Center as a measure of self-competence. It has an index of reproducibility as a Guttman Scale of .94 (see Douvan & Walker, 1956).

11. This estimate is conservative: The count of 57 comparisons includes comparisons that are not independent (e.g., adult criminal record and crimes after the age of 25), but only 7 independent significant relationships have been counted. If comparisons for any stress-related disease, for NORC ranking of occupation, and for job satisfaction without controlling work status are counted, 10 out of 60 comparisons were significant.

12. Such conflicts seem to have been aroused by intervention in the lives of hard-core unemployables (Padfield & Williams, 1973).

References

Adorno, T. W., E. Frenkel-Brunswik, D. J. Levinson, and R. N. Sanford. 1950. *The Authoritarian Personality*. New York: Harper.

Craig, M. M. and P. W. Furst. 1965. What happens after treatment? A study of potentially delinquent boys. *Social Service Review* 39: 165–171.

Douvan, E. and A. M. Walker. 1956. The sense of effectiveness in public affairs. *Psychological Monographs* 70 (22, Whole No. 429).

Empey, L. T. and M. L. Ericson. 1972. *The Provo Experiment: Evaluating Community Control of Delinquency*. Lexington, Mass.: Lexington Books.

Ewing, J. A. and B. A. Rouse. 1970. *Identifying the "Hidden Alcoholic."* Paper presented at the 29th International Congress on Alcohol and Drug Dependence, Sydney, New South Wales, Australia, February 3.

Hackler, J. C. 1966. Boys, blisters, and behavior: The impact of a work program in an urban central area. *Journal of Research in Crime and Delinquency* 12: 155–164.

McCord, J. and W. McCord. 1959a. A follow-up report on the Cambridge-Somerville youth study. *Annals of the American Academy of Political and Social Science* 322: 89–96.

McCord, W. and J. McCord. 1959b. *Origins of Crime*. New York: Columbia University Press.

Miller, W. B. 1962. The impact of a "total community" delinquency control project. *Social Problems* 10: 168–191.

Padfield, H. and R. Williams. 1973. *Stay Where You Were: A Study of Unemployables in Industry*. Philadelphia, Pa.: Lippincott.

Powers, E. and H. Witmer. 1951. *An Experiment in The Prevention of Delinquency: The Cambridge-Somerville Youth Study*. New York: Columbia University Press.

Robin, G. R. 1969. Anti-poverty programs and delinquency. *Journal of Criminal Law, Criminology, and Police Science* 60: 323–331.

Sanford, F. H. and J. J. Older. 1950. *A Short Authoritarian-Equalitarian Scale* (Progress Report No. 6, Series A). Philadelphia, Pa.: Institute for Research in Human Relations.

CHAPTER TWO

Consideration of Some Effects of a Counseling Program*

T HOSE WHO spend their lives providing psychological services generally do not have the opportunity to learn about the long-term effects of their efforts. The opportunity to study men who once were members of the Cambridge-Somerville Youth Study provides a rare exception.

The Cambridge-Somerville Youth Study was designed, during the years of the Great Depression, with the hope that it would help prevent delinquency. Its organizers solicited the names of young boys who lived in designated (generally deteriorated) areas of two communities in eastern Massachusetts. By intention, the program included "average" as well as "difficult" children. Between 1935 and 1939, a Selection Committee gathered information from elementary school teachers, the courts, physicians, and parents regarding the children whose names had been submitted. On the basis of this information, pairs of boys similar in age, family backgrounds, home environments, intelligence, and delinquency-prone histories were identified. The matching procedure justified a belief that both members of a pair reasonably could be expected to have similar life chances in the absence of intervention. A flip of a coin determined which member in each pair would receive treatment; the other member was placed into the control group.[1]

Retrospective comparisons indicated that the treatment and control groups were indeed similar. No reliable differences were discovered in comparisons of age, IQ, whether the boy had been referred to the Youth Study as "difficult" or "average," or the delinquency prediction scores assigned by the Selection Committee on the basis of the boys' histories and home environments. No reliable differences appeared in comparisons of ratings for the boys' physical health, mental health, social adjustment, acceptance of authority, or social aggressiveness. Nor were

*Reprinted from McCord, J. 1981. Consideration of some effects of a counseling program. In *New Directions in the Rehabilitation of Criminal Offenders*, edited by S. E. Martin et al., 394–405 Washington, DC: The National Academy of Sciences; with permission from National Academies Press.

reliable differences found in ratings of delinquency in the home, adequacy of discipline, standard of living, status of the occupation of the father, "social status level" of the elementary school attended (as measured by sampled occupational levels of the parents), or neighborhoods as likely or unlikely to produce delinquency (see Powers and Witmer, 1951, Ch. 6).

By May 1939 each of the 325 boys in the treatment group had been assigned to a social worker who was expected to build close relations with the boy and be available to provide assistance to both the boy and his family. In addition to 10 social workers, the staff included a psychologist, tutors, a shop instructor, consulting psychiatrists, and medical doctors. Counselor turnover and the recognition that case loads were too heavy led to a decision to drop some of the boys from the program. When a boy was dropped from the treatment group, his "matched mate" was dropped from the control group. By 1942, 253 matched pairs of boys remained in the program. These 506 boys are the subjects in the present study.

When the program terminated in 1945, the 253 boys in the treatment group had been visited (on the average) twice a month for five and a half years. Over half had been tutored in academic subjects; over 100 received medical or psychiatric attention; almost half had been sent to summer camps; and most of the boys had participated in such activities as swimming, visits to local athletic competitions, and work in the project's woodshop. Boys in the treatment group were encouraged to join the YMCA or other community youth programs. Social workers from the Youth Study were specifically prohibited from working with boys in the control group.

The current follow-up study began in 1975. The names (and pseudonyms) of all 506 men were traced through records of the Massachusetts Board of Probation, the Department of Mental Health, the Division of Alcoholism, and the Department of Vital Statistics. Subsequently, over 100 alcoholism treatment centers in Massachusetts and the criminal justice services departments of other states have added information about the men. By January 1979, 98 percent of the men had been located. Almost four out of five were found in Massachusetts. The men were asked to respond to a questionnaire and, later, to consent to an interview. Data from these sources provide the bases for evaluating effects of the Youth Study.

Prior data analyses (McCord, 1978) had indicated that men from the treatment group differed subtly from men who had been in the control group. The differences suggested that treatment may have had damaging effects. The present study considers this possibility.

Each of the 506 men was classified as having or not having an "undesirable outcome." If and only if a man had been convicted for a crime indexed by the FBI, or had died prior to the age of 35, or had received medical diagnoses of alcoholism, schizophrenia, or manic-depressive was a man's outcome counted as undesirable. Using this criteria, 105 men from the treatment group (42%), as compared with 81 men from the control group (32%), had undesirable outcomes ($z=2.28$, $p=0.0226$).[2]

Although the overall impact of treatment appeared to have been damaging, it seemed reasonable to search for positive effects in variations of treatment. Beneficial effects might have resulted from starting treatment when the child was particularly young, from providing frequent help, or from treatment being available over an especially long period of time. Or, alternatively, the program might have been successful in helping those with whom the counselor had developed close relationships; or, perhaps, in helping those assigned male (or female) counselors. Perhaps boys whose counselors had focused on a particular type of assistance had an advantage: counselor emphases had been classified as dealing with academics, health, group participation, personal problems, or family problems.

To assess the possibilities that subsets of the treatment group had been benefited, the outcome of each man from the treatment group was compared with the outcome of his match in the control group. A pair was placed into one of four categories: neither had an undesirable outcome; only the man from the control group had an undesirable outcome (i.e., the treatment group had a better outcome); only the man from the treatment group had an undesirable outcome (i.e., the control group had a better outcome); or both had undesirable outcomes. The sign test, two-tailed, was used to evaluate the reliability of obtained differences.

The comparisons did not support a view that early intervention was beneficial. Nor was there evidence that intense or close or long-term assistance was helpful. Furthermore, none of the types of assistance resulted in outcomes generally better for the treatment group than for the control group. On the contrary, more intense contact and longer exposure to the treatment were related to a particularly strong adverse impact. Table 2.1 shows how outcome was related to variations in treatment.

As shown in Table 2.1 none of the treatment variations revealed a subset of clients in which boys from the treatment group had outcomes better than would have been expected by chance. Rather, several of these subsets seemed to have been particularly harmed: those boys who were between the ages of 9 and 11 when first assigned a counselor ($p=0.012$); those who had been visited at least every other week for a minimum period of 6 months ($p=0.008$); those in the program for at least 6 years ($p=0.001$); and those whose counselors had focused on personal ($p=0.003$) or family problems ($p=0.002$).

Analyses of effects from treatment differences point to the conclusion that "more" was "worse." Several possible explanations are worth considering.

1. Counselors, with their middle-class values, may have imposed these values upon the boys; such imposition, it could be argued, might lead to trouble in a lower-class milieu.
2. Since counselors were available and eager to provide assistance, they may have increased or heightened dependency among members of the treatment group; with removal of support (due to termination of the program), it could be argued, these boys were less able than their matches to cope with their problems.
3. Although the Youth Study included "average" as well as "difficult" boys, the presence of counselors may have suggested that help was necessary: a "labeling effect," it could be argued, created the behaviors that would justify the help received.

TABLE 2.1 Desirable Outcomes: Treatment Versus Control (number of pairs in each category)

Treatment variables	Undesirable outcome ($T=C$)	Undesirable outcome only for control case	Undesirable outcome only for treatment case	Undesirable outcome for both ($T=C$)
Age at beginning of treatment				
Under 9	30	8	12	9
9 to under 11	40	16	35*	19
11 to 13	39	15	16	14
Frequency of counselor visits to subject				
Every other week	21	5	19**	14
Once a month	27	10	23*	18
Less often	61	24	21	10
Frequency of counselor visits to family				
Every other week	16	4	15*	9
Once a month	28	14	20	19
Less often	65	21	28	14
Quality of counselor/subject relationship				
Close	19	6	13	12
Friendly	57	19	27	19
Distant	33	14	23	11
Length of treatment				
Less than 4 years	43	13	15	9
4 to less than 6 years	26	16	14	9
At least 6 years	40	10	34***	24
Number of counselor(s)				
One	31	17	15	7
Two	44	12	21	13
Three of more	34	10	27**	22
Sex of counselor(s)				
Male	61	19	40**	29
Female	22	14	9	1
Both	26	6	14	12
Counselor focused on				
Academics	52	22	39*	26
Health	35	16	34*	16
Group participation	52	19	33	17
Personal problems	26	8	28**	15
Family problems	33	9	28**	17

*$p < 0.05$. **$p < 0.01$. ***$p < 0.001$.

4. The supportive attitudes of the counselors may have filtered reality for the boys, leading them to expect more from life than they could receive: disillusionment based on perceived deprivation, it could be argued, produced those symptoms that differentiated treatment and control groups.

These explanations were evaluated by comparing treatment and control groups for evidence of middle-class achievement values, evidence of dependency, evidence of a labeling effect, and evidence of disillusionment. Responses from 343 men, 178 from the treatment group and 165 from the control group, provided data for these analyses. In the treatment group, excluding men who had died prior to successful contact, 67 percent of those who had "undesirable outcomes" (as defined above) and 85 percent of those who did not have "undesirable outcomes" responded to the questionnaire or were interviewed. The corresponding figures for the control group were 61 percent and 77 percent.

One measure of achievement orientation is the amount of formal education received. During the interview, men were asked how far they had gone in school. Although the groups had been matched for IQ, and although almost equal proportions of interview respondents among the treatment and control groups (36% and 33%, respectively) had been considered dull, slow, or retarded prior to the beginning of the treatment program, men from the treatment group were less likely to have graduated from high school ($\chi^2(1)=4.91$, $p=0.027$).

Almost equal proportions of the high school graduates from the treatment and control groups (69% and 64%, respectively) attended college; among these, 15 percent of the treatment group and 30 percent of the control group graduated. Among respondents who had dropped out before graduating from high school, 18 percent in the treatment group and 20 percent in the control group eventually received high school degrees. Among high school graduates, 10 percent from the treatment group and 19 percent from the control group received a college degree.

Other measures of achievement orientation also showed no support for the hypothesis that counselor intervention produced difficulties through imposing middle-class values on the boys. During the interview, the men were read the following two stories:

At the age of 32, Mr. X has been working on an assembly line for 10 years. A friend of his has told him about an opening in the front office which he thinks Mr. X can get. His salary would be about $10 a week less than the wages he is now making. Should Mr. X apply for the job?

Mr. M is 22 and has two job offers. He can go to work in a factory where he is assured of steady pay and union benefits—but is not likely to rise. He can join a new company, where—if things work out well—he may become a foreman. Which job should Mr. M accept?

Responses to these stories did not differentiate between treatment and control group.

The men were asked to describe their children. Reasoning that people talk about what they consider to be important, the mention of a child's education (regardless of what was said) was considered to be a sign that achievement was relevant to the respondent. There were 120 men in the treatment group and 105 men in the control group who had at least one child over 18; 47 percent of the former and 50 percent of the latter mentioned education in describing their children.

The men were asked to identify and describe people whom they admired. The treatment and control groups did not differ in proportions who mentioned success, hard work, achievement, or abilities as grounds for their admiration.

In short, none of the comparisons indicates that treatment had increased the achievement orientation attributed to holding middle-class values.

The second possible explanation suggested that treatment increased dependency. Three measures of dependency were gleaned from the interviews. Respondents were asked whether they generally asked others for an opinion when faced with a difficult decision. As compared with men from the control group, men from the treatment group were slightly less likely to respond affirmatively to this question. Men were asked whether they were active in any clubs; 62 percent of the men from the treatment group and 65 percent of those from the control group reported that they were or had been. Men were asked about the frequency of visits with their parents: 41 percent of the treatment group respondents and 45 percent of the control group respondents reported seeing their parents at least once a week.

The questionnaire provided one measure of dependency; it inquired about use of leisure time. Completed questionnaires were received from 125 men in the treatment group and 129 men in the control group: responses to the question on use of leisure time were classified as activities that are generally performed alone, activities in which interaction is peripheral, and activities in which interaction is essential. Almost half of each group (47% and 44% for treatment and control, respectively) reported that they spend at least part of their leisure time in activities in which interaction is central.

In sum, none of the measures of dependency indicates that the treatment program had encouraged dependency.

The third possible explanation suggested that treatment implied the need for help through a "labeling effect." Several measures were considered as indirect means for discovering a labeling effect. These involved measures of self-confidence, reports of psychosomatic illnesses, and the taking of medication.

Questionnaires included a measure of feelings of competence (Douvan and Walker, 1956). This measure asked the men to evaluate their satisfaction with life, their chances for leading the kind of life they would like to have, and whether they could plan ahead. Differences in responses were unrelated to having been in the treatment group.

A measure of self-confidence was included in the interview (modified from Rosenberg, 1965). Differences in self-confidence, too, were unrelated to having been in the treatment group.

During the interview, men were asked whether they get headaches; 66 percent of the treatment group respondents and 68 percent of the control group respondents reported that they did. Asked whether they take any medicines, 38 percent of the treatment group respondents and 34 percent of the control group respondents reported affirmatively. Both interviews and questionnaires provided information about psychosomatic diseases: arthritis, gout, emphysema, depression, high blood pressure, asthma, ulcers, heart trouble, allergies. Among respondents from the treatment group, 43 percent reported one or more of the psychosomatic disorders; among respondents from the control group, 36 percent reported one or more of these disorders. If members of the treatment group had been affected by a labeling process, one would expect to find evidence that they viewed themselves as sick. None of the measures designed to detect a self-definition as "ill" support the hypothesis that such a perception had been a result of the treatment program.

The fourth explanation suggested that treatment encouraged unrealistic expectations. The hypothesis that treatment laid the seeds for disillusionment did receive support.

As compared with men from the control group, men from the treatment group had apparently been less satisfied with their first marriages. Although treatment and control group members had been almost the same ages when first married ($\bar{x}$=24.4 for each group), a higher proportion among the treatment group had been separated, divorced, or remarried ($\chi^2(1)$=5.56, p=0.018).

Current marriages, too, seemed less satisfying for men in the treatment group. Several questions in the interview provided information about a man's perception of his wife. Men were asked what sort of things they did with their wives and whether their wives knew most of their friends. Men were free to include their wives in responses to questions about what makes a good marriage, about what they generally do when stuck by a decision, about the sorts of things that annoy or anger them, about people they admire and people who have made a difference in the way their lives have turned out. After reading these responses, as well as notes about the interaction that had been recorded by the interviewer, coders indicated whether the respondent demonstrated warmth toward his (current) wife. Among the 126 men from the treatment group for whom a rating could be made, 47% were coded as demonstrating warmth; that proportion was reliably lower than the 65% of 104 men from the control group who demonstrated warmth toward their wives ($\chi^2(1)$=7.94, p=0.005).

As the interview drew to a close, the interviewer asked, "If we were to try to get in touch with you in 10 years or so, what would be a good way of reaching you?" Responses were coded to identify those that suggested permanence or continuity (e.g., "I'll probably still be here"; "My daughter keeps in touch"; "I'll still be working for..."). Responses from the control group were more likely to indicate belief in continuity (84%) than were responses from the treatment group (79%) ($\chi^2(1)$=8.95, p=0.003).

In the questionnaire, the men were asked whether they found their work satisfying. Responses were linked to ratings of occupational status (Hollingshead and Redlich, 1958) ($F(4,243)$=3.02. p=0.019). With occupational status controlled, those who had been in the treatment group were less likely to report being satisfied ($F(1,243)$=4.32. p=0.039).

The relative frequency of divorce and dissatisfaction among the treatment group is consistent with a view that treatment laid the groundwork for subsequent disillusionment. Alternatively, however, the greater frequency of reported dissatisfaction among men in the treatment group could be due to a reporting bias if men from the treatment group were merely more honest in reporting problems.

Responses to questions about problems that would not also represent disillusionment were used to check this latter possibility.

Almost equal proportions of the treatment and control groups (20% and 18%, respectively) reported having committed serious crimes during childhood. In describing their childhood years, 77 percent of the treatment group and 74 percent of the control group described financial and/or psychosocial problems; in recalling things that stand out in their lives, 35 percent of the treatment group and 40 percent of the control group mentioned problems. Forty-nine percent in the treatment group and 46 percent in the control group reported that their fathers, and 25 percent in each group reported that their mothers, had been harsh or very harsh as disciplinarians. Among the treatment group, 18 percent reported having been unemployed for a year or more, as did 16 percent of those in the control group.

Since members of the treatment group were *not* systematically reporting having more problems than were members of the control group, it seems reasonable to interpret reports of dissatisfaction with jobs, marriage, and life as representing real (as opposed to merely reported) differences.

To review: Inspection of objective evidence used to compare 253 men who had been assigned to a treatment program with 253 men who had been matched with them prior to treatment suggested that the treatment program may have been harmful. Consideration of variations in treatment provided between 1939 and 1945, as these variations were related to objective measures of outcome, gave additional support to that view: longer and more intense treatment appeared to have been particularly damaging. These results, initially detected 30 years after termination of the treatment program, lead to two methodological questions. Could the adverse impact of the program have been detected at an earlier date? Could it have been detected in the absence of a control group? Figure 2.1 provides a visual display of the relationship between age and adverse outcomes.[3]

The figure illustrates a relatively constant rate in the development of adverse impacts to the age of 35. Since the slope of the development of adverse outcomes for the treatment group is greater than the slope for the control group, the impact of treatment appears to have been one that affected internal phenomena (e.g., attitudes or beliefs). If the treatment had affected behaviors more directly, one would expect to find a difference in intercepts rather than in slopes.

Treatment seems to have affected expectations, which in turn affected probabilities for behaviors. Using the objective criteria, differences between treatment and control group became statistically reliable by the age of 35 ($z=2.58$, $p=0.010$).[4]

Had there been no control group, evaluation of the program might have led to radically different conclusions. Client evaluation seems to have been favorable. Completed questionnaires were received from 125 former members of the treatment group, yielding a 59 percent response rate from men who were still living and whose addresses were known. The questionnaire asked how, if at all, the Cambridge-Somerville Youth Study had been helpful. Two-thirds of the men responded that the program had been helpful. Most of these men amplified their responses by specifying ways in which their counselors or their experiences with

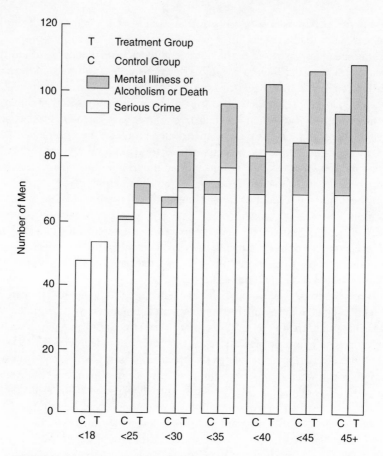

FIGURE 2.1   Age and undesirable outcomes.

the program had improved their lives. The men mentioned that the program had kept them off the streets, taught them to be more understanding, showed them that there were people around who cared; they wrote of the opportunity the program provided for learning, for having someone around who listened and understood, and for doing things that they might not otherwise have done.

The subjective reports served as testimonials for the project. They also provide evidence that such scars as were caused by the treatment program were not those of resentment. The clients' favorable judgments of the program are, however, consistent with a view that supportive attitudes of the counselors led the boys to expect more from life than they were likely to receive.

TO SUMMARIZE: As measured by objective criteria, men in the treatment group were more likely than men in the control group to have had undesirable outcomes. Since the differential between treatment and control groups was greatest among those subsets who had been given more treatment, the relationship appears to be causal. Four "dynamic" interpretations were proposed. These postulated increases in different intervening variables were increase in achievement-oriented values, increase in dependency, increase in perceptions of the self as needing help, and increase in expectations for satisfactions. On the basis of evidence adduced from questionnaires and interviews, the first three interpretations were rejected; the fourth gained support. The Cambridge-Somerville Youth Study seems to have raised the expectations of its clients without also providing the means for increasing satisfactions. The resulting disillusionment seems to have contributed to the probability of having an undesirable outcome.

Notes

This study was supported by U.S. Public Health Service Research Grant No. RO1 MH26779, National Institute of Mental Health (Center for Studies of Crime and Delinquency). It was conducted jointly with the Department of Probation of the Commonwealth of Massachusetts. The author wishes to express appreciation to the Division of Criminal Justice Services of the State of New York, to the Maine State Bureau of Identification, and to the states of Florida, Michigan, New Jersey, and Washington for supplemental data about the men, though they are responsible neither for the statistical analyses nor for the conclusions drawn from this research.

1. Eight cases were matched after treatment began; the assignment to the treatment group for these eight was not random. All brothers were assigned to that group that was the assignment of the first brother matched.

2. In 39 pairs, only the man from the control group had an "undesirable outcome," whereas only the man from the treatment group had an "undesirable outcome" among 63 pairs. When serious criminality is defined by multiple criminal convictions (rather than a single conviction for an indexed crime), differences between the treatment and control groups are larger.

3. The graph includes death to the age of measurement (rather than prior to the age of 35) as an adverse outcome.

4. In 35 pairs, only the man from the control group had an "undesirable outcome," whereas only the man from the treatment group had an "undesirable outcome" among 59 pairs.

References

Douvan, E. and A. M. Walker. 1956. The sense of effectiveness in public affairs. *Psychological Monographs* 70 (22, Whole No. 429).

Hollingshead, A. B. and F. F. Redlich. 1958. *Social Class and Mental Illness*. New York: Wiley.

McCord, J. 1978. A thirty-year follow-up of treatment effects. *American Psychologist* 33(3): 284–289.

Powers, E. and H. Witmer. 1951. *An Experiment in the Prevention of Delinquency: The Cambridge-Somerville Youth Study*. New York: Columbia University Press.

Rosenberg, M. 1965. *Society and the Adolescent Self-Image*. Princeton, N.J.: Princeton University Press.

CHAPTER THREE

The Cambridge-Somerville Study

A Pioneering Longitudinal Experimental Study of Delinquency Prevention*

CLAIMS LINKING FAMILY inadequacies with criminal behavior are far from new. In the seventeenth century, for example, William Gouge (1627) described the duties of family members toward one another by writing that "children well nurtured and by correction kept in filiall awe, will so carry themselves, as their parents may rest somewhat secure" (p. 311). In the nineteenth century, convinced that "all sources of crime ... may be traced to one original cause, namely, the neglect of parents as to a proper care of their children," Jevons urged that parents, rather than their children, be punished for their children's delinquency (1834/1970, p. 153). In 1848, the New York City chief of police described the delinquents he encountered as "the offspring of always careless, generally intemperate, and oftentimes immoral and dishonest parents" (Matsell, 1850, p. 14).

By the first quarter of the twentieth century, such observations had become common enough to encourage a movement aimed at preventing crime through use of child guidance clinics. As part of this movement, teams of workers consisting of a psychologist, a psychiatrist, and a social worker joined forces to combat problems believed to be at the root of crime. In 1917, Judge Frederick Cabot invited William Healy, M.D., director of the Juvenile Psychopathic Institute in Chicago, to become head of the Judge Baker Foundation (Mennel, 1973).

Healy (1917) believed that delinquents lacked close emotional ties. Delinquents, he wrote, "never had any one near to them, particularly in family life, who supplied opportunities for sympathetic confidences" (p. 327).

As director of the Judge Baker Foundation (later known as the Judge Baker Guidance Centre), Healy and his codirector, Augusta Bronner, worked closely with Judge Cabot. The Judge Baker Foundation reviewed juvenile court cases, making recommendations to the court regarding placement and treatment.

*Reprinted from McCord, J. 1992. The Cambridge-Somerville Study: A pioneering longitudinal-experimental study of delinquency prevention. In *Preventing Antisocial Behavior*, edited by J. McCord and R. E. Tremblay, 196–206. New York: Guilford.

Careful case reviews not only served as bases for their recommendations but also enabled Healy and Bronner (1926) to identify common features in the backgrounds of delinquents. Among the discoveries they reported was the fact that less than 10 percent of 2,000 young recidivists had come from "reasonably good conditions for the upbringing of a child" (p. 129). When they compared delinquents with their nondelinquent siblings, they gained additional support for the view that lack of warm interaction in the family was at least partially responsible for crime. Healy and Bronner (1936) discovered that the nondelinquents received more affection. Naturally, recommendations made by the Judge Baker Foundation reflected the perspective of its directors.

Meanwhile, Sheldon Glueck, who had taken a seminar with Richard Clark Cabot (a cousin of Judge Cabot) in 1925, began to study the impact of the juvenile justice system on later criminal careers (Glueck and Glueck, 1945). As part of this assessment, Sheldon and Eleanor T. Glueck retraced delinquents 5 years after official control by the Boston court ended. Disconcertingly, Glueck and Glueck (1934) reported that of the 905 delinquents who could have become recidivists, 798 (88.2%) had done so. Rates of recidivism were only slightly lower among the subset of cases in which the Judge Baker recommendations had been followed. These results produced calls for stronger interventions and greater attention to the broader life setting of delinquents. Healy had suggested attacking the problem of delinquency as it could "be seen developing in school life" (1934, p. 94). This was the climate into which the Cambridge-Somerville Youth Study was born.

In 1934 Dr. Cabot retired from Harvard, where he had served as professor of clinical medicine and of social ethics. His medical work included texts on diagnosis. He had made a mark in the field by showing how to differentiate typhoid fever from malaria, and his etiological study of heart disease was widely recognized as an important medical contribution. Cabot introduced social services to Massachusetts General Hospital and became president of the National Conference on Social Work in 1931. He wrote about social work, the relationship between psychotherapy and religion, and the meaning of right and wrong. His scientific writing and teaching had been broadly critical, and it was reported that the Massachusetts Medical Society considered expelling him for publicly criticizing general practitioners by claiming that most diagnoses were wrong (Deardorff, 1958).

Richard C. Cabot reviewed the Gluecks' study of recidivism for the journal *Survey* and was convinced of the need for more information about the development of criminal behavior. He concluded his review with an expression of admiration that shaped the future of his work: "What piece of social work ... is able to declare (with good grounds for its belief) that it has not failed in 88 percent of its endeavors? I honor the Judge Baker Foundation and the Boston Juvenile Court for having welcomed this piece of investigation. They have trusted in the spirit of science though their hopes of success may perish at the hands of that spirit" (1934, p. 40).

Cabot hypothesized that even rebellious youths from ghastly families "may conceivably be steered away from a delinquent career and toward useful citizenship if a devoted individual outside his own family gives him consistent emotional support, friendship, and timely guidance" (Allport, 1951, p. vi). The Cambridge-Somerville Youth Study would test this hypothesis.

Method

The Cambridge-Somerville Youth Study grafted scientific methods onto a social action program. The Youth Study was designed both to learn about the development of delinquent youngsters and to test Cabot's belief about how a child could be steered away from delinquency. Cabot selected as the sites for his study an area of eastern Massachusetts in which poverty was widespread and crimes were common. Within these areas, boys whose ages were less than 12 became potential targets for intervention.

To avoid stigmatizing participants, boys without difficulties as well as those who seemed headed for trouble were included in the program. Between 1935 and 1939 the Youth Study staff used information collected from schools, neighborhoods, courts, physicians, and families to match pairs of boys similar in age, intelligence, physiques, family environments and backgrounds, social environments, and delinquency-prone histories. In the absence of intervention, both boys in a pair would be expected to have similar lives. The selection committee flipped a coin to decide which member of the pair would receive treatment and which would be placed in the control group.[1]

Each boy in the treatment group was assigned to a social worker who tried to build a close personal relationship with the boy and assist both the boy and his family in a variety of ways. Counselors were not allowed to have contact with criminal justice agencies or with boys in the control group, though, naturally, no attempt was made to prevent their receiving assistance from other sources.

Supported by the Ella Lyman Cabot Foundation, the program started with 325 matched pairs of boys. This number was reduced as the United States entered World War II, counselors joined the armed forces, and gas rationing made it more difficult to travel. When a boy was dropped from the treatment program, his "matched mate" was dropped from the control group. In 1942, when 253 boys remained in the treatment program and an equal number remained in the control group, the research staff compared the groups (Powers and Witmer, 1951).

No reliable differences were discovered in comparisons of age, IQ, or whether referral to the Youth Study had been as difficult or not difficult. The two groups had almost identical delinquency prediction scores, as these were assigned by the selection committee summarizing the boys' family histories and home environments. No reliable differences appeared in comparisons regarding the boys' physical health as rated by the doctor after a medical examination, or in mental health, social adjustment, acceptance of authority, or social aggressiveness as reflected by teachers' descriptions of the boys. Nor were reliable differences found in ratings regarding adequacy of the home, disruption of the home, delinquency in the home, adequacy of discipline, standard of living, occupational status of the father, "social status level" of the elementary school attended by the boy (a measure based on the occupational levels of fathers whose children attended the school), or quality of the neighborhood in which the boys resided (Powers and Witmer, 1951).

The average age of the boys at the start of treatment was 10.5. Social workers, psychologists, tutors, a shop instructor, consulting psychiatrists, and medical doctors formed the treatment staff. Boys were seen in their homes, on the streets, and in the headquarters of the project.

To the innovative design in which matched groups provided a basis for random assignment to a treatment or control group, Cabot added the requirement of keeping excellent records. Following any encounter of the staff with a boy in the study or his family, the staff member dictated a report about what had transpired. Throughout the years of the project, counselors reviewed case records at staff meetings. (See Powers and Witmer, 1951, for further details.)

Case workers offered the boys as well as their parents counseling for personal problems; they referred cases to specialists when that seemed advisable. When the program terminated in 1945, boys in the treatment group had been visited, on the average, two times a month for $5^{1}/_{2}$ years. Over half the boys had been tutored in academic subjects; over 100 received medical or psychiatric attention; almost half had been sent to summer camps; and most of the boys had participated with their counselors in such activities as swimming, visits to local athletic competitions, and woodwork in the project's shop. Boys in the treatment group were encouraged to join the YMCA and other community youth programs. The boys and their parents called upon the social workers for help with a variety of problems including illness and unemployment.

Boys assigned to the control group were excluded from activities provided to the treatment group. Members of the control group did receive help, of course. Families, churches, and community organizations provided assistance. The difference between treatment and control groups was not whether boys received help, but rather whether boys received the integrated, friendly guidance provided by the Cambridge-Somerville Youth Study.

Results

The men were born between 1925 and 1934 (mean=1928; SD=1.7). The most recent follow-up began when the men were an average of 47 years old. The Youth Study had been designed to prevent antisocial behavior, so measures of criminal behavior were particularly appropriate to its evaluation. Court records had the advantage of objectivity and were independent of self-reporting biases. Although court records yield incomplete records of criminal activities and are likely to reflect cultural, racial, and social class biases, the treatment and control groups would be equally affected by these influences.

In order to evaluate the impact of treatment, names and pseudonyms of the 506 men were checked through the Massachusetts Department of Probation centralized records in 1975–76. If treatment and control group men had migrated differentially from Massachusetts, the evaluations might have produced biased results. To check this possibility, we searched for the men themselves. By the end of 1979, 248 men from the treatment group and 246 men from the control group had been found. Equal proportions in each group, 76 percent, were living in Massachusetts.

As we discovered the men, we expanded record searches to the states where men were known to have lived. To obtain additional objective information about the men, files of the Massachusetts Department of Mental Health, the Division

TABLE 3.1   Effects of Treatment

Outcome	Number
Neither an undesirable outcome	109 pairs
Both an undesirable outcome	42 pairs
Only control group man an undesirable outcome	*39 pairs
Only treatment group man an undesirable outcome	*63 pairs
TOTAL	253

*z=.0226, two-tailed test.

of Alcoholism, state alcoholic clinics, and the Department of Vital Statistics were searched. Records of these agencies yielded information showing which of the men had died and which had been treated for mental illness or alcoholism.

To use a single objective measure for evaluating whether the Cambridge-Somerville Youth Study had affected the lives of its clients, each of the 506 men was classified as having or not having an objectively defined "undesirable" outcome. If and only if a man had been convicted for a crime indexed by the FBI, had died prior to age 35, or had received a medical diagnosis as alcoholic, schizophrenic, or manic-depressive was a man's outcome counted as undesirable. All other men were classified as having no undesirable outcome. Each pair was then placed in one of four categories: (1) neither the man from the treatment group nor the man from the control group had an undesirable outcome; (2) both men had undesirable outcomes; (3) only the man from the control group had an undesirable outcome; or (4) only the man from the treatment group had an undesirable outcome.

Discrepancies within pairs would be interpreted as evidence for effects of the treatment program. Pairs in which only the man from the control group had an undesirable outcome would be considered pairs in which the treatment program had been helpful.

Unfortunately, the objective measure for evaluating outcome indicated that the program had an adverse effect. (See Table 3.1.)

If some of the families resented intervention, failures might be due to their refusals to accept assistance or to that resentment. It therefore seemed reasonable to look at differences in effects of treatment based on whether the treatment group boys had been recipients of the intended program. To make the comparison, families were divided into those who presented problems of cooperation and those who did not. Counselors dictated reports about each of their interactions with the boys or the families, so that most of the case records included several hundred pages. Cases were considered to have shown problems of cooperation if the counselor reported such difficulties or if the case record was exceptionally short (fewer than 25 pages), indicating little interaction. The results, shown in Figure 3.1, indicate that only the cooperative families were affected by the treatment program.

Among the pairs in which the treatment family was uncooperative, the control and treatment boys were equally likely to turn out badly. Among the pairs in which the treatment family was cooperative, however, there were 27 pairs in which the treatment boys turned out better but 52 pairs in which the treatment

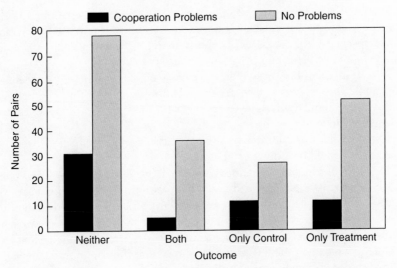

FIGURE 3.1   Case-control comparison: bad outcomes (convicted for Index crime, treated for psychoses or alcoholism, or died before age 35).

boys turned out worse. These findings strongly suggest that the treatment itself had been harmful.

The general impact of treatment appeared to have been damaging. Nevertheless, some subgroups of those who received treatment might have been helped. Beneficial effects might have resulted from starting treatment when the child was particularly young, from providing more frequent help, or from treatment being available over an especially long period of time. None of these possibilities received support. Nor was there evidence to show that some particular variation of treatment had been effective. Moreover, when comparisons were restricted to those with whom a counselor had particularly good rapport or those whom the staff believed it had helped most, the objective evidence failed to show that the program had been beneficial. (See McCord, 1981, 1990a, for details.)

Discussion

Why did the treatment have harmful effects? Part of the reason, it seems to me, has been the compensatory model on which treatment was based. Cabot—and many others—have assumed that an appropriate treatment would undo deficits in backgrounds of people at high risk for developing problems. This can be a critical error. A child rejected by parents may not be best served by someone else who tries to take the role of parent. Such a strategy might result in an exaggerated sense of loss; it might produce expectations for or dependence on assistance.

We know that supervision or "monitoring" is an efficient predictor of socialized behavior. But absence of supervision is likely to have resulted in a set of expectations, adaptations, and (perhaps) skills. So a child who has not been supervised may become *more* antisocial if he is placed under close supervision.

Children who are not good in school may not be best served by tutoring them. Self-identity or peer labeling may make such tutoring reinforce perceptions of inadequacy. Timing could be critical in determining whether a particular intervention would be beneficial or harmful.

In a strange sort of way, we may have come close to assuming that there is a single mold that would be appropriate for all. So we assume that children who are not loved should be given love; children who are doing badly in school should be taught to do better.

Certainly there are alternatives to academic success for satisfactory lives. The same might be said regarding social success.

Despite failure of the treatment program, the records of the Cambridge-Somerville Youth Study provided a rich field for mining information about the homes of 253 boys. These records were coded in 1957, prior to collection of the follow-up data. They therefore were not contaminated by retrospective biases. (See McCord and McCord, 1960, for a complete description of the coding.)

Analyses based on these records have shown that the criminogenic impact of paternal absence depends largely on the nature of the family interaction (McCord, 1990b), that differences between families with and without alcoholic fathers are permeating in terms of variables related to child rearing (McCord, 1988), and that home environments during early adolescence are strong predictors of both juvenile delinquency and of adult criminal behavior (McCord, 1991a).

It has been possible to learn, also, that some patterns of family interaction seem to promote alcoholism (McCord, 1988), while others contribute to competence (McCord, 1991b). It is doubtful that these relationships could have been discovered had not evidence been collected by direct observation and over a relatively long period of time. The opportunity for observation was generated by the treatment provided (Cabot, 1940).

On the one hand, the Cambridge-Somerville Youth Study could be considered a failure because it harmed some of the boys given treatment through its auspices. On the other hand, the study should be considered a success. It was a success because:

1. It showed the importance of using random assignment to treatment and control groups in order to assess the validity of cherished beliefs about helping others. Despite good intentions, iatrogenic effects occurred.
2. It showed that providing supportive friendly guidance was not a sufficient antidote for criminogenic conditions.
3. It showed that careful records collected in the process of providing treatment can yield scientifically valuable information about developmental issues.
4. It demonstrated that intervention can have long-term effects.

On a theoretical level, results of the Cambridge-Somerville Youth Study have two implications. First, they provide grounds for doubting that deficit approaches to reducing crime can be effective. And second, they provide grounds for doubting the adequacy of control theory as an explanation for crime.

Control theory explains crime as the result of failure to develop attachments to family, school, and norms. The Cambridge-Somerville Youth Study succeeded in developing conventional ties—but nevertheless failed to prevent deviant behavior.

Notes

This study was partially supported by U.S. Public Health Service Research Grant MH26779, National Institute of Mental Health (Center for Studies of Crime and Delinquency). The author expresses appreciation to the Department of Probation of the Commonwealth of Massachusetts, to the Division of Criminal Justice Services of the State of New York, to the Maine State Bureau of Identification, and to the states of California, Florida, Michigan, New Jersey, Pennsylvania, Virginia, and Washington for supplemental data about the men. The author thanks Richard Parente, Robert Staib, Ellen Myers, and Ann Cronin for their work in tracing the men and their records and Joan Immel, Tom Smedile, Harriet Sayre, Mary Duell, Elise Goldman, Abby Brodkin, and Laura Otten for their careful coding. The author is responsible for the statistical analyses and for the conclusions drawn from this research.

1. An exception to random assignment was made for eight cases who were matched after the treatment began. In addition, brothers were assigned to that group to which the first of the siblings was randomly assigned. This involved 21 boys in the treatment group and 19 in the control group.

References

Allport, G. 1951. Foreword. In E. Powers and H. Witmer, *An experiment in the prevention of delinquency: The Cambridge-Somerville Youth Study.* New York: Columbia University Press.

Cabot, P. S. deQ. 1940. A long-term study of children: The Cambridge-Somerville Youth Study. *Child Development* 11: 143–151.

Cabot, R. C. 1934. 1000 delinquent boys: First findings of the Harvard Law School's survey of crime. *Survey* 70(2): 38–40.

Deardorff, N. R. 1958. Richard Clarke Cabot. In *Dictionary of American Biography*, edited by R. L. Schuyler and E. T. James (Supplement 2, pp. 83–85). New York: Scribner's.

Glueck, S. and E. T. Glueck. 1934. *One Thousand Juvenile Delinquents.* Cambridge: Harvard University Press.

———. 1945. *After-conduct of Discharged Offenders.* London: Macmillan.

Gouge, W. 1627. *The works of William Gouge: vol. 1 Domestical Duties.* London: John Beal.

Healy, W. 1917. *Mental Conflicts and Misconduct.* Boston: Little Brown.

———. 1934. Comments. *Survey* 70(3): 94.

Healy, W. and A. F. Bronner. 1926. *Delinquents and Criminals: Their Making and Unmaking.* New York: Macmillan.

———. 1936. *New Light on Delinquency and its Treatment.* New Haven: Yale University Press.

Jevons, T. 1834/1970. Remarks on criminal law; with a plan for an improved system and observations on the prevention of crime. London. Reprinted in *Juvenile Offenders For a Thousand Years*, edited by W. B. Sanders, 152–154. Chapel Hill: University of North Carolina Press.

Matsell, G. W. 1850. Report of the chief of police concerning destitution and crime among children in the city. In *Juvenile Depravity and Crime in Our City*, edited by T. L. Harris, 14–15. New York: Norton.

McCord, J. 1981. Consideration of some effects of a counseling program. In *New Directions in the Rehabilitation of Criminal Offenders*, edited by S. E. Martin, L. R. Sechrest, and R. Redner, 394–405. Washington, D.C: National Academy of Sciences.

McCord, J. 1988. Identifying developmental paradigms leading to alcoholism. *Journal of Studies on Alcohol*, 49(4): 357–362.

McCord, J. 1990a. Crime in moral and social contexts. *Criminology*, 28(1): 1–26.

McCord, J. 1990b. Long-term perspectives on parental absence. In *Straight and Devious Pathways from Childhood to Adulthood*, edited by L. N. Robins and M. Rutter, 116–134. Cambridge: Cambridge University Press.

McCord, J. 1991a. Family relationships, juvenile delinquency, and adult criminality. *Criminology*, 29(3): 397–417.

McCord, J. 1991b. Competence in long-term perspective. *Psychiatry*, 54(3): 227–237.

McCord, W., and McCord, J. 1960. *Origins of Alcoholism*. Stanford, CA: Stanford University Press.

Mennel, R. M. 1973. *Thomas and Thistles: Juvenile Delinquents in the United States 1825–1940*. Hanover, NH: University Press of New England.

Powers, E., and H. Witmer, 1951. *An Experiment in the Prevention of Delinquency: The Cambridge-Somerville Youth Study*. New York: Columbia University Press.

CHAPTER FOUR

Cures That Harm

Unanticipated Outcomes of Crime Prevention Programs*

T HE *NEW YORK TIMES* published an article on Thursday, 4 April 2002 announcing that "a trade group representing British pharmaceutical companies publicly reprimanded Pfizer for promoting several medicines for unapproved uses and marketing another drug before it received government approval" (p. C5). The reprimand was justified because the drugs had not been appropriately tested for safety. Pfizer risked causing harm. No such reprimand could possibly occur in the fields of social intervention.

Researchers, practitioners, and policy makers have begun to understand that evidence is required to identify effective programs to reduce crime. Yet they typically couple the desire for evidence with an inappropriately narrow focus. They ask, Does the program work or not? This question is too narrow because it fails to recognize that some treatments cause harm. Intervention programs may, for example, increase crime or the use of drugs. They may decrease the punitive impact of sanctions available to the criminal justice system. They may, perhaps, result in reductions in the ability to cope with life—or even in premature death. Unless social programs are evaluated for potential harm as well as benefit, safety as well as efficacy, the choice of which social programs to use will remain a dangerous guess.

No public reservoir of data permits evaluating whether a given type of program meets even minimum requirements to provide benefits and avoid harm either to recipients of the social programs or to the communities from which they come. Yet social harm is costly to the public, perhaps even more costly than physical harm.

Reluctance to recognize that good intentions can result in harm can be found in biased investigating and reporting. Many investigators fail to ask whether an

*Reprinted from McCord, J. 2003. Cures that harm: Unanticipated outcomes of crime prevention programs. In *Annals of the American Academy of Political Science* 587: 16–30; with permission from Sage Publications and Corwin Press.

intervention has had adverse effects, and many research summaries lack systematic reporting of such effects (Sherman et al., 1997).

What has been called a publication bias appears when analyses show that a higher proportion of studies that reinforce popular opinions than those that do not get into peer-reviewed journals (Dickersin and Min, 1994; Easterbrook et al., 1991; Scherer, Dickersin, and Langenberg, 1994). In summarizing the results of studies evaluating publication bias, Colin Begg (1994) reported that "most studies of the issue have consistently demonstrated that positive (statistically significant) studies are more likely to be published" (p. 401).

One reason for what appears to be a code of silence about adverse effects is fear that all social programs will be tainted by the ones that are harmful. That fear, perhaps justified in some quarters, would be like blocking publication of potentially damaging effects of Celebrex, thalidomide, or estrogen because the publication could slow experimental work in disease prevention. Social programs deserve to be treated as serious attempts at intervention, with possibly toxic effects, so that a science of intervention can prosper.

What follows is a discussion of some social programs that have been carefully evaluated using experimental designs with random assignment to a treatment and a comparison group. They have been found to have harmful effects, and for this reason, they are important experiments. Knowledge that well-designed, carefully implemented social programs can produce unwanted results should set a solid foundation for insisting that all social programs should be coupled with evaluations that have scientific credibility.

The Cambridge-Somerville Youth Study

The Cambridge-Somerville Youth Study was a carefully designed, adequately funded, and well-executed intervention program. Furthermore, a scientifically credible research design played a central role in its construction.

Richard Clark Cabot funded, designed, and, until his death, directed the Cambridge-Somerville Youth Study. As a professor of clinical medicine and social ethics at Harvard, Cabot had made a mark in medicine by showing how to differentiate typhoid fever from malaria. His etiological study of heart disease was widely recognized as an important contribution to the field. He had introduced social services to Massachusetts General Hospital and had been president of the National Conference on Social Work. Not surprisingly, in turning to the problem of crime, Cabot insisted on using a scientific approach, one that aimed to alleviate the probable causes of crime but also one that would permit adequate tests of the results of intervention.

Cabot's beliefs about the causes of crime derived in part from the work of William Healy and Augusta Bronner, prominent researchers who codirected the Judge Baker Foundation (later known as the Judge Baker Guidance Centre) in Boston. Healy and Bronner reviewed four thousand delinquent cases, half from Chicago and half from Boston. Having discovered that less than 10 percent of the delinquents in their study had come from good homes, Healy and Bronner (1926) concluded that "where to place a large measure of responsibility, where to direct a strong attack in treatment and for prevention of delinquency stands out with striking clearness" (p. 129).

Cabot hypothesized that even rebellious youth from ghastly families "may conceivably be steered away from a delinquent career and toward useful citizenship if a devoted individual outside his own family gives him consistent emotional support, friendship, and timely guidance" (Allport, 1951, vi). The Cambridge-Somerville Youth Study would test this hypothesis.

The study began with a matched case design. Staff hired by the youth study solicited names of boys younger than ten who were living in the congested urban environments of Cambridge and Somerville, Massachusetts. To avoid stigmatizing the program, scout leaders as well as the police contributed to the pool of names.

Laboriously, the staff gathered information about the boys, their families, and the neighborhoods of their homes. Each boy was matched to another of similar age, social background, somatotype, and temperament. A toss of a coin determined which member of each matched pair would be placed into the treatment group and which into the control group.

When a match was identified and the coin had been tossed, a counselor visited the home of the treatment boy. These caseworkers visited the homes as frequently as weekly, when that seemed necessary, but the average frequency was twice a month. Treatment lasted an average of five and one-half years.

The logic of the study required being convinced that the treatment and control groups would have turned out similarly but for the introduction of treatment. Therefore, the groups were compared after a reduction of caseloads due to wartime gas restrictions had taken place in 1942. After the reduction, 253 matched pairs of boys remained in the program. No biases were discovered in the comparisons.

No reliable differences were discovered in comparisons of age, intelligence, whether referral to the youth study had been as "difficult" or "average," or the delinquency prediction scores assigned by the selection committee on the basis of the boys' family histories and home environments. No reliable differences appeared in comparisons regarding the boys' physical health as rated by the doctor after a medical examination, in mental health, in social adjustment, in acceptance of authority, or in social aggressiveness as reflected by teachers' descriptions of the boys. Nor were reliable differences found in ratings of adequacy of the home, disruption of the home, delinquency in the home, adequacy of discipline, standard of living, occupational status of the father, social status level of the elementary school attended by the boy (a measure based on the occupational levels of fathers whose children attended the school), or quality of the neighborhood in which the boys resided. Thus, the randomization within matched pairs had succeeded in producing two groups of boys who were substantially similar prior to the beginning of the treatment program.

During the period of treatment, counselors (most of whom had professional degrees in social work) provided friendly guidance to the boys, counseled parents, assisted the families in a variety of ways, and referred the boys to specialists when that seemed advisable. Boys in the treatment group were tutored, taken to a variety of sports events, and encouraged to participate in the woodwork shop provided by the youth study. Counselors encouraged the boys to join community youth groups and helped them get jobs. Many were sent to summer camps to take them away from the heat of the city.

Counselors were not permitted to accompany the boys to court. Nor were they permitted to include boys from the control group for any of their activities. Of course, boys in the control group received whatever services were provided by other organizations.

When the program terminated in 1945, more than half the treatment boys had been tutored in academic subjects, more than one hundred received medical or psychiatric attention, almost half had been sent to summer camps, and most of the boys had participated with their counselors in such activities as swimming, visits to local athletic competitions, and woodwork in the project's shop. The boys and their parents called on the social workers for help with such problems as illness and unemployment. They talked with their counselors about their hopes and ambitions as well as about their fears and defeats.

Although a discouraging number of boys in the treatment group were known to have broken the law, at the close of treatment, many boys identified as maladjusted when they entered the program had made fairly good adjustments. Had improvement from prediction been accepted as the measure of success, the program might have been judged effective.

To determine whether the improved adjustment should be attributed to treatment, interviewers tracked down 148 boys who had been in the control group. The interviewers gathered information from the boys, their families, and their school principals. Dr. Helen Witmer was brought into the program to help in its evaluation. She classified each boy among the 148 pairs in terms of adjustment. Disconcertingly, the results indicated that almost equal numbers of the control and the treatment group did better than had been anticipated at the beginning of the project. (See Powers and Witmer, 1951, for a more complete description of the program and its early evaluation.)

Additional disappointment came in 1948 from the Massachusetts Department of Probation. Court records showed that a slightly larger number of boys in the treatment group had been in court, 96 versus 92, and they had been charged with a slightly larger number of offenses, 264 versus 218.

Gordon Allport, president of the Board of Directors for the Ella Lyman Cabot Foundation, called for patience. He believed that the program might have prepared the boys to benefit from experience. If so, treatment effects might appear as the youth matured.

Between 1975 and 1981, when the boys were reaching middle age, my research assistants and I retraced the 253 matched pairs who had remained in the program after the cut in 1942. We located 98 percent of them. Questionnaires sent to men from the treatment group asked how, if at all, the program had helped them. Two-thirds of the respondents claimed that the program was helpful, with most of these men amplifying their judgments by specifying ways in which the project or the counselors had improved their lives. These testimonials included claims that the program had helped the men become law-abiding citizens, that it had helped to provide a better understanding of people, and that it had provided evidence that there were "people around who care." Many mentioned that the program had kept them "off the streets," that they were helped by having someone with whom they could talk, and that the counselors had affected their values. Some noted that the program had put them on the right track. Others mentioned the friendships encouraged or the talents acquired. With these subjective endorsements in hand, we sought objective evidence of the program's effects.

We tracked court records both in Massachusetts and in the states to which the men had migrated. We tracked mental hospital records and records from facilities for treatment of alcoholism. We obtained death records to confirm deaths when this was reported, and we searched death records for men who had not been found.

Comparisons between the treatment and control groups showed that for the majority of pairs (n=150), treatment had no measured effect on the objective outcomes. Nevertheless, for the 103 pairs who had different outcomes, those who had been in the treatment program were more likely to have been convicted for crimes indexed by the Federal Bureau of Investigation as serious street crimes. Those who had been in the treatment program had died an average of five years younger. And those who had been in the treatment program were more likely to have received a medical diagnosis as alcoholic, schizophrenic, or manic depressive (McCord, 1978, 1981, 1992).

In 1945, counselors had identified thirty-eight boys as having received the most benefit from the program. Among this select group, twenty-two appeared neither better nor worse than their matches in the control group. Four of the men turned out better than their matches, but twelve turned out worse. Thus, even among those whom the staff believed it had helped most, the objective evidence failed to show that the program had been beneficial.

One might argue that these results had nothing to do with the treatment program. Two comparisons suggest that this argument is wrong.

The first is that adverse treatment effects increased with increased intensity and duration of treatment. That is, the treatment program appeared to reflect a dose response. Boys whose counselors more frequently visited them and those in the treatment program the longest were most likely to fare badly as compared with their matched mates in the control group.

The second is that adverse effects occurred only among boys whose families had cooperated with the program. Families were divided into those who presented problems of cooperation and those who did not. Counselors had dictated reports about each of their interactions with the boys or the families, so most of the case records included several hundred pages. Cases were considered to have shown problems of cooperation if the counselor reported such difficulties or if the case record was exceptionally short (fewer than twenty-five pages), indicating little interaction.

Among the pairs in which the treatment family was uncooperative, the control and treatment boys were equally likely to turn out badly. Among the pairs in which the treatment family was cooperative, however, there were twenty-seven pairs in which the treatment boys turned out better but fifty-two pairs in which the treatment boys turned out worse. These comparisons strongly suggest that the treatment itself had been harmful.

To evaluate effects of the various treatment approaches, I computed an adverse odds ratio by dividing the number of pairs in which the treatment boy did worse than his match by the number of pairs in which the treatment boy did better than his match for each of the major emphases of the treatment program. Adverse odds ratios less than 1 indicate benefits of the treatment program. Conversely, ratios greater than 1 indicate harmful effects of the treatment program.

The odds ratio for bad outcomes for an emphasis on encouraging the boy to participate in community youth groups such as Boy Scouts and YMCA was 1.75 (35:20). That for an emphasis on providing academic help was 1.91 (42:22). The odds ratio for an emphasis on personal problems was 3.5 (28:8). And that for an emphasis on family problems was 3.75 (30:8). No emphasis seemed to have produced benefits from treatment.

Treatment in the Cambridge-Somerville Youth Study had specifically included summer camp. The camps selected for placement were not designed for troublesome kids. They catered to a general population, one for which summer camping offered an alternative to city heat and boredom as well as the pleasures of outdoor activities.

In part because I had developed a theory that would predict increased deviance through close association with peers one wanted to impress, I focused on effects of summer camp (Dishion, McCord, and Poulin, 1999). The construct theory of motivation suggests that people construct their motives through the way they perceive choices and that these perceptions are influenced by perceived actions of their associates (McCord, 1997, 1999, 2000). At summer camp, misbehaving boys would have unsupervised time during which they would be likely to brag about deviance. A bragging effect would be particularly noticeable among those sent to camp more than once. After the first summer, these boys would have known what camp was like and be in a position to estimate the effects of their reported daring (whether or not these reports were factual).

Among the 253 matched pairs assessed for follow-up, 125 of the treatment boys had been sent to summer camp, and 128 were not. The odds ratio for bad outcomes among those not sent to summer camp was 1.12 (28:25), that for the 59 boys sent to summer camp once was 1.33 (16:12), and that for the 66 boys sent to summer camp at least twice was 10.0 (20:2). In short, none of the treatment approaches showed measurable benefits, and some, particularly repeated placement in summer camps, resulted in harm.

I will summarize with the following list:

1. The Cambridge-Somerville Youth Study was carefully planned.
2. It was based on knowledge that poor families in disorganized neighborhoods were at high risk for crime.
3. Counselors had been trained to carry out their roles, and weekly conferences ensured that they were doing so.
4. Counselors integrated services provided by other available agencies with their own.
5. The program included youth with good as well as bad prognoses so that participation was not stigmatizing.

6. The youth study aimed to change many features of the environment, providing the boys with prosocial guidance, social skills, and healthful activities.
7. The program gave medical assistance and tutoring as well as guidance to both parents and youth.
8. Clients, for the most part, were satisfied with the program.
9. The program lasted five and one-half years, covering the period when the boys were between the ages of 10.5 and 16.
10. The program could be scientifically evaluated because its founder insisted that evaluation was central to the advance of social intervention practices.

Had there been no control group, evaluators might have concluded that the program was beneficial because so many of the treatment boys were better adjusted than anticipated. Or because two-thirds reported beneficial effects for themselves, evaluators might have judged that the program was effective. But these judgments would have been contrary to objective evidence that the program resulted in adverse outcomes for many of the participants.

Let me emphasize again the fact that the Cambridge-Somerville Youth Study was effective. The intervention had lasting effects. These effects were not beneficial.[1] The important legacy of the program, however, is its contribution to the science of prevention. Because the design supports scientifically credible conclusions, it showed that social interventions can have long-term effects. The results also serve to remind anyone willing to heed the warning that we do not yet know how to ensure benefits for youth in need of assistance.

Other Counterproductive Programs

The Cambridge-Somerville Youth Study is not alone in showing that sensible ideas and adequate implementation may produce interventions that fail to achieve their beneficial goals. The following sections describe some others.

Court Volunteers

Many courts in the United States encourage volunteer counselors to work with delinquents. Few of these receive adequate evaluation. An exception occurred when Martin Gold, who was director of the Program on Children, Youth, and Family Life at the University of Michigan Institute for Social Research, arranged to evaluate Volunteers in Probation. The program had already won community respect.

Police, caseworkers, or judges could assign probationers to the Volunteers in Probation program. Participation required consent from both the juvenile and his or her guardian. The consent form requested participation in a study involving Volunteers in Probation. Random assignment took place after this consent was obtained, with two out of three being assigned to the program and one of three to a control group. Those in the control group received the ordinary services of

the court, whereas those in the participation group were assigned to group counseling, individual counseling, and tutoring services provided by the volunteers.
Evaluations occurred after six months and again after twelve months.

Both self-reports and official records showed that participation in the program
inhibited a decline in criminality. Those assigned to the control group and those
who had been assigned to the volunteer program but had not participated in it
decreased their rates of crime. Those who participated in the volunteer program,
however, increased the number of crimes they reported committing. Their court
records, too, showed increases in crime as measured by the number of their police
contacts (Berger et al., 1975).

Berger et al. (1975) summarized, "While we found some ways that the volunteer service was delivered that seem superior to other ways, none of these
proved superior to providing no volunteer service at all" (p. VIII-2). Surprised
and disappointed by the results of their study, Berger et al. cautioned,

> To those who may feel that other such programs, perhaps their own, are
> so much superior or so different from this program that our findings and
> recommendations are irrelevant to them, we urge caution. The staff
> responsible for this program has reasons good enough for them to feel
> that their program was effective when this study began, and without this
> study might still have no reason to feel otherwise. If there is anything
> that such a study as this one demonstrates, it is the danger of relying
> exclusively on faith in good works in the absence of systematic data. (Pp.
> VIII-1–VIII-2)

Group Interaction Training

Several studies have reported deficiencies in the social skills of delinquents. Hoping to reduce delinquency, many schools developed programs designed to increase
the social skills of potential delinquents by giving them practice in discussing
issues with well-adjusted peers. Typically, adult leaders guide the discussions. The
programs have been called Positive Peer Culture, Peer Culture Development,
Peer Group Counseling, and Guided Group Interaction. Several of the programs
claim to be highly successful. Few have been evaluated using scientifically credible designs.

In 1982–1983, Gary Gottfredson (1987) arranged to have students in public
schools of Chicago randomly selected for inclusion in either the treatment or the
control group of a Guided Group Interaction program. Positive leaders, negative
leaders, troublesome children, and average children were included in the pool.
Fifty-one percent of both the treatment group and the control group were male,
Caucasians were approximately equally distributed between the groups, and the
groups were equivalent in terms of the prestige of parental occupations, prior
police contacts, and age. School tardiness, attachment to parents, self-reported
delinquency, and waywardness were used as measures of outcome.

Overall, the results for elementary school children showed no effects. For
the high school students, however, the Guided Group Interaction program tended

to increase misbehavior and delinquency. Gottfredson (1987) summarized the posttreatment comparisons: "the present results lend no support to any claim of benefit of treatment. . . . For the high school students, the effects appear predominantly harmful" (p. 708).

A somewhat different approach toward training young adolescents to have increased social skills has backfired in a program administered by the Oregon Social Learning Center. There, aggressive youngsters were randomly assigned to one of four groups: a teen training group that encouraged self-regulation and socialized behavior, a parental training group that encouraged parents to track their youngsters' behavior and to praise them for positive deeds, both, or one in which tapes and booklets substituted for group interaction. Whereas the parental training group (without peer training) seemed to show benefits, both groups assigned to peer training turned out worse than the no-interaction controls (Dishion and Andrews, 1995).

Activities Programs

Because of the poverty in which so much delinquency is embedded, many observers have concluded that delinquency might be reduced if alternative recreation were available. The Social Options for Teenagers Like You (SOFTLY) program in Australia was designed as an activities program to provide healthful recreation to delinquent adolescents. In addition, the program was designed

> to develop socially relevant skills, develop an awareness of options, teach skills to create further options, teach decision-making, planning and organizational skills (being at the same time aware of the effects of the choice on self and others), and reduce recidivism. (Dufty and Richards, 1978, ii)

The program consisted in group activities guided by peer group leaders trained by a supervisor to attend to the participating teenagers' interests. Weekly meetings provided support to the leaders.

Normally, groups met twice a week. Attempts were made to include parents in the meetings, a process facilitated by rotating meeting places among participants' homes. During the first weekly meeting, the group planned the activity to be carried out during the second meeting. Peer groups lasted between ten and twelve weeks.

The experimental group included ten peer groups with four to seven participants in each. Although forty-six teenagers were originally selected, only thirty-nine participants took part in both baseline and follow-up evaluation. A control group of teenagers was matched on sex, age, offending history during six months prior to the initial interview, guardianship, race, nationality of parental figures, work involvement of parental figures, and intellectual capacity.

Assessments were carried out for the experimental group just before the groups were formed and again six months later. For the comparison group, assessments were carried out when a match was identified and then six months after this identification.

The evaluation included measures of school and work involvement as well as delinquent activity. Reliable differences were not found for the former.

Court records identified a greater number of offenders among the treatment group during the first three months following completion of the intervention. Both groups decreased their rates of offending, but only the control group showed a significant decrease in the number of offenses committed. Dufty and Richards (1978) concluded that "this means that SOFTLY as it currently operates has a detrimental effect on the 'delinquently inclined' by increasing recidivism once the intervention ceases" (p. 42). As a consequence of the evaluation, the SOFTLY program was disbanded.

Scared Straight

Inmates designed a program, popularly known as Scared Straight, on an assumption that delinquency could be prevented by giving wild youngsters a taste of what it would be like to be imprisoned. The project started in Rahway Prison in New Jersey, where its endorsement by judges helped to make a convincing film that popularized the program.

Without scientifically respectable evaluations, Scared Straight projects were adopted in thirty-eight states. Congress held hearings about the program because researchers were skeptical. Miller and Hoelter (1979) found the town from which thirteen of seventeen youngsters in the film had come. They learned that some of the teenagers in the film claimed to have committed crimes to prove they were not scared.

Finally, careful research was carried out, with random assignment to San Quentin's Squires Program or to a control group. Twelve months later, 81 percent of the experimental group and 67 percent of the control group had been arrested (Lewis, 1983). Other scientifically credible evaluations, too, have shown that attempts to scare teenagers into better behavior is not a successful enterprise (Petrosino, Turpin-Petrosino, and Buehler, 2002).

Summary and Conclusions

I have described five types of programs that seemed promising but had harmful effects. Evidence about two of these—those involving court volunteers and those providing healthful group activities—appear in what has been called the fugitive literature. That is, despite solid research designs, the results have not been published. Evidence about adverse effects from social programs is hard to find in part because of a strong bias against reporting adverse effects of social programs. Authors of studies that fail to produce evidence of beneficial outcomes sometimes do not bother to submit their reports for publication. But also, those who do submit for publication tend to receive delays or rejections attributable to the unpalatable message they convey.

Many people seem to be willing to believe favorable results of inadequate evaluation designs. Some accept testimonials from clients who express their appreciation of a program. Against the claim that these provide valid evidence of effect, it should be noted that each of the programs described above would have been counted as successful by this criterion. Yet the clients would have been better off had they not participated in the programs.

Some argue that without comparison groups, measures taken before and after intervention can be used for valid evaluations. But changes over time occur for a variety of reasons, many of which are not documented. If changes are favorable and are more likely to occur in the absence of a program, the program should not be considered beneficial. The Cambridge-Somerville Youth Study might have been considered beneficial had improvements over prediction been accepted as the measure of outcome.

Often, one finds resistance to scientifically credible evaluations on the grounds that one ought not deprive some clients of the benefits given to others. Yet each of the harmful programs described above had been considered beneficial prior to its evaluation. Without appropriate equivalent comparisons in which both efficacy and safety are evaluated, we cannot know which treatments ought to be considered beneficial.

I have read several final reports of intervention programs that describe outcomes that are significantly worse than those in the comparison but include in the executive summary only results favorable to the program, often adding that the size of the sample precludes obtaining significant differences favoring treatment.

When results of the Cambridge-Somerville study were first published (and they were published only on the condition that a critical article would be coupled with its publication), I received threatening phone calls and notes. When I gave talks about these results, in many audiences, people shouted ugly names at me.

Researchers typically fail to consider whether social programs have had adverse effects, looking only for favorable results of treatment. Government agencies sponsor intervention programs with no provision for adequate evaluation. These are problems for the advancement of social well-being.

Yet providers of social services do not have a right to harm their clients. Nor do most providers wish to do so. But the social climate that buries evidence of harm is powerful. That social climate must be changed.

Clearly, social programs can have enduring effects. Although some popular interventions have harmful effects, of course, other intervention programs benefit their clients. Without scientifically credible evaluations, we cannot learn which programs are beneficial and which are harmful.

It is not enough to evaluate a program once. As noted by Weisburd and Taxman (2000), "The strength of experimental designs in specifying treatment impacts for specific populations does not in itself overcome the weaknesses associated with single site research studies" (p. 316).

Even when replications suggest that a particular type of program is effective, we should not assume that the program will work under new conditions. Historical changes, for example, in the definitions of crime or availability of drugs or of employment might alter the outcome of particular interventions. Demographic differences such as age, sex, or ethnicity might affect whether an intervention is effective. Different places, with different practices (e.g., regarding day care,

medical coverage, or education), might reflect the influence of unmeasured variables on the relationship between interventions and outcomes. As Peter Grabosky
(1996) noted in his review of unintended consequences of crime prevention
strategies, "What works in Wollongong might fail on Palm Island" (p. 39).

Canada bears many similarities to the United States. Nevertheless, the Center for Children and Families in the Justice System wisely recognized that programs effective in some environments might not be effective in different environments. It brought the promising multisystemic therapy (Henggeler, Melton,
and Smith, 1992; Henggeler et al., 1993) from the United States to Ontario,
Canada. The Canadian program involved a multisite design with random assignment to treatment and comparison groups. The comparison groups received the
usual treatments in each of the four sites involved in the study. Program fidelity
was monitored. Survival curves for convictions of 407 youth at six months, 363
at one year, 239 at two years, and 115 at three years give no indication of benefit from the program. Alison Cunningham (2002), director of research and plan-
ning for the project wrote, "Because the control group has the same outcomes as
the MST [multisystemic therapy] recipients, it is unsafe to conclude that the two
American studies are sufficient evidence to justify the wide-spread adoption of
MST in Canada" (p. 11).

Social programs can cause crime as well as reduce it. They also can increase
illness and reduce the ability of clients to cope with life's challenges. Effects of
criminal justice interventions on education, mental health, and job performance
deserve attention. A practice that decreases crime but increases alcoholism or
mental illness might not be considered a net gain either by the clients or by the
community that supported the program.

Potentially harmful effects of drugs have been recognized, and drug companies are required to keep track of reports of problems with the medications they
advertise and sell. These can be subject to periodic review. Similar standards
might be embraced for social programs. Recognizing that programs can have
harmful effects may be critical to acceptance of experimental designs for evaluating social interventions.

Clearly, if social practice is to be improved, continuing evaluation should be
an integral part of social interventions. Whenever possible, these evaluations
should employ random assignment of similar people to either treatment or comparison groups. Always, the outcome should be measured in ways that do not rely
on the typically favorable biases of clients, program providers, and sponsors. The
evaluations should, of course, include a check for evidence of adverse effects as
well as benefits.

We do not know the dimensions of variation that affect social programs.
Careful collection of data to document the process of treatments and their effects
should become as essential in the field of criminology as it is in the field of highway or airline safety.

It would be extremely useful to have not only a data repository that provides
systematic reviews of high-quality research, as will the Campbell Collaboration
(Farrington and Petrosino 2001), but also one that collects information about
particular programs in specific venues. If evaluation becomes an expected part of

program administration, and all well-designed programs and their evaluations contribute toward such a data repository, knowledge about the safety and effectiveness of social programs would begin to accumulate, and informed decisions could be made.

Note

The author thanks David Weisburd and Anthony Petrosino for their helpful comments on an earlier draft of this article.

1. Discussion of possible causes for these effects can be found in McCord (1978, 1981) and Dishion, McCord, and Poulin (1999).

References

Allport, Gordon. 1951. Foreword. In *An Experiment in the Prevention of Delinquency: The Cambridge-Somerville Youth Study*, edited by E. Powers and H. Witmer. New York: Columbia University Press.

Begg, Colin B. 1994. Publication bias. In *The Handbook of Research Synthesis*, edited by Harris Cooper and Larry V. Hedges. New York: Russell Sage.

Berger, R. J., J. E. Crowley, M. Gold, J. Gray, and M. S. Arnold. 1975. *Experiment in a Juvenile Court: A Study of a Program of Volunteers Working with Juvenile Probationers*. Ann Arbor: Institute for Social Research, University of Michigan.

Cunningham, Alison. 2002. *One Step Forward: Lessons Learned from a Randomized Study of Multisystemic Therapy in Canada*. London, Canada: Center for Children and Families in the Justice System.

Dickersin, Kay and Y.-I. Min. 1994. Publication bias: The problem that won't go away. *Annals of the New York Academy of Sciences* 703: 135–146.

Dishion, Thomas J. and David W. Andrews. 1995. Preventing escalation in problem behaviors with high-risk young adolescents: Immediate and 1-year outcomes. *Journal of Consulting and Clinical Psychology* 63(4): 538–548.

Dishion, Thomas J., Joan McCord, and François Poulin. 1999. When interventions harm: Peer groups and problem behavior. *American Psychologist* 54(9): 1–10.

Dufty, B. J. and W. Richards. 1978. Evaluation of S.O.F.T.L.Y. Unpublished manuscript, Australian Institute of Criminology, Canberra.

Easterbrook, P. J., J. A. Berlin, R. Gopalan, and D. R. Matthews. 1991. Publication bias in clinical research. *Lancet* 337: 867–872.

Farrington, David P. and Anthony Petrosino. 2001. The Campbell Collaboration Crime and Justice Group. *Annals of the American Academy of Political and Social Science* 578: 35–49.

Gottfredson, Gary D. 1987. Peer group interventions to reduce the risk of delinquent behavior: A selective review and a new evaluation. *Criminology* 25(3): 671–714.

Grabosky, Peter N. 1996. Unintended consequences of crime prevention. *Crime Prevention Studies* 5: 25–56.

Healy, William and Augusta F. Bronner. 1926. *Delinquents and Criminals: Their Making and Unmaking*. New York: Macmillan.

Henggeler, Scott W., Gary B. Melton, and Linda A. Smith. 1992. Family preservation using multisystemic therapy: An effective alternative to incarcerating serious juvenile offenders. *Journal of Consulting & Clinical Psychology* 60: 953–961.

Henggeler, Scott W., Gary B. Melton, Linda A. Smith, Sonja K. Schoenwald, and J. H. Hanley. 1993. Family preservation using multisystemic therapy: Longterm follow-up to a clinical trial with serious juvenile offenders. *Journal of Child & Family Studies* 2: 283–293.

Lewis, Roy V. 1983. Scared Straight—California style. *Criminal Justice and Behavior* 10(2): 284–289.

McCord, Joan. 1978. A thirty-year follow-up of treatment effects. *American Psychologist* 33(3): 284–289.

———. 1981. Consideration of some effects of a counseling program. In *New Directions in the Rehabilitation of Criminal Offenders*, edited by Susan E. Martin, Lee B. Sechrest, and Robin Redner. Washington, DC: National Academy of Sciences.

———. 1992. The Cambridge-Somerville Study: A pioneering longitudinal-experimental study of delinquency prevention. In *Preventing Antisocial Behavior: Interventions from Birth through adolescence*, edited by Joan McCord and Richard E. Tremblay. New York: Guilford.

———. 1997. He did it because he wanted to … In *Motivation & Delinquency*. vol. 44 of *Nebraska Symposium on Motivation*, edited by D. Wayne Osgood. Lincoln: University of Nebraska Press.

———. 1999. Understanding childhood and subsequent crime. *Aggressive Behavior* 25: 241–253.

———. 2000. A theory of motivation and the life course. In *Social Dynamics of Crime and Control: New Theories for a World in Transition*, edited by Susanne Karstedt and Kai-D Bussmann. Portland, OR: Hart.

Miller, Jerome G. and Herbert H. Hoelter. 1979. *Prepared Testimony: Oversight on Scared Straight.* Washington, DC: Government Printing Office.

The New York Times. 2002. 4 April, p. C5.

Petrosino, Anthony, Carolyn Turpin-Petrosino, and John Buehler. 2002. *The Effects of Scared Straight and Other Juvenile Awareness Programs on Delinquency.* Issue 3 of *Cochrane Library.* Oxford, UK: Update Software.

Powers, Edwin and Helen Witmer. 1951. *An Experiment in the Prevention of Delinquency: The Cambridge-Somerville Youth Study.* New York: Columbia University Press.

Scherer, Roberta W., Kay Dickersin, and Patricia Langenberg. 1994. Full publication of results initially presented in abstracts: A meta-analysis. *Journal of the American Medical Association* 272: 158–162.

Sherman, Lawrence W., Denise C. Gottfredson, Doris L. MacKenzie, John E. Eck, Peter Reuter, and Shawn D. Bushway. 1997. *Preventing Crime: What Works, What Doesn't, What's Promising.* Washington DC: U.S. Department of Justice, National Institute of Justice.

Weisburd, David and Faye S. Taxman. 2000. Developing a multicenter randomized trial in criminology: The case of HIDTA. *Journal of Quantitative Criminology* 16: 315–340.

PART II

The Effects of Child Rearing

CHAPTER FIVE

Some Child-Rearing Antecedents of Criminal Behavior in Adult Men*

D ESPITE A MASSIVE literature emphasizing the importance of child rearing, conscientious critics (e.g., Clarke & Clarke, 1976; Yarrow, Campbell, & Burton, 1968) have raised legitimate doubts regarding the impact of parental behavior on personality development. Many of the studies that link parental behavior with personality development rely upon a single source of information for both sets of variables; systematic reporting biases could thus cause obtained relationships. Most of the remaining studies have depended upon concurrent measurements, leaving doubt as to the direction of influence between parents' behavior and characteristics of the child. Questions about interpreting the results of both types of studies serve to highlight the importance of longitudinal research.

A few researchers have gathered information through longitudinal studies, using independent sources for measuring child rearing and for measuring personality. Robins (1966) analyzed information from clinic records gathered during childhood and related that information to data gathered when the subjects were adults. Robins pioneered assessment of long-term effects of child rearing, and her study raises doubts about the validity of retrospective reports on family socialization. Nevertheless, since predictor models combined variables describing child rearing with other types of variables (empirically linked with outcome), the research fails to provide convincing evidence that child-rearing differences affected adult behavior.

Block (1971) evaluated character development among subjects in the Berkeley longitudinal studies. Dividing 63 subjects into five types and checking differences in their backgrounds, Block reached the conclusion: "What comes through, for both sexes and without exception in viewing the various types, is an

*Reprinted from McCord, J. 1979. Some child-rearing antecedents of criminal behavior in adult men. In *Journal of Personality and Social Psychology* 37 (9): 1477–1486; with permission from Sage Publications and Corwin Press.

unequivocal relationship between the family atmosphere in which a child grew up and his later character structure" (p. 258). Although Block reports many statistically reliable differences, his analyses do not permit the reader to evaluate the strength of relationships between family atmosphere and character structure.

In 1973–1974, Werner and Smith (1977) retraced 88 percent of the children born on Kauai Island in 1955. Interviews with the mothers provided evidence about the family environment of subjects when they were newborn infants, age 2, and age 10. Although combined measures tended to account for a relatively high proportion of variance in several problem areas, the authors did not assess specific child-rearing models as predictors of outcome behavior.

Lefkowitz, Eron, Walder, and Huesmann (1977) used a main effects model in stepwise multiple regression for their longitudinal study of aggression. Only two of the six variables that together accounted for about a quarter of the variance in male aggressiveness at age 18 were related to child rearing at age 8. Since the model included both redundant measures of child rearing and heterogeneous variables (e.g., child's preference for girls' games, parents' religiosity, and ethnicity of family), effects of differences in child rearing may have been masked by collinearity (Blalock, 1963; Gordon, 1968; Mosteller & Tukey, 1977).

The paucity of evidence to support a view that child rearing affects personality has led some authors (e.g., Clinard, 1974; Jessor & Jessor, 1977) to the conclusion that home atmosphere during childhood has a negligible effect upon personality development. Such authors present the challenge to which the present research is addressed: if parental behavior has an important impact upon personality development, differences in child rearing ought to contribute to variations in subsequent behavior.

Method

Subjects for this study were selected from a treatment program designed to prevent delinquency. The youths ranged in age, at the time of their introduction to the program, from 5 to 13 ($M=10.5$, $SD=1.6$).

Counselors visited 253 boys twice a month, for an average 5-year period between 1939 and 1945. With the exception of one who was a nurse, the counselors had been trained as social workers. After each visit, the counselor recorded observations about the family as well as the child.[1]

Case records from the treatment program described, in detail, whatever activities the counselors had observed on their visits to the homes. The records included reports of conversations with parents, friends, neighbors, and teachers as well as with the boys. Counselor turnover (a potential problem from a treatment perspective) produced a benefit for research: most of the families were visited by more than one counselor.

To justify treatment of family backgrounds as independent units for analyses, only one subject from a family was included. Boys not reared by their natural mothers were also excluded. After eliminating brothers ($n=21$) and those not reared by their natural mothers ($n=36$), 201 cases remained for analysis.[2]

In 1957, coders read each case thoroughly in order to form judgments about the home and family interaction. These coders had no access to information about the subjects other than that contained in treatment records. A 10 percent random sample of the records was read independently by a second coder to yield an estimate of the reliability of the coding.[3] Variables from the coded case records were used in the present study.

The mother's attitude toward her son had been classified as actively affectionate (if there had been considerable interaction, without continual criticism, between mother and child, $n=95$), passively affectionate (if there had been little interaction between mother and son, though the mother had shown concern for her child's welfare, $n=51$), ambivalent or passively rejecting (if there had been marked alternations in the mother's attitude toward her son so that she had seemed sometimes to be actively affectionate and sometimes rejecting, or if the mother had seemed unconcerned about the child's welfare, $n=43$), or actively rejecting (if the mother had appeared to be constantly critical of the boy, $n=11$). Independent reading of 25 cases resulted in the same ratings for 80 percent.

Two ratings from the original codes were combined to evaluate effects of supervision. One described whether the child's activities outside of school were governed by an adult. This scale was divided to indicate whether supervision was generally present, occasionally present, or absent. Independent coding yielded identical ratings for 84 percent of the 25 randomly selected cases. The second rating described parental expectations regarding the boys' activities. Coders were instructed to rate expectations as "high" if the child was given responsibility for care of his younger siblings, for preparation of meals, for contributing to the financial support of the family, or for doing "extremely well" in school. Independent ratings yielded agreement for 76 percent of 25 cases. The scales from the 1957 codes were combined to classify subjects into one of four categories: supervision generally present and high expectations for the child to accept responsibilities ($n=40$), supervision generally present without evidence that high expectations were placed on the child ($n=78$), occasional supervision ($n=60$), and supervision absent ($n=23$).[4]

A rating of parental conflict was based on counselors' reports of disagreements between the parents. Raters were instructed to look for conflicts about the child and conflicts about values, about money, about alcohol, and about religion. Parental conflict was coded into one of four categories: no indication, apparently none, some, or considerable. For the present research, cases were divided into those whose parents evidenced considerable conflict ($n=68$) and those coded in alternative categories. Independent readers agreed, for this division, on 80 percent of the cases checked for reliability.

Three measures from the 1957 codes were combined to identify aggressive parents. Coders classified the aggressiveness of each parent by looking for evidence that the parent "used little restraint" when angry. Case records included reports on parents who threw things (e.g., one father threw a refrigerator down the stairs in the midst of an argument with his wife), hit people, broke windows, and shouted abuses. Independent coders agreed on 84 percent of the fathers and 92 percent of the mothers in classifying parents as aggressive. The coders described paternal discipline; the category "consistently punitive" identified fathers who regularly used physical force (e.g., beating a child) or very harsh verbal abuse. Independent coders agreed on 92 percent of the cases for ratings regarding this classification. If a parent was coded as aggressive or the father was coded as consistently punitive, the child was classified as having an aggressive parent ($n=75$).[5]

The 1957 codes included a measure of the mother's self-confidence. A rating as self-confident was assigned if that mother showed signs of believing in her own abilities ($n=55$). Other possibilities for this rating were "no indication of general attitude; evidence that mother saw herself as a victim or pawn in a world about which she could do nothing; and neutral, that is, generally seemed merely to accept things as they came." For this variable, independent raters agreed in classifying 84 percent of the 25 cases used to estimate reliability.

In 1957, coders rated a father as alcoholic if the case record indicated that he had lost jobs because of repeated drinking, if marital problems were attributed primarily to his excessive drinking, if welfare agencies had repeatedly pointed to the father's drinking as grounds for family problems, or if the father had received treatment specifically for alcoholism. Independent coders agreed for 96 percent of the ratings on this variable. In 1948, after termination of the treatment program, criminal records on the family members of subjects were collected; these records were locked in a file separate from the case histories. In 1975, after names had been replaced by numerical identifiers, an assistant unfamiliar with the case records coded these criminal records. For the present study, a father was considered "deviant" if the case record indicated that he was an alcoholic, if the criminal record showed that he had been convicted at least three times for drunkenness, or if his criminal record showed that he had been convicted for a serious crime (i.e., theft, burglary, assault, rape, attempted murder, or murder). These criteria led to identification of 86 fathers as deviant.[6]

Case records included information about family structure. A father was considered "absent" if his residence was not with the subject's mother. Independent coding of 25 cases yielded agreement on 96 percent regarding whether or not the boy was living with both natural parents.[7] The 71 boys having absent fathers ranged in age, at the time when the loss occurred, from birth to 16 ($M=7.01$, $SD=5.03$). The father-absent subjects were subclassified to identify those whose natural fathers had been present during their first 5 years ($n=48$) and those for whom the absence had occurred prior to the age of 5 ($n=23$).

These seven variables (mother's affection, supervision, parental conflict, parental aggression, mother's self-confidence, father's deviance, and paternal absence) were used to depict the home atmosphere of subjects during childhood. The first three are regarded as directly related to child rearing. Relationships among these measures are shown in Table 5.1.

Subjects had been selected from congested urban neighborhoods. Nevertheless, differences in social status could contribute to subsequent differences in behavior. Two measures of social status were available. The case records supplied information about the father's occupation. Coders classified these occupations as white-collar (9.6%), skilled tradesmen (32.8%), or unskilled workers (57.6%). The reliability check yielded agreement on 96 percent of the ratings. A second

TABLE 5.1 Relationships Among Variables Describing Home Atmosphere (Cramer's V)

	Supervision	Parent conflict	Parent aggression	Mother's self-confidence	Father's deviance	Father's absence
Mother's affection	.241***	.209*	.184*	.199*	.209*	.110
Supervision		.267**	.106	.308***	.230*	.187*
Parent conflict			.188**	.109	.381***	.375***
Parent aggression				.289***	.144*	.024
Mother's self-confidence					.125	.087
Father's deviance						.206*

*p < .05. **p < .01. ***p < .001.

measure of social status was provided by a rating of the neighborhoods in which the boys were raised. These ratings had been made, in 1938 and 1939, as part of the selection procedures. The ratings took into account delinquency rates, availability of recreational facilities, and proximity to bars, railroads, and junkyards. These ratings were coded on a 4-point scale from better to worst neighborhoods. The two measures tended to covary, Cramer's V (6)=.218, p=.0044.

Between 1975 and 1978, the subjects were retraced. Among the 201 men included in the study, 153 (76%) were alive and in Massachusetts at least until the age of 40[8]; 16 (8%) had died prior to their fortieth birthdays; 29 (14%) had migrated from Massachusetts; and 3 (1%) remained to be found.

During 1975 and 1976, the names (and pseudonyms) of all the men who had been in the program were checked through court records in Massachusetts.[9] These criminal records were traced and coded by different people from those who coded other records. Coders of the criminal records (and those who traced them) had no access to other information about the subjects. The court records showed the dates of court appearances and the crimes for which the subjects had been convicted. They were coded to show the type of crime and the age of the person when he was convicted. Convictions for serious property crimes (larceny, auto theft, breaking and entering, arson) and serious personal crimes (assault, attempted rape, rape, attempted murder, kidnapping, and murder) were used as dependent measures for this study.

Among the 201 men, 71 had been convicted for at least one serious crime; 53 had been convicted for property crimes and 34 for personal crimes (including 15 convicted for both types). Their ages when first convicted ranged from 8 to 38, with a mean of 18.7 (SD=8.7) and a median of 20. Those convicted prior to their 18th birthdays were classified as juvenile delinquents (n=43); those convicted after reaching the age of 18 were classified as adult criminals (n=48, including 20 who had been juvenile delinquents).

After analyzing the relationship to crime of each of the childhood variables separately, multiple regression analyses (General Linear Model Procedure, Barr, Goodnight, Sall, and Helwig, 1976) were used to ascertain the contribution of child rearing to the variance in number of serious property and personal crimes. To test the degree to which knowledge of home atmosphere could enable accurate prediction of subsequent behavior, the six central variables describing home atmosphere were used in discriminant function analyses to identify criminals.

As a more stringent test of the contribution of home atmosphere to subsequent crime, the discriminant function analyses were also used to predict criminals among the subsample whose criminal records provided the most complete histories of convictions: those men living in Massachusetts at least until the age of 40. If this function identified criminality more accurately for the total group than for those living in Massachusetts, there would be grounds for suspecting an interaction effect between home background and unmeasured variables. If this function identified criminality at least as accurately for those alive in Massachusetts at the age of 40, there would be additional support for a conclusion that home atmosphere during childhood contributes to criminality.

Results

As a first step toward learning whether parental behavior contributes to subsequent differences in criminality, the seven scales describing home atmosphere and the two scales describing social status were individually analyzed for their contributions to the variance in number of serious crimes against property and persons. (See Table 5.2.)

With the exception of father's absence, each of the scales describing home atmosphere accounted for a statistically significant ($p < .05$) proportion of the variance in number of crimes against property, persons, or both.[10] Neither of the measures of social status was significantly related to these types of crimes.

Supervision and mother's self-confidence were related to both crimes against property and crimes against persons; mother's affection and father's deviance were related to property crimes (though not to personal crimes); conflict and parental aggression were related to personal crimes (though not to property crimes). The boys who lacked maternal affection, who lacked supervision, whose mothers lacked self-confidence, and whose fathers were deviant were more often subsequently convicted for property crimes. The boys who lacked supervision, whose

TABLE 5.2   Relationships Between Variables Describing Home Background and Crimes

		Property crimes			Personal crimes		
	df	R^2	F	Prob. $> F$	R^2	F	Prob. $> F$
Mother's affection	3,196	.092	6.60	.0003	.029	1.92	.1261
Supervision	3,197	.152	11.77	.0001	.071	5.04	.0023
Parent conflict	1,199	.008	1.76	.1866	.035	7.14	.0081
Parent aggression	1,199	.012	2.38	.1242	.036	7.36	.0073
Mother's self-confidence	1,199	.022	4.50	.0350	.024	4.98	.0268
Father's deviance	1,199	.024	4.81	.0295	.000	0.00	.9569
Father's absence	2,198	.005	0.47	.6286	.026	2.67	.0715
Neighborhood	3,197	.028	1.87	.1335	.016	1.10	.3513
Father's occupation	2,195	.008	0.74	.4798	.012	1.15	.3181

mothers lacked self-confidence, and who had been exposed to parental conflict and to aggression were subsequently more often convicted for personal crimes.

The relationships to criminality of individual variables describing home atmosphere, though statistically significant, each accounted for a relatively small proportion of the variance. More important, since "criminogenic" conditions tended to be related to one another, these relationships could not be taken as evidence that the differences in home background that they represented resulted in differences in subsequent behavior.

To evaluate the contribution of parental behavior to subsequent behavior, the six central variables describing home atmosphere were divided into two sets. The first set included those variables that described characteristics of the parents, characteristics that might be viewed as antecedent to child-rearing practices: parental aggressiveness, paternal deviance, and mother's self-confidence. The second set included the three variables that described interpersonal behavior: parental conflict, supervision, and mother's affection; these were considered to be direct measures of child rearing. The effect of this division was to classify families in two ways. The first classification took account of relationships among the variables describing the parents; the second took account of relationships among the variables describing child rearing.

Sequential multiple regression models were used. They introduced the measure of social status (the interaction of father's occupation and neighborhood) as the first variable. The regression procedure next evaluated the sequential contribution to explained variance of parental characteristics (the interaction of paternal deviance, maternal self-confidence, and parental aggression). After controlling effects of both social status and parental characteristics, the procedure evaluated effects of child rearing (i.e., the interaction of supervision, parental conflict, and the mother's affection).

Child rearing, as measured in this longitudinal study, clearly accounts for a significant proportion of the variance in subsequent criminality. Table 5.3 describes the decomposition of the regression models.

As predictors of property crimes, the model accounts for 39.1 percent of the variance, $F(45, 151)=2.15$, $p=.0003$. Parental aggression, paternal deviance, and maternal self-confidence account for 6.1 percent of the variance after controlling social status, $F(7, 151)=2.16$, $p=.0404$. Parental conflict, supervision, and maternal affection contribute significantly to the variance after effects of social status and parental characteristics have been controlled, $R^2=.261$, $F(27, 151)=2.40$, $p=.0003$.

As predictors of personal crimes, the model accounts for 35.7 percent of the variance, $F(45, 151)=1.87$, $p=.0028$. The three more direct measures of child rearing contribute significantly to the variance after effects of social status and parental characteristics have been removed, $R^2=.244$, $F(27, 151)=2.13$, $p=.0023$.

As predictors of the total number of serious crimes for which the men had been convicted, the model accounts for 39.1 percent of the variance, $F(45, 151)=2.16$, $p=.0003$. Parental characteristics account for 5.9 percent of the variance after effects of social status have been controlled, $F(7, 151)=2.45$, $p=.0209$. The child-rearing variables account for 26.0 percent of the variance, $F(27, 151)=2.39$, $p=.0005$, after removing effects of both social status and parent characteristics.

TABLE 5.3   Home Environment and Subsequent Criminality

Sequential contribution	df	R^2	F	Prob. > F
PREDICTING PROPERTY CRIMES[a]				
Social status	11	.0688	1.55	.1185
Parental characteristics	7	.0610	2.16	.0404
Child rearing	27	.2612	2.40	.0005
PREDICTING PERSONAL CRIMES[b]				
Social status	11	.0541	1.16	.3222
Parental characteristics	7	.0588	1.97	.0616
Child rearing	27	.2444	2.13	.0023
PREDICTING TOTAL CRIMES[c]				
Social status	11	.0620	1.40	.0620
Parental characteristics	7	.0691	2.45	.0209
Child rearing	27	.2601	2.39	.0005

[a]Model: R^2=.391; $F(45, 151)$=2.15; p=.0003.

[b]Model: R^2=.3573; $F(45, 151)$=1.87; p=.0028.

[c]Model: R^2=.3912; $F(45, 151)$=2.16; p=.0003.

Adding information about whether or not a man had been reared in a home marked by paternal absence did not reliably increase the accuracy of any of the predictions.[11]

Within the (relatively restricted) range of social class represented in the study, the contribution of social status to the variance in crimes was not statistically reliable. On the other hand, both parental characteristics and child-rearing practices were reliably related to the number of crimes for which the subjects had been convicted.[12]

Approximately a third of the 200 men coded on all six variables describing home atmosphere had been convicted for at least one serious crime. A discriminant function based on the variables describing home atmosphere for these 200 men correctly identified 147 (73.5%) as criminals or noncriminals; random predictions based on prior probabilities would be expected to identify only 54.2 percent correctly,[13] z=5.48, p < .0001. The function based on parental aggression, maternal self-confidence, paternal deviance, supervision, maternal affection, and parental conflict correctly identified 76.7 percent of the noncriminals and 67.6 percent of the criminals. (See Table 5.4.)

Forty-eight men had been convicted for serious crimes after their 18th birthdays. The six variables describing home atmosphere provided a discriminant function which correctly identified 27 (56.3%) of the 48 adult criminals and 133 (87.5%) of the 152 men without records for convictions as adults. Predictions based on the descriptions of home atmosphere provided a 16.5 percent improvement over the 63.5 percent expected from random predictions based on prior probabilities, z=4.85, p < .0001. (See Table 5.4.)

TABLE 5.4   Results of Discriminant Function Analyses

Dependent and independent variables	Correct as criminals		Correct as noncriminals		Overall accuracy		% improvement over chance	$z < p$
	N	%	N	%	N	%		
ALL SUBJECTS								
Ever criminal home atmosphere	71	67.6	129	76.7	200	73.5	19.3	.0001
Adult criminal home atmosphere	48	56.3	152	87.5	200	80.0	16.5	.0001
MEN LIVING IN MASSACHUSETTS THROUGH THE AGE OF 40								
Ever criminal home atmosphere	60	81.7	92	70.7	152	75.0	22.8	.0001
Adult criminal home atmosphere	42	71.4	110	84.6	152	80.9	20.9	.0001
Juvenile delinquency record	42	45.2	110	83.6	152	73.0	13.0	.0011

After discarding men who had died before the age of 40, migrated from Massachusetts, or who had not yet been found, 152 men who were living in Massachusetts at least until the age of 40 and whose case records had been coded for all six variables describing home atmosphere remained for discriminant function analyses. Among these men, the discriminant function correctly identified 75.0 percent, a slight improvement over the rate of correct identification among the total group of men and a 22.8 percent improvement over random procedures based on prior probabilities, $z=5.63$, $p < .0001$. (See Table 5.4.) This discriminant function correctly identified 81.7 percent of the 60 criminals and 70.7 percent of the 92 noncriminals.

A breakdown of the results shows that the discriminant function had correctly classified as criminal 78.1 percent of those convicted only for property crimes, 78.6 percent of those convicted only for personal crimes, and 92.9 percent of those convicted for both property and personal crimes.

Among the 60 men convicted for serious crimes and still living in Massachusetts at the age of 40, 18 (30.0%) had been convicted only as juveniles, 23 (38.7%) had first been convicted after the age of 18, and 19 (31.7%) had been convicted both as juvenile and as adults. Were one to predict that only and all juvenile delinquents would be convicted as adults, the prediction would be correct for 73.0 percent, an improvement over an expectation of 60.0 percent from random procedures based on prior probabilities, $z=3.27$, $p=.0011$. This prediction would be correct for 45.2 percent of the adult criminals and for 83.6 percent of the men not convicted as adults. Predictions based on juvenile records would, of course, be right for *none* of the men first convicted as adults (54.8% of the adult criminals) and for only 51.4 percent of the juvenile delinquents.

Among men living in Massachusetts at the age of 40, the discriminant function analysis based on home atmosphere during childhood correctly identified 80.9 percent as criminal or noncriminal after the age of 18. (See Table 5.4.) Use of the variables describing home atmosphere during childhood resulted in a 20.9 percent improvement over chance identification, $z=5.26$, $p < .0001$, and a 7.9 percent improvement over predictions based on the subjects' juvenile criminal histories, $z=2.19$, $p=.0282$. This function correctly identified 71.4 percent of the adult criminals and 84.6 percent of the noncriminals. The discriminant function based on home atmosphere correctly identified as criminals 65.2 percent of the men who had first been convicted as adults. In terms of their subsequent criminal records, this discriminant function correctly sorted 78.4 percent of the juvenile delinquents and 81.7 percent of those who had not been juvenile delinquents.[14]

Summary and Discussion

Recent criticism of the assumption that child-rearing practices have an important impact on personality development posed the issue addressed in this research. In order to evaluate the assumption, records describing home atmosphere during childhood, recorded during childhood, were linked with records of subsequent criminality, gathered when the subjects were middle-aged. The two sources of information were independent: data collection had been separated by several decades, the data had been coded by different people, and the coders had no access to information other than that which they were coding. Therefore, measures of home atmosphere were uncontaminated by retrospective biases and measures of subsequent behavior were uncontaminated by knowledge of home background.

Records describing home atmosphere had been written between 1939 and 1945. These records were case reports of counselors' repeated home visits to the 201 boys included in this study. The case records were coded, in 1957, to provide descriptions of home atmosphere.

Information about criminal behavior was gathered from court records, 30 years after termination of the program from which descriptions of home atmosphere had been collected. Subjects were considered criminals if they had been convicted for serious crimes (those indexed by the Federal Bureau of Investigation).

In preliminary analyses, six of seven variables describing home atmosphere were reliably related to criminal behavior. Only father's absence failed to distinguish criminals from noncriminals. Considering the emphasis given to broken homes as a source of subsequent criminality (e.g., Bacon, Child, and Barry, 1963; Glueck and Glueck, 1951; Wadsworth, 1979; Willie, 1967), this finding is worthy of note.

Multiple regression analyses indicated that six variables describing home atmosphere in childhood account for a significant proportion of the variance in number of convictions for serious crimes. After controlling effects of differences in social status, parental characteristics and child-rearing variables accounted for 32.2 percent of the variance in number of convictions for property crimes and 30.3 percent of the variance in number of convictions for personal crimes. The three most direct measures of child rearing (supervision, mother's affection, and parental conflict) accounted for approximately a quarter of the variance in number of convictions for serious crimes—after effects of both social status and parental characteristics had been removed.

Discriminant function analyses based on the six variables describing home atmosphere correctly identified 73.5 percent of the men as either subsequently criminal or noncriminal; further, these six variables provided a function that for 80 percent of the men correctly discriminated between those convicted and those not convicted for serious crimes as adults.

As compared with analyses for the total sample, the discriminant function analyses were (slightly) more accurate when used to predict behavior among the men whose criminal records provided the most complete histories of convictions. Among men living in Massachusetts at least to the age of 40, these functions correctly identified 75 percent as ever criminal or as noncriminal and 80.9 percent as criminal or noncriminal after the age of 18. Limiting analyses to men living in Massachusetts controlled any differences contributing to migration or early death; therefore, the accuracy of discriminant functions among this subsample is interpreted as supporting the view that home atmosphere during childhood contributes to criminality.

When used to identify men convicted as adults, the discriminant function identified as criminals almost two-thirds of the men first convicted after the age of 18. This function also correctly sorted more than three-quarters of the juvenile delinquents, distinguishing between those who were and those who were not adult criminals.

Although the discriminant functions based on home atmosphere were surprisingly successful in identifying men who were to become criminals, it would be a mistake to conclude that the longitudinal design of this research has led to recognition of the causes of crime. This research is limited not only by its subjects (all of whom were reared in congested urban areas during the thirties and early forties) but also by the hypotheses considered. In this research, parental aggression, paternal deviance, maternal self-confidence, supervision, mother's affection, and parental conflict indexed home atmosphere; unconsidered variables might better describe the features in the child's home that affect his behavior. In this research, the possibly confounding variable of social status was considered; other conditions might account for the apparent link between home atmosphere and crime. Nevertheless, the evidence from this study suggests that parental behavior does have an important impact on subsequent behavior: predictions of adult criminality based on knowledge of home atmosphere were not only markedly more accurate than chance—they were also more accurate than predictions based on the individuals' juvenile criminal records.

Notes

This study was supported by U.S. Public Health Service Research Grant 2 RO1 MH26779, National Institute of Mental Health (Center for Studies of Crime and Delinquency). It was conducted jointly with the Department of Probation of the Commonwealth of Massachusetts. The author wishes to express appreciation to the Division of Criminal Justice Services of the State of New York and to the Maine State Bureau of Identification for supplemental data from criminal records, though they are responsible neither for the statistical analyses nor for the conclusions drawn from this research.

1. The project included a matched control group. Since records on family life, for the control group, were limited to information gathered during the intake interviews supplemented by information from secondary sources, the control group was not used in this study. Originally, 325 boys were included in both the treatment group and the control group. By January 1942, 253 boys remained in each group. (See Powers and Witmer, 1951, for details regarding selection of cases and a description of the treatment program.)

2. The criteria are not mutually exclusive. Five men were eliminated through both of the selection criteria.

3. See McCord and McCord (1960) for a complete description of the coding.

4. Only nine boys exposed to high expectations had not been rated as generally supervised.

5. Fifty of the subjects were classified as having aggressive parents by the direct description of parental aggression.

6. Forty-nine had been convicted for serious crimes.

7. Of the 86 deviant fathers, 40 were also absent fathers.

8. Among them, 147 were in Massachusetts through their 45th birthdays.

9. These records were supplemented by court records from the states of New York, Maine, Michigan, Nebraska, and Florida, where some of the men had resided.

10. The Duncan multiple range test, modified for unequal groups (Kramer, 1956), indicated that boys without supervision, reliably ($p < .05$) more than boys in the other three categories, were convicted for both property and personal crimes. This a posteriori test showed that boys rejected by their mothers were most likely to be convicted for property crimes, and boys who had affectionate mothers were least likely.

11. R^2 was increased by .002 for property crimes, .007 for personal crimes, and .001 for total crimes.

12. Without controlling for social status, parental characteristics and child-rearing variables accounted for 36.7 percent of the variance in property crimes, $F(34, 162)=2.76$, p .0001, 30.8 percent of the variance in personal crimes, $F(34, 162)=2.12$, $p=.0010$, and 36.3 percent of the variance in total number of serious crimes, $F(34, 162)=2.71$, $p \leq .0001$.

13. The model used to estimate predictions based on chance assumes that the number of predictions as criminal would be proportional to the actual distribution of criminals among subjects. Alternative models that might be considered range from assuming that each individual is as likely to be convicted as not (which would result in an expectation for correct predictions among half the noncriminals and half the criminals) to assuming that all or no individuals would be convicted. Although a "rational bet" would maximize correct predictions by predicting that all individuals would fall into the larger class, this model is inappropriate when the interest is incorrect identification of those in the smaller class. An equiprobability model for the discriminant function analysis based on family atmosphere resulted in correct sorting of 68 percent of the men (62% of the noncriminals and 79% of the criminals) in terms of whether or not they had been convicted for serious crimes.

14. The "rational bet" that men not convicted as juveniles would not be convicted as adults would be correct for 80 percent of the men not convicted as juveniles. Since this bet would be correct only for the noncriminals, the prediction would fail to identify correctly any of the critical group: men first convicted as adults.

References

Bacon, M. K., I. L. Child, and H. A. Barry. 1963. Cross-cultural study of correlates of crime. *Journal of Abnormal and Social Psychology* 66: 291–300.

Barr, A. J., J. H. Goodnight, J. P. Sall, and J. T. Helwig. 1976. *A User's Guide to SAS 76*. Raleigh, N.C.: SAS Institute.

Blalock, H. M. 1963. Correlated independent variables: The problem of multicollinearity. *Social Forces 42*: 233–237.

Block, J. 1971. *Lives Through Time*. Berkeley, Calif.: Bancroft Books.

Clarke, A. M. and A. D. B. Clarke. 1976. *Early Experience: Myth and Evidence*. New York: Free Press.

Clinard, M. B. 1974. *Sociology of Deviant Behavior*. (4th ed.) New York: Holt, Rinehart and Winston.

Glueck, S. and E. Glueck. 1951. *Unraveling Juvenile Delinquency*. Cambridge, Mass.: Harvard University Press.

Gordon, R. A. 1968. Issues in multiple regression. *American Journal of Sociology 73*: 592–616.

Jessor, R. and S. L. Jessor. 1977. *Problem Behavior and Psychosocial Development*. New York: Academic Press.

Kramer, C. Y. 1956. Extension of multiple range tests to group means with unequal numbers of replication. *Biometrics 12*: 307–310.

Lefkowitz, M. M., L. D. Eron, L. O. Walder, and L. R. Huesmann. 1977. *Growing Up to Be Violent: A Longitudinal Study of Aggression*. New York: Pergamon Press.

McCord, W. and J. McCord. 1960. *Origins of Alcoholism*. Stanford, Calif.: Stanford University Press.

Mosteller, F. and J. W. Tukey. 1977. *Data Analysis and Regression*. Reading, Mass.: Addison-Wesley.

Powers, E. and H. Witmer. 1951. *An Experiment in the Prevention of Delinquency: The Cambridge-Somerville Youth Study*. New York: Columbia University Press.

Robins, L. N. 1966. *Deviant Children Grown Up*. Baltimore, Md.: Williams & Wilkins.

Wadsworth, M. E. J. 1979. *Roots of Delinquency*. New York: Barnes & Noble.

Werner, E. E. and R. S. Smith. 1977. *Kauai's Children Come of Age*. Honolulu: University Press of Hawaii.

Willie, C. V. 1967. The relative contribution of family status and economic status to juvenile delinquency. *Social Problems 14*: 326–335.

Yarrow, M. R., J. D. Campbell, and R. V. Burton. 1968. *Child Rearing*. San Francisco: Jossey-Bass.

CHAPTER SIX

A Longitudinal View of the Relationship Between Paternal Absence and Crime*

FOR MORE THAN 2,000 years, concern with the existence of crime has been coupled with a belief that child rearing is linked to antisocial behaviour. Aristotle identified the relationship in *Nicomachean Ethics* (Book II, ch. 3, 1104b).

> For moral excellence is concerned with pleasures and pains; it is on account of the pleasure that we do bad things, and on account of the pain that we abstain from noble ones. Hence we ought to have been brought up in a particular way from our very youth, as Plato says, so as both to delight in and to be pained by the things that we ought; for this is the right education.

To delight in and to be pained by things that we ought, many have argued, requires being reared in a united, nuclear family (Fenichel, 1945; Freud, 1953; Goode, 1956; Meerloo, 1956; Murdock, 1949; Parsons and Bales, 1955). Many studies have gone further and produced evidence showing some relationship between broken homes and delinquency. Reviewers have failed to notice that different and often contrary relationships have been reported. Before looking anew at the relationship between paternal absence and crime, an examination of this previously acquired evidence is appropriate.

Less than two decades after Lombroso's treatise stressing the importance of biological bases of criminal behaviour was translated into English, broken homes were implicated in the search for causes of crime. Slawson (1923) published the results of a study comparing boys in four New York State reformatories with boys

---

in three New York City public schools. The incidence of broken homes was twice as great among delinquents as among the children in public schools. Shortly thereafter, Burt (1925) published results of his comparison between delinquents and nondelinquents in London: 61 percent of the former and 25 percent of the latter were from broken homes.

Over the years, reports of high incidence of broken homes among delinquents have peppered the literature. Shaw and McKay (1932) found that the incidence of broken homes among youths who appeared in the Chicago juvenile court was greater than that among 10- to 17-year-olds in the Chicago public schools. Merrill (1947, p. 66) found that over half of 300 cases referred to court in a rural California county had come from "homes in which one or both parents were divorced, separated, dead, or had deserted"; among school children from the same county, 27 percent had come from broken homes. Glueck and Glueck (1950), comparing 500 incarcerated delinquents with 500 nondelinquents from the same neighbourhoods in Massachusetts, found that 60 percent of the former and 34 percent of the latter were from broken homes. Monahan (1957) inspected Philadelphia court records of 1949 to 1954. This inspection plus his review of the literature led him to conclude (p. 258):

> ... the place of the home in the genesis of normal or delinquent patterns of behavior should receive greater practical recognition. The relationship is so strong that, if ways could be found to do it, a strengthening and preserving of family life among the groups which need it most, could probably accomplish more in the amelioration and prevention of delinquency and other problems than any other single program yet devised.

Noting that policemen and the courts use more serious sanctions in response to a child from a broken home, Nye (1958) depended upon self-reports for assessing the relationship between broken homes and crime. In his sample of high school students in the state of Washington, Nye found broken homes over-represented among those reporting greater frequencies of such delinquent behaviours as truancy, running away from home, buying or drinking alcohol, and having heterosexual relations. Delinquency was unrelated to the age of the child at the time of parental loss. Nye cautioned (p. 43): "Present data provide additional evidence, therefore, of a slight relationship between broken homes and delinquent behavior, but indicate that as an etiological factor its importance can be easily overestimated."

Seeking to uncover the aetiological roots of delinquency in a birth cohort sample of legitimate children in Great Britain, Wadsworth (1979) reports on one of the most ambitious studies of health ever undertaken. Criminal records for the cohort were traced to the age of 21. In Britain, as in the United States, there was evidence indicating that for similar crimes, boys from broken homes were more likely to be placed in custodial care. Boys from broken homes, especially those who had been infants at the time of the break, were also more likely to be convicted for the least socially acceptable crimes. Even after statistically controlling effects of adverse financial conditions attributable to family disruption, Wadsworth found a reliable relationship between broken homes and subsequent delinquency. He concluded (p. 115): "The most striking findings concerned family life, where disruption of parent-child relationship in early life, through parental death, divorce or separation, was associated with later delinquency, and chiefly with the most unacceptable kinds of offences."

As part of the Freudian legacy, paternal absence has been thought to result in compensatory masculine behavior, of which delinquency is thought to be an example (Lamb, 1976; Miller, 1958; Whiting et al., 1958). To test this theory, Bacon et al. (1963) used ethnographies describing 48 nonliterate cultures. Coders rated the frequency of theft and personal crimes in each of the cultures. The theft scale yielded a correlation of –0.58 and the personal crime scale a correlation of –0.44 with a scale describing the cultures in terms of "opportunity to identify with the father." The authors summarized (p. 299): " ... the cross-cultural method supports the theory that lack of opportunity for the young boy to form a masculine identification is in itself an important antecedent of crime."

A perceived link between broken homes and crime seemed to establish the importance of masculine sex-role identification and the villainy of maternal dominance while simultaneously providing an account for the relatively high rates of crime among the disadvantaged and blacks (Moynihan, 1965). Nonwhites and members of the lower class have the highest rates of broken homes (Bachman, 1970; Bernard, 1966; Cutright, 1971; Goode, 1956; Hillman, 1962; Hollingshead, 1950; Kephart, 1955; Udry, 1966). As measured by official statistics, these are the same groups who are over-represented among criminals (Hindelang et al., 1979; Wolfgang et al., 1972).

Using court referrals of 10- to 17-year-old youths as his measure of criminality, Willie (1967) analysed data from 115 census tracts in the District of Columbia. Willie classified the tracts along two dimensions: wealth and proportion of broken homes. For both whites and nonwhites, within both affluent and poor communities, delinquency rates were higher in census tracts which had many broken homes. Willie specified his perception of the relationship between delinquency and broken homes (p. 335): "The preventive potential of two-parent households against juvenile delinquency tends to be impaired by circumstances of poverty. The preventive potential of affluent economic status against juvenile delinquency tends to be impaired by family instability."

Seeking a dynamic explanation of the relationship between delinquency and broken homes, Toby (1957) reasoned that parental absence would reduce the amount of control which a family could exert. If reduction in control accounted for criminogenic properties of broken homes, Toby reasoned, broken homes ought to have their most potent impact upon the groups whose behaviour normally is most susceptible to parental control: females and pre-adolescents. Since urban areas contain higher proportions of broken homes than do rural areas, Toby classified the 21 New Jersey counties according to the proportions of their populations who lived in cities. Since nonwhites have higher proportions of broken homes, Toby computed delinquency rates separately for whites and nonwhites. Using male adolescent delinquency rate as a base, Toby showed that females and pre-adolescents had relatively higher delinquency rates in more urbanized counties and, within county-type, among nonwhites. Toby concluded (p. 512): "The better integrated the family, the more successful it is as a bulwark against anti-social influences emanating from the neighborhood or the peer group."

Despite crime rate variations which seem to link broken homes to crime, several studies have shown that among blacks, crime rates are not higher for those who come from broken homes. Broken homes failed to predict who would become delinquent in a longitudinal study of black males (Robins and Hill, 1966). Chilton and Markle (1972), after controlling for sex and race, found broken homes related to seriousness of crime only for white males. Austin (1978) found no relationship between broken homes and crime for black males and learned that among females, black girls from broken homes were "least vulnerable" to criminogenic pressures.

Similarly, among poverty groups, broken homes do not seem to increase crime. In a study of London schoolboys, Gibson (1969) found that broken homes were not related to delinquency if the family had low income or poor housing. Chilton and Markle (1972) learned that broken homes were not related to seriousness of criminal record among those whose family income was under $3,000 in 1969. These authors concluded (p. 98): "For children from families with very low income, it would appear that the family's economic situation and not its composition is the more important factor in understanding the child's apprehension for delinquency."

Studies of crime in the middle class, too, raise doubts about the existence of a causal relationship between broken homes and crime. Hennessy et al. (1978) asked school students in a Midwest suburb to report on their delinquent activities and their families. No significant correlation between measures of delinquency and broken homes was found.

Grinnell and Chambers (1979) used court records to gather information about the relationship between broken homes and delinquency among Caucasians whose families had annual incomes of at least $10,000. Broken homes "did not contribute to explaining the observed variance in the offenses committed" (p. 398). Grinnell and Chambers note that in their study, as in the previously reported study by Hennessy et al. (1978), broken homes appeared less frequently than would be expected by chance among those convicted for auto theft, injury to property, and breaking and entering.

Theoretical underpinnings which support a link between broken homes and crime depend on an over-representation of broken homes among serious, repetitive criminals whose behaviour could plausibly be explained as "beyond control" or compensatory acting out. Yet Weeks (1940), using court records in the state of Washington, and Power et al. (1974), using court records in London, found that broken homes were linked only with nonserious, status crimes.

Evidence on the relationship between recidivism and broken homes is contradictory. Guze (1964), Meade (1973), and Ganzer and Sarason (1973) failed to find a relationship between recidivism and broken homes, though West and Farrington (1977), in their longitudinal study of London youths, found high representation of broken homes among the 50 men who had been convicted both as juveniles and as adults. Buikhuisen and Hoekstra (1974) discovered that having been reared in a broken home was a reliable predictor of recidivism among male juveniles released from prison in England.

Careful inspection of the Glueck and Glueck (1950) data indicate that homes in which the missing parent was not replaced by a surrogate were not over-represented among the delinquents. Of the 500 delinquents, 230 had lived with a substitute parent and 72 had lived continuously with just one parent; of the 500 nondelinquents, 60 had lived with a substitute parent and 111 had lived continuously with just one parent. (These figures are obtained by combining Gluecks' Tables XI-12 and XI-10.) The Gluecks' evidence suggests that broken homes that remain broken may be insulators against crime.

After reviewing the sorry state of research into the relationship between broken homes and crime, Rosen and Neilson (1978) reached the conclusion: "The most one can say at present is that the empirical evidence does not support the thesis that the broken home is a significant factor in the development of delinquent tendencies" (p. 414).

In a similar vein, Lamb (1979, p. 940) coupled his critical review of research with the observation "that the effects of a father leaving a family will be markedly different depending on the nature of the preceding father-child, mother-father, and mother-child relationships. Greater progress will be made if researchers recognize the multiple determinants of father absence and the heterogeneity of father-absent families."

To understand effects of paternal absence, the context in which a broken home has developed as well as the circumstances which follow the break ought to be considered. If relevant differences in the contexts of broken and united homes go unnoticed, the impact of context would be confused with that of the structural variable. Several models which incorporate effects of context could provide an account of the disparate findings in prior research:

1. Possibly, broken homes appear to be criminogenic because of the relative frequency with which a child from a broken home has previously been exposed to parental discord. The broken home, however, may not be the factor conducive to delinquency.

   Several studies provide evidence to suggest that parental conflict causes crime (e.g., Dinitz et al., 1962; Glueck and Glueck, 1950; McCord, 1979). More importantly, several studies have shown that unhappy, discordant homes with two parents are more criminogenic than broken homes. Nye (1957) used self-reports of a sample of high school students in Washington State to evaluate the relationship between home situations and delinquency. Students living in a united home with parents who were unhappy, often quarrelled or argued, and lacked mutual interests, were more likely to be among the more serious delinquents than those living with "solo mothers." Rutter (1971), who used official records to measure delinquency, concluded that marital disharmony rather than parent separation was related to antisocial behaviour. West and Farrington (1973), in their longitudinal study of London children, reached a similar conclusion. Power et al. (1974) discovered that among the 246 delinquents who had at least one court appearance in the inner London bureau whose records they studied, recidivism was more likely to occur for those living in intact families with problems than for those from broken homes.

If exposure to parental discord promotes criminality, it is reasonable to argue that divorce or separation could reduce the exposure and thereby decrease the probability of crime. Thus, this first model proposes a negative relationship between parental loss and criminality.

2. Possibly, the link between broken homes and crime rests on some characteristic of individuals who tend to be involved in broken homes—a characteristic antecedent to parental discord and itself directly criminogenic. Maternal rejection appears as a candidate for such a characteristic. It would not be unreasonable to guess that women who reject their children are likely to be cold towards their husbands—a behaviour which could increase the probability of divorce or separation. Many studies provide evidence to suggest that maternal rejection is criminogenic (Austin, 1978; Bender, 1947; Bowlby, 1940; Glueck and Glueck, 1934; Goldfarb, 1945; McCord, 1979).

A second possible characteristic which might create the appearance of a causal relationship between broken homes and crime is paternal deviance. A *prima facie* case can be made for paternal deviance as a cause of parental conflict and separation. Studies have shown that paternal criminality and/or alcoholism are related to antisocial behaviour (Farrington, 1973; Glueck and Glueck, 1950; McCord, 1977; McCord et al., 1963; McCord and McCord, 1960; Robins, 1966).

Assuming that maternal rejection and/or paternal deviance are conditions which precede and are not caused by parental separation—though they sometimes cause separation—this model proposes a positive, *but not causal*, relationship between broken homes and crime in some samples.

3. Possibly, broken homes are potentially criminogenic, requiring "catalytic agents." Broken homes might lead to crime, for example, if the child of such a home is unsupervised. There is reason to believe that single parents may be less capable of providing supervision: not only might it be necessary for the sole parent to leave the child in order to work, but also there are likely to be fewer relatives in the extended family available to give help (Spicer and Hampe, 1975). Several studies have shown a relationship between poor supervision and delinquency (Glueck and Glueck, 1950; Hirschi, 1969; Jensen, 1972; Maccoby, 1958; McCord, 1979). If being a single parent increases the probability of poor supervision of the child, and if poor supervision of the child causes delinquency, the link between broken homes and crime would be causal, albeit indirect. Furthermore, the indirect, causal relationship might depend on further conditions, such as availability of alternative child-care facilities, for it to be

operative. Thus, this model proposes a conditional, causal relationship between broken homes and crime.

Each of the above models provides an account of a possible relationship between broken homes and crime which would accommodate at least some of the apparent inconsistencies in prior research.
It remains possible, however, that the apparent link between broken
homes and crime is an artifact of the selection procedures which
promote publication only when relationships of interest (to the
reviewers) tend to be confirmed. The inconsistent results of studies
assessing the relationship between broken homes and crime led
Wilkinson (1974, p. 737) to suggest: "The recognition that ideologi-
cal bias has tended to control the acceptance and rejection of this
variable should justify its reexamination before completely eliminating it from consideration."

A longitudinal study in which qualitative differences in family
life during childhood could be correlated with subsequent antisocial
behaviour provided data to assess alternative views about the relationship between broken homes and crime.

Method

The study is based on information about men who were part of a counselling programme aimed at preventing delinquency. The programme, active between 1939
and 1945, had included both "difficult" and "average" youngsters from congested
areas of eastern Massachusetts.[1] Approximately twice a month, for more than 5
years, counsellors visited the homes of 253 boys who, at the time of their introduction to the programme were between the ages of 5 and 13 years ($\bar{x}=10.5$,
$SD=1.6$). The counsellors provided assistance to the boys and their families and
recorded their observations after each visit. The case records from this project are
rich with details about family interactions as well as information about the boys
and their parents.

In 1957, coders read each case record thoroughly to form judgments about
the home and family interaction. These coders had no access to information
about the subjects other than that contained in treatment records.[2] A second
coder independently read the case records of 25 randomly selected cases to provide an estimate of reliability of the coding. Variables from the coded case
records were used in the present study. These records contained descriptions of
family life during childhood, from a third-person perspective, uncontaminated by
retrospective bias.

Between 1975 and 1978, the men were retraced. Almost 80 percent of the
248 men who have been located were found in Massachusetts. Court records
from Massachusetts, supplemented by information on criminal histories in Florida, Maine, Michigan, New York, Virginia, and Washington, were used to learn
which of the men had been convicted for crimes. Men convicted for larceny, auto
theft, burglary, assault, attempted rape, rape, attempted murder, kidnapping, or
murder were considered to have committed "serious" crimes. Trespass, truancy,

disturbing the peace, drunkenness, nonsupport, destruction of property are examples of crimes considered to be "minor" ones.

To justify treatment of family backgrounds as independent units for analyses, only one subject from a family was included in the present study. To reduce the source of variance in unmeasured background factors, boys not reared by their natural mothers were also excluded. Of the 201 men who met the selection criterion of having been reared by their natural mothers, 71 were from homes broken by absence of their natural fathers. Their mean age at the time of paternal loss was 7.01 (SD=5.03).

Descriptions from the case records were used to classify cases on four qualitative dimensions: parental conflict, maternal affection, paternal deviance, and supervision of the child.

To rate parental conflict, raters had been instructed to look for disagreements between the parents about the child, values, money, alcohol, and/or religion. For the present research, cases were divided into those whose parents evidenced considerable conflict and those in alternative categories (no indication, apparently no conflict, or some conflict). For this division, independent readers agreed on 80 percent of the cases used to estimate reliability of coding.

Raters had evaluated the quantity and quality of maternal interaction recorded in the case records. A mother was classified as actively affectionate if there had been considerable interaction without continual criticism of the boy. For the present research, cases were divided into those whose mothers evidenced active affection and those in alternative categories (passively affectionate, ambivalent or passively rejecting, or actively rejecting). Independent reading by a second coder resulted in the same ratings among 84 percent of the randomly selected cases used to estimate reliability on this coding.

Coders rated a father as alcoholic if the case record indicated that he had lost jobs because of repeated drinking, if marital problems were attributed primarily to his excessive drinking, if welfare agencies had repeatedly pointed to the father's drinking as ground for family problems, or if the father had received treatment specifically for alcoholism. Independent coders agreed on 96 percent of the ratings on this variable. In 1948, after termination of the counselling programme, criminal records for the family members of subjects were collected; these records were locked in a file separate from the case histories. An assistant unfamiliar with the subjects' case records coded these criminal records. A father was considered as criminal if he had been convicted for theft, burglary, assault, rape, attempted murder, or murder.

Supervision of the boy was rated on the basis of whether or not the child's activities outside of school were governed by an adult. Two raters agreed on 88 percent of the cases read independently regarding this classification.

Evidence to assess the suggested models of the nature of the relationship between broken homes and crime was garnered by comparing subsets of broken and intact homes. To test whether parental loss might be beneficial as an option to living in the midst of parental conflict, crime rates of sons reared by affectionate mothers in broken homes were compared with crime rates of sons reared by two parents who disagreed considerably. To test whether the link between broken homes and crime depends on the prevalence of parental characteristics which are criminogenic, main effects and interaction effects of maternal rejection, paternal absence, and paternal deviance on crime rates were considered. To assess the possibility that broken homes contribute to crime by promoting criminogenic conditions, the relationships of family structure to supervision and of supervision to crime were considered.

Results

Court records gathered 30 years after termination of the counselling project during which information about childhood had been collected showed that 70 of the 201 men had been convicted for serious crimes. An additional 46 men had been convicted only for minor crimes.

Among the 71 men from broken homes, 41 percent were convicted for serious crimes and an additional 20 percent were convicted for minor crimes only. These rates were similar to those for the 130 boys reared by two parents, 32 percent of whom were convicted for serious crimes and an additional 25 percent for minor crimes.

Age of the boy at the time of paternal loss did not contribute to a reliable prediction of subsequent criminality. Among the 30 men who had lost their fathers prior to their sixth birthdays, 40 percent had been convicted for serious crimes and an additional 23 percent had been convicted for minor crimes; among the 24 men who had lost their fathers between their sixth and twelfth birthdays, 42 percent had been convicted for serious crimes and an additional 13 percent had been convicted for minor crimes; among the 17 men who had their twelfth birthdays prior to loss of their fathers, 41 percent had been convicted for serious crimes and an additional 24 percent were convicted for minor crimes. Criminal rates for boys reared in broken homes varied little in relation to age at the time of loss.

In order to test whether divorce or separation might be beneficial with respect to crime, united homes were divided into two types: those in which considerable conflict had been noted (N=27) and those in which considerable conflict had not been noted (N=103). Although conflict need not precede separation or divorce, it seemed reasonable to assume that a relatively high proportion of divorced or separated parents had been in conflict. Thus, crime rates for homes with conflict provide an appropriate comparison against which to evaluate crime rates in broken homes.

Prior research and theory suggest that maternal affection influences crime rates in broken homes. Since the question of benefit or harm from separation often appears in a context in which the alternative to raising a child in a home with conflict is raising the child in a broken but affectionate home, a division of broken homes into those which provided maternal affection and those which did not seemed appropriate.

Table 6.1 shows that conviction rates were not randomly distributed among the four types of homes, χ^2 (6)=20.79, p=0.002. Over half the men who had been reared in the midst of conflict acquired criminal records for serious crimes. This

TABLE 6.1   Family Type and Criminal Records

	United homes		Broken homes	
Convictions	Without conflict (N=103)	With conflict (N=27)	Affectionate mothers (N=37)	Not affectionate mothers (N=34)
No crimes, %	46.6	33.3	51.4	26.5
Only minor crimes,[a] %	27.2	14.8	27.0	11.8
Serious crimes, %	26.2	51.9	21.6	61.8
	100.0	100.0	100.0	100.0

$$\chi^2(6)=20.79, p=0.002$$

[a]Traffic offences have been excluded. Hence, men whose only convictions were for traffic offences would be included with nonoffenders.

proportion is only slightly lower than the proportion of men from *rejecting* broken homes who were convicted for similar crimes.

Among men from unbroken homes with conflict serious criminality occurred with more than twice the frequency of that among men from broken homes whose mothers had been affectionate, $\chi^2(1)=6.32$, $p=0.012$. Living with parental conflict appears to be far more criminogenic than living with an affectionate mother in a broken home. Broken homes which provided maternal affection produced no more criminals than did unbroken homes without conflict.

A generalized least squares procedure for categorical data that provides minimum chi-square estimates similar to the F-ratio estimates in analysis of variance (Sall, 1979) was used to evaluate the main effect of paternal absence and the nested effects of conflict in united homes and affection in broken homes. Paternal absence was not reliably related to predictions of criminal behavior, $\chi^2(1)=0.05$, $p=0.826$, whereas conflict in united homes ($\chi^2(1)=6.19$, $p=0.013$) and absence of affection in broken homes ($\chi^2(1)=11.00$, $p=0.0009$) accounted for reliable proportions of the variation in criminal records.

Of the 27 mothers living with their husbands despite considerable conflict, only 8 (30%) had been actively affectionate towards their sons. Among the 8 sons, half had been convicted for serious crimes; thus, there was no evidence that maternal affection decreased the criminogenic effects of parental conflict. Rather, the evidence appears to support the view that divorce could be beneficial if the alternative would be living in the midst of conflict.

To test whether links between high crime rates and broken homes were functions of parental, criminogenic characteristics which happened to vary concomitantly with paternal absence, the 201 homes were successively divided on two dimensions: maternal affection and paternal deviance. Slightly over half (52%) of the mothers in broken homes had been actively affectionate; slightly under half (45%) of the mothers in unbroken homes had been actively affectionate.

Of the 58 men who had been reared by affectionate mothers in intact families, 22 percent were convicted for serious crimes. That proportion is the same as was found among men reared by affectionate mothers in broken homes, but reliably

TABLE 6.2   Home Backgrounds and Serious Crimes

	Intact homes	Broken homes
Mother affectionate	(N=58) 22.4	(N=37) 21.6
Mother not affectionate	(N=72) 39.0	(N=34) 61.9
	$\chi^2(1)=3.96, p=0.047$	$\chi^2(1)=11.00, p=0.0009$
Father not alcoholic or criminal	(N=84) 23.8	(N=31) 29.0
Father alcoholic or criminal	(N=46) 45.7	(N=40) 50.0
	$\chi^2(1)=6.38, p=0.012$	$\chi^2(1)=3.11, p=0.078$
Child supervised	(N=87) 23.0	(N=31) 25.8
Child not supervised	(N=43) 48.8	(N=40) 52.5
	$\chi^2(1)=8.55, p=0.004$	$\chi^2(1)=4.97, p=0.026$

Note: These figures show the percentage in each category who were convicted for serious crimes.

lower than the 39 percent convicted among the 72 men reared by nonaffectionate mothers in intact homes, χ^2 (1)=3.96, p=0.047 (see Table 6.2).

Although the evidence did not show maternal rejection to be more prevalent among broken than intact homes, the data do indicate that broken homes may magnify effects of maternal rejection. Among sons of rejecting mothers, those reared in broken homes were more likely to have been convicted for serious crimes, χ^2 (1)=4.86, p=0.028.

Over half, 56 percent, of the fathers of boys reared in broken homes were known to be alcoholics or criminals; this proportion was reliably greater than the 35 percent of fathers in united homes known to be alcoholics or criminals, χ^2 (1)=8.24, p=0.004. Close to half the sons of alcoholic or criminal men, whether reared in broken or unbroken homes, had been convicted for serious crimes. Paternal absence seemed neither to ameliorate nor to exacerbate criminogenic effects of paternal deviance (see Table 6.2).

To test whether broken homes increase crime by reducing the probability that supervision would be available, broken and intact homes were divided into those which did and those which did not provide supervision for the boy. Among the 130 intact homes, 67 percent provided supervision; among the 71 broken homes, only 44 percent provided supervision, χ^2 (1)=10.25, p=0.005. Supervision, a form of control more likely to occur when a child was raised by two parents, accounted for a reliable proportion of the variation in crime, χ^2 (2)=13.53, p=0.0012 (see Table 6.2).

Whether supervision was provided varied not only as a function of whether two parents were present, but also as a function of maternal affection. In united homes, 81 percent of the boys with loving mothers as compared with 56 percent of the boys without loving mothers had been supervised, χ^2 (1)=9.42, p=0.002. In broken homes, 65 percent of the loving mothers and only 21 percent of the rejecting mothers provided supervision for their sons, χ^2 (1)=14.12, p=0.0002. The concomitant variation of affection and supervision make it difficult to evaluate effects of the latter. Only 13 boys from broken homes were reared by affectionate mothers who failed to provide supervision; just 3 (23%) were convicted for serious crimes.

One theme seems to run through the analyses: *the quality of home life rather than the number of parents affects crime rates.* Thirty-five of the men from intact homes and fourteen from broken homes had affectionate mothers, nondeviant fathers, and had been supervised during childhood. Their rates of crime were the same: 14 percent of each group were convicted for serious crimes. The categorical analogue of analysis of variance indicated that mother's rejection (χ^2 (1)=4.37, p=0.037), father's deviance (χ^2 (1)=5.23, p=0.022), and supervision (χ^2 (1)=6.48, p=0.011) contribute reliably to an explanation of criminal convictions; *paternal absence did not* (χ^2 (1)=0.18, p=0.671).

Conclusion

A review of prior evidence regarding the link between broken homes and criminal behaviour led to the suggestion of three possible specifications of the relationship. Each proposed relationship acknowledged the potential importance of the context in which a break occurred. Each of the suggested models for specifying the relationship between broken homes and criminality was tested using data from a longitudinal study. The 201 men in the longitudinal study had been reared by their natural mothers; data about their families of orientation had been collected when they were children; data about their criminal behaviour had been collected from court records when they were middle-aged.

Hypothesis 1

If exposure to parental conflict increases the probability of future criminality, termination of that exposure might decrease the probability. The data showed higher criminal rates for men reared by two parents in an atmosphere of conflict than for men reared by affectionate mothers in broken homes. The comparison may be interpreted as providing evidence that, by terminating conflict, paternal absence (under some conditions) may be beneficial.

Hypothesis 2

Systematic character differences between parents who separate and those who remain together are responsible for the apparent relationship between broken homes and crime. After controlling for maternal affection and for paternal deviance, criminal rates for broken and intact homes were compared. The results could be interpreted as evidence that although paternal absence might magnify a criminogenic impact of maternal rejection, paternal absence itself was not criminogenic.

Hypothesis 3

A criminogenic impact from paternal absence might depend upon intervening conditions. Comparisons indicated that boys were more likely to be supervised if they had intact homes and they were less likely to be criminal if supervised. The data could be interpreted as suggesting an indirect criminogenic effect from paternal absence.

THESE ANALYSES SUGGEST that results of prior studies appeared contra-dictory because they were incomplete. Some of the characteristics of parents seem to be both criminogenic and conducive to broken homes; attribution to broken homes of the resultant criminality produces an error important both for theory and for practice.

Although the present research has taken a step towards clarifying contextual effects, it would be a mistake to assume that causal relationships have been correctly identified. Unconsidered conditions might provide a more adequate account of the relationship between broken homes and criminal behaviour. Nevertheless, on the basis of present information, it seems appropriate to suggest a focus upon quality rather than quantity of parenting.

Notes

This study was supported by U.S. Public Health Service Research Grant No. R01 MH26779, National Institute of Mental Health (Center for Studies of Crime and Delinquency). It was conducted jointly with the Department of Probation of the Commonwealth of Massachusetts. The author wishes to express appreciation to the Division of Criminal Justice Services of New York State, to the Maine State Bureau of Identification, and to the states of Florida, Michigan, New Jersey, and Washington for supplemental data about the men, though only the author is responsible for the statistical analyses and for the conclusions drawn from this research.

1. See Powers and Witmer (1951) for details about selection of the men. The project included a matched control group. Since records for the control group on family life were limited to information gathered during the intake interviews, supplemented by information from secondary sources, the control group was not used in this study. Originally, 325 boys were included in both the treatment group and the control group. By January 1942, 253 boys remained in each group.

2. See McCord and McCord (1960) for a more complete description of the coding.

References

Austin, R. L. 1978. Race, father-absence, and female delinquency. *Criminology* 15: 487–504.

Bachman, J. G. 1970. The impact of family background and intelligence on tenth grade boys. In *Youth in Transition*, vol. II, Ann Arbor: Institute for Social Research.

Bacon, M. K., I. L. Child, and H. Barry. 1963. A cross-cultural study of correlates of crime. *Journal of Abnormal and Social Psychology* 66: 291–300.

Bender, L. 1947. Psychopathic behavior disorders in children. In *Handbook of Correctional Psychology*, edited by R. M. Linder and R. V. Seliger. New York: Philosophical Library.

Bernard, J. 1966. Marital stability and patterns of status variables. *Journal of Marriage and the Family* 28: 421–439.

Bowlby, J. 1940. The influence of early environment on neurosis and neurotic character. *International Journal of Psychoanalysis* 21: 154.

Buikhuisen, W. and H. A. Hoekstra. 1974. Factors related to recidivism. *British Journal of Criminology* 14: 63–69.

Burt, C. 1925. *The Young Delinquent*. New York: D. Appleton and Co.

Chilton, R. J. and G. E. Markle. 1972. Family disruption, delinquent conduct and the effect of subclassification. *American Sociological Review* 37: 93–99.

Cutright, P. 1971. Income and family events: Marital stability. *Journal of Marriage and the Family* 32: 291–306.

Dinitz, S., F. R. Scarpitti, and W. C. Reckless. 1962. Delinquency vulnerability: A cross group and longitudinal analysis. *American Sociological Review* 27: 515–517.

Farrington, D. P. 1973. Self-reports of deviant behavior: Predictive and stable? *Journal of Criminal Law and Criminology* 64: 99–110.

Fenichel, O. 1945. *The Psychoanalytic Theory of Neurosis*. New York: Norton.

Freud, S. 1953. Three essays on sexuality. In *Standard Edition*. vol. VII, London: Hogarth.

Ganzer, V. J. and I. G. Sarason. 1973. Variables associated with recidivism among juvenile delinquents. *Journal of Consulting and Clinical Psychology* 40: 1–5.

Gibson, H. B. 1969. Early delinquency in relation to broken homes. *Journal of Child Psychology and Psychiatry* 10: 195–204.

Glueck, S. and E. T. Glueck. 1934. *One Thousand Juvenile Delinquents*. Cambridge: Harvard University Press.

———. 1950. *Unraveling Juvenile Delinquency*. Cambridge: Harvard University Press.

Goldfarb, W. 1945. Psychological privation in infancy and subsequent adjustment. *American Journal of Orthopsychiatry* 15: 247–255.

Goode, W. J. 1956. *After Divorce*. Glencoe, Ill: Free Press.

Grinnell, R. M., Jr. and C. A. Chambers. 1979. Broken homes and middle-class delinquency: A comparison. *Criminology* 17: 395–400.

Guze, S. B. 1964. A study of recidivism based upon a follow-up of 217 consecutive criminals. *Journal of Nervous and Mental Disease* 138: 575–580.

Hennessy, M., P. J. Richards, and R. A. Berk. 1978. Broken homes and middle-class delinquency: A reassessment. *Criminology* 15: 505–528.

Hillman, K. G. 1962. Marital instability and its relation to education, income, and occupation: An analysis based on census data. In *Selected Studies in Marriage and the Family*, edited by R. F. Winch, R. McGinnis, and H. R. Barringer. New York: Holt, Rinehart and Winston.

Hindelang, M. J., T. Hirschi, and J. G. Weis. 1979. Correlates of delinquency: The illusion of discrepancy between self-report and official measures. *American Sociological Review* 44: 995–1014.

Hirschi, T. 1969. *Causes of Delinquency*. Berkeley: University of California Press.

Hollingshead, A. B. 1950. Class differences in family stability. *Annals of the American Academy of Political and Social Science* 272: 39–46.

Jensen, G. F. 1972. Parents, peers, and delinquent action: A test of the differential association perspective. *American Journal of Sociology* 78: 562–575.

Kephart, W. M. 1955. Occupational level and marital disruption. *American Sociological Review*, 20: 456–465.

Lamb, M. E. 1976. The role of the father: An overview. In *The Role of the Father in Child Development*, edited by M. E. Lamb. New York: Wiley.

Lamb, M. E. 1979. Paternal influences and the father's role: A personal perspective. *American Psychologist* 34: 938–943.

Maccoby, E. E. 1958. Effects upon children of their mothers' outside employment. In *The Lives of Married Women* (National Manpower Council). New York: Columbia University Press.

McCord, J. 1977. A comparative study of two generations of native Americans. In *Theory in Criminology*, edited by R. F. Meier. Beverly Hills: Sage.

McCord, J. 1979. Some child-rearing antecedents of criminal behavior in adult men. *Journal of Personality and Social Psychology* 37: 1477–1486.

McCord, J., W. McCord, and A. Howard. 1963. Family interaction as antecedent to the direction of male aggressiveness. *Journal of Abnormal and Social Psychology* 66: 239–242.

McCord, W. and J. McCord. 1960. *Origins of Alcoholism*. Stanford: Stanford University Press.

Meade, A. 1973. Seriousness of delinquency, the adjudicative decision and recidivism: A longitudinal configuration analysis. *Journal of Criminal Law and Criminology* 64: 478–485.

Meerloo, J. A. M. 1956. The father cuts the cord: The role of the father as initial transference figure. *American Journal of Psychotherapy* 10: 471–480.

Merrill, M. A. 1947. *Problems of Child Delinquency*. New York: Houghton Mifflin.

Miller, W. B. 1958. Lower class culture as a generating milieu of gang delinquency. *Journal of Social Issues* 14: 5–19.

Monahan, T. 1957. Family status and the delinquent child: A reappraisal and some new findings. *Social Forces* 35: 251–258.

Moynihan, D. 1965. *The Negro Family: The Case for National Action*. Washington, DC: US Government Printing Office.

Murdock, G. P. 1949. *Social Structure*. New York: Macmillan.

Nye, F. I. 1957. Child adjustment in broken and in unhappy unbroken homes. *Marriage and Family Living* 19: 356–361.

Nye, F. I. 1958. *Family Relationships and Delinquent Behavior*. New York: Wiley.

Parsons, T. and R. F. Bales. 1955. *Family, Socialization and Interaction Process*. Glencoe, III.: Free Press.

Power, M. J., P. M. Ash, E. Shoenberg, and E. C. Sirey. 1974. Delinquency and the family. *British Journal of Social Work* 4: 13–38.

Powers, E. and H. Witmer. 1951. *An Experiment in the Prevention of Delinquency: The Cambridge-Somerville Youth Study*. New York: Columbia University Press.

Robins, L. N. 1966. *Deviant Children Grown Up*. Baltimore: Williams and Wilkins.

Robins, L. N. and S. Y. Hill. 1966. Assessing the contribution of family structure, class and peer groups to juvenile delinquency. *Journal of Criminal Law, Criminology, and Police Science* 57: 325–334.

Rosen, L. and K. Neilson. 1978. The broken home and delinquency. In *Crime in Society* edited by, L. D. Savitz and N. Johnston. New York: Wiley.

Rutter, M. 1971. Parent-child separation: Psychological effects on the children. *Journal of Child Psychology and Psychiatry* 12: 233–260.

Sall, J. P. 1979. *SAS Users Guide*. Raleigh, NC: SAS Institute, Inc.

Shaw, C. and H. D. McKay. 1932. Are broken homes a causative factor in juvenile delinquency? *Social Forces* 10: 514–524.

Slawson, J. 1923. Marital relations of parents and juvenile delinquency. *Journal of Delinquency* 8: 280–283.

Spicer, J. W. and G. D. Hampe. 1975. Kinship interaction after divorce. *Journal of Marriage and the Family* 37: 113–119.

Toby, J. 1957. The differential impact of family disorganization. *American Sociological Review* 22: 505–512.

Udry, R. 1966. Marital instability by race, sex, education, and occupation using 1960 census data. *American Journal of Sociology* 72: 203–209.

Wadsworth, M. 1979. *Roots of Delinquency*. New York: Barnes and Noble.

Weeks, H. A. 1940. Male and female broken home rates by type of delinquency. *American Sociological Review* 5: 601–609.

West, D. J. and D. P. Farrington. 1973. *Who Becomes Delinquent?* London: Heinemann.

———. 1977. *The Delinquent Way of Life*. London: Heinemann.

Whiting, J. W. M., R. Kluckhohn, and A. Anthony. 1958. The function of male initiation ceremonies at puberty. In *Readings in Social Psychology*, edited by E. E. Maccoby, T. M. Newcomb, and E. L. Hartley. New York: Holt, Rinehart and Winston.

Wilkinson, K. 1974. The broken family and juvenile delinquency: Scientific explanation or ideology? *Social Problems* 21: 726–739.

Willie, C. V. 1967. The relative contribution of family status and economic status to juvenile delinquency. *Social Problems* 14: 326–335.

Wolfgang, M. E., R. M. Figlio, and T. Sellin. 1972. *Delinquency in a Birth Cohort*. Chicago: University of Chicago Press.

CHAPTER SEVEN

A Forty Year Perspective on Effects of Child Abuse and Neglect*

T HE PRESENT STUDY has been designed to assess long-term effects of child abuse and neglect. The data are part of a longitudinal study of the lives of 253 men reared in 232 families prior to World War II in eastern Massachusetts. Randomly selected for the study because they lived in transitional neighborhoods, were between the ages of five and nine, and could be matched with a similar boy of similar background (who was not included in the group assigned counselors, and therefore, for whom evidence on childhood was skimpy), the men have been traced to their late forties.

Method

Study Population as Boys

Information about the lives of the men begins with reports of elementary school teachers, collected by the selection committee for the Youth Study. In 1936–1937, teachers filled out "trait record cards" that were lists of words or descriptive phrases (e.g., "needs constant directions"), checking those that described the child. On these check lists, teachers noted which of the boys got in fights, bullied their classmates, or generally teased others. For purposes of the present research, such boys were considered aggressive.

Information about the behavior of the parents had been written as case reports between 1939 and 1945 by social workers participating in the project (which had been designed in hopes of preventing delinquency). These social workers visited the homes of the youngsters approximately twice a month for five and one-half

*Reprinted from McCord, J. 1983. A forty year perspective on effects of child abuse and neglect. In *Child Abuse and Neglect*, 7: 265–270. Copyright © 1982, with permission from Elsevier. An earlier version of this article was presented at the Fourth International Congress on Child Abuse and Neglect, Paris, France, September 1982.

years. Shortly after each encounter with a boy or his family, the social workers described what had occurred.

Coding. These running records were coded, in 1957, to yield descriptions of the conditions under which a child had been reared. Trained coders read each case record and classified the material on a series of categorical scales. Reliability was assessed by having a second coder read the case histories of a randomly selected 10 percent.

Counselors' descriptions of how the boy and his parents interacted provided the basis for coding the attitude of each parent to the child. A parent was considered loving if the parent seemed genuinely concerned for the child's welfare and if criticism was absent from most of the parent-child interactions. A parent was considered as rejecting if the parent demonstrated repeated displeasure with the child. And a parent was considered as neglecting if there tended to be little emotional commitment to the child. Two raters agreed for 76 percent of the fathers and 80 percent of the mothers for this coding of parental attitude to the boy.

Since the counselors would appear at various times of the day and throughout the week, they often encountered parents in the process of disciplining their children. In addition, both the boys and the parents would talk about discipline. Raters coded a parent as punitive if corporal punishments formed the regular basis for the parent's attempt to control the boy. Two raters agreed for 88 percent of the ratings of fathers and for all of the ratings about mothers for this coding.

A measure of the level of parental expectations of the parents for the boy's behavior depended on whether the boy was expected to care for younger siblings, assist in preparation for meals, contribute to the financial support of the family, or do "extremely well" in school. Evidence for any of these expectations was sufficient to classify a boy as exposed to high demands. Independent codings yielded agreement on 76 percent of the cases.

Parents were rated as aggressive if the parent yelled, threw things, or attempted to injure someone in response to frustration or annoyance. For these ratings, independent coders agreed on 92 percent of the mothers and on 84 percent of the fathers. A boy was rated as having or not having at least one unrestrained, aggressive parent.

To rate parental conflict, raters looked for disagreements between the parents about the child, values, money, alcohol, or religion. Independent readers agreed on 80 percent of the parents regarding whether or not they were in considerable conflict.

To rate parental dominance, coders looked for parental disagreements, then counted that parent as dominant whose opinions seemed to control the actual decisions. Independent readings resulted in 88 percent agreement regarding whether or not the father was dominant.

Homes were considered broken if one or both parents did not reside with the child for at least six months. Coders agreed on 96 percent of the cases read to assess reliability. Socioeconomic status (SES) was rated from father's occupation and an eleven-point rating of the neighborhood in terms of its likelihood for promoting delinquency. The latter rating was made by counselors in 1938. Boys whose fathers were unskilled and who lived in the worst neighborhoods were considered to be from the lowest SES.

Fathers had been considered alcoholics if they had lost jobs through their drinking, if marital problems had been caused by repeated drunkenness, if they had been arrested at least three times for public drunkenness or driving under the influence of alcohol, or if they had received treatment for alcoholism or a related physical disease. Fathers were considered criminals if they had been convicted for crimes that are indexed by the Federal Bureau of Investigation—that is, for theft, burglary, assault, rape, attempted murder, or murder.

Study Population as Adults

Between 1975 and 1979, the men were retraced. Records were checked for information about the men. Court records yielded information about their criminal behavior. Mental hospital and clinic records indicated which had received treatment for such problems as manic-depression, schizophrenia, or alcoholism. Death records, voting registrations, and driver licenses provided some information about occupations. A search for the men themselves resulted in location of 248 (98%). Questionnaires mailed to the men and an interviewer visiting them helped give a more complete picture of them as middle-aged.

Nonduplicating numbering systems protected the privacy of individuals while also enabling collation of the information about individuals. Those checking records and those retracing the men had no access to information about the childhoods of the men being studied. Nor were the records of adult behavior available to the interviewer.

For analysis of the data, the codes from 1957 were used to divide the men into four categories on the basis of how their parents treated them when they were children. Only one man from a family was included in the analyses. Men who had been subjected to consistently punitive, physical punishments were classified as *abused*. Those whose parents interacted with them infrequently, showing neither affection nor rejection, were classified as *neglected*. Among those not abused, the ones who had at least one parent who seemed concerned for the child's welfare and generally pleased with his behavior were classified as *loved*. And the remaining group, those neither abused nor neglected but also not loved, were classified as *rejected*. The study compares the parents and the men in these four groups: 49 classified as abused, 48 as neglected, 34 as rejected, and 101 as loved.

Analyses were directed toward detecting differences in characteristics of the parents that seem to be linked with abuse and neglect; differences in the subsequent behavior of those who had been abused, neglected, rejected, and loved; and conditions that might mitigate adverse effects of neglect and abuse. Statistical tests compared observed values with expected values among the four groups. Differences reported as significant have a probability $<.05$, using chisquare with 3 degrees of freedom. In addition, observed differences between the rejected and loved groups were compared with their expected values. For these comparisons, too, differences reported as significant have a probability $<.05$ (with 1 degree of freedom).

TABLE 7.1 Social Context and Child Relations (percent of type for which description applies)

	Neglected (N = 48)	Abused (N=49)	Rejected (N=34)	Loved (N=101)
Lowest SES	54	39	62	48
Broken home	40	33	59	47
Father alcoholic or criminal*	46	37	56	37

*Difference between rejected and loved. df=1; $p < .05$.

Results

Within the rather restricted range in social class among the men from the Youth Study, low socioeconomic status did not appear to increase the probability for abuse or neglect. Nor were the groups reliably different in proportion to who were reared in broken homes. Although the prevalence of paternal alcoholism and criminality failed to differentiate loved from abused or neglected boys, loved boys were significantly less likely than rejected boys to have criminal or alcoholic fathers. (See Table 7.1.)

Though neglected, abused, and rejected boys shared in being deprived of consistent, affectionate parental guidance, their childhoods differed systematically in other ways. Abused children were likely to have parents whose behavior was generally aggressive. These parents also tended to expect their children to accept responsibilities at an early age. Abused children were likely also to have had fathers who were clearly the dominant members of their families. Rejected children were most likely to be exposed to aggressive parents who had low expectations for their behavior; their fathers were *not* likely to be the dominant person in the homes. Neglected children were least likely to be exposed to parental conflict. Those children reared in loving homes were most likely to have self-confident mothers and least likely to have aggressive parents. Table 7.2 shows the percent of men in each type of child-rearing background who had aggressive parents, high demands, dominant fathers, parents in conflict, and self-confident

TABLE 7.2 Parental Behavior and Child Relations (percent of type for which description applies)

	Neglected (N = 48)	Abused (N = 49)	Rejected (N = 34)	Loved (N = 101)
Parents aggressive*	21	35	44	15
High demands*	17	37	6	30
Father dominant*	53	76	20	51
Parental conflict*	23	35	56	28
Mother self-confident*	21	20	21	43

Note: Numbers are not constant within categories since some variables are missing for some subjects.
*df=3; $p < .01$.

TABLE 7.3 Criminal Behavior and Child Relations (percent of type for which description applies)

	Neglected (N=48)	Abused (N=49)	Rejected (N=34)	Loved (N=101)
Juvenile only	15	10	29	7
Juvenile and adult	8	12	21	4
Adult only	13	16	3	12
Ever convicted	35	39	53	23

Note: Groups differ for juvenile crime. df=3; $p < .0001$.

mothers. Statistical tests showed that each of these variables reliably distinguished among the four groups.

Rejected children had significantly higher rates of juvenile delinquency than did loved children. As juveniles, half the rejected children had been convicted for serious crimes such as theft, auto theft, breaking and entering, burglary, or assault. Among the children from loving homes, only 11 percent had been convicted for these types of crimes. And among both the abused and neglected, approximately one in five had been convicted for serious juvenile crimes.

Apparently the antisocial impact from parental abuse, neglect, and rejection is largely reflected in juvenile delinquency. With about four out of ten of the juvenile delinquents again convicted as adults, a slightly higher proportion of the neglected, abused, and rejected than of the loved boys had been convicted after the age of eighteen. Adult criminality seems to have been less affected than juvenile delinquency by parental rejection or abuse. Disregarding adults who began their criminal careers as juveniles, the loved were more likely than the rejected and almost as likely as the neglected or abused to become criminals as adults. (See Table 7.3.)

The four groups did not differ reliably in proportions of men who had become alcoholics. Nor did they differ as adults in terms of occupational status, frequency of visits to their parents, marital status, or proportions returning to schools for further education.

As adults, the rejected children were more likely than neglected, abused, or loved children to remember their parents as having been harsh. But the abused were not more likely than the loved to perceive their parents as harsh. According to their responses to a question asking how they punish (or formerly punished) their children when discipline was needed, parents from the four types of family backgrounds were about equally likely to use physical punishments.

The data suggest that some people are relatively invulnerable to adverse effects from parental abuse and neglect. Among the 97 neglected or abused children, 44 had become criminal, alcoholic, mentally ill, or had died before reaching age 35, and 53 showed none of these signs of having been damaged. Results of comparing these groups suggest conditions that affect the probability that child neglect and abuse will have adverse effects.

TABLE 7.4 Vulnerability among Abused and Neglected Children (percent of type for which description applies)

	Vulnerable (*N*=44)	Not vulnerable (*N*=53)
Alcoholic or criminal father*	55	30
Parents aggressive*	39	19
Affectionate parent	25	28
Mother self-confident**	5	31
Aggressive as child*	59	36
Held back in school	77	62
Teacher liked boy	61	53
Returned to school*	42	70

Note: Vulnerable=alcoholic, criminal, manic-depressive, schizophrenic, or died prior to age 35.
df=1; *p < .05. **p < .01.

Paternal alcoholism and criminality had not been related to the occurrence of child abuse; yet they were related to damage from such abuse. Paternal alcoholism and crime as well as parental aggressiveness appear to increase the probability that child abuse and neglect will be damaging to future development. The two groups were about equally likely to have some parental affection. The vulnerable group, however, had mothers who lacked self-confidence. In addition, early aggression by the child appeared to signal vulnerability. (See Table 7.4.)

Although their early schooling had not indicated that they were better students or that their teachers liked them more, the group who appeared to be less vulnerable to their parents' neglect or abuse were more likely to have returned to school having once terminated their education. (See Table 7.4.)

Summary and Implications

On the basis of case records written between 1939 and 1945, and coded in 1957, 232 males were placed into one of four categories reflecting interactions with their parents. These categories were "Neglected," "Abused," "Rejected," and "Loved." Social contexts and parental behaviors among the four were compared. The groups were similar in terms of poverty and proportions from broken homes. Evidence from this study suggests that with poverty and parental absence controlled, the occurrence of child abuse and neglect is only coincidentally related to paternal alcoholism or criminality.

In distinction from the other groups, the abused boys were more likely to have also been exposed to aggressive models, high expectations for adult behaviors, and dominant fathers. The rejected boys were most likely to have been exposed to aggressive, criminal or alcoholic models, parental conflict, and low demands.

Both the men and their criminal records were retraced (by different groups of researchers) thirty years after the parent-child interactions had been recorded. The records showed higher rates of juvenile delinquency among the rejected, abused, and neglected boys than among those raised by loving parents. Rates of alcoholism, divorce, and occupational success, however, were similar among the four groups.

Close to half (45%) of the abused or neglected boys had been convicted for serious crimes, became alcoholics or mentally ill, or had died when unusually young. Those who showed these signs of having been damaged tended also to have had aggressive, alcoholic, or criminal parents and to have been aggressive themselves. Such conditions seem to presage enduring problems that are likely to bring a child to the attention of authorities. Evidence from the present study suggests that it would be erroneous to conclude, however, that alcoholic or criminal fathers are particularly likely to be neglecting or abusive.

Slightly over half of the abused or neglected children seem to have come through the experience without permanent damage. Maternal self-confidence and education appear to have contributed to their relative invulnerability.

This longitudinal study, tracing children into adulthood, suggests that child abuse and neglect tend to produce juvenile delinquency. Parental rejection, however, appears to be an even more powerful instigator of crime. The effects of abuse and neglect seem to be greatest among those who have aggressive parents and are aggressive themselves. The study also hints that education may help to deflect the potential damage of having neglecting or abusive parents.

CHAPTER EIGHT

Family Relationships, Juvenile Delinquency, and Adult Criminality*

Theoretical Perspective

HISTORICALLY, family interactions have been assumed to influence criminal behavior. Plato, for example, prescribed a regimen for rearing good citizens in the nursery. Aristotle asserted that in order to be virtuous, "we ought to have been brought up in a particular way from our very youth" (Bk. II, Ch. 3:11048). And John Locke wrote his letters on the education of children in the belief that errors "carry their afterwards-incorrigible taint with them, through all the parts and stations of life" (1693:iv).

Twentieth-century theorists ranging from the analytic to the behavioral seem to concur with the earlier thinkers in assuming that parental care is critical to socialized behavior. Theorists have suggested that inadequate families fail to provide the attachments that could leverage children into socialized life-styles (e.g., Hirschi, 1969). They note that poor home environments provide a backdrop for children to associate differentially with those who have antisocial definitions of their environments (e.g., Sutherland and Cressey, 1974). And they point out that one feature of inadequate child rearing is that it fails to reward desired behavior and fails to condemn behavior that is not desired (e.g., Akers, 1973; Bandura and Walters, 1959).

Over the past several decades, social scientists have suggested that crime is a product of broken homes (e.g., Bacon et al., 1963; Burt, 1925; Fenichel, 1945; Freud, 1953; Goode, 1956; Murdock, 1949; Parsons and Bales, 1955; Shaw and McKay, 1932; Wadsworth, 1979), maternal employment (e.g., Glueck and Glueck, 1950; Nye, 1959), and maternal rejection (Bowlby, 1940, 1951; Goldfarb, 1945; Newell, 1934, 1936). Some have linked effects from broken homes with the impact parental absences has on sex-role identity (Bacon et al., 1963; Lamb,

*Reprinted from McCord, J. 1991. Family relationships, juvenile delinquency, and adult criminality. In *Criminology* 29: 397–417; with permission.

1976; Levy, 1937; Miller, 1958; Whiting et al., 1958), and others have suggested that parental absence and maternal employment affect crime through contributing to inadequate supervision (e.g., Dornbusch et al., 1985; Hirschi, 1969; Hoffman, 1975; Maccoby, 1958; Nye, 1958).

Despite this long tradition, empirical support demonstrating the link between child rearing and criminal behavior has been weak. Accounting for this fact, Hirschi (1983) suggested that attributing behavioral differences to socialization practiced in the family is "directly contrary to the metaphysic of our age" (p. 54). Hirschi criticized the few studies that refer to family influences for using global measures of inadequacy, noting that they cannot yield information about the practices or policies that might reduce criminality.

Most of the evidence made available since Hirschi's appraisal has depended on information from adolescents who have simultaneously reported their parents' behavior and their own delinquencies (e.g., Cernkovick and Giordano, 1987; Hagan et al., 1985; Jensen and Brownfield, 1983; van Voorhis et al., 1988). Because these studies are based on data reporting delinquency and socialization variables at the same time, they are unable to disentangle causes from effects.

Two studies based on adolescents' reports have addressed the sequencing issue. Both used data collected by the Youth in Transition project from adolescents at ages 15 and 17 years (Bachman and O'Malley, 1984). Liska and Reed (1985) looked at changes in delinquency related to parent-adolescent interaction; their analyses suggest that friendly interaction with parents (attachment) retards delinquency, which in turn, promotes school attachment and stronger family ties. Wells and Rankin (1988) considered the efficacy of various dimensions of direct control on delinquency; their analyses suggest that restrictiveness, but not harshness, inhibits delinquency. Although the same data base was used for the two studies, neither considered variables that appeared in the other, so the issues of relative importance and of collinearity among child-rearing parameters were not examined.

Relying on adolescents to report about their parents' child-rearing behavior assumes that the adolescents have correctly perceived, accurately recalled, and honestly reported the behavior of their parents. There are grounds for questioning those assumptions.

Experimental studies show that conscious attention is unnecessary for experiences to be influential (Kellogg, 1980); thus adolescents may not notice salient features of their socialization. Studies have shown that reports of family interaction tend to reflect socially desirable perspectives (J. McCord and W. McCord, 1962; Robins, 1966; Weller and Luchterhand, 1983; Yarrow et al., 1970); thus adolescents' reports reflecting this bias would tend to blur real differences in upbringing.

In addition, studies of perception and recall suggest that reports about child rearing are likely to be influenced by the very features under study as possible consequences of faulty child rearing. For example, abused children tend to perceive their parents as less punitive than revealed by objective evidence (Dean et al., 1986; J. McCord, 1983a); aggressive children tend to perceive behavior justifying aggression (Dodge and Somberg, 1987); and painful experience tends to exaggerate recall of painful events (Eich et al., 1990). Yet, criminologists have paid little attention to measurement issues related to ascertaining the impact of socialization within families.

Studies of the impact of child rearing suffer from special problems. When the source of data is children's reports on their parents' behavior, effects and causes are likely to be confounded. When parents report on their own behavior, they are likely to have a limited and biasing perspective and to misrepresent what they are willing to reveal. These biases have been shown in a study that included home observations as well as mothers' reports. The child's compliance was related to observed, although not to reported, behavior of the mother (Forehand et al., 1978). Eron and his coworkers (1961) discovered that even when fathers and mothers reported similarly about events, "the relation to other variables was not the same for the two groups of parents" (p. 471). Additionally, regardless of the source of information, if data are collected after the onset of misbehavior, distortions of memory give rise to biases.

Attention to problems of measurement characterize two studies of juvenile crime. In one, Larzelere and Patterson (1990) combined interviews with the child and his parents, observations, and the interviewer's impressions to create measures of discipline and monitoring. They found strong collinearity and therefore used a combined measure of "parental management." Data on family management were collected when the children were approximately nine years old. This variable mediated a relationship between socioeconomic status and delinquency as reported by the boys when they were 13. Larzelere and Patterson acknowledge that their measure of delinquency may be premature, but they point out that early starters tend to become the more serious criminals.

In the other study, Laub and Sampson (1988) reanalyzed data from the files compiled by Sheldon Glueck and Eleanor Glueck (1950). They built measures of family discipline, parent-child relations, and maternal supervision from multiple sources of information. The variables indicated that child-rearing processes bore strong relations to juvenile delinquency, as measured through official records. Laub and Sampson concluded that "family process and delinquency are related not just independent of traditional sociological controls, but of biosocial controls as well" (p. 374).

Other researchers have focused on different parts of the child-rearing process. Selection seems to be more a matter of style than a result of considered evidence. In reviewing studies of family socialization, Loeber and Stouthamer-Loeber (1986) concluded that parental neglect had the largest impact on crime. They also suggested the possibility of a sleeper effect from socialization practices, although they noted that reports by different members of the family have little convergence.

Problems in collecting information make the few extant longitudinal data sets that include family interactions particularly valuable. The Cambridge-Somerville Youth Study data provided evidence about childhood milieu and family interaction collected during childhood. The data were based on observations of family processes by a variety of people over a period of several years.

Prior analyses of the data, based on a follow-up when the men were in their late twenties, have provided evidence of predictive validity for many of the measures. The results of these earlier studies suggested that child-rearing practices mediate the conditions under which sons follow the footsteps of criminal fathers (J. McCord and W. McCord, 1958). They showed that child-rearing practices are correlated with concurrent aggressive behavior among nondelinquents (W. McCord et al., 1961) and contribute to promoting antisocial directions for aggressive behavior (J. McCord et al., 1963a). Analyses also indicated that the stability of family environments mediated results of maternal employment on concurrent characteristics of dependency and sex anxiety; only among unstable families did maternal employment seem to contribute to the subsequent delinquency (J. McCord et al., 1963b). Probably the most critical test of the predictive worth of the coded variables appeared in the analyses of their relation to alcoholism (W. McCord and J. McCord, 1960). Spurred on by these results, I collected additional information from and about the men two decades later.

Prior analyses from this extended data base have suggested that parental affection acts as a protective factor against crime (J. McCord, 1983b, 1986) and alcoholism (J. McCord, 1988). Analyses also suggested that how parents responded to their son's aggressive behavior influences whether early aggression continued through adolescence and emerged as criminal behavior (J. McCord, 1983b).

In tracing the comparative results of child abuse, neglect, and rejection, analyses indicated both that parental rejection was more criminogenic than either abuse or neglect and that vulnerability to alcoholism, mental illness, early death, and serious criminality was increased by having had an alcoholic, criminal, or aggressive parent (J. McCord, 1983a).

Prior analyses from these data have also shown that single-parent families are not more criminogenic than two-parent families—provided the mother is affectionate (J. McCord, 1982). Additional analyses of family structure indicated that although parental absence had a detrimental effect on delinquency, only when compounded by other family-related stresses did it have an apparent effect on serious criminal behavior, alcoholism, or occupational achievement (J. McCord, 1990).

Theories have emphasized one or another description of family life as important to healthy child development. Research concerned with bonding to, or identification with, socialized adults has focused on affection of parents for their children (e.g., Hirschi, 1969; W. McCord and J. McCord, 1959). Research based on either conditioning or dissonance theories has emphasized discipline and controls (e.g., Bandura and Walters, 1959; Baumrind, 1968, 1978, 1983; Lewis, 1981). And differential association and social learning theories give special weight to the nature of available models (e.g., Akers, 1973; Bandura and Walters, 1963; Sutherland and Cressey, 1974).

Because criminologists have rarely gone beyond describing home environments in globally evaluative terms, the same data could be interpreted as confirming the importance of family bonding or of providing firm control. In order to distinguish among effects, equally valid and reliable measurement of the different dimensions is needed, and collinearity among the measures must be taken into account. Although it is known that child rearing influences adult criminality (J. McCord, 1979, 1983b), there is little ground for judging the extent to which one or another dimension of child rearing is important at different times. Thus, the question remains: In what ways does child rearing affect criminal behavior?

This study addresses two questions: (1) Are there particular features of child rearing that influence criminal outcomes or does only the general home atmosphere of childhood account for the relationship between conditions of socialization and crime? (2) Do similar influences operate to increase criminality at different ages?

Method

This study includes 232 boys who had been randomly selected for a treatment program that, although designed to prevent delinquency, included both well-behaved and troubled youngsters. The boys were born between 1926 and 1933. They lived in congested urban areas near Boston, Massachusetts. Counselors visited their homes about twice a month over a period of more than five years. Typically, the boys were between their tenth and sixteenth birthdays at the time of the visits.

One emphasis of the youth study was on developing sound case reports. Staff meetings included discussion of cases not only from the perspective of treatment but also to provide rounded descriptions of the child's life circumstances. After each visit with a boy or his parents, counselors dictated reports about what they saw and heard (see Powers and Witmer, 1951). The reports from visits to the boys' homes provided the raw material for subsequent analyses.

Child-Rearing Variables

In 1957, records were coded to describe the 232 families of the 253 boys who had remained in the program after an initial cut in 1941 (see W. McCord and J. McCord, 1960). Codes included ratings of family structure, family conflict, esteem of each parent for the other, parental supervision and disciplinary characteristics, parental warmth, self confidence, role, and aggressiveness. Codes also included parental alcoholism and criminality. The coding was designed for global assessments; this type of rating helps to circumvent problems that would occur when measures depend on specific items of information that might be missing from any particular data collection effort.

Among the 232 families, 130 were intact through the boys' sixteenth year. There were 60 families in which mothers were not living with a man; 23 fathers had died and 37 were living elsewhere. There were 30 families with mother substitutes and 29 with fathers substitutes, including 17 in which both natural parents were absent. Information about absent parents came from their concurrent interactions with the boys or their mothers. Thirteen substitute fathers and 13 substitute mothers were rated.

Rating for the mother's self-confidence were based on how she reacted when faced with problems. If she showed signs of believing in her ability to handle problems, she was rated as self-confident ($N=60$). Alternative ratings were "no indication," "victim or pawn," and "neutral."

The attitude of a parent toward the boy was classified as "affectionate" if that parent interacted frequently with the child without being generally critical. Among the parents, 110 mothers and 59 fathers were rated as affectionate.

Alternative classifications were "passively affectionate" (if the parent was concerned for the boy's welfare, but there was little interaction), "passively rejecting" (if the parent was unconcerned for the boy's welfare and interacted little), "actively rejecting" (if the parent was almost constantly critical of the boy), "ambivalent" (if the parents showed marked alternation between affection and rejection of the child), and "no indication."

Parental conflict reflected reports of disagreements about the child, values, money, alcohol, or religion. Ratings could be "no indication," "apparently none," "some," or "considerable." Parents were classified as evidencing ($N=75$) or not evidencing considerable conflict.

A rating of each parent's esteem for the other was based on evidence indicating whether a parent showed respect for the judgment of the other. Ratings could be "no indication," "moderate or high," or "low." In this study, each parent was classified as showing or not showing moderate or high esteem for the other. Almost an equal number of mothers ($N=109$) and fathers ($N=106$) revealed relatively high esteem for their spouse.

Maternal restrictiveness was rated as "subnormal" if a mother permitted her son to make virtually all his choices without her guidance ($N=83$). Alternative ratings were "no indication," "normal," and "overly restrictive."

Parental supervision was measured by the degree to which the boy's activities after school were governed by an adult. Supervision could be rated "present" ($N=132$) or, alternatively, "sporadic," "absent," or "no information."

Demands placed on a child were considered "high" if they involved doing well at school and performing tasks at home or if they included unusually high standards for either school or home ($N=58$). Alternative ratings were "moderate," "low," and "no information."

Discipline by each parent was classified into one of six categories. "Consistently punitive, including very harsh verbal abuse," identified a parent who used physical force to control the boy. A parent who used praise, rewards, or reasoning to control the boy was rated as "consistent, nonpunitive." Alternative categories were "erratically punitive," "inconsistent, nonpunitive," "extremely lax, with almost no use of discipline," and "no information." Fathers were difficult to classify for consistency, so for this analyses, their discipline was coded as "punitive" ($N=39$) or "other." Mother's discipline was coded as "consistent and nonpunitive" ($N=70$) or "other."

A mother's role in the family was classified as "leader," "dictator," "martyr," "passive," "neglecting," or "no indication." The leadership role involved participating in family decisions. Mothers in this analysis were classified either as being ($N=144$) or not being leaders.

The aggressiveness of each parent was rated as "unrestrained" if that parent regularly expressed anger by such activities as shouting abuses, yelling, throwing or braking things, or hitting people. Thirty-seven fathers and 23 mothers were rated as aggressive. Alternative classifications were "no indication," "moderately aggressive," "greatly inhibited."

To estimate the reliability of the coding, two raters independently read a 10 percent random sample of the cases. Agreement for those ratings ranged from 76

TABLE 8.1   Interrater Reliability: Dichotomous Variables (2 raters on 10 percent random sample)

Characteristic	Percent agreement	Scott's Pi[*]
Mother's self-confidence	84	.60
Mother's discipline	84	.62
Mother's attitude to son	84	.68
Mother's leadership	96	.91
Father's attitude to son	84	.57
Father's esteem for mother	84	.68
Mother's esteem for father	88	.76
Father's aggressiveness	84	.41
Family conflict	80	.55
Boy's supervision	88	.76
Demands for boy	76	.35
Mother's restrictiveness	84	.65
Mother's aggressiveness	92	.56
Father's discipline	88	.52

[*]$Pi=(P_o-P_e)/(1-P_e)$. P_o=percent agreement observed. P_e=percent agreement expected: $P_e=(p)^2 + (q)^2$, where p=proportion having the characteristic and $q=1-p$.

percent to 96 percent. Since chance agreement between rates varies in relation to distribution, Scott's (1955) interrater reliability coefficient, pi, was computed to indicate improvement over chance.[1] (See Table 8.1.)

Correlation among the measures of child rearing showed that supervision was strongly related to each of the other measures. Only mothers' aggression and fathers' discipline were not strongly correlated with the other measures. As Table 8.2 indicates, correlations among some of the variables suggested that they might be measures of similar dimensions.

A clustering procedure, Varclus (SAS, 1985), was used to identify the dimensional structure of the 14 variables. The procedure searches for unidimensional factors in terms of combinations of variables that will maximize variance among cluster centroids. The first cluster included (in order of contribution) mother's discipline, self-confidence, affection for her son, and role. The factor appeared to represent Mother's Competence. A second dimension included (in order of contribution) mother's esteem for the father, father's esteem for the mother, parental conflict, father's affection for his son, and father's aggressiveness. The factor appeared to represent Father's Interaction with the family. A third dimension included (in order of contribution) maternal restrictiveness, supervision, and demands. The factor represented Family Expectations. A fourth dimension included father's punitiveness and mother's aggressiveness, weighted in opposite directions. The factor appeared to measure something like Disciplinarian. This factor was dropped, however, because 75 percent of the families scored at the midpoint. Table 8.3 shows descriptive characteristics of the clusters representing Mother's Competence, Father's Interaction, and Family Expectations.

The predictive validity of home observations had been proven in prior studies, but problems of collinearity precluded using the individual scales for the

TABLE 8.2 Correlation among Child-Rearing Variables

		2	3	4	5	6	7	8	9	10	11	12	13	14
1	Mother's self-confidence	40*	22*	30*	14	17	23*	20	13	24*	32*	-15	-15	-18
2	Mother's discipline	37*	24*	13	21	13	-11	-13	33*	16	-24*	-19	-15	
3	Mother's attitude to son	32*	28*	10	13	-11	-14	23*	19	-24*	-11	-01		
4	Mother's leadership	03	09	17	-22	-11	29*	-04	-23*	-19	-10			
5	Father's attitude to son	40*	34*	-23*	-19	23*	10	-15	-09	-02				
6	Father's esteem for mother	65*	-28*	-47*	27*	07	-16	-16	-04					
7	Mother's esteem for father	-34*	-56*	26*	10	-18	-11	-10						
8	Father's aggressiveness	30*	-22*	-09	17	-03	18							
9	Family conflict	-24*	-10	17	14	03								
10	Boy's supervision	26*	-57*	16	00									
11	Demands for boy	-29*	-06*	01										
12	Mother's restrictiveness	02	-02											
13	Mother's aggressiveness	-07												
14	Father's discipline													

Note: Decimal points have been omitted.

*p < .001.

TABLE 8.3   Cluster Analysis

	R^2		
Group variable	Highest	Second	Scoring coefficient
Mother's competence			
Consistent discipline	.553	.104	.386
Self-confidence	.479	.087	.359
Affection for son	.472	.084	.357
Role	.422	.054	.337
Father's interaction			
Father's esteem for mother	.669	.053	.320
Mother's esteem for father	.720	.058	.332
Parental conflict	.532	.049	−.286
Father's affection for son	.323	.045	.222
Father's aggressiveness	.312	.050	−.219
Family expectations			
Mother's restrictiveness	.710	.096	−.478
Supervision	.692	.154	.472
Demands	.360	.054	.341

	Correlations		
	A	B	C
A Mother's competence	1.00		
B Father's interaction	0.29	1.00	
C Family expectations	0.41	0.31	1.00

purpose of detecting differential impact. The Varclus clustering procedure reduced collinearity to acceptable levels, but a conservative view would recognize the resultant measures as having only ordinal properties. To stabilize and simplify the scales, items in each factor were given equal weights and scored so that higher scores represent more socially desirable behaviors: greater mother's competence; more approving, less aggressive father's interaction; and higher family expectations. Scores on Mother's Competence ranged from 0 to +4; on Father's Interaction, from −2 to +3; and on Family Expectations, from −1 to +2. Each factor was divided as close to the median as possible so that a family could be described as high or low in terms of each of the variables.

Follow-up Measures

Between 1975 and 1980, when they ranged from 45 to 53 years in age, the former youth study participants were retraced. Twenty-four were found through their death records.[2] Police and court records had been collected in 1948. Those records of juvenile delinquency were combined with records gathered in 1979 from probation departments in Massachusetts and in other states to which the men had migrated.

The measure of criminality depended on official records of convictions. Such records do not reflect all crimes committed (Murphy et al., 1946), but they do appear to identify those who commit serious crimes and those who break the law frequently (Morash, 1984). In addition, several studies show convergence between results from official records and from well-designed self-reporting instruments for measuring serious criminality (Elliott and Ageton, 1980; Farrington, 1979; Hindelang et al., 1979; Reiss and Rhodes, 1961).

A boy was considered a juvenile delinquent if he had been convicted for an Index crime prior to reaching the age of 18 years. Fifty boys had been convicted for such serious crimes as auto theft, breaking and entering, and assault. Of the 50 juveniles convicted for serious crimes, 21 also were convicted for serious crimes as adults; additionally, 29 men not convicted as juveniles were convicted for at least one Index crime as an adult.

The strength of relationships was tested using chi-square. Catmod (SAS, 1985), a method for analyzing categorical data, was used to detect the impact of family interaction on delinquency and on adult criminality. Catmod uses a log-linear procedure that fits a linear model on generalized logits. Where analysis of variance estimates are based on individual scores, the log-linear procedure estimates are based on cell frequencies.

Results

Comparisons for the impact of child rearing showed that Mother's Competence, Father's Interaction with the family, and Family Expectations were related to juvenile delinquency. Considered separately, poor child rearing in each of these domains reliably increased risk of delinquency (Table 8.4).

Joint effects of poor child rearing can be seen by examining their combinations in relation to juvenile delinquency. Only 5 percent of the boys reared by compe-

TABLE 8.4 Child-Rearing Variables and Juvenile Delinquency (percent who were juvenile delinquents)

			Prob.
Mother's competence=high	(123) 11	Low (109) 34	.000
Self-confident	(66) 8	Not (166) 27	.001
Consistent nonpunitive	(70) 9	Not (162) 27	.002
Affectionate	(110) 10	Not (122) 32	.000
A leader	(144) 16	Not (88) 31	.008
Father's interaction=good	(123) 14	Bad (109) 30	.002
Esteem for mother high	(106) 9	Not (126) 32	.000
Mother's esteem for father high	(109) 12	Not (123) 30	.001
Family conflict much	(75) 35	Not (157) 15	.001
Aggressive	(37) 38	Not (195) 18	.009
Affectionate	(59) 5	Not (173) 27	.000
Family expectations=high	(125) 11	Low (107) 34	.000
Mother control little	(83) 35	Not (149) 14	.000
Boy supervised	(132) 12	Not (100) 34	.000
Demands for boy high	(58) 10	Not (174) 25	.017

Note: Numbers in parentheses are N's.

TABLE 8.5   Family Constellations and Juvenile Delinquency (percent delinquent in each type of family)

		Mother's competence	
		Low	High
Father's interaction	Family expectations		
Bad	Weak	(38) 47	(24) 29
Bad	Strong	(25) 24	(22) 9
Good	Weak	(29) 34	(16) 6
Good	Strong	(17) 18	(61) 5

	Analysis of variance (CATMOD)		
	df	Chi sq.	Prob.
Intercept	1	55.65	.0001
Mother's competence	1	8.72	.0031
Father's interaction	1	3.67	.0554
Family expectations	1	8.60	.0034
Residual	4	1.32	.8574

Note: Numbers in parentheses are *N*'s.

tent mothers in families with good paternal interaction and high expectations had become delinquents. In contrast, almost half (47%) had become delinquents among those who had been raised by incompetent mothers in homes that had poor paternal interaction and low expectations (Table 8.5).

Serious criminality as a juvenile was strongly related to both the mother's competence and to family expectations for the boy. Together, these accounted for 12 percent of the variance in juvenile delinquency, $p = .0001$. Father's poor interaction with the family showed a weaker relationship with juvenile delinquency; it accounted for an additional 1.5 percent of the variance, $p = .0617$.

A different picture emerges from analyses of the impact of child-rearing variables on adult criminality (see Table 8.6).[3] Father's interaction with the family increased in importance. With the exception of affection, each of the variables contributing to this dimension was related to adult criminality. The impact of the mother's competence had weakened—only the mother's self-confidence clearly contributed to adult criminality. The dimension of family expectations was not reliably related to adult convictions, although supervision and maternal control apparently had enduring effects. The categorical analysis of variance, controlling collinearity, indicated that only the father's interactions bore a significant independent relationship to adult criminality (Table 8.7).

Conviction as a juvenile was related to being convicted as an adult. As noted above, among the 50 boys who had been juvenile delinquents, 21 (42%) had been convicted for serious crimes as adults. In contrast, among 182 boys who had not been convicted for serious crimes as juveniles, 27 (15%) had been convicted for serious crimes as adults, $\chi^2_{(1)} = 17.64$, $p < .001$.

To test the degree to which paternal interaction independently influenced adult crime above and beyond effects through juvenile delinquency, juvenile

TABLE 8.6 Child-Rearing Variables and Adult Criminality (percent who were adult criminals)

			Prob.
Mother's competence=high	(123) 15	Low (109) 27	.036
Self-confident	(66) 6	Not (166) 27	.001
Consistent nonpunitive	(70) 13	Not (162) 24	NS
Affectionate	(110) 15	Not (122) 25	NS
A leader	(144) 17	Not (88) 26	NS
Father's interaction=good	(123) 14	Bad (109) 28	.006
Esteem for mother high	(106) 11	Not (126) 29	.001
Mother's esteem for father high	(109) 13	Not (123) 28	.005
Family conflict much	(75) 32	Not (157) 15	.003
Aggressive	(37) 43	Not (195) 16	.000
Affectionate	(59) 15	Not (173) 23	NS
Family expectations=high	(125) 18	Low (107) 24	NS
Mother control little	(83) 28	Not (149) 17	.049
Boy supervised	(132) 15	Not (100) 28	.017
Demands for boy high	(58) 12	Not (174) 24	NS

Note: Numbers in parentheses are N's.

TABLE 8.7 Family Constellations and Adult Criminality (percent criminal in each type of family)

		Mother's competence	
		Low	High
Father's interaction	Family expectations		
Bad	Weak	(38) 34	(24) 29
Bad	Strong	(25) 32	(22) 14
Good	Weak	(29) 14	(16) 13
Good	Strong	(17) 24	(61) 11

	Analysis of variance (CATMOD)		
	df	Chi sq.	Prob.
Intercept	1	63.44	.0001
Mother's competence	1	2.09	NS
Father's interaction	1	4.88	.0271
Family expectations	1	0.12	NS
Residual	4	2.18	.7028

Note: Numbers in parentheses are N's.

TABLE 8.8 Predictors of Adult Criminality (stepwise discriminant analysis)

Step	Variable	Partial r^2	F	Prob. >F
1	Juvenile delinquency	.076	18.926	.0001
2	Father's interaction	.018	4.109	.0438

delinquency and the three child-rearing dimensions were introduced into a stepwise discriminant function analysis (Table 8.8). The results show that juvenile delinquency accounted for 7.6 percent of the variance in adult criminality, $p = .0001$. The father's interactions during childhood accounted for an additional 1.8 percent, $p < .0438$. None of the other child-rearing variables approached a significant contribution to variance in adult criminality (with a criterion of entry set at $p < .15$) once juvenile criminality had been taken into account.

Summary and Discussion

This study reexamined the ways in which family interactions during childhood influence criminal behavior. By considering families whose socioeconomic backgrounds were similar, it was possible to look beyond effects of poverty, social disorganization, and blighted urban conditions.

Case records based on repeated visits to the homes of 232 boys allowed analyses that included the dynamics of family interactions. The variables resulting from observations in the homes were reduced to three dimensions in order to minimize problems of collinearity. A reasonable conclusion from the data is that the mother's competence and family expectations influenced the likelihood that a son became a juvenile delinquent.

Competent mothers seem to insulate a child against criminogenic influences even in deteriorated neighborhoods. Competent mothers were self-confident and provided leadership; they were consistently nonpunitive in discipline and affectionate. Coupled with high family expectations, maternal competence seems to reduce the probability that sons become juvenile delinquents. The influence of these child-rearing conditions on adult criminality appears to be largely through their impact on juvenile delinquency.

Compared with the mother's influences, the father's interactions with his family appeared less important during the juvenile years. Father's interactions with the family became more important, however, as the boys matured.

Fathers who interact with their wives in ways exhibiting high mutual esteem, who are not highly aggressive, and who generally get along well with their wives provide models for socialized behavior. Conversely, fathers who undermine their wives, who fight with the family, and who are aggressive provide models of antisocial behavior. Both types of fathers, it seems, teach their sons how to behave when they become adults.

The evidence from this study raises doubts abut two currently prevalent views. One view holds that regardless of the age of the criminal, crime is merely a particular symptom of a single underlying "disorder." The other view holds that causes of crime are basically the same at all ages. This study indicates that the causes of juvenile crime are different from those of adult criminality. Juvenile delinquency might be explained through elements of control, as represented by maternal competence and high expectations, but adult criminality appears to add a component based on role expectations. If these interpretations are correct, criminality cannot be attributed to a single type of cause, nor does it represent a single underlying tendency.

Notes

This study was partly supported by U.S. Public Health Service Research Grant MH26779. I thank Richard Parente, Robert Staib, Ellen Myers, and Ann Cronin for tracing the men and their records; Joan Immel, Tom Smedile, Harriet Sayre, Mary Duell, Elise Goldman, Abby Brodkin, and Laura Otten for coding the follow-up. I also express appreciation to the Massachusetts Department of Probation, the New York Division of Criminal Justice Services, the Maine Bureau of Identification, and to California, Florida, Michigan, New Jersey, Pennsylvania, Virginia, and Washington for supplying supplemental data about the men. In addition, I thank the anonymous reviewers whose criticisms have greatly improved the product. Only the author is responsible for the statistical analyses and conclusions.

1. Scott's pi differs from kappa (Cohen, 1960) regarding expected values. Whereas kappa assumes fixed marginals for both raters, pi assumes only a single distribution.

2. None of the subjects died before the age of 20. Of those who died in their twenties, nine had no convictions and one was convicted only as a juvenile. Of those who died in their thirties, three had no convictions, two were convicted only as juveniles, and two were convicted only as adults. Of those who died in their forties, three were not convicted, two were convicted only as adults, and two were convicted both as juveniles and as adults.

3. The range in age among the 20 who had died prior to the follow-up and did not have criminal records as adults was 20 to 50 years. The median age was 39. Only six were under age 25. Because there was no attempt to ascertain rates of criminality, no correction was attempted for time of "exposure."

References

Akers, R. L. 1973. *Deviant Behavior: A Social Learning Approach*. Belmont, Calif. Wadsworth.

Aristotle. 1941. Ethica Nicomachea. Translated by W. D. Ross. In *The Basic Works of Aristotle*, edited by R. McKeon. New York: Random House.

Bachman, J. G. and P. M. O'Malley. 1984. The youth in transition project. In *Handbook of Longitudinal Research*, edited by S. A. Mednick, M. Harway, and K. M. Fineilo. New York: Holt, Praeger.

Bacon, M. K., I. L. Child, and H. Barry, Jr. 1963. A cross-cultural study of correlates of crime. *Journal of Abnormal and Social Psychology* 66: 291–300.

Bandura, A. and R. H. Walters. 1959. *Adolescent Aggression*. New York: Ronald.

———. 1963. *Social Learning and Personality Development*. New York: Holt, Rinehart and Winston.

Baumrind, D. 1968. Authoritarian vs. authoritative parental control. *Adolescence* 3: 255–272.

———. 1978. Parental disciplinary patterns and social competence in children. *Youth and Society* 9(3): 239–276.

———. 1983. Rejoinder to Lewis's reinterpretation of parental firm control effects: Are authoritative families really harmonious? *Psychological Bulletin* 94(1): 132–142.

Bowlby, J. 1940. The influence of early environment on neurosis and neurotic character. *International Journal of Psychoanalysis* 21: 154.

———. 1951. Maternal care and mental health. *Bulletin of the World Health Organization* 3: 355–534.

Burt, C. 1925. *The Young Delinquent*. New York: Appleton and Co.

Cernkovich, S. A. and P. C. Giordano. 1987. Family relationships and delinquency. *Criminology* 25(2): 295–319.

Cohen, J. 1960. A coefficient of agreement for nominal scales. *Educational and Psychological Measurement* 20: 37–46.

Dean, A. L., M. M. Malik, W. Richards, and S. A. Stringer. 1986. Effects of parental maltreatment on children's conceptions of interpersonal relationships. *Developmental Psychology* 22(5): 617–626.

Dodge, K. Q. and D. R. Somberg. 1987. Hostile attributional biases among aggressive boys are exacerbated under conditions of threats to the self. *Child Development* 58: 213–224.

Dornbusch, S. M., J. M. Carlsmith, S. J. Bushwall, P. L. Ritter, H. Leiderman, A. H. Hastorf, and R. T. Gross. 1985. Single parents, extended households, and the control of adolescents. *Child Development* 56: 326–341.

Eich, E., S. Rachman, and C. Lopatka. 1990. Affect, pain, and autobiographical memory. *Journal of Abnormal Psychology* 99(2): 174–178.

Elliot, D. S. and S. S. Ageton. 1980. Reconciling race and class differences in self-reported and official estimates of delinquency. *American Sociological Review* 45: 95–110.

Eron, L. D., T. J. Bants, L. O. Walder, and J. H. Laulicht. 1961. Comparison of data obtained from mothers and fathers on child-rearing practices and their relation to child aggression. *Child Development* 32(3): 455–472.

Farrington, D. P. 1979. Environmental stress, delinquent behavior, and convictions. In *Stress and Anxiety*, vol. 6, edited by I. G. Sarason and C. D. Spielberger. New York: John Wiley and Sons.

Fenichel, O. 1945. *The Psychoanalytic Theory of Neurosis*. New York: Norton.

Forehand, R., K. C. Wells, and E. T. Sturgis. 1978. Predictors of child noncompliant behavior in the home. *Journal of Consulting and Clinical Psychology* 46(1): 179.

Freud, S. 1953. *Three Essays on the Theory of Sexuality*. In Standard Edition, vol. 7. London: Hogarth.

Glueck, S. and E. T. Glueck. 1950. *Unraveling Juvenile Delinquency*. New York: Commonwealth Fund.

Goldfarb, W. 1945. Psychological privation in infancy and subsequent adjustment. *American Journal of Orthopsychiatry* 15: 247–255.

Goode, W. J. 1956. *After Divorce*. Glencoe, Ill.: Free Press.

Hagan, J., A. R. Gillis, and J. Simpson. 1985. The class structure of gender and delinquency: Toward a power-control theory of common delinquent behavior. *American Journal of Sociology* 90: 1151–1178.

Hindelang, M. J., T. Hirschi, and J. G. Weis. 1979. Correlates of delinquency: The illusion of discrepancy between self-report and official measures. *American Sociological Review* 44: 995–1014.

Hirschi, T. 1969. *Causes of Delinquency*. Berkeley: University of California Press.

———. 1983. Crime and the family. In *Crime and Public Policy*, edited by J. Q. Wilson. San Francisco: Institute for Cotemporary Studies.

Hoffman, L. W. 1975. Effects on child. In *Working Mothers*, edited by L. W. Hoffman and F. I. Nye. San Francisco: Jossey-Bass.

Jensen, G. F. and D. Brownfield. 1983. Parents and drugs. *Criminology* 21(4): 543–555.

Kellogg, R. T. 1980. Is conscious attention necessary for long-term storage? *Journal of Experimental Psychology* 6(4): 379–390.

Lamb, M. E. 1976. The role of the father: An overview. In *The Role of the Father in Child Development*, edited by M. E. Lamb. New York: John Wiley and Sons.

Larzelere, R. E. and G. R. Patterson. 1990. Parental management: Mediator of the effect of socioeconomic status on early delinquency. *Criminology* 28(2): 301–323.

Laub, J. H. and R. J. Sampson. 1988. Unraveling families and delinquency: A reanalysis of the Gluecks' data. *Criminology* 26(3): 355–380.

Levy, D. 1937. Primary affect hunger. *American Journal of Psychiatry* 94: 643–652.

Lewis, C. 1981. The effects of parental firm control: A reinterpretation of findings. *Psychological Bulletin* 90(3): 547–563.

Liska, A. E. and M. D. Reed. 1985. Ties to conventional institutions and delinquency: Estimating reciprocal effects. *American Sociological Review* 50(Aug): 547–560.

Locke, J. 1693. *Some Thoughts Concerning Education*, vol. 8, Collected Works, 9th ed. London: T. Longman.

Loeber, R. and M. Stouthamer-Loeber. 1986. Family factors as correlates and predictors of juvenile conduct problems and delinquency. In *Crime and Justice*, vol. 7, edited by M. Tonry and N. Morris. Chicago: University of Chicago Press.

Maccoby, E. E. 1958. Effects upon children of their mothers' outside employment. In *Work in the Lives of Married Women*, National Manpower Council. New York: Columbia University Press.

McCord, J. 1979. Some child-rearing antecedents of criminal behavior in adult men. *Journal of Personality and Social Psychology* 37: 1477–1486.

———. 1982. A longitudinal view of the relationship between paternal absence and crime. In *Abnormal Offenders, Delinquency, and the Criminal Justice System*, edited by J. Gunn and D. P. Farrington. Chichester: John Wiley and Sons.

———. 1983a. A forty year perspective on effects of child abuse and neglect. *Child Abuse and Neglect* 7: 265–270.

———. 1983b. A longitudinal study of aggression and antisocial behavior. In *Prospective Studies of Crime and Delinquency*, edited by K. T. Van Dusen and S. A. Mednick. Boston: Kluwer-Nijhoff.

———. 1986. Instigation and insulation: How families affect antisocial aggression. In *Development of Antisocial and Prosocial Behavior*, edited by J. Block, D. Olweus, and M. R. Yarrow. New York: Academic Press.

———. 1988. Identifying developmental paradigms leading to alcoholism. *Journal of Studies on Alcohol* 49(4): 357–362.

———. 1990. Longterm effects of parental absence. In *Straight and Devious Pathways from Childhood to Adulthood*, edited by L. Robins and M. Rutter. New York: Cambridge University Press.

McCord, J. and W. McCord. 1958. The effects of parental role model on criminality. *Journal of Social Issues* 14(3): 66–75.

———. 1962. Cultural stereotypes and the validity of interviews for research in child development. *Child Development* 32(2): 171–185.

McCord, J., W. McCord, and A. Howard. 1963a. Family interaction as antecedent to the direction of male aggressiveness. *Journal of Abnormal and Social Psychology* 66: 239–242.

McCord, J., W. McCord, and E. Thurber. 1963b. The effects of maternal employment on lower class boys. *Journal of Abnormal and Social Psychology* 67(1): 177–182.

McCord, W. and J. McCord. 1959. *Origins of Crime*. New York: Columbia University Press.

———. 1960. *Origins of Alcoholism*. Stanford, California: Stanford University Press.

McCord, W., J. McCord, and A. Howard. 1961. Familial correlates of aggression in nondelinquent male children. *Journal of Abnormal Psychology and Social Psychology* 1: 79–93.

Miller, W. B. 1958. Lower class culture as a generating milieu of gang delinquency. *Journal of Social Issues* 14: 5–19.

Morash, M. 1984. Establishment of a juvenile police record: The influence of individual and peer group characteristics. *Criminology* 22: 97–111.

Murdock, G. P. 1949. *Social Structure*. New York: Macmillan.

Murphy, F. J., M. M. Shirley, and H. L. Witmer. 1946. The incidence of hidden delinquency. *American Journal of Orthopsychiatry* 16: 686–696.

Newell, H. W. 1934. The psycho-dynamics of maternal rejection. *American Journal of Orthopsychiatry* 4: 387–401.

————. 1936. A further study of maternal rejection. *American Journal of Orthopsychiatry* 6: 576–589.

Nye, F. I. 1958. *Family Relationships and Delinquent Behavior*. New York: John Wiley & Sons.

————. 1959. Maternal employment and the adjustment of adolescent children. *Marriage and Family Living* 21(August): 240–244.

Parscaus, T. and R. F. Bales. 1955. *Family, Socialization and Interaction Process*. Glencoe, Ill.: Free Press.

Plato. 1937. Laws. In *The Dialogues of Plato*, translated B. Jowett. New York: Random House.

Powers, E. and H. Witmer. 1951. *An Experiment in the Prevention of Delinquency: The Cambridge-Somerville Youth Study*. New York: Columbia University Press.

Reiss, A. J., Jr. and A. L. Rhodes. 1961. Delinquency and class structure. *American Sociological Review* 26(5): 720–732.

Robins, L. N.1966. *Deviant Children Grown Up*. Baltimore: Williams & Wilkins.

SAS Institute. 1985. *SAS User's Guide: Statistics*. 1985 ed. Cary, N.C.: SAS Institute.

Scott, W. A. 1955. Reliability of content analysis: The case of nominal scale coding. *Public Opinion Quarterly* 19(3): 321–325.

Shaw, C. and H. D. McKay. 1932. Are broken homes a causative factor in juvenile delinquency? *Social Forces* 10: 514–524.

Sutherland, E. H. and D. R. Cressey. 1974. *Criminology* 1924. 9th ed. Philadelphia: Lippincott.

van Voorhis, P., F. T. Cullen, R. A. Mathers, and C. C. Garner. 1988. The impact of family structure and quality on delinquency: A comparative assessment of structural and functional factors. *Criminology* 26(2): 235–261.

Wadsworth, M. 1979. *Roots of Delinquency*. New York: Barnes and Noble.

Weller, L. and E. Luchterhand. 1983. Family relationships of "Problem" and "Promising" youth. *Adolescence* 18(69): 43–100.

Wells, L. E. and J. H. Rankin. 1988. Direct parental controls and delinquency. *Criminology* 26(2): 263–285.

Whiting, J. W. M., R. Kluckhohn, and A. Anthony. 1958. The function of male initiation ceremonies at puberty. In *Readings in Social Psychology*, edited by E. E. Macccby, T. M. Newcomb, and E. L. Hartley. New York: Holt, Rinehart & Winston.

Yarrow, M. R., J. D. Campbell, and R. V. Burton. 1970. Recollections of childhood: A study of the retrospective method. *Monographs of the Society for Research in Child Development* 35(1): 1–83.

PART III

Punishment and Discipline

CHAPTER NINE

Questioning the Value of Punishment*

"SPARE THE ROD and spoil the child," many have argued. "No," say others, as they refer to evidence that physical punishment leads to, rather than prevents, violent behavior. Yet only a few, it seems, have whispered that we should question the value of every type of punishment, including psychological punishments and deprivation of privileges as well as physical punishments.

When attention has been focused only on physical punishment, critics typically note that such discipline provides a model for the use of force, thereby teaching people to use force. Murray Straus, for example, argues that corporal punishment contributes to a cycle of violence that includes violent crime, child abuse, spouse abuse, nonviolent crimes, ineffective family socialization, and ineffective schooling. Straus accounts for correlations between the use of physical punishment, on the one hand, and antisocial or dysfunctional behaviors on the other by means of Cultural Spillover Theory. This theory is an amalgam of explanations that consider behavior to be learned through imitation of models and adoption of norms supported by groups with whom an individual associates. In this view, individuals come to accept the use of violence—and to be violent—because they see violence as legitimated through its use by role models, and they generalize the behavioral norm to include illegitimate uses of violence.

While Straus is correct that physical punishments tend to increase aggression and criminal behavior, I believe he takes too narrow a view about the mechanisms that account for the relationships. My conclusion is grounded in evidence from longitudinal studies about the transmission of violence from one generation to the next. I offer a competing theory, one that merges evidence from experimental studies designed by psychologists to understand the conditions under which children learn and that considers critical issues related to the learning of

*Reprinted from McCord, J. 1991. Questioning the value of punishment. *Social Problems* 38 (2): 167–179. Copyright © 1991 by the Society for the Study of Social Problems, Inc; with permission.

language. The competing theory, which I call the Construct Theory, suggests how the same mechanism that links physical punishments to aggression can be triggered by nonphysical punishments and neglect. Before turning to the competing theory, I present empirical evidence that physical punishment leads to aggression and criminal behavior and then show that the Cultural Spillover Theory inadequately explains the relationship.

Problems with the Cultural Spillover Explanation

Much of the research to which Straus refers in his analysis of the relationship between physical punishment and misbehavior is cross-sectional. With such data, as Straus acknowledges, one cannot determine whether punishments were a cause or an effect of the behavior. Three longitudinal studies that measured discipline prior to the age serious antisocial behavior began, however, suggest temporal priority for punitive discipline. Comparing children whose parents depended on physical punishments with those whose parents did not in Finland (Pulkkinen, 1983), Great Britain (Farrington, 1978), and in the United States (McCord, 1988), researchers found that those whose parents used harsh physical punishments had greater probabilities for subsequently committing serious crimes. Longitudinal studies of victims of child abuse, too, suggest that violence tends to increase the probability that victims will commit serious crimes (McCord, 1983; Widom, 1989).

The theory of Cultural Spillover, like similar theories that attempt to explain pockets of violence, postulates acceptance of norms exhibited by the subculture using violence. Although longitudinal studies suggest that violence in the family precedes violence in society, they contain data incongruent with a theory that explains the causal mechanism as socialization into norms that legitimize violence.

One incongruence is revealed in my study of long-term effects of child abuse in which I compared abused sons with neglected and rejected and loved sons (McCord 1983). The classifications were based on biweekly observations in the homes when the boys were between the ages of 8 and 16 years and living in high-crime areas. Records of major (FBI Index) crime convictions were collected thirty years after the study ended. Twenty-three percent of those reared in loving families and 39 percent of those reared in abusing families had been convicted; but the conviction rate was 35 percent for the neglected and 53 percent for the rejected boys. That is, the data show almost as much violence produced from neglect as from abuse, and greater violence from rejection without abuse than from abuse. Because neglect and rejection typically lead to socialization failure, these results raise doubts that acceptance of norms of violence account for transmission of violence. It would be an anomaly if the very conditions that undermine acceptance of other types of norms promoted norms of violence.

One might argue that Cultural Spillover Theory accounts for violence among the abused and some other theory accounts for violence among neglected and rejected children. Yet neglect and rejection have enough in common with abuse to suggest that a more parsimonious account would be desirable. Furthermore, as

TABLE 9.1   Paternal Criminality, Physical Punishment, and Criminality

| | Father's physical punishment? | | | |
| | No | | Yes | |
Paternal criminality	% sons criminal	Number	% sons criminal	Number
No	14	56	37	52
Yes	33	6	63	16

will be shown, when neglect is combined with abuse, the result is not increased violence as one would expect were there different causes involved.

My data from the Cambridge-Somerville Youth Study records permitted further checks on the Cultural Spillover Theory. The data include parental criminal records as well as coded descriptions of family life between 1939 and 1945. Sons' criminal records had, as noted, been collected in 1978, when the sons were middle-aged. Among the 130 families containing two natural parents, 22 included a father who had been convicted for an Index crime. Fifty-five percent (12) of their sons were convicted for an Index crime. In comparison, 25 percent (27) of the 108 sons of noncriminal men had been convicted ($\chi^2_{(1)}$=7.60, p=.006). The criminal fathers were more likely to use physical punishment: 73 percent compared with 48 percent ($\chi^2_{(1)}$=4.43, p=.035). Further, the combined impact of a criminal father using physical punishment appeared to be particularly criminogenic (Table 9.1).

These data support the view that use of physical punishment increases the likelihood that sons of criminals will be criminals. Cultural Spillover Theory suggests that the increase comes about because sons adopt the norms displayed through physical punishments. If the theory were correct, then the transmission of norms of violence should be particularly effective under conditions that promote acceptance of other types of norms as well. The evidence, however, gives another picture.

Many studies have shown that warmth or affection facilitates acceptance of social norms (e.g., Austin, 1978; Bandura and Huston, 1961; Bandura and Walters, 1963; Baumrind, 1978; Bender, 1947; Bowlby, 1940; Glueck and Glueck, 1950; Goldfarb, 1945; Hirschi, 1969; Liska and Reed, 1985; Maccoby, 1980; McCord, 1979; Olson, Bates, and Bayles, 1990; Patterson, 1976). Parental

TABLE 9.2   Child-Rearing and Criminality

Parents	% sons criminal	Number
Non-punitive	18	40
Punitive and affectionate	28	47
Punitive and not affectionate	44	43

$\chi^2(2)$=7.219; p=.027.

affection for the child should increase concordance if a similar mechanism for acceptance of norms accounts for a connection between parents' and children's aggression. To test this hypothesis, the 130 families were divided into three groups: those not using physical punishment, those using physical punishment and also expressing affection for the child, and those using physical punishment and not expressing affection for the child.

The data show that parental affection did not increase acceptance of norms of violence, but the opposite (Table 9.2). For individuals reared with physical punishment, those whose parents were affectionate were *less* likely to become criminals. This result does not easily fit an assumption that normative acquisition accounts for the violence.

Another inconsistency is apparent in a longitudinal study that at first glance might appear to support the Cultural Spillover Theory. Widom (1989) retraced children reported to have been victims of abuse or neglect prior to the age of 11. Using records from elementary schools and hospitals at birth, Widom was able to match 667 of 908 children on sex, race, and age with children not known to have been either abused or neglected. Widom's analyses, based either on aggregate data combining abuse with neglect or matched and unmatched cases, have led her to conclude that violence breeds violence. I reanalyzed her data (Widom, 1990) to differentiate effects of neglect from effects of violence.

The matched pairs were divided into those in which the child had experienced sexual abuse (85 females, 15 males), neglect but not physical abuse (205 females, 254 males), physical abuse but not neglect (14 females, 35 males), and both physical abuse and neglect (29 females, 30 males). Assuming that acceptance of a norm of violence accounts for the high rates of crime that Widom found to follow abuse, crime would be considerably more prevalent among those who had been physically abused than among those who had been neglected but not abused.

Using Widom's codes of the individuals' criminal records, I compared each case with the matched control to see which had the worse criminal record. If both had been convicted of at least one crime, the one convicted for more crimes was counted as being worse.

TABLE 9.3   Child Abuse/Neglect and Crimes

	Sexual abuse	Neglect	Physical abuse	Abuse and neglect
Females	(N=85)	(N=205)	(N=14)	(N=29)
Equal	53	59	57	66
Control worse	22	15	7	3
Case worse	25	26	36	31
Males	(N=15)	(N=254)	(N=35)	(N=30)
Equal	13	22	26	47
Control worse	20	26	17	17
Case worse	67	52	57	37

Note: Percent in each category.

TABLE 9.4 Child Abuse/Neglect and Violent Crimes

	Sexual abuse	Neglect	Physical abuse	Abuse and neglect
Females	(N=85)	(N=205)	(N=14)	(N=29)
Equal	88	97	79	97
Control worse	4	1	0	3
Case worse	8	2	21	0
Males	(N=15)	(N=254)	(N=35)	(N=30)
Equal	67	68	83	77
Control worse	13	9	6	0
Case worse	20	23	11	23

Note: Percent in each category.

The data show that neglect is about as criminogenic as sexual abuse and physical abuse (Table 9.3). Moreover, the combined effects of neglect and abuse are not worse than those of either alone as would be expected if each had separate causal impact. Comparisons of cases and controls for crimes of violence (e.g., assault, murder, attempted murder) produced similar results (Table 9.4).

These comparisons again suggest that continuity in violence among abusing families has been mistakenly attributed to transmission of norms of violence. Among males, neglect and sexual abuse were in fact more likely than physical abuse to lead to violence. Yet if transmission of social norms accounts for violence, physical abuse should create more. The reanalysis of these data suggest that one ought to search for a common cause, for something shared by neglect and abuse that might lead to violence.

In sum, violence seems to beget violence, but studies of child abuse and of family socialization undermine the argument that violence begets violence *through acceptance of family (subcultural) norms of violence*. Because neglect, rejection, and physical abuse result in similarly high rates of crime, it seems appropriate to search for a cause in terms of what they have in common.

A sound understanding of the way children learn can explain why physical abuse, neglect, and rejection lead to antisocial behavior. Below I develop such an understanding to show that a norm of self-interest, rather than a norm of violence, underlies the education shared by those who are rejected, neglected, and abused. It is the norm of self-interest that leads to violence in some circumstances.

Undermining Some Assumptions

Side stepping the issue of how infants learn, many psychologists have simply assumed that babies are completely self-centered. In contrast, the evidence shows that how much children care about their own pleasures and pains and what they will consider pleasurable and painful is largely a function of the way they are taught.

It may, for instance, be tempting to believe that an infant "instinctively" cries for food, to be held, or to have dirty diapers removed, but evidence points to large contributions from experience. In a study of neonates, Thoman, Korner, and Benson-Williams (1977) randomly assigned primiparous healthy newborns to conditions in which one third were held when they awakened. As anticipated by the authors, the babies who were held spent more time with their eyes open and cried less vigorously while being held; unexpectedly, however, they spent more time crying during nonstimulus periods. The babies had been equated for pretrial behaviors, so the authors suggest that the infants had come to associate their crying with being picked up during the 48 hour training period.

In another study also showing that neonates learn from their environments, Riese (1990) compared 47 pairs of monozygotic twins, 39 pairs of dizygotic twins of the same sex, and 72 pairs of dizygotic twins of the opposite sex. Using standardized tests for irritability, resistance to soothing, activity level when awake, activity level when asleep, reactivity to a cold disk on the thigh and to a pin prick, and response to cuddling, she found significant correlations for the dizygotic twins (both same and opposite sex), indicating shared environmental influences, but no significantly larger correlations among the monozygotic pairs. Riese concluded that "environment appears to account for most of the known variance for the neonatal temperament variables" (1236).

Just as neonates can learn to cry in order to be picked up, children learn what to consider painful. Variability in recognizing sensations as painful has been dramatically evidenced through studies of institutionalized infants who received serious injuries without seeming to notice (Goldfarb, 1958). During the period of observation, one child caught her hand in the door, injuring a finger so severely that it turned blue; yet the child did not cry or otherwise indicate pain. Another child sat on a radiator too hot for the teacher to touch. Observed injuries also included a child who was cutting the palm of his own hand with sharp scissors and another who had removed from her cornea a steel splinter that had been imbedded for two days without any report of pain. All the children, however, gave pain responses to a pin prick, dispelling the hypotheses that they had a higher than normal threshold for pain. Goldfarb reasonably concluded: "The perception of pain and the reaction to pain-arousing stimuli are episodes far more complex than is implied in the concept of pure, unencumbered sensation" (1945:780–781).

Often, children show no signs of pain after a fall until adults show that they expect a "pained" response. Studies with college students show that feeling pain is influenced by pain exhibited by models (Craig and Theiss, 1971), role playing as calm or upset (Kopel and Arkowitz, 1974), and feedback from one's own responsive behavior (Bandler, Madaras, and Bem, 1968). My personal experience and reports from students suggest that children whose mothers do not respond to their cuts with anxious concern do not exhibit such pain-behavior as crying when they fall.

Not only do children learn what is painful, but they attach pleasure to circumstances intended to result in pain. Solomon (1980) demonstrated that over a range of behaviors, pain-giving consequences acquire positive value through repetition (see Shipley, 1987; Aronson, Carlsmith, and Darley, 1963; Walster, Aronson, and Brown, 1966). Studies showing that children learn to repeat behaviors that result in "reinforcement" through negative attention demonstrate that expectations are only one basis for the attraction of "pain-giving" stimuli (Gallimore, Tharp, and Kemp, 1969; Witte and Grossman, 1971).

Children also learn without extrinsic reinforcement. Curious about why so many young children appeared to increase their aggressiveness in experimental situations, Siegel and Kohn (1959) measured aggression both with and without an adult in the room. Only when adults were present did escalation occur. The authors drew the sensible conclusion that young children assume that what is not forbidden is permitted.

The egocentric motivational assumption that underlies classic theories of socialization has been subjected to a series of criticism, most notably by Butler (1726) and Hume (1960 [1777]). These authors pointed out that the plausibility of the egocentric assumption rests on circular reasoning. The fact that a voluntary action must be motivated is confused with an assumption that voluntary actions must be motivated by desire to benefit from them. Often the only evidence for self-interest is the occurrence of the act for which a motive is being sought.

Raising further questions about the assumption of egocentrism in children, some studies indicate that altruistic behavior is not always egoistic behavior in disguise (Batson et al., 1988; Grusec and Skubiski, 1970). In fact, altruistic behavior turns up at very young ages (Rheingold and Emery, 1986; Zahn-Waxler and Radke-Yarrow, 1982; Zahn-Waxler et al., 1988), suggesting that even babies are not exclusively interested in themselves.

The prevalent view that children require punishment in order to learn socialized behavior rests on three erroneous assumptions. The first two—that children are motivated by self-interest and that what gives them pain is "fixed"—have been shown to lack support in empirical research. The third—that unless there are punishments rules have no power—is addressed in my proposal of Construct Theory.

An Alternative: Construct Theory

Construct Theory states that children learn what to do and what to believe in the process of learning how to use language. In simplest form, Construct Theory claims that children learn by constructing categories organized by the structure of the language in their culture. These categories can be identified by descriptions, much as one might identify a file, for example, "accounting," "things to do," "birthdays," "Parsons, T.," "true." Some categories are collections of objects, but others are actions that can be identified by such descriptions as "to be done" or "to be believed" or "to be doubted."

Learning a language requires learning more than concepts. Children learn not only what to count as tables and chairs, cars and trucks, but also what to count as painful or pleasant, undesirable or desirable, and worth avoiding or pursuing. In learning labels, in learning how to name and to re-identify objects, children are constructing classifications. The classification systems they develop will permeate what they notice and how they act as well as what they say.

Construct Theory explains the fact that different people consider similar events to have different affective characteristics—for example, as undesirable and desirable—because individuals construct different classifications of the events.

This theory can account for relations between knowledge and action that have led many theorists to conjure "pro-attitudes" as the means by which some knowledge sometimes changes behavior (e.g., Kenny, 1963; Milligan, 1980; Müller, 1979; Nowell-Smith, 1954). According to Construct Theory, those reasons that move one to action are classified as "reasons worth acting upon"; no special entity need also be attached to them.[1] Construct Theory also explains how language can be learned and how people can communicate, for it shows the way in which meanings can be made public through the categories that are constructed.[2]

Learning a language involves learning to formulate sentences as well as learning how to use words. At its most fundamental level, sentences involve stringing together what logicians call "predicates" (which can be thought of as classes) and functional relations among them. Perhaps no component of a sentence is so critical to understanding how punishment works as the connective "if ... then," for on this connective punishments rely. This connective also gives linguistic expression to what the neonates described above learned when they cried and were picked up (if I cry, then I will be picked up), what an infant learns by pushing a ball (if I push, then it will roll), and what the child learns when discovering natural consequences in the physical world.

Both natural and artificial contingencies provide information to the child who is learning about consequences. When a child is credibly threatened with punishment, the information conveyed extends beyond the intended message that the child ought not do something. A punishment is designed to give pain. Unless the chosen event is thought by the punisher to be painful, it would not be selected as a means for controlling the child's behavior. What is selected as a punishment, then, shows what the punisher thinks to be painful.[3]

A child also perceives the intention of the punisher to give pain (and may attempt to thwart the intention by saying such things as "I didn't like the dessert anyway" or "There's nothing good on TV anyhow"). So the use of punishment shows the child that the punisher is willing to hurt the threatened or punished child. This knowledge may decrease the child's desire to be with the punisher or to care how the punisher feels, thereby reducing the socializing agent's influence.

An interesting study illustrates another feature of punishment: it conveys information about what (according to the punisher) is valuable, thus potentially enhancing the value of the forbidden. Aronson and Carlsmith (1963) asked preschool children, individually, to compare five toys until they established stable transitive preferences. The experimenter then said he had to leave the room for a few minutes and placed on a table the toy ranked second-favorite by the child. The child was told not to play with that toy but that playing with the others was permissible. Half of the 44 children were randomly assigned to each of two conditions. In the "mild threat" condition, the experimenter said he would be annoyed if the child played with the forbidden toy. In the "severe threat" condition, the experimenter said that if the child played with the forbidden toy, the experimenter would be very angry and would take all the toys and never come back. The experimenter left the child for 10 minutes. Approximately 45 days later, the children were again asked to rank the five toys. For this ranking, 4 of the children from the mild threat condition ranked the forbidden toy as a favorite whereas 14 of those in the severe threat condition regarded the forbidden toy as the favorite. Conversely, 8 of those who were merely told that the experimenter would be annoyed had decreased their preference for the forbidden toy whereas none of the children who were threatened with punishment had they played with the toy decreased their preference for it.

In a near replication, Lepper (1973) found that, two weeks later, children from his stronger threat condition were more likely to cheat in a game. There are two explanations for this. Lepper explained the findings by suggesting that the children who resisted with severe threat reasoned: "I am the sort of person who would break the rules except for the fact that I would be punished." In contrast, according to this self-referential theory, the children under mild threat defined themselves as the sorts of people who generally conform to rules and requests.

I suggest an alternative explanation: The different exposures in the experiment taught the children something about the world and about other people—not primarily something about themselves. The more severe threats taught the children that they ought to orient their behavior around estimates of consequences *to themselves*. In the process of assessing their self-interests, the children looked for attractive features of that which had been forbidden. The "mild threat" condition in both experiments, however, implied only that the child should be concerned about how the experimenter might feel.

Punishments are invoked only when rules are disobeyed, so that telling a child about rules in conjunction with information about punishments for infractions informs a child that he or she has a choice: obey, or disobey-and-accept-the-consequences named as punishment.

Negative correlations between a parent's use of punishments and insistence that rules be followed were so strong in their study of misbehavior that Patterson, Dishion, and Bank (1984) could not use both measures in their model. Believing that punishments were more important, they dropped the follow-through measure. The data, however, show equally that a parent who insists that rules be followed need not use punishments to socialize children.

It might be tempting to argue that rewards circumvent the unwanted effects of punishment as a means for teaching norms. That would be a mistake. Although using rewards does not hazard rejection of the purveyor, rewarding shares many of the characteristics of punishing. Rewards as well as punishments employ the "if … then" relationship. Laboratory studies have demonstrated, as predicted from the Construct Theory, that contingent reinforcements sometimes interfere with the discovery of general rules (Schwartz 1982). Studies have demonstrated, also as predicted from Construct Theory, that incentives larger than necessary to produce an activity sometimes result in devaluation of the activity being rewarded (Greene and Lepper, 1974; Lepper, Greene, and Nisbett, 1973; Lepper et al., 1982; Ross, 1975; Ross, Karniol, and Rothstein, 1976).

Like those involved in punishments, contingencies that use rewards convey more information than intended when a socializing agent uses them to convince a child to do something. A reward is designed to be attractive, so rewards contain information about what the rewarder believes to be valuable. When a reward is clearly a benefit to the person being promised the reward, rewarding teaches the child to value his or her own benefit.[4]

In addition to learning that whatever requires reward is probably considered unpleasant, children learn that the reward is something considered valuable by the reward-giver. That children *learn* to perceive rewards as valuable has been demonstrated in the laboratory (Lepper et al., 1982). Children were told a story about a mother giving her child two supposed foods; children in the study were asked which the child in the story would prefer: "hupe" or "hule." Children in the experimental group were told that the mother explained to her child that (s)he could have one ("hupe" or "hule" for different children) if (s)he ate the other. In this condition, the contingent relation led the children to suppose that the second food was a reward for eating the first. The children overwhelmingly thought the second food would be preferred—and gave grounds for the choice in terms of its tasting better. The experiment showed that the continguent relation, rather than the order of presentation, influenced preference because children in the control condition who were told only that the child's mother gave the child first one and then the other food either refused to make a choice or gave no reason for a selection (which they equally distributed between the two). In other experiments with preschool children, play objects have been manipulated similarly, showing that an activity that is arbitrarily selected as the one to be rewarded will be "discounted" whereas the arbitrarily selected inducement gains value (e.g., Lepper et al., 1982; Boggiano and Main, 1986). These studies show that children learn what to value as well as how to act from perceiving the ways in which rewards are used.[5]

The Construct Theory explains why punishments tend to increase the attraction of activities punished—and why extrinsic rewards tend to reduce the value of activities rewarded. The categorizing that children learn as they learn sentences in a language can be schematically represented by formal logic. When children become aware of the logical equivalence between the conditional (if *x* then *y*) and the disjunctive (either not-*x* or *y*), they learn that *rewards and punishments weaken the force of a rule by introducing choices*. If rewards are designed to give pleasure to the child and punishments are designed to give the child pain, then their use teaches children that they ought to value their own pleasure and to attempt to reduce their own pain.

Conclusion

Rewards and punishments are used to manipulate others. They often result in short-term gains, but their use teaches children to look for personal benefits. Like rewards and punishments, neglect and rejection teach egocentrism. Children brought up among adults who do not attend to their well-being are given no grounds for learning to consider the welfare of others.

Using punishments seems particularly short-sighted. Punishments may increase the attraction of forbidden acts. They also risk desensitizing children both to their own pains and to the pains of others (Cline, Croft, and Courrier, 1973; Pearl, 1987; Thomas et al., 1977). Although severe penalties may force compliance in specific instances, the behavior being punished is actually more likely to occur at a time or place when opportunities for detection are reduced (Bandura and Walters, 1959).

No increase in punishment or in reward can guarantee that children will make the choices adults wish them to make. Several studies show, however, that children are more likely to want to do what an adult wishes if the adult generally does as the child desires. In one study, randomly selected mothers of preschoolers were trained to respond to their children's requests and to avoid directing them during a specified period of time each day for one week. Their children complied with more of the mother's standardized requests in the laboratory than the comparison group of children whose mothers used contingency training (Papal and Maccoby, 1985). The results are mirrored in a natural setting with the discovery that children reared at pre-school age in a consensual environment were among the most likely to value autonomy, intellectual activity, and independence as well as to have high educational aspirations ten years later (Harrington, Block, and Block, 1987).

In another study, mothers and children were observed at home for three-months when the children were between 9 and 12 months in age. Mothers were rated for their sensitivity to their babies, a rating based on their perceived ability to see things from the baby's perspective, positive feelings expressed toward the baby, and adaptations favoring the baby's arrangements of his or her own behavior. Discipline was rated for verbal commands as well as for frequency of any physical interventions. The baby's compliance was a simple measure of the proportion of verbal commands the baby obeyed without further action by the mother. Compliance turned out to be practically unrelated to discipline, although it was strongly related to the mother's responsiveness. The authors note: "The findings suggest that a disposition toward obedience emerges in a responsive, accommodating social environment without extensive training, discipline, or other massive attempts to shape the infant's course of development" (Stayton, Hogan, and Ainsworth, 1971:1065).

Punishments—nonphysical as well as physical—teach children to focus on their own pains and pleasures in deciding how to act. If parents and teachers were to substitute nonphysical punishments for physical ones, they might avoid teaching children to hit, punch, and kick; yet, they would nevertheless perpetuate the idea that giving pain is a legitimate way to exercise power. If the substitute for physical punishment were to be nonphysical punishments, the consequences could be no less undermining of compassion and social interests.

Children do not require punishments if their teachers will guide them consistently, and they do not require rewards if intrinsic values of what they ought to do are made apparent to them. I am not suggesting that a child will be constantly obedient or agree completely with the values of those who do not punish. No techniques will guarantee a clone. Rather, I do suggest that children can be taught to follow reasonable rules and to be considerate—and that the probabilities for their learning these things are directly related to the use of reason in teaching them and to the consideration they see in their surroundings.

Straus turns a spotlight on physical punishment, suggesting that by using violence to educate, adults legitimize the use of violence. I paint a broader canvas, suggesting that by using rewards and punishments to educate, adults establish self-interest as the legitimate grounds for choice.

Notes

1. This interpretation of language provides a modification of the Aristotelian notion that action is the conclusion of a practical syllogism; it adds a proviso that the syllogism must correctly represent the classification system of the actor, and then "straightway action follows." The interpretation also reflects the Humean claim that reason alone cannot account for action. It does so by including motivational classifications as separate from purely descriptive classifications.

2. Wittgenstein (1958) demonstrated the implausibility of accounting for language through private identification of meanings.

3. Thus, there is the irony that when teachers use school work, parents use performing chores, and both use being by oneself as punishments, they are likely to create distaste for learning, doing chores, and being alone.

4. One could, of course, reward a child by permitting some action beneficial to others or by permitting the child a new challenge.

5. The phenomenon is well enough known to have produced several theories, ranging from balance theory (Heider 1946) and Theory of Cognitive Dissonance (Festinger 1957) to Psychological Reactance (Brehm 1966; Brehm and Brehm 1981). None to my knowledge has tied the phenomenon with language.

References

Aronson, Elliot and J. Merrill Carlsmith. 1963. Effect of the severity of threat on the devaluation of forbidden behavior. *Journal of Abnormal and Social Psychology* 66: 584–588.

Aronson, Elliot, J. Merrill Carlsmith, and John M. Darley. 1963. The effects of expectancy on volunteering for an unpleasant experience. *Journal of Abnormal and Social Psychology* 66: 220–224.

Austin, Roy L. 1978. Race, father-absence, and female delinquency. *Criminology* 15: 487–504.

Bandler, Richard J., George R. Madaras, and Daryl J. Bem. 1968. Self-observation as a source of pain perception. *Journal of Personality and Social Psychology* 9: 205–209.

Bandura, Albert and Aletha C. Huston. 1961. Identification as a process of incidental learning. *Journal of Abnormal and Social Psychology* 63: 311–318.

Bandura, Albert and Richard H. Walters. 1959. *Adolescent Aggression*. New York: Ronald.

———. 1963. *Social Learning and Personality Development*. New York: Holt, Rinehart, and Winston.

Batson, C. Daniel, Janine L. Dyck, J. Randall Brandt, Judy G. Batson, Anne L. Powell, M. Rosalie McMaster, and Cari Griffitt. 1988. Five studies testing two new egoistic alternatives to the empathy-altruism hypothesis. *Journal of Personality and Social Psychology* 55: 52–77.

Baumrind, Diana. 1978. Parental disciplinary patterns and social competence in children. *Youth and Society* 9: 239–276.

Bender, Loretta. 1947. Psychopathic behavior disorders in children. In *Handbook of Correctional Psychology*, edited by R. Lindner and R. Seliger, 360-377. New York: Philosophical Library.

Boggiano, Ann K. and Deborah S. Main. 1986. Enhancing children's interest in activities used as rewards: The bonus effect. *Journal of Personality and Social Psychology* 31: 1116–1126.

Bowlby, John. 1940. The influence of early environment on neurosis and neurotic character. *International Journal of Psychoanalysis* 21: 154–178.

Brehm, Jack W. 1940. *A Theory of Psychological Reactance*. New York: Academic Press.

Brehm, Sharon S. and Jack W. Brehm. 1981. *Psychological Reactance: A Theory of Freedom and Control*. New York: Academic Press.

Butler, Joseph. 1726. *Fifteen Sermons (including "Three Sermons Upon Human Nature")*. London.

Cline, Victor B., Richard G. Croft, and Steven Courrier. 1973. Desensitization of children to television violence. *Journal of Personality and Social Psychology* 27: 360–365.

Craig, Kenneth D. and Stephen M. Theiss. 1971. Vicarious influences on pain-threshold determinations. *Journal of Personality and Social Psychology* 19: 53–59.

Farrington, David P. 1978. The family backgrounds of aggressive youths. In *Aggression and Antisocial Behaviour in Childhood and Adolescence*, edited by Lionel A. Hersov and Michael Berger, 73–93. Oxford: Pergamon.

Festinger, Leon. 1957. *A Theory of Cognitive Dissonance*. Stanford, Calif.: Stanford University Press.

Gallimore, Ronald, Ronald G. Tharp, and Bryan Kemp. 1969. Positive reinforcing function of "negative attention." *Journal of Experimental Child Psychology* 8: 140–146.

Glueck, Sheldon and Eleanor T. Glueck. 1950. *Unraveling Juvenile Delinquency*. New York: Commonwealth Fund.

Goldfarb, William. 1945. Psychological privation in infancy and subsequent adjustment. *American Journal of Orthopsychiatry* 15: 247–255.

———. 1958. Pain reactions in a group of institutionalized schizophrenic children. *American Journal of Orthopsychiatry* 28: 777–785.

Greene, David and Mark R. Lepper. 1974. Effects of extrinsic rewards on children's subsequent intrinsic interest. *Child Development* 45: 1141–1145.

Grusec, Joan E. and Sandra L. Skubiski. 1970. Model nurturance demand characteristics of the modeling experiment and altruism. *Journal of Personality and Social Psychology* 14: 352–359.

Harrington, David M., Jeanne H. Block, and Jack Block. 1987. Testing aspects of Carl Roger's theory of creative environments: Child-rearing antecedents of creative potential in young adolescents. *Journal of Personality and Social Psychology* 52: 851–856.

Heider, Fritz. 1946. Attitudes and cognitive organization. *Journal of Psychology* 21: 107–112.

Hirschi, Travis. 1969. *Causes of Delinquency*. Berkeley: University of California Press.

Hume, David. [1777]1960. *An Enquiry Concerning the Principles of Morals*. La Salle, Ill.: Open Court.

Kenny, Anthony. 1963. *Action, Emotion and Will*. London: Routledge and Kegan Paul.

Kopel, Steven A. and Hal S. Arkowitz. 1974. Role playing as a source of self-observation and behavior change. *Journal of Personality and Social Psychology* 29: 677–686.

Lepper, Mark. 1973. Dissonance, self-perception and honesty in children. *Journal of Personality and Social Psychology* 25: 65–74.

Lepper, Mark R., David Greene, and Richard E. Nisbett. 1973. Undermining children's intrinsic interest with extrinsic rewards. *Journal of Personality and Social Psychology* 28: 129–137.

Lepper, Mark R., Gerald Sagotsky, Janet L. Dafoe, and David Greene. 1982. Consequences of superfluous social constraints: Effects on young children's social influences and subsequent intrinsic interest. *Journal of Personality and Social Psychology* 41: 51–65.

Liska, Allen E. and Mark D. Reed. 1985. Ties to conventional institutions and delinquency: Estimating reciprocal effects. *American Sociological Review* 50: 547–560.

Maccoby, Eleanor E. 1980. *Social Development*. New York: Harcourt, Brace, Jovanovich.

McCord, Joan. 1979. Some child-rearing antecedents of criminal behavior in adult men. *Journal of Personality and Social Psychology* 37: 1477–1486.

———. 1983. A forty year perspective on effects of child abuse and neglect. *Child Abuse and Neglect* 7: 265–270.

———. 1988. Parental behavior in the cycle of aggression. *Psychiatry* 51: 14–23.

Milligan, David. 1980. *Reasoning and the Explanation of Actions*. Atlantic Highlands, N.J.: Humanities Press.

Müller, Anselm W. 1979. How theoretical is practical reason? In *Intention and Intentionality: Essays in Honor of G.E.M. Anscombe*, edited by Cora Diamond and Jenny Teichman, 91–108. Ithaca, N.Y.: Cornell University Press.

Nowell-Smith, P. H. 1954. *Ethics*. Middlesex, Eng.: Penguin.

Olson, Sheryl L., John E. Bates, and Kathryn Bayles. 1990. Early antecedents of childhood impulsivity: The role of parent-child interaction, cognitive competence, and temperament. *Journal of Abnormal Child Psychology* 18: 317–334.

Parpal, Mary and Eleanor E. Maccoby. 1985. Maternal responsiveness and subsequent child compliance. *Child Development* 56: 1326–1344.

Patterson, Gerald R. 1976. The aggressive child: Victim and architect of a coercive system. In *Behavior Modification and Families: Vol. 1. Theory and Research*, edited by Eric J. Mash, Lee A. Hamerlynck, and Leo C. Handy, 267–316. New York: Brunner/Mazel.

Patterson, Gerald R., Thomas J. Dishion, and L. Bank. 1984. Family interaction: A process model of deviancy training. *Aggressive Behavior* 10: 253–267.

Pearl, David. 1987. Familial, peer and television influences on aggressive and violent behavior. In *Childhood Aggression and Violence: Sources of Influence, Prevention, and Control*, edited by David H. Crowell, Ian M. Evans, and Clifford R. O'Donnell, 231–247. New York: Plenum.

Pulkkinen, Lea. 1983. Search for alternatives to aggression in Finland. In *Aggression in Global Perspective*, edited by Arnold P. Goldstein and Marshall H. Segall, 104–144. Elmsford, N.Y.: Pergamon Press.

Rheingold, Harriet and Gena N. Emery. 1986. The nurturant acts of very young children. In *Development of Antisocial and Prosocial Behavior*, edited by Dan Olweus, Jack Block, and Marian Radke-Yarrow, 75–96. New York: Academic Press.

Riese, Marilyn L. 1990. Neonatal temperament in monozygotic and dizygotic twin pairs. *Child Development* 61: 1230–1237.

Ross, Michael. 1975. Salience of reward and intrinsic motivation. *Journal of Personality and Social Psychology* 32: 245–254.

Ross, Michael, Rachel Karniol, and Mitch Rothstein. 1976. Reward contingency and intrinsic motivation in children: A test in the delay of gratification hypothesis. *Journal of Personality and Social Psychology* 33: 442–447.

Schwartz, Barry. 1982. Reinforcement-induced behavioral stereotypes: How not to teach people to discover rules. *Journal of Experimental Psychology* 111: 23–59.

Shipley, Thomas E., Jr. 1987. Opponent process theory. In *Psychological Theories of Drinking and Alcoholism*, edited by Howard T. Blane and Kenneth E. Leonard, 346–387. New York: Guilford Press.

Siegel, Alberta E. and Lynette G. Kohn. 1959. Permissiveness, permission, and aggression: The effects of adult presence or absence on aggression in children's play. *Child Development* 36: 131–141.

Solomon, Richard L. 1980. The ópponent-process theory of acquired motivation: The costs of pleasure and the benefits of pain. *American Psychologist* 35: 691–712. Stayton, Donelda J., Robert Hogan, and Mary D. Ainsworth. 1971. Infant obedience and maternal behavior: The origins of socialization reconsidered. *Child Development* 42: 1057–1069.

Thoman, Evelyn B., Anneliese F. Korner, and Lynn Benson-Williams. 1977. Modification of responsiveness to maternal vocalization in the neonate. *Child Development* 48: 563–569.

Thomas, Margaret H., Robert W. Horton, Elaine C. Lippincott, and Ronald S. Drabman. 1977. Desensitization to portrayals of real-life aggression as a function of exposure to television violence. *Journal of Personality and Social Psychology* 35: 450–458.

Walster, Elaine, Elliot Aronson, and Zita Brow. 1966. Choosing to suffer as a consequence of expecting to suffer: An unexpected finding. *Journal of Experimental Social Psychology* 2: 400–406.

Widom, Cathy S. 1989. Child abuse, neglect, and adult behavior: Research design and findings on criminality, violence, and child abuse. *American Journal of Orthopsychiatry* 59: 355–367.

————. 1990. Child Abuse, Neglect, and Violent Criminal Behavior (Data Set JU.2428, K.J. Kuipers and J. L. Peterson, Archivists) [machine-readable data files and documentation]. Bloomington, Ind.: Indiana University, Departments of Criminal Justice and Psychology (Producer). Los Altos, Calif.: Sociometrics Corporation, Data Resources Program of the National Institute of Justice (Distributor).

Witte, Kenneth L. and Eugene E. Grossman. 1971. The effects of reward and punishment upon children's attention, motivation, and discrimination learning. *Child Development* 42: 537–542.

Wittgenstein, Ludwig. 1958. *Philosophical Investigation*, translated by by G.E.M. Anscombe. New York: Macmillan.

Zahn-Waxler, Carolyn and Marian Radke-Yarrow. 1982. The development of altruism: Alternative research strategies. In *The Development of Prosocial Behavior*, edited by Nancy Eisenberg, 109–137. New York: Academic Press.

Zahn-Waxler, Carolyn, Marian Radke-Yarrow, Elizabeth Wagner, and Claudia Pyle. 1988. *The Early Development of Prosocial Behavior*. Presented at the ICIS meetings, Washington, D.C., April.

CHAPTER TEN

Deterrence and the Light Touch of the Law*

Deterrence of Labelling?

TRADITIONALLY, two claims regarding effects of punishment have competed in the arena of criminal justice. The older claim can be traced to Protagoras, with Beccaria (1764) and Bentham (1789) as picadors. To Protagoras, Plato attributed the argument: "He who desires to inflict rational punishment does not retaliate for a past wrong which cannot be undone; he has regard to the future, and is desirous that the man who is punished and he who sees him punished may be deterred from doing wrong again" (Plato: *Protagoras*, 324). Proponents of this claim believe that fear of punishment deters crime (Boland and Wilson, 1978; Hart, 1968; Jeffery, 1965; Jensen, 1969; Mednick, 1977; Tullock, 1980; van den Haag, 1975; Wilson, 1980).

The second claim evolves from a neo-Hegelian view, for which Cooley (1922), Mead (1918), Tannenbaum (1938), and Thomas (1923) have been banderilleros. Historically rooted in the sociopolitical argument that crime originates in the eye of the beholder, this claim asserts that punishment produces behaviour to confirm the label as criminal (Ageton and Elliott, 1974; Becker, 1963; Durkheim, 1933; Erikson, 1964; Garfinkel, 1956; Kitsuse, 1962; Lemert, 1951; Payne, 1973; Schur, 1971).

Negative correlations between perceived risk of punishment and crime appear to confirm the view that punishment deters crime. Positive correlations between deviant behaviour and labelling appear to corroborate the view that crime is a response to encounters with agents for its control.

If fear of punishment deters crime, a reduction in crime rates should correspond with increases in the expected negative value of punishment. And if the

*Reprinted from McCord, J. 1985. Deterrence and the light touch of the law. In *Reactions to Crime: The Public, the Police, Courts and Prisons*, edited by D. P. Farrington and J. Gunn, 73–85. Copyright © 1985 John Wiley & Sons Limited; with permission.

expected value of punishment is a function of certainty and severity, changes in clearance rates and in severity of sentences should alter crime rates.

Studying crime rates in the United States for the years 1959–1963, Tittle (1969) found evidence to support the deterrence position—at least with regard to certainty. Tittle devised a measure of certainty based on the ratio of conviction to crime rates and a measure of severity based on length of sentence. Comparisons among the states showed strong negative correlations between offence rates and certainty, but a slight positive correlation between offence rates and severity. Tittle acknowledged the possibility that both crime rates and certainty of punishment could be functions of the attitudes towards crime, thus creating the erroneous appearance of a causal link between them.

After expanding the data base to cover three time periods, Chiricos and Waldo (1970) concluded that relationships between crime rates and both certainty and severity were inconsistent and probably rightly attributed to chance. Using similar measures for crime rate, severity, and certainty, Antunes and Hunt (1973) developed models that could be interpreted as showing that certainty, or the interaction of certainty with severity, but not severity alone, had deterrent effects.

In her review of evidence about effects of penalties, Crowther (1969) pointed out the constancy of recidivism rates across punishments and the irrelevance of length of sentence as a predictor of crime rates. She noted that, although punishments for attacking policemen had increased between 1961 and 1965, the rate of attack had also increased from 8.4 to 15.8 per 100 officers per year. She noted that although penalties for marijuana offences had increased between 1961 and 1967, the number of arrests had also increased. And she noted that administrative and judicial decisions which resulted in early release had not resulted in increased recidivism. Crowther's support for labelling theory seemed to rest most heavily, however, on a study of matched pairs of men. The men had been convicted for first- or second-degree robbery and burglary. They were matched for ethnicity, crime, prior history, and parole region. One member of each pair had been incarcerated more than the median time and the other had been incarcerated less than the median time. The parole agency identified as having a favorable outcome more of the men who had served shorter sentences. Crowther recommended that "alternatives to arrest and intake into any *large* system should be developed immediately" (p. 158).

Attempting to detect effects of labelling as well as deterrence, Klein (1974) compared recidivism rates in jurisdictions that released high proportions of arrested juveniles with rates in jurisdictions that released low proportions of arrested juveniles. Klein assumed that the result of few releases was frequent labelling. In jurisdictions that released few arrested juveniles, first offenders had higher rates of recidivism than did first offenders in jurisdictions that released high proportions of arrested juveniles. An opposite trend, though not statistically significant, appeared in comparisons of multiple offenders. Klein concluded that both labelling and deterrent effects had been uncovered. In subsequent reviews, Tittle (1975, 1980) argued that the labelling position had been poorly specified and inadequately tested, and that the deterrence position had been inadequately measured, thus producing "contradictory findings."

Crime rates in 98 cities of the United States provided evidence for evaluating deterrence over time. As potential influences on the relationship between clearance rates and crime rates, Greenberg and Kessler (1982) considered population, population density, percentage of the labour force unemployed, median income, proportion of households headed by women, and skewness of income. Cross-sectional analyses produced an appearance of deterrent effects of certainty (as measured by clearance rates). The relationship disappeared, however, when "background" (as measured by the variables above) was controlled, and crime rates were assumed to have an influence on clearance rates, with a lag of either 2 or 3 years.

Agreeing that correlational studies have inadequately demonstrated a deterrent effect, Cook (1977) pointed to "natural experiments" that appear to show that some increases in certainty of punishment have reduced crime. With increased policing of New York City subways, crimes decreased; despite rising crime in most precincts, a 40 percent increase in police surveillance appeared to have controlled the rise in one, Cook argued. Also, advertised rules about arrests for drunk driving under the British Road Safety Act of 1967 resulted in a 25 percent reduction in accidents.

Studies of crime rates have shed some light on the controversy between those who argue that criminal sanctions deter crime and those who argue that they encourage crime. Evidence about some crucial questions, however, must depend on studies of individuals. Proponents of the labelling theory believe that the criminal justice system affects criminality by altering a person's perception of himself. Proponents of the deterrence theory believe that people are motivated to avoid their own pain and that, therefore, the expectation of punishment will decrease crime. Changes in actual conviction rates or in the duration of punishment might be unrelated to sanctioning severity or certainty as *perceived* by potential criminals.

Through interviews with university students, Waldo and Chiricos (1972) sought evidence for a link between perceived punishments and crime. Students estimated penalties for marijuana use and for theft, and the likelihood of arrest for each. They also reported their own use and their own thefts. Both marijuana use and theft were related to the perceived likelihood of arrest. But since respondents more often confessed to thefts and also more often overestimated penalties for theft, the authors argued that deterrence effects were stronger for marijuana use. Further analysis of the data (Anderson et al., 1977) showed that severity, as reflected in the estimated likelihood of receiving a maximum sentence, was not significantly related to marijuana use. The students' estimates regarding the likelihood of being caught served as a measure of certainty and *was* negatively correlated with use.

On the other hand, Meier and Johnson (1971) found virtually no correlation between perceived certainty of punishment and marijuana use in a national probability sample of adults in the United States. Furthermore, the Meier and Johnson analysis uncovered a positive correlation between perceived severity of punishment and marijuana use.

Pointing to general inadequacies of prior attempts to test deterrent effects of sanctions, Grasmick and Bryjak (1980) emphasized the importance of the interaction between severity and certainty. They noted that only if being apprehended is perceived as a cost can the certainty of apprehension deter; and only if arrest is perceived as reasonably certain should the perceived severity of a penalty be expected to deter. Grasmick and Bryjak asked randomly selected people about eight illegal activities. For each, subjects reported whether they had or had not committed the crime, estimated the chance of being arrested if they had, estimated the chance that they would be put in jail if arrested, and reported on the severity of problems that would be created by a plausible punishment. Like Meier and Johnson, Grasmick and Bryjak found a positive correlation between illegal behaviour and perceived severity *as measured by estimates of the probability of being put in jail if arrested.* Both the measure of certainty and the *subjective* evaluation of severity, however, were negatively correlated with illegal behaviour. Most importantly, the subjective evaluation of severity was significantly related to crimes only for the highest quartile of certainty, and certainty was related to crimes only for the top three quartiles of subjective severity.

The study by Grasmick and Bryjak seems to vindicate some of the assumptions of utilitarian theorists. Yet, as Erickson et al. (1977) pointed out, a link between subjective estimates of probability and severity has little practical value unless subjective estimates can be tied to actual sanctions.

The Children and Young Persons Act of 1969 introduced "cautioning" to the London courts. This formal warning procedure was believed to be both less serious and less stigmatizing than court processing. Its introduction appeared to enlarge the range of the criminal justice system's actions. To analyse effects of police cautioning, Farrington and Bennett (1981) examined files of juveniles who had been less than 15 when first arrested. Of the 202 sent to court, 44 percent had been rearrested within the follow-up period of 34 months. Of the 705 issued a police caution, 25 percent had been rearrested. Disposition appeared to have been strongly influenced by age and seriousness of the offence. But independent of effects from sex, age, race, social class, area, and seriousness, those who received cautions were less likely to be rearrested. Forty-seven cases were selected for deeper analysis. Records of home visits provided information about family size, attitudes of the parents and the juveniles, academic performance, and school behaviour. "Negative attitudes" of the juveniles appeared as the strongest predictor for court dispositions and for rearrests. After controlling for the effects of the juvenile's attitudes, rearrest rates following cautions exceeded those following court dispositions.

After World War II, the movement to provide diversion from the courts in order to avoid labelling gained wide currency in the United States. Evaluations have demonstrated that the projects envelop youngsters who would otherwise not be included in activities of the criminal justice system, and that they have not had a beneficial impact (Elliott et al., 1978; Gibbons and Blake, 1976; Klein, 1979; Van Dusen, 1981).

Probably the most coherent study of possible labelling effects has been produced in a longitudinal study of London youths. Beginning with 411 8- or 9-year-old boys in six school districts of London, West and Farrington (1977) traced delinquency through self-reports at ages 14–15, 16–17, and 18–19. They reviewed court records when the youths turned 21. Farrington (1977) coordinated court records with the self-reports of 383 youths who had been interviewed all three times. The 98 found guilty and therefore publicly labelled prior to reaching the age of 18 reported committing more crimes than the remaining 285. The 53 who had been first convicted between the ages of 14 and 18 had reported committing more crimes than the unconvicted at age 14. Since selection for labelling was thereby shown to be non-random, Farrington matched 27 who had been first convicted between ages 14 and 16 with 27 who had similar self-report scores at age 14. By comparing self-reports at the two ages, Farrington cleverly teased out an "amplification" or labelling effect. Those convicted by 16 admitted more acts at this age than those who were not convicted. From the different proportions of crimes that were concealed (or forgotten), Farrington concluded that about half the difference between the groups as measured by self-reports of delinquency at age 16 could be attributed to decreased concealment; half could be attributed to labelling. Farrington noted that those who had been labelled tended also to have increased their hostility toward police. Official police cautions and motoring convictions had no apparent labelling effects.

Farrington et al. (1978) pursued the relationship between increased hostility towards the police and self-reported delinquency by comparing changes in hostility with changes in reported delinquencies among youths first convicted between ages 18 and 21 and among those first convicted prior to age 14. For the former group, both hostility towards police and self-reported delinquencies increased; for the latter, self-reported delinquencies declined without corresponding reductions in hostile attitudes. Analysis of the delinquency reports by the men first convicted between 18 and 21 showed that, among those who had been fined as a penalty, practically no increase in delinquency occurred between 18 and 21. Among those who had been discharged, however, the self-reports showed marked increases.

Most reviews emphasize the paucity of empirical support for either deterrence or labelling theory (Cook, 1977; Gibbs, 1979; Hepburn, 1977; Hirschi, 1975; Hood and Sparks, 1970; Klein, 1979; Maltz et al., 1980; Morris and Zimring, 1969; Tittle, 1980; Wolfgang et al., 1972). The present research provides some evidence by which to evaluate these rival claims and gives grounds for suggesting that neither theory has been correct.

Background and Method

Data for this analysis were drawn from the criminal histories of 506 men who had been included in a youth study designed to prevent delinquency (Powers and Witmer, 1951). The youth study included youngsters born between 1925 and 1932 (mean=1928) who, at the time of the programme (1936–1945), were living in eastern Massachusetts. In 1948, as part of a follow-up evaluation, police records were searched for arrests of former members of the programme. The police records indicated that 231 had been picked up as juveniles. Among them were 34 whose first arrests culminated in convictions for serious (index) crimes and 197 first booked for minor crimes. The 275 who had no police records as juveniles were dropped from consideration in the present analysis.

In 1975, when their average age was 47, the men were retraced. Court records from ten states, including Massachusetts, provided information about criminal convictions. The local police department had established a Crime Prevention Bureau in 1938. Through this Bureau, police could give informal warnings to boys picked up for minor crimes. Of the 197 boys whose first recorded encounters with the criminal justice system had been for such transgressions as trespass, truancy, malicious mischief, and petty larceny, 163 were processed by the Crime Prevention Bureau and 34 were taken to court.

Of the 34 delinquents sent to court for minor offences, 15 received probation or release, 11 paid fines, and 8 went to reform school. In order not to confuse effects of incarceration with effects of criminal processing, the youngsters whose first arrests resulted in incarceration were not included in comparisons between boys taken to court and boys sent home by the Crime Prevention Bureau.

Various researchers have suggested the possibility that police discretion increases the scope for discriminatory handling of youngsters (Arnold, 1971; Lundman, 1976; Nejelski, 1976). In the present study, evidence of racial bias was not present. The vast majority of both groups were Caucasian: 96 percent of those sent to court and 83 percent of those processed by the Crime Prevention Bureau. Nor was there evidence for a social class bias. Fathers of 65 percent of the boys sent to court and of 56 percent of the boys processed by the Crime Prevention Bureau were unskilled workers. Also approximately the same proportions had broken homes: 50 percent of the boys sent to court and 44 percent of those processed by the Crime Prevention Bureau.

Several studies suggest that age affects the decision to divert a juvenile away from court (Boland and Wilson, 1978; Farrington and Bennett, 1981; McEachern and Bauzer, 1967). Among the youths in the present study, too, age appeared to influence disposition. Whereas half the youths processed by the Crime Prevention Bureau (53 percent) were under 13, only four of those taken to court but not incarcerated (plus three of the incarcerated boys) were so young. Although both groups ranged in age from 7 to 17, the mean age for those processed by the Crime Prevention Bureau was 12.1 (s.d.=1.9) and for those referred to court, excluding those incarcerated, 15.0 (s.d.=3.0).

Among the boys processed by the Crime Prevention Bureau, 138 subsequently appeared in court and were convicted. The mean age at the time of first conviction for this group was 18.5 (s.d.=6.5). Thus, the court-processed group was older when first picked up, but younger at the age of the first *official* record.

Age has been shown to be related to recidivism (Ganzer and Sarason, 1973; Gibbens and Ahrenfeldt, 1966; Sellin, 1958; Wolfgang et al., 1972) as well as to disposition. Differences in recidivism can be interpreted as showing either that those who commence a criminal career at younger ages have worse characters, or that their special treatment by the courts leads them towards different expectations regarding consequences of criminal behaviour—and so, to more criminal behaviour.

The court and police records were used to evaluate two hypotheses:

1. through use of legal sanctions, juvenile court convictions have a deterrent effect on crime; and
2. criminal convictions produce criminality by labelling boys whose behaviour has been no worse than that of their peers.

The first hypothesis predicts *less* crime among the minority of boys whose first arrests resulted in court convictions, whereas the second hypothesis predicts *more* crime among them than among the group for whom a first encounter with police resulted in no official action by the criminal justice system. Differential outcomes from different court dispositions for similar crimes enabled a further check on effects of court sanctions.

Results

The study gives no support to a conclusion that diversion decreases criminality. Among the 163 boys first processed through the Crime Prevention Bureau, 83 (51%) were subsequently convicted for at least one Index crime. That proportion was significantly higher than the 6 of 26 (23%) of the boys convicted and fined, released, or placed on probation ($\chi^2(1)=6.977$, $p=0.0083$). Forty-nine of the first group (30%) were convicted for more than one Index crime, whereas 2 (8%) of the latter were recidivists ($\chi^2(1)=5.695$, $p=0.0170$). Both recidivists from the court group (and none of the remainder of the court group) had also been processed by the Crime Prevention Bureau for crimes discovered after their first convictions.

On first glance, it may seem as though a more *serious* penalty assists in deterring crime. That interpretation, however, does not receive support from the evidence. The records include 110 men whose first court convictions had been for minor crimes. Ten of these spent time in reform school as the penalty. Half subsequently committed Index crimes. Since 35 percent of those placed on probation or released, and only 13 percent of those fined, subsequently were convicted for Index crimes, the evidence is against the hypothesis that a severe sanction deters recidivism. Table 10.1 shows the criminogenic effects of court sanctions both with and without prior processing through the Crime Prevention Bureau.

The 40 boys first processed by the Crime Prevention Bureau and placed on probation or released when convicted for a minor crime averaged 12.7 years of age at the time of their first encounters with the police. The 34 boys first processed

TABLE 10.1   First Official Offence a Minor Crime (percentage later convicted for an Index crime)

Sanction	Prior processing	No prior processing	Total
Probation/release	38% (N=40)	27% (N=15)	35% (N=55)
Fine	12% (N=34)	18% (N=11)	13% (N=45)
Incarceration	100% (N =2)	38% (N=8)	50% (N=10)

TABLE 10.2   First Official Offence an Index Crime (percentage later convicted for another Index crime)

Sanction	Prior processing	No prior processing	Total
Probation/release	63% (N=52)	61% (N=28)	63% (N=80)
Fine	33% (N=3)	—	33% (N=3)
Incarceration	57% (N=7)	83% (N=6)	69% (N=13)

by the Crime Prevention Bureau and fined when convicted for a minor crime averaged 12.1 years of age at the time of their encounters with the police. These two groups, similar in age at the time of first encounters with the police, had been treated differently by the courts. A smaller proportion of those who received fines (12%) than of those released or placed on probation (38%) subsequently were convicted for Index crimes.

Table 10.2 shows criminogenic effects of differential penalties among boys whose first convictions were for serious crimes. These data provide no evidence that incarceration deters recidivism.

Summary and Discussion

The study reports on the criminal histories of 231 boys who committed crimes between the ages of 7 and 17. Traced to middle age, the histories of those deflected from the courts at the time of their first offence gave no support for a belief that such deflection prevented crime. Contrary to a labelling theory prediction that an official label as a delinquent would promote crime, those juveniles processed through the courts were less likely to be convicted subsequently for serious crimes. Contrary to a deterrence theory prediction that more serious punishments would prevent crime, recidivism rates among previously incarcerated boys were not lower than recidivism rates among those who received more lenient sanctions.

Despite the widespread belief that court processing for minor crimes increases crime (Rutter and Giller, 1983), results of the present study join others that have shown lower recidivism rates following official processing. Among those delinquents arrested for minor crimes in a Philadelphia cohort, relatively few were sent to court; yet those sent to court were less likely to be recidivists (Wolfgang et al., 1972). In the Uniform Crime Reports for the United States, rearrest rates appeared higher among those whose cases were dismissed or who were acquitted than among those incarcerated, fined, or placed on probation (Ward, 1972). Among Chicago youths, restrictive sanctions were more effective deterrents of criminality than more permissive responses (Murray and Cox, 1979). In a study of juveniles in London, with attitude towards police controlled, those cautioned by the police had higher rearrest rates than those sent to court (Farrington and Bennett, 1981).

Longitudinal data collected in Philadelphia (Wolfgang, 1976) and in California (Crowther, 1969) have also shown, as did the present study, that severity of response is not well correlated with effectiveness in deterring crime.

Perhaps, as several authors suggest, in providing ceremonial condemnation, the courts clarify boundaries for acceptable behaviour (Ball, 1955; Erikson, 1964; Merton, 1957; Stephen, 1980; van den Haag, 1975). Conversely, diversion from the courts may have contributed to crime by blurring the boundaries between acceptable and unacceptable behaviour.

Many years ago, Siegel and Kohn (1959) used a laboratory study to demonstrate that children become more aggressive in the presence of an adult who failed to respond to their aggressive play. Both in the laboratory and in the criminal justice system, children are being taught what to expect as well as how to act. Reasonably, one can argue (as has Klein, 1981) that failure to respond to criminal behaviour reinforces the legitimacy of delinquency. Glaser (1978, 1979) suggests that an adequate theory of the causes of crime would link biological, psychological, and sociological theories through showing how these lead to differences in expectations. Reasonably, one could also argue that delinquents who are diverted from the courts anticipate receiving help or being excused for their delinquent conduct.

Writing about "techniques of neutralization," Sykes and Matza (1957) suggested that delinquents prepare themselves for criminal behaviour by creating a system of beliefs that will rationalize their future antisocial actions. The diversionary programmes may help create a system of rationalizations to be used subsequently in justifying criminal behaviour.

Rationalizations include justifications and excuses. Whereas justifications show that an act is not wrong, excuses reduce an actor's responsibility for the action (Austin, 1961; Hart, 1968). In being given a second chance, whether by the police or through probation or release, a delinquent may come to see his delinquencies as excusable.

Suppose that a delinquent explains broken windows as playfulness, stealing apples as due to hunger, or truancy as due to peer pressure. If he or she is not penalized, the delinquent has reason to believe either that what is done playfully or when hungry or in response to peer pressure is not wrong—or that playfulness, hunger, or peer pressures diminish moral responsibility. The courts, having accepted certain forms of justifications or excuses, may tend to promote crime through implicit endorsement.

Whether courts influence crime through their effects on excuses, on expectations, or on ceremonial boundaries, it seems time to abandon the traditional approaches to analysing the relationship between crime and criminal sanctions. Neither labelling theory nor deterrence theory has brought us close to understanding how to decrease crime.

Note

This study was supported by U.S. Public Health Service Research Grant No. R01 MH26779, National Institute of Mental Health (Center for Studies of Crime and Delinquency). It was conducted jointly with the Department of Probation of the Commonwealth of Massachusetts. The author wishes to express appreciation to the Division of Criminal Justice Services of the State of New York, to the Maine State Bureau of Identification, and to the states of California, Florida, Michigan, New Jersey, Pennsylvania, Virginia, and Washington for supplemental data about the men, though only the author is responsible for the statistical analyses and for the conclusions drawn from this research. Additionally, the author would like to thank Richard Parente, Robert Staib, Ellen Myers, and Ann Cronin for their work in tracing men and their records, and to thank Daniel Glaser, Neil Weiner, and Laura Otten for their comments on earlier versions of this paper.

References

Ageton, S. and D. S. Elliott. 1974. The effects of legal processing on delinquent orientations. *Social Problems* 22: 87–100.

Anderson, L. S., F. G. Chiricos, and G. P. Waldo. 1977. Formal and informal sanctions: A comparison of deterrent effects. *Social Problems* 25: 103–114.

Antunes, G. and A. L. Hunt. 1973. The impact of certainty and severity of punishment on levels of crime in American states: An extended analysis. *Journal of Criminal Law and Criminology* 64: 489–493.

Arnold, W. R. 1971. Race and ethnicity relative to other factors in juvenile court dispositions. *American Journal of Sociology* 77: 211–227.

Austin, J. L. 1961. A plea for excuses. In *Philosophical Papers*, edited by J. O. Urmsan and G. J. Warnock. Oxford: Clarendon Press.

Ball, J. C. 1955. The deterrence concept in criminology and law. *Journal of Criminal Law, Criminology, and Police Science* 46: 347–354.

Beccaria, C. B. 1764, 1963. *On Crimes and Punishments.* Indianapolis: Bobbs-Merrill.

Becker, H. S. 1963. *Outsiders.* Glencoe: Free Press.

Bentham, J. 1939. An introduction to the principles of morals and legislation. In *The English Philosophers from Bacon to Mill*, edited by E. Burtt. New York: Random House.

Boland, B. and J. Q. Wilson. 1978. Age, crime, and punishment. *Public Interest* 51: 22–34.

Chiricos, T. G. and G. P. Waldo. 1970. Punishment and crime: An examination of some empirical evidence. *Social Problems* 18: 200–217.

Cook, P. J. 1977. Punishment and crime: A critique of current findings concerning the preventive effects of punishment. *Law and Contemporary Problems* 41: 164–204.

Cooley, C. H. 1922. *Human Nature and the Social Order.* New York: Charles Scribner's Sons.

Crowther, C. 1969. Crimes, penalties and legislatures. *Annals of the American Academy of Political and Social Science* 381: 147–158.

Durkheim, E. 1893, 1933. *The Division of Labor in Society.* New York: Free Press.

Elliott, D. S., F. W. Dunford, and B. A. Knowles. 1978. Diversion—a study of alternative processing practices: An overview of initial study findings. Boulder, Colo.: Behavioural Research Institute.

Erickson, M., J. P. Gibbs, and G. F. Jensen. 1977. The deterrence doctrine and the perceived certainty of legal punishments. *American Sociological Review* 42: 305–317.

Erikson, K. T. 1964. Notes on the sociology of deviance. In *The Other Side*, edited by H. S. Becker. Glencoe: Free Press.

Farrington, D. P. 1977. The effects of public labelling. *British Journal of Criminology* 17: 112–125.

Farrington, D. P. and T. Bennett. 1981. Police cautioning of juveniles in London. *British Journal of Criminology* 21: 123–135.

Farrington, D. P., S. G. Osborn, and D. J. West. 1978. The persistence of labelling effects. *British Journal of Criminology* 18: 277–284.

Ganzer, V. J. and I. G. Sarason. 1973. Variables associated with recidivism among juvenile delinquents. *Journal of Consulting and Clinical Psychology* 40: 1–5.

Garfinkel, H. 1956. Conditions of successful degradation ceremonies. *American Journal of Sociology* 61: 420–424.

Gibbens, T. C. N. and R. H. Ahrenfeldt. 1966. *Cultural Factors in Delinquency.* London: Tavistock.

Gibbons, D. C. and G. F. Blake. 1976. Evaluating the impact of juvenile diversion programs. *Crime and Delinquency* 22: 411–420.

Gibbs, J. P. 1979. Assessing the deterrence doctrine: A challenge for the social and behavioral sciences. *American Behavioral Scientist* 22: 653–677.

Glaser, D. 1978. *Crime in Our Changing Society*. New York: Holt, Rinehart and Winston.

Glaser, D. 1979. A review of crime-causation theory and its application. In *Crime and Justice*, vol. 1, edited by N. Morris and M. Tonry. Chicago: University of Chicago Press.

Grasmick, H. G. and G. J. Bryjak. 1980. The deterrent effect of perceived severity of punishment. *Social Forces* 59, 471–491.

Greenberg, D. and R. C. Kessler. 1982. The effect of arrests on crime: A multivariate panel analysis. *Social Forces* 60, 771–790.

Hart, H. L. A. 1968. *Punishment and Responsibility*. Oxford: Oxford University Press.

Hepburn, J. R. 1977. The impact of police intervention upon juvenile delinquents. *Criminology* 15, 235–262.

Hirschi, T. 1975. Labelling theory and juvenile delinquency: An assessment of the evidence. In *The Labelling of Deviance*, edited by W. R. Gove. New York: Wiley.

Hood, R. and R. Sparks. 1970. *Key Issues in Criminology*. London: World University Library.

Jeffery, C. R. 1965. Criminal behavior and learning theory. *Journal of Criminal Law, Criminology, and Police Science* 56, 294–300.

Jensen, G. 1969. "Crime doesn't pay": Correlates of a shared misunderstanding. *Social Problems* 17: 189–201.

Kitsuse, J. I. 1962. Societal reaction to deviant behavior. *Social Problems* 9: 247–256.

Klein, M. W. 1974. Labelling, deterrence and recidivism: A study of police dispositions of juvenile offenders. *Social Problems* 22: 292–303.

Klein, M. W. 1979. Deinstitutionalization and diversion of juvenile offenders: A litany of impediments. In *Crime and Justice*, vol. I, edited by N. Morris and M. Tonry. Chicago: University of Chicago Press.

Klein, M. W. 1981. A judicious slap on the wrist: Thoughts on early sanctions for juvenile offenders. In *New Directions in the Rehabilitation of Criminal Offenders*, edited by S. E. Martin, L. B. Sechrest, and R. Redner. Washington DC: National Academy Press.

Lemert, E. M. 1951. *Social Pathology*. New York: McGraw Hill.

Lundman, R. J. 1976. Will diversion reduce recidivism? *Crime and Delinquency* 22: 428–437.

Maltz, M. D., A. C. Gordon, D. McDowall, and R. McCleary. 1980. An artifact in pretest-posttest designs: How it can mistakenly make delinquency programs look effective. *Evaluation Review* 4: 225–240.

McEachern, A. W. and R. Bauzer. 1967. Factors related to disposition in juvenile police contacts. In *Juvenile Gangs in Context*, edited by M. W. Klein. Englewood Cliffs: Prentice Hall.

Mead, G. H. 1918. The psychology of punitive justice. *American Journal of Sociology* 23: 577–602.

Mednick, S. A. 1977. A bio-social theory of the learning of law-abiding behavior. In *Biosocial Bases of Criminal Behavior*, edited by S. A. Mednick and K. O. Christiansen. New York: Gardner Press.

Meier, R. F. and W. T. Johnson. 1971. Deterrence as social control: The legal and extralegal production of conformity. *American Sociological Review* 42: 292–304.

Merton, R. K. 1957. *Theory and Social Structure*. Glencoe: Free Press.

Morris, N. and F. Zimring. 1969. Deterrence and corrections. *Annals of the American Academy of Political and Social Science* 381: 137–146.

Murray, C. A. and L. A. Cox. 1979. *Beyond Probation*. Beverly Hills: Sage.

Nejelski, P. 1976. Diversion: The promise and the danger. *Crime and Delinquency* 22: 393–410.

Payne, W. D. 1973. Negative labels: Passageways and prisons. *Crime and Delinquency* 19: 33–40.

Plato. 1956. *Protagoras*. Indianapolis: Bobbs-Merrill.

Powers, E. and H. Witmer. 1951. *An Experiment in the Prevention of Delinquency: The Cambridge-Somerville Youth Study*. New York: Columbia University Press.

Rutter, M. and H. Giller. 1983. *Juvenile Delinquency: Trends and Perspectives*. Harmondsworth: Penguin.

Schur, E. M. 1971. *Labelling Deviant Behaviour: Its Sociological Implications*. New York: Harper and Row.

Sellin, T. 1958. Recidivism and maturation. *National Probation and Parole Association Journal* 4: 241–250.

Siegel, A. E. and I. G. Kohn. 1959. Permissiveness, permission, and aggression: The effects of adult presence of absence on aggression in children's play. *Child Development* 36: 131–141.

Stephen, J. F. 1980. *A History of the Criminal Law of England*. New York: Garland Publications.

Sykes, G. and D. Matza. 1957. Techniques of neutralization: A theory of delinquency. *American Sociological Review* 22: 667–670.

Tannenbaum, F. 1938. *Crime and the Community*. Boston: Ginn and Company.

Thomas, W. I. 1923. *The Unadjusted Girl*. Boston: Little, Brown.

Tittle, C. R. 1969. Crime rates and legal sanctions. *Social Problems* 14: 409–422.

Tittle, C. R. 1975. Labelling and crime: An empirical evaluation. In *The Labelling of Deviance*, edited by W. R. Gove. New York: Wiley.

Tittle, C. R. 1980. Evaluating the deterrent effects of criminal sanctions. In *Handbook of Criminal Justice Evaluation*, edited by M. W. Klein and K. S. Teilmann. Beverly Hills: Sage.

Tullock, G. 1980. Does punishment deter crime? In *The Economics of Crime*, edited by R. Andreano and J. J. Siegfried. New York: Wiley.

van den Haag, E. 1975. *Punishing Criminals*. New York: Basic Books.

Van Dusen, K. T. 1981. Net widening and relabelling: Some consequences of deinstitutionalization. *American Behavioral Scientist* 24: 801–810.

Waldo, G. P. and T. G. Chiricos. 1972. Perceived penal sanction and self-reported criminality: A neglected approach to deterrence research. *Social Problems* 19: 522–540.

Ward, P. 1972. "Careers in crime": The FBI story. *Journal of Research in Crime and Delinquency* 7: 207–218.

West, D. J. and D. P. Farrington. 1977. *The Delinquent Way of Life*. London: Heinemann.

Wilson, J. Q. 1980. "What works?" revisited: New findings on criminal rehabilitation. *Public Interest* 61: 3–17.

Wolfgang, M. E. 1976. Seriousness of crime and policy of juvenile justice. In *Delinquency, Crime, and Society*, edited by J. F. Short. Chicago: University of Chicago Press.

Wolfgang, M. E., R. M. Figlio, and T. Sellin. 1972. *Delinquency in a Birth Cohort*. Chicago: University of Chicago Press.

CHAPTER ELEVEN

On Discipline*

PARENTAL DISCIPLINE CONSTITUTES one of the more salient and, perhaps, malleable features of child-rearing. Knowing how to bring about desired results in children's behavior is likely, therefore, to be particularly valuable. Yet research designed to understand effects of variations in timing, techniques, or context of discipline has been surprisingly rare. For this reason alone, the research reported by Deater-Deckard and Dodge in their target article is welcome.

Deater-Deckard and Dodge suggest that physical discipline affects children's aggression, with the magnitude of the influence depending on "the severity of the discipline, the cultural group in which the discipline occurs (and meaning that it conveys), the parent-child relationship context in which discipline occurs, and the gender of the parent and child." Specifically, they suggest that "when physical discipline is administered in the context of a cold parent-child relationship . . . its effects will be magnified." Deater-Deckard and Dodge report short-term results confirming their hypotheses regarding effects of corporal punishment on aggressive behavior. In the pages that follow, I evaluate these hypotheses from the perspective of a 30-year follow-up study.

Method

Data for analysis of the long-term impact of corporal punishment come from the Cambridge-Somerville Youth Study. The Youth Study was designed for the dual purposes of preventing delinquency and measuring development of boys who lived in impoverished, crowded urban environments. Referrals to the program included Boy Scouts as well as school truants so that participation would not stigmatize the boys.

*Reprinted from McCord, J. 1997. On discipline. *Psychological Inquiry* 8 (3): 215–217; with permission from Lawrence Erlbaum Associates, Inc.

The program involved a matched-pair design with one member of each pair randomly assigned to treatment. As part of the information gathered in order to match pairs of boys, teachers were asked to describe the behavior of boys in their classes. The boys were between the ages of 4 and 9 at the time these ratings were made.

Treatment began in 1939, when the boys averaged 10.5 years in age. It lasted for approximately 5.5 years. As part of the treatment program, case workers visited the homes of the clients, reporting what they saw and heard after each visit. The case records were coded in 1957.

The attitude of a parent toward the boy was classified as warm (affectionate) if that parent interacted frequently with the child, without being generally critical. Alternative classifications were: passively affectionate (if the parent was concerned for the boy's welfare, but there was little interaction), passively rejecting (if the parent was unconcerned for the boy's welfare and interacted little), actively rejecting (if the parent was almost constantly critical of the boy), ambivalent (if the parent showed marked alternation between affection and rejection of the child), and no indication. Two raters reading a 10 percent random sample of the cases agreed on 84 percent of the ratings for mothers and for fathers regarding parental attitudes toward their sons.

Discipline by each parent was classified as corporal punishment (punitive) if the parent used very harsh verbal abuse or physical force to control the boy. Alternative ratings were nonpunitive (used praise, rewards, or reasoning), extremely lax (almost no use of discipline), and no information. Two raters reading a 10 percent random sample of the cases agreed on 96 percent of the ratings for discipline by mothers and 76 percent by fathers.

To discern whether corporal punishment as measured through the case records should be considered a response to prior misbehavior, teachers' ratings were used to identify the particularly troublesome children, children whose teachers described them as fighters, truants, blaming others for their own misbehavior, and so forth (see McCord, 1994). Neither the mothers' nor the fathers' use of corporal punishment was reliably related to prior general misbehavior.

Data regarding the mother's affection and discipline were available for 224 of 232 families. The data were available for 173 of the fathers.

Not surprisingly, lack of maternal warmth and use of corporal punishment were related. Whereas only 35 percent of the 108 punitive mothers were warm, 60 percent of the 116 nonpunitive mothers were warm, χ^2 (1)=14.18, p=.000. Similarly, lack of paternal warmth and corporal punishment were related. Whereas only 22 percent of the 102 punitive fathers were warm, 42 percent of the 71 nonpunitive fathers were warm, χ^2 (1)=8.52, p=.004. Maternal warmth was not reliably related to paternal use of corporal punishment. Nor was paternal warmth reliably related to maternal use of corporal punishment.

In 1979, the youths (who had become adults) were retraced and their criminal records obtained. These records tracked the participants for 30 years after the last home visit and more than 20 years after the case records had been coded. Men were classified as criminals if they had been convicted for crimes indexed by the FBI. These included the violent crimes of assault, attempted assault, kidnapping, robbery, rape, abuse of a female child, weapons charges, manslaughter, intent to murder, or murder, as well as the nonviolent crimes of burglary, larceny, larceny of auto, breaking and entering, or receiving stolen property. Seventy-five men had been convicted for at least one of these crimes. Thirty-four of the men had been convicted for violent crimes.

Prior reports have indicated that child-rearing variables provide strong predictions both for juvenile delinquency and for adult criminality (McCord, 1979, 1991) and that they do so after controlling for childhood misbehavior (McCord, 1994). These prior analyses, however, have not focused on understanding the role of corporal punishment in relation to subsequent aggression. To evaluate the latter, categorical analyses were used to test the degree to which warmth, corporal punishment, and their interaction affected rates of serious criminality and violence.

Results

As shown in Tables 11.1 and 11.2, a mother's warmth seemed to protect boys from criminogenic influences regardless of the techniques she used to enforce control.

Paternal warmth, too, reduced the probability that sons would become criminal. Corporal punishment, however, seemed to increase the likelihood of criminality among sons of both warm and not-warm fathers. Almost half the sons of fathers who were not warm and who used corporal punishment had been convicted for Index crimes.

Although a mother's use of corporal punishment did not independently influence the rate of general criminality, it did appear to affect the rates of violence. Neither a father's affection nor his corporal punishment seemed to affect the rate of violence among sons (Tables 11.3 and 11.4).

TABLE 11.1   Serious Crimes, Parental Warmth, and Corporal Punishment

	N	% criminal
Mother		
Not warm		
Corporal punishment	70	51
Not	46	33
Warm		
Corporal punishment	38	21
Not	70	23
Father		
Not warm		
Corporal punishment	80	49
Not	41	27
Warm		
Corporal punishment	22	27
Not	30	13

TABLE 11.2 Maximum-Likelihood Analysis of Variance Table: Serious Crimes

Source	df	χ^2	p
Mother			
Intercept	1	26.01	.000
Warmth	1	8.84	.003
Punishment	1	1.16	.281
Warmth × Punishment	1	2.00	.158
Father			
Intercept	1	22.05	.000
Warmth	1	4.68	.031
Punishment	1	4.92	.027
Warmth × Punishment	1	0.01	.940

TABLE 11.3 Violence, Parental Warmth, and Corporal Punishment

	N	% violent
Mother		
Not warm		
Corporal punishment	70	29
Not	46	9
Warm		
Corporal punishment	38	13
Not	70	7
Father		
Not warm		
Corporal punishment	80	23
Not	41	15
Warm		
Corporal punishment	22	18
Not	30	7

TABLE 11.4 Maximum-Likelihood Analysis of Variance Table: Violence

Source	df	χ^2	p
Mother			
Intercept	1	75.49	.000
Warmth	1	1.78	.183
Punishment	1	5.66	.017
Warmth × Punishment	1	0.73	.394
Father			
Intercept	1	46.05	.000
Warmth	1	1.18	.278
Punishment	1	2.49	.114
Warmth × Punishment	1	0.33	.563

Discussion

These analyses of long-term effects of corporal punishment suggest that disciplinary techniques deserve attention as potentially powerful ways to affect personality. In using corporal punishments, parents demonstrate that power can be legitimately used to enforce desires.

The data show that parental warmth reduces the likelihood of serious criminality. They do not suggest, however, that effects of corporal punishment are rendered harmless by the presence of parental warmth. Corporal punishment by mothers increased the likelihood of violence even when coupled with maternal warmth; corporal punishment by fathers increased the likelihood of serious criminality even when coupled with paternal warmth.

Deater-Deckard and Dodge indicate that cultural acceptance of corporal punishment might mitigate its effects. They specifically note that in some communities, one hears the argument that corporal punishment is a part of the culture and a way of indicating love. Nevertheless, or perhaps for this reason, it is worth noting that teaching another generation that love involves inflicting pain may not be the best way to generate considerate and law-abiding behavior.

It would be a mistake to leave discussion of corporal punishment with the general impression that discipline requires the use of punishments. *Punishment*, defined as the intentional use of pain as retribution for specific behavior or to prevent repetition of a type of behavior, can be considered as a mark of failure in socialization.

Socialization failure can occur for three reasons:

1. The socializing agent has not been clear enough in teaching.
2. The child is unable to comply.
3. The child disagrees with the socializing agent regarding whether compliance is a good idea.

Many children are expected to guess what their parents want them to do and they are punished for having made mistaken guesses. The punishments reduce incentives to try to guess what their parents want. Severe or frequent pain may lead to escapes from parental supervision. Parents could become more effective were they to see transgressions as a sign that they have not successfully taught a child how to act under the given circumstances. Were they to take a teaching perspective, parents might discover ambiguities in their ideas of appropriate behavior or in their presentation of cues regarding how to act. These could be clarified and the child would be more likely to comply.

If a child does not understand what is expected, compliance is unlikely. Parents sometimes assume that children can remember longer than they can or are capable of doing things they are not yet able to do. In such cases, of course, misbehavior is inevitable. Sometimes compliance can be increased through the use of reminders; sometimes, a reduction in expectations of the parents is appropriate.

Children sometimes disagree with their parents about what should be done. Neither the use of corporal punishment nor its absence will eliminate such disagreement. If parents generally have good reasons for the behavior they require, they are more likely to be able to teach their children that such behavior is warranted than if they give the children pain for having chosen alternative behavior.

Most Americans have been victims of corporal punishment (Straus, 1994). Two mistaken beliefs seem to underpin the American proclivity to use corporal punishment. The first is that children will act to avoid physical pain. The popularity of contact sports should be considered evidence that this is not an accurate assumption. The second is that if one does not punish, all behavior is permissible.

High standards that are maintained clearly need not be coupled with punishment. Reasonably, some parents note that it is more difficult to rear well-behaved children in environments where lures for misbehavior are plentiful. Such parents need to be especially careful to set and enforce clear standards. Enforcing obedience, however, ought not be confused with punishing disobedience. Corporal punishment may, in fact, make enforcement of socialized behavior far more difficult.

References

McCord, J. 1979. Some child-rearing antecedents of criminal behavior in adult men. *Journal of Personality and Social Psychology* 37: 1477–1486.

McCord, J. 1991. Family relationships, juvenile delinquency, and adult criminality. *Criminology* 29: 397–417.

McCord, J. 1994. Family socialization and antisocial behavior: Searching for casual relationships in longitudinal research. In *Cross-national Longitudinal Research on Human Development and Criminal Behavior*, edited by I. G. M. Weitekamp and H-J Kerner, 217–227. Dordrecht, Netherlands: Kluwer.

Straus, M. A. 1994. *Beating the Devil out of Them: Corporal Punishment in American Families*. New York: Lexington.

CHAPTER TWELVE

Discipline and the Use of Sanctions*

OFTEN, WHEN PARENTS and advisors discuss discipline, they refer only to punishment. Yet punishment is to discipline, I suggest, as crumbs are to a banquet. Punishments are tiny, largely undesirable, pieces of the delicious feast provided by well-prepared discipline. Discipline, which is far larger and more valuable than the crumbs of punishment, includes rules, norms, and values as well as external sanctions.

Indeed, thoughtful consideration of discipline should include at least three areas: (a) Characteristics of the rules, norms, and values to which a child is being socialized; (b) The nature of the enforcement; and (c) The substance and effects of external sanctions: that is, of rewards and punishments.

Characteristics of Rules, Norms, and Values

Rules, norms, and values are part of the substance of discipline. They should be considered in terms of content, clarity, consistency, number, and appropriateness to the child's ability to learn.

Although it has become popular in some circles to recognize that adequate child rearing requires more than biological capacity to become a parent, much too little attention has been paid to parents having a consistent and reasonable set of expectations for children.

Unrealistic or inconsistent expectations increase the probability of misbehavior. The literature on child abuse suggests that unrealistic expectations regarding what particular children are able to do constitutes one of the risk factors for abuse (Herrenkohl and Herrenkohl, 1981; Reid, Patterson, and Loeber, 1982). More commonly, the socialization literature indicates that inconsistency in expectations constitutes a risk factor for most children's misbehavior (Patterson, 1995; Rutter,

*Reprinted from McCord, J. 1997. Discipline and the use of sanctions. In *Aggression and Violent Behavior* 2 (4): 313–319; with permission from Elsevier.

Bolton, Harrington, Le Couteur, Macdonald, and Simonoff, 1990; Stouthamer-Loeber, 1991). On the other hand, flexibility and clear expectations promote prosocial behavior, independence, and competence (Grolnick and Ryan, 1989; Zahn-Waxler, Radke-Yarrow, and King, 1979).

Prior to becoming a parent, many people fail to reflect upon what they value and why. Yet such self-understanding may be the most fundamental basis for rearing children whom one can genuinely enjoy. A first step in adequate discipline, therefore, is recognition or creation of a clear and consistent set of values that the socializing agents would like to convey.

Norms for behavior should be clearly expressed and consistently transmitted. Frequently, parents tell their children to do things they do not do themselves—or tell them not to do things they themselves do. Some examples:

A parent who hopes to teach her child not to lie may ask that child to tell someone who calls on the telephone that the parent is not home.

A parent who hopes to teach her child to be generous and to share may grab her own possessions when the child reaches for them.

A parent who would like to teach her child to avoid hurting others may willingly give unnecessary pain to her child.

Perhaps most commonly, a parent who would like to have a child do as the *parent* requests may consistently refuse to do as the *child* asks.

Studies indicate that hypocrisy is imitated, and that both doing and explaining what should be done is more likely to be effective than is a verbal message alone (Gelfand, Hartmann, Lamb, Smith, Mahon, and Paul, 1974; Grusec and Skubiski, 1970; Midlarsky, Bryan, and Brickman, 1973). In fact, modelling behavior has a greater impact than giving directions.

In one powerful study, Parpal and Maccoby (1985) demonstrated effects of modelling on children's compliance. The researchers randomly selected mothers of preschool children to train in being responsive to their children. The researchers taught these mothers to imitate their children in play and to avoid directing them, lessons the mothers practiced during a specified short period each day for 1 week. At the end of the week, the mother-child pairs came to the child-study laboratory which contained toys. Mothers trained to be responsive demonstrated what they learned for 15 minutes before their children were tested for compliance. For comparison, half of the remaining mothers filled out a questionnaire that took approximately 15 minutes. These mothers paid little attention to their children as the children played. A third group of mothers, called the "contingency training" group, played with their children for 15 minutes, using whatever rewards and punishments they normally used.

Mother-child pairs were evaluated by standardized requests for compliance. Each mother made 17 requests to the child, using the words dictated by the experimenter. Overall, children of mothers in the no-attention and the responsive play groups were more compliant than those in the group in which mothers behaved as they usually do. The authors discovered that "the Responsive condition was especially effective with children who are perceived to be 'difficult'" (Parpal and Maccoby, 1985, p. 1333).

Typically, at least in the United States, parents begin to think about what they teach their children when the children break an unacknowledged rule, that is, when the parent objects to something the child does. Under such circumstances, parents may state a rule or issue a punishment.

By the time a child has done something correctable, of course, the child has picked out features of the environment that could form the bases for values. The child, in other words, has begun to make choices and to recognize certain types of behavior as pleasant and others as unpleasant.

Let us suppose that what the child does—to which the parent objects—is something the child believes to be pleasant. Suppose the child asks why he should not continue doing the thing. Compare the values taught by a parent who says "because it might hurt your little brother" with the values taught by parents who say "because I told you to stop" or "because you'll get spanked if you don't."

In the first case, the child is being taught to regard injuring his little brother as something not to be done because of his brother's possible pain. He is thus taught to attend to and value the well-being of another. In the second case, the child is being taught that parents (who are powerful) can make arbitrary rules and that avoiding parents may be advisable. In the third case, the child is being taught to do things to avoid being spanked, and thus, to attend to his own discomfort rather than the welfare of others.

The Nature of the Enforcement

Monitoring or supervision turns out to be one of the strongest predictors of compliant behavior (Loeber and Stouthamer-Loeber, 1986; Peeples and Loeber, 1994; Sampson & Groves, 1989). The fact that single-parent families are less likely to provide supervision than are intact families seems to account for a measurable amount of the criminogenic effects often attributed to single-parent families (McCord, 1982; Sampson and Groves, 1989). Indeed, when supervision and mother's affection are controlled, single-parent families are not more criminogenic than intact families.

For effective monitoring, timing is critical. Monitoring is most effective when it is used to enforce compliance rather than to detect noncompliance. That is, monitoring as a prelude to punishment or reward is less effective in teaching a child how to behave than is monitoring when used to see that a child behaves appropriately in the first place.

For very young children, parents can adjust what they ask to that which they can enforce. For example, a parent who tells a child to stop doing something should be able to enforce that command by holding the child long enough to stop the forbidden action. A child told to go someplace should be led, if necessary, to where he or she is told to go.

Effective monitoring can take place for children who are told to go to bed (with a parent prepared to enforce the command), but monitoring cannot enforce going to sleep. Effective monitoring can take place for children who are told to leave the table or the room, but not for commands to eat or to be quiet. In short, the first timing consideration is one that requires socializing agents to become aware of the nature of the commands they issue, so that they can monitor compliance to them. If children are to learn what it means to "leave the table," their parents may need to enforce the action. Only after having learned the meaning of the words is it reasonable to expect a child to follow instructions or requests.

Parents should be conscious of the fact that they are teaching children the meaning of words at the same time that they teach children how to act. If parents use words like "stop hitting" in conjunction with their own hitting of the child, they give a confusing message.

When children are learning how to act, their parents can combine enforcement with teaching. By joining their children in the acts they request, they show what to do while also lending credibility to the claim that the requested behavior is desirable. For example, if parents want a child to clean a room, an effective way to achieve this goal is to clean the room with the child.

Timing also is critical in relation to the nature of the child whose actions are monitored. According to my own longitudinal study of boys reared in Cambridge and Somerville, Massachusetts (McCord, 1994), monitoring seemed to have different effects on disruptive and compliant children. Although monitoring seemed to protect compliant boys from subsequent criminality, it did not reduce criminogenic tendencies of conduct-disordered boys. Children who have already become disruptive require more than supervision to change their behavior.

Disruptive boys appear to attribute aggressive intentions to others. Changing these sets of beliefs has been shown to have beneficial effects in at least one experiment. Hudley and Graham (1993) assigned 3rd through 5th grade boys to one of three groups: an attributional training group, an attention training group, or a no-treatment control group. Approximately two thirds of the boys were considered unpopular and aggressive by both peers and teachers; the remaining third were both nonaggressive and popular. Attributional training, which lasted for 6 weeks, focused on teaching the boys how to pick out cues for understanding others' intentions, using role play in social situations. Attention training also used role play, though the situations involved nonsocial problem solving.

Teachers who did not know the group assignment of the children rated them 2 weeks after the training ended. Only children who had received attributional training were rated as less aggressive. Teachers' ratings regarding prosocial behavior did not change, indicating the specificity of the change. Results of an experimental evaluation of the training were even more encouraging. The boys were tested in a frustrating situation where they might have won toys but for a putative mix-up by an unseen classmate. Those who had received attributional training were less likely to attribute hostile intent for the error and less likely to complain or criticize their partners. The authors note that cognitive and behavioral change was unaccompanied by change in anger.

External Sanctions: Rewards and Punishments

External sanctions, for purposes of this discussion, are rewards and punishments contingent on actions of a child. In the case of rewards, they are intended to give pleasure. In the case of punishments, they are intended to give pain.

External sanctions have several effects that are likely to be overlooked by those who use them. First, external sanctions show that misbehavior is permissible.

Parents can tell a child not to walk in the street. An adult can enforce the prohibition by holding the child. The prohibition can be explained by referring to possible injury to the child. Suppose, however, the child is told not to go into the street or he will be punished. The child is informed by the choice given that going into the street is possible. The child may well wonder why the parent objects to one form of possible injury while threatening to give another. The child may also conclude that going into the street is desirable when no adult is around to punish him.

Alternatively, suppose the child is told that if he does not go into the street he will be allowed to play with a special toy. The child is still informed by the choice that going into the street is possible. If playing with the special toy appears less desirable than going into the street, the child has reason to select the street rather than the toy.

The examples of the use of sanctions show why external sanctions diminish the power of proper discipline. Sanctions present alternatives; they suggest that a child need not follow desired rules.

A second effect of using external sanctions is that they mask the cues children require to learn how to act when socializing agents are unavailable. Parents can tell a child to brush her teeth. An adult can take the child and do the brushing, should that be necessary. The behavior can be justified in terms of caring for the health of the child. Suppose, however, the parent says that if the child brushes her teeth she can stay up for a special television program. By using a reward, the parent has undermined the value of doing things for the sake of health, while also providing an option for the child should she not want to watch television.

Barry Schwartz (1982) demonstrated that even among college students, contingent positive reinforcements interfere with the discovery of general rules. In his study, students were presented with a game in which winning depended on pressing complicated key sequences. When they were rewarded for each correctly pressed sequence, they failed to recognize the rule, a rule that was discovered by those told to find the rule and by those simply asked to play the game.

A third reason why external sanctions diminish the worth of clearly expressed values is that sanctions endorse egocentric motivations. If children are to be taught to consider the welfare of others, then reasons for action should invoke the welfare of others as justification. If a parent wants to teach a child not to make a mess in the house of a neighbor, the parent can help the child to keep her toys neat or to eat carefully. If the parent couples a request to avoid making a mess with a threat of punishment or promise of reward, the parent has shifted grounds for action from consideration for others to the child's own pains and pleasures.

A fourth reason to be skeptical of using external sanctions is that they tend to have perverse consequences. Rewards tend to diminish the value of what is rewarded and punishments tend to enhance the value of what is attached to punishment.

If we assume that children are generally rational, the reason for these "perverse" consequences becomes clear. No one suggests a reward for doing something that is instrinsically pleasant. Rewards are the sorts of things that people attach to unattractive alternatives. So a child offered a reward will look for reasons why the reward is thought to be necessary.

Studies have demonstrated that offering incentives in the form of rewards sometimes results in devaluation of the activity being rewarded (Greene and Lepper, 1974; Lepper, Greene, and Nisbett, 1973; Lepper, Sagotsky, Dafoe, and Greene, 1982; Ross, 1975; Ross, Karniol, and Rothstein, 1976). These studies are based on a model in which some children, randomly selected, are offered rewards for doing such things as drawing with special crayons. Those not invited to draw for the sake of a reward were more likely to freely choose drawing with the crayons at a later time.

In an ideal model of the conditions under which children learn values and language simultaneously, Lepper et al. (1982) had one of two types of stories read to children. Both stories were about a mother giving two foods to her child: "hupe" and "hule." The children in the experiment were asked to say which the child in the story would prefer. In one story, the mother explained to her child that she could have "hupe" if she ate the "hule" (or, for alternate children, "hule" if she ate the "hupe"). In this condition, one in which the second food was a reward for eating the first, children believed that the child in the story would prefer the second food, giving as their reasons the fact that it tastes better. The control condition used a similar story except that the two foods were not contingently related. The mother simply gave the child two foods, presented in alternate order for different children. Children in this condition either refused to identify a preferred food or chose one without providing a reason for the selection. Similar studies have shown that play objects can be manipulated so that what is selected as rewarding gains value while that which is rewarded tends to be discounted (Boggiano and Main, 1986).

Just as no one suggests a reward for doing something that is instrinsically pleasant, people do not need to threaten punishment for something thought to be undesirable. Therefore, a child given threat of punishment for doing something recognizes that the to-be-punished for must be desirable.

An experiment by Aronson and Carlsmith (1963) provided clear demonstration of the enhancing value of punishments. Individually, preschool children ranked preferences for five toys, using paired comparisons. The experimenter placed the toy ranked second on the table. Every child was told not to play with the toy on the table. Half the children were also told that if they disobeyed, the experimenter would be very angry and would take away all the toys and never come back. The other half were told only that the experimenter would be annoyed if the child played with the forbidden toy. The experimenter left for 10 minutes. Although none of the children played with the forbidden toy, when the children re-ranked the toys, there were marked differences related to whether or not the child had been exposed to threat of punishment. Only 4 of the 22 children in the mild threat condition increased the value of the forbidden toy, whereas 14 of the 22 children in the threatened punishment condition increased its value. Conversely, eight of those in the mild threat condition, but none of those in the punishment condition, decreased the value placed on the forbidden toy.

In addition to the general effects of external sanctions as undermining important elements of discipline, punishments have additional disadvantages. These include the following:

1. Punishments demonstrate the possibility for legitimate use of pain-giving.
2. The use of punishments tends to increase the probability of a child's lying in order to avoid the consequences of honesty.
3. The use of punishment also tends to make the company of a punisher risky. Punishments, therefore, diminish the influence of a parent.

Summary

Proper discipline should begin with parental reflection. Parents should consider their values and priorities among them. Ideally, this reflection should occur prior to the birth of a child so that parents will not teach undesirable habits that must later be corrected.

Proper discipline also includes establishing habits consistent with the values one hopes to teach. Having established priorities, parents should consider techniques to teach their children the values through using them as grounds for governing the children's behavior. When teaching fails, parents should shift their techniques, reconsidering their own behavior as teachers.

Discipline may fail for three reasons: (a) The socializing agent has not been clear enough in teaching. (b) The child may be unable to comply. (c) The child disagrees with the socializing agent regarding whether compliance is a good idea. If punishments are issued in order to insure compliance, they are likely to corrupt the point that a socializing agent has tried to teach and unlikely to persuade the child that compliance (for its own sake) is reasonable. In short, when enforcement has been properly negotiated, punishments are both unnecessary and undesirable.

Note

This paper was prepared for the NICHD/Discipline Conference, April 25 and 26, 1996, Chapel Hill, NC. Correspondence should be addressed to Joan McCord, 623 Broad Acres Road, Narbeth, PA 19072.

References

Aronson, E. and J. M. Carlsmith. 1963. Effect of the severity of threat on the devaluation of forbidden behavior. *Journal of Abnormal and Social Psychology* 66: 584–588.

Boggiano, A. K. and D. S. Main. 1986. Enhancing children's interest in activities used as rewards: The bonus effect. *Journal of Personality and Social Psychology* 31: 1116–1126.

Gelfand, D., D. Hartmann, A. Lamb, C. Smith, M. Mahon, and S. Paul. 1974. The effects of adult models and described alternatives on children's choice of behavior management techniques. *Child Development* 45: 585–593.

Greene, D. and M. R. Lepper. 1974. Effects of extrinsic rewards on children's subsequent intrinsic interest. *Child Development* 45: 1141–1145.

Grolnick, W. S. and R. M. Ryan. 1989. Parent styles associated with children's self-regulation and competence in schools. *Journal of Educational Psychology* 81: 143–154.

Grusec, J. E. and S. L. Skubiski. 1970. Model nurturance demand characteristics of the modeling experiment and altruism. *Journal of Personality and Social Psychology* 14: 352–359.

Herrenkohl, R. C. and E. C. Herrenkohl. 1981. Some antecedents and developmental consequences of child maltreatment. In *Developmental Perspectives on Child Maltreatment*, edited by R. Risley and D. Cicchetti, 57–76. San Francisco: Jossey-Bass.

Hudley, C. and S. Graham. 1993. An attributional intervention to reduce peer-directed aggression among African-American boys. *Child Development* 64: 124–138.

Lepper, M. R., D. Greene, and R. E. Nisbett. 1973. Undermining children's intrinsic interest with extrinsic rewards. *Journal of Personality and Social Psychology* 28: 129–137.

Lepper, M. R., G. Sagotsky, J. L. Dafoe, and D. Greene. 1982. Consequences of superfluous social constraints: Effects on young children's social influences and subsequent intrinsic interest. *Journal of Personality and Social Psychology* 41: 51–65.

Loeber, R. and M. Stouthamer-Loeber. 1986. Family factors as correlates and predictors of juvenile conduct problems and delinquency. In *Crime and justice*, edited by M. Tonry and N. Morris, vol. 7: 29–149. Chicago: University of Chicago Press.

McCord, J. 1982. A longitudinal view of the relationship between paternal absence and crime. In *Abnormal Offenders, Delinquency and the Criminal Justice System*, edited by J. Gunn and D. P. Farrington, 113–128. Chichester, England: John Wiley & Sons.

McCord, J. 1994. Family socialization and antisocial behavior: Searching for causal relationships in longitudinal research. In *Cross-national Longitudinal Research on Human Development and Criminal Behavior*, edited by E. G. M. Weitekamp and H-J. Kerner, 177–188. Dordrecht, Netherlands: Kluwer.

Midlarsky, E., J. H. Bryan, and P. Brickman. 1973. Aversive approval: Interactive effects of modeling and reinforcement on altruistic behavior. *Child Development* 44: 321–328.

Parpal, M. and E. E. Maccoby. 1985. Maternal responsiveness and subsequent child compliance. *Child Development* 56: 1326–1344.

Patterson, G. R. 1995. Coercion as a basis for early age of onset for arrest. In *Coercion and punishment in long-term perspectives*, edited by J. McCord, 81–105. New York: Cambridge University Press.

Peeples, F. and R. Loeber. 1994. Do individual factors and neighborhood context explain ethnic differences in juvenile delinquency? *Journal of Quantitative Criminology* 10: 141–157.

Reid, J. B., G. R. Patterson, and R. Loeber. 1982. The abused child: Victim, instigator, or innocent bystander? In *Proceedings of the Nebraska Symposium on Motivation: Response Structure and Organization*, edited by D. J. Bernstein and H. E. Howe. Lincoln: University of Nebraska Press.

Ross, M. 1975. Salience of reward and intrinsic motivation. *Journal of Personality and Social Psychology* 32: 245–254.

Ross, M., R. Karniol, and M.Rothstein. 1976. Reward contingency and intrinsic motivation in children: A test in the delay of gratification hypothesis. *Journal of Personality and Social Psychology* 33: 442–447.

Rutter, M., P. Bolton, R. Harrington, A. Le Couteur, H. Macdonald, and E. Simonoff. 1990. Genetic factors in child psychiatric disorders-I. A review of research strategies. *Journal of Child Psychology and Psychiatry and Allied Disciplines* 31: 3–37.

Sampson, R. J. and W. B. Groves. 1989. Community structure and crime: Testing social-disorganization theory. *American Journal of Sociology* 94: 774–802.

Schwartz, B. 1982. Reinforcement-induced behavioral stereotypy: How not to teach people to discover rules. *Journal of Experimental Psychology* III, 23–59.

Stouthamer-Loeber, M. 1991. Young children's verbal misrepresentations of reality. In *Children's personal trust*, edited by K. J. Rotenberg, 21–42. New York: Springer-Verlag.

Zahn-Waxler, C., M. Radke-Yarrow, and R. A. King. 1979. Child-rearing and children's pro-social initiations toward victims of distress. *Child Development* 50: 319–330.

PART IV

Crime in the Family

CHAPTER THIRTEEN

Patterns of Deviance*

OVER THE LAST FEW decades, studies of crime have yielded enough information to raise some interesting questions about patterns of deviance. For example, studies of young criminals have linked their behavior to parental rejection, parental conflict, and to criminal role models (Bandura and Walters, 1959; Farrington, 1973; Glueck and Glueck, 1950; Havighurst et al., 1962; McCord et al., 1963; McCord and McCord, 1959 and 1960; Nye, 1958; Palmore and Hammond, 1964; Peck et al., 1960; Robins, 1966). Follow-up studies of delinquents generally indicate that they are likely to continue to commit crimes as adults (Chaitin and Dunham, 1966; Glueck and Glueck, 1940; Robins and O'Neal, 1958). Yet studies of adult criminals have failed to find relationships between childhood family disruption or parental criminality and recidivism (Buikhuisen and Hoekstra, 1974; Guze, 1964; Meade, 1973).

Cross-sectional data have shown that types of crimes are age-related (Federal Bureau of Investigation, 1974). Yet, Wolfgang et al. (1972) failed to find significant patterns of progression among juveniles from one type of crime to another.

Studies of criminals have indicated that alcoholism contributes to adult recidivism (Guze, 1964 and 1976; Guze and Cantwell, 1965; Guze et al., 1962 and 1968; Nicol et al., 1973). Yet backgrounds of alcoholics and of criminals appear to be distinguishable (McCord 1972; McCord and McCord 1959 and 1960).

The evidence gives rise to three questions: (1) Why is it that rejection, family conflict, and parental criminal models are seemingly unrelated to adult crime? (2) Does a typology based on official records show promise for the understanding of criminal behavior? and (3) Are there distinctive patterns of antisocial behavior which might help to distinguish between alcoholic and nonalcoholic criminals?

*Reprinted from McCord, J. 1980. Patterns of deviance. In *Human Functioning in Longitudinal Perspective: Studies of Normal and Psychopathological Populations*, edited by S. B. Sells et al., 157–167. Baltimore: Williams & Wilkins; with permission

Method

A sample of 506 men who had participated in the Cambridge-Somerville Youth Study between 1939 and 1943 has been retraced to 1975. Tracing included a search of criminal records, mental hospital records, records from alcoholic treatment centers, and death records in Massachusetts.

Although these subjects had not been sought since 1948, information about the current location of 93 percent has been obtained: 83 percent were living in Massachusetts at the time of death or their fortieth birthday. Additional information about alcoholism has been gathered from responses to questionnaires and through interviews.[1]

Data regarding criminal behavior are based on court convictions through 1975 and on records of the Crime Prevention Bureau gathered in 1945. Almost a third of the men (29%) had been convicted for serious crimes ranging from arson and larceny to murder; an additional 43 percent had records for less serious offenses.

Men were considered alcoholics if they described themselves as alcoholic, had received treatment for alcoholism, answered "yes" to at least three out of the four questions from the CAGE test for alcoholism (Ewing and Rouse, 1970), or had been convicted at least three times for drunkenness. By these criteria, 99 men (20%) were identified as alcoholics.

All subjects are male, and most were reared in the congested areas of Cambridge and Somerville, Massachusetts. Their median age in 1975 was 47.

Results

Histories of deviant behavior among the 506 men have been organized to allow consideration of the relationship between juvenile delinquency and adult criminality, patterns of criminality among men who committed various types of crimes, and comparisons between alcoholics and nonalcoholics in terms of their criminal behavior.

Juvenile Delinquency and Adult Criminality

Of the 365 men who had been convicted for at least one crime, 139 (38%) had records as juvenile delinquents.[2]

Although three-fourths (79%) of the juvenile delinquents committed at least one crime as an adult, only a third of the men convicted as adults also had records as juvenile delinquents. Thus, although juvenile delinquents tended to become adult criminals (χ^2=13.93; p < .001), a majority of adult criminals had no history as juvenile delinquents.

Both incarceration and being young when first convicted appeared to increase the probability of subsequent serious crimes. Almost half of the juveniles convicted for serious crimes had been sentenced to reform school. Records for men who had been incarcerated as juveniles were compared with those for men who,

TABLE 13.1 Percent of Adult Criminals Who Had Records for Serious Crimes as Juvenile Delinquents

Crimes as adults	% convicted for juvenile crimes
Property and persons (N=19)	63
Property (not persons) (N=35)	57
Persons (not property) (N=36)	31
Only minor crimes (N=275)	21

χ^2=32.2; df=3; p < .001.

as juveniles, had committed serious crimes but had not been incarcerated; 56 percent of the former and 33 percent of the latter committed serious crimes as adults (χ^2=5.06; p < .025).

Before reaching age 16, 103 delinquents had been convicted for at least one crime. The average age at first conviction among them was 12.5 years. Subsequently, 67 percent committed at least one serious crime. Since only 19 percent of the 36 men first convicted when 16 or 17 subsequently committed a serious crime, recidivism was considerably more prevalent among those who became delinquent before their 16th birthday (χ^2=24.33; p < .001). This same group of men—those first convicted as youngsters—were likely to be convicted for serious crimes between the ages of 18 and 24 (χ^2=7.3; p < .01) and also after their 25th birthday (χ^2=6.9; p < .01).

The relationship between adult crimes and serious juvenile delinquency appears in Table 13.1.

Patterns of Criminality

To search for meaningful patterns of deviance, crimes were classified into groups: those against ordinances (status offenses, traffic violations, etc.); those against order (disturbing the peace, lewd and lascivious behavior, neglecting family, malicious mischief, crimes without victims, etc.); those against property (arson, larceny, breaking and entering, receiving stolen property, theft); and those against persons (rape, attempted rape, assault, kidnapping, manslaughter, murder, and attempted murder). In terms of seriousness, these four types were ordered from low to high as listed above: crimes against ordinances, order, property, and persons. Each man who had been convicted for at least one crime was classified by the most serious of his crimes.

Among the 112 men classified as criminals only for crimes against ordinances, 14 percent had juvenile records: also 14 percent of those whose most serious crime was against order (N=104) had juvenile records. Differences were marked, however, between men convicted for crimes against persons and those convicted for crimes against property but not against persons; whereas 84 percent of those whose most serious crime was against property (N=80) had juvenile records, only 39 percent of those who had committed crimes against persons (N=69) had been juvenile delinquents (χ^2=10.99; p < .001).

TABLE 13.2   Percentage of Subjects Grouped by Age at First Conviction by Type of Most Serious Crime

	% by type of most serious crime			
Age	Ordinance	Order	Property	Persons
Under 16 (N=103)	5	7	54	34
16 or 17 (N=36)	31	22	31	17
18–20 (N=65)	34	34	15	17
21–24 (N=63)	40	43	5	13
Over 24 (N=98)	50	41	0	9

$\chi^2=165.46$; df=12; $p < .0001$.

Comparisons of these groups (classifying men by their most serious crimes) show distinguishable trends in the ages when they were first convicted. The probability that a person would commit no crime more serious than one against order increased with age at first conviction: the probability that a criminal would commit crimes against property or against persons decreased with age at first conviction, although the decline was sharper for those whose worst crimes were against property (Table 13.2).

Using a somewhat different classification, men were selected who had been convicted for larceny (including breaking and entering or auto theft) for assault (including rape and attempted murder), and for both larceny and assault. Criminals convicted of both larceny and assault had been convicted about twice as often as men convicted only of larceny ($t=2.89$; $p < .005$) or only of assault ($t=1.99$; $p < .05$). Even omitting convictions for crimes against ordinances or order, the men convicted for both larceny and assault committed significantly more crimes ($t=4.13$ and 5.33; $p < .0002$).

Men convicted for assault but not for larceny tended to be older at the time of their first conviction than either men convicted only for larceny ($t=7.04$; $p < .0001$) or men convicted both for larceny and assault ($t=4.54$; $p < .0001$).

When first convicted for a *serious* crime, men convicted only for larceny had been younger than either those convicted for both larceny and assault ($t=7.22$; $p < .0001$) or those convicted only for assault ($t=7.34$; $p < .0001$).

The comparisons suggest that men who commit both larceny and assault can be distinguished by their youthful crimes from those who commit only larceny; those who will commit both larceny and assault tend to begin their criminal careers with relatively minor crimes. Although men who commit both larceny and assault and those who commit only assault tend to commit their first *serious* crimes at approximately the same ages, those who commit both types of crimes more typically have prior histories for less serious offenses and are more likely to commit future crimes.

Alcoholism and Patterns of Deviance

Among the 99 men identified as alcoholics, 86 percent had been convicted for some crime. Among nonalcoholics, 69 percent had court convictions ($\chi^2=11.14$;

TABLE 13.3 Adult Alcoholism and Patterns of Serious Crimes[a]

% with	Adult alcoholics (N=57)	Adult nonalcoholics (N=92)
Juvenile record only	21	50
Juvenile and adult record	39	24
Adult record only	40	26

$\chi^2=12.5$; df=2; $p < .01$.

[a]Arson, larceny and related crimes, assault, rape, attempted murder, and murder.

$p < .001$). Furthermore, alcoholics were disproportionately represented among the men who committed serious crimes (those ranging from arson to murder). Among those who had been convicted for some crime, 67 percent of the alcoholics and only 33 percent of the nonalcoholics had been convicted for a serious crime ($\chi^2=31.57$; $p < .001$).

Among juvenile delinquents, those who became alcoholics were more likely to commit serious crimes as adults. Also, among men without serious juvenile records, alcoholics were more likely than nonalcoholics to commit serious crimes as adults (Table 13.3).

The Bureau of Crime Prevention records contained information about crimes committed by juveniles. These records showed that 171 men had committed crimes, as juveniles, for which they were not convicted. When both official and unofficial crimes were taken into account, men who later became alcoholics were found more frequently in the group that had been convicted for some—but not all—of their known crimes than among those either convicted for all or for none of their known crimes ($\chi^2=12.2$; d.f.=3; $p < .01$).[3] Over half (56%) of the men whose first conviction was for larceny became alcoholics. Criminal records following first convictions indicated that alcoholics had more frequently committed at least one subsequent crime which was more serious than that for which they had first been convicted ($\chi^2=25.99$; $p < .001$).

Summary and Discussion

This research has been directed toward providing answers for three questions suggested from analyses of prior research. To answer these questions, the lives of 506 men have been traced through official records, questionnaires, and interviews. Now in their mid- to late forties, 149 of these men have criminal records for committing crimes ranging from arson to murder; an additional 216 had records for less serious offenses. One out of five has been (or is) alcoholic.

The data from this study agree with other studies in showing that very young delinquents tend to have the worst prognoses, that types of crimes are age-related, and that there is a large overlap between alcoholics and criminals.

The data go beyond this, however, in suggesting tentative answers to the three questions posed earlier.

1. Rejection, parental criminality, and parental conflict may be causes—not merely predictors—of delinquency and yet may not be related to adult criminality because so large a proportion of adult criminals have not also been juvenile delinquents.
2. Typologies based on official criminal records do seem to provide meaningful categories among criminals. Classifications based on "most serious crime" suggest differences in criminal patterns. It appears reasonable to expect to find different backgrounds among those who commit crimes against property and those who commit crimes against persons.
3. Alcoholics who are criminals have patterns of deviance which distinguish them from nonalcoholic criminals. It seems advisable, therefore, to differentiate among alcoholic criminals, nonalcoholic criminals, and noncriminal alcoholics in attempting to understand both alcoholism and crime.

Notes

This paper is a report of research in progress. The research has been conducted jointly with the Department of Probation of the Commonwealth of Massachusetts. The author wishes to express appreciation to the Division of Alcoholism, the Department of Mental Health, the Cambridge and Somerville Program for Alcoholism Rehabilitation, the Department of Motor Vehicles, the Department of Corrections, the National Institute of Law Enforcement through their Grant NI 74-0038 to Ron Geddes) and to the many individuals who helped in this research. The research has been generously supported by the NIMH (Grant 5 RO1 MH26779).

1. By September 1976, 42 men were known to have died, 216 had responded to the questionnaire, and 83 men had been interviewed. Among the 429 men located and not known to be dead, over half (55%) had provided current information about themselves. Excluding those for whom we had information but no means of contact, the rate of response was 61%.

2. Excluding status, traffic, and auto violations, 124 men had juvenile records—76 percent for larceny and 13 percent for assault. Excluding traffic and auto violations, 219 men had been convicted for at least one crime after reaching the age of 18 (25% for larceny and 25% for assault).

3. This finding is particularly interesting in relation to the theory that alcoholism is a self-punitive response.

References

Bandura, A. and R. Walters. 1959. *Adolescent Aggression*. Ronald Press, New York.

Buikhuisen, W. and H. A. Hoekstra. 1974. Factors related to recidivism. *Br. J. Criminol. Delinquency, Deviant Soc. Behav.* 14: 63–69.

Chaitin, M. R. and H. W. Dunham. 1966. The juvenile court in its relationship to adult criminality: A replicated study. *Soc. Forces* 45: 114–119.

Ewing, J. A. and B. A. Rouse. 1970. *Identifying the hidden alcoholic.* Paper presented at the 29th Alcoholic Congress, February 3, Sydney, N, S. W., Australia.

Farrington, D. P. 1973. Self-reports of deviant behavior: Predictive and stable? *J. Criminal Law Criminol.* 64: 99–110.

Federal Bureau of Investigation. 1975. *Crime in the United States, 1974, Uniform Crime Reports.* U.S. Government Printing Office, Washington, D.C.

Glueck, S. and E. Glueck. 1940. *Juvenile Delinquents Grown Up*. The Commonwealth Fund, New York.

———. 1950. *Unraveling Juvenile Delinquency*. The Commonwealth Fund, New York.

Guze, S. B. 1964. A study of recidivism based upon a follow-up of 217 consecutive criminals. *J. Nerv. Ment. Dis.* 128: 575–580.

———. 1976. *Criminality and Psychiatric Disorders*. Oxford University Press, New York.

Guze, S. B. and D. P. Cantwell. 1965. Alcoholism, parole observations and criminal recidivism: A study of 116 parolees. *Am. J. Psychiatry* 122: 436–439.

Guze, S. B., V. B. Tuason, P. D. Gatfield, M. A. Stewart, and B. Picken. 1962. Psychiatric illness and crime with particular reference to alcoholism: A study of 223 criminals. *J. Nerv. Ment. Dis.* 134: 512–521.

Guze, S. B., E. D. Wolfgram, J. K. McKinney, and D. P. Cantwell. 1968. Delinquency, social maladjustment and crime: The role of alcoholism. *Dis. Nerv. System* 29: 238–243.

Havighurst, R. J., P. H. Bowman, G. P. Liddle, C. V. Matthews, and J. V. Pierce. 1962. *Growing Up in River City*. Wiley, New York.

McCord, J. 1972. Some differences in backgrounds of alcoholics and criminals. *Ann. N.Y. Acad. Sci.* 197: 183–187.

McCord, J., W. McCord, and A. Howard. 1963. Family interaction as antecedent to the direction of male aggressiveness. *J. Abnorm. Soc. Psychol.* 66: 239–242.

McCord, W. and J. McCord. 1959, 1960. *Origins of Alcoholism*. Stanford University Press, Stanford.

Meade, A. 1973. Seriousness of delinquency, the adjudicative decision and recidivism— A longitudinal configuration analysis. *J. Criminal Law Criminol.* 64: 478–485.

Nicol, A. R., J. C. Gunn, J. Gristwood, R. H. Forggitt, and J. P. Watson. 1973. The relationship of alcoholism to violent behavior resulting in long-term imprisonment. *Br. J. Psychiatry* 123: 47–51.

Nye, F. I. 1958. *Family Relationships and Delinquent Behavior*. Wiley, New York.

Palmore, F. B. and P. E. Hammond. 1964. Interacting factors in juvenile delinquency. *Am. Sociol. Rev.* 29: 848–854.

Peck, R. F., R. J. Havighurst, R. Cooper, J. Lilienthal, and D. More. 1960. *The Psychology of Character Development*. Wiley, New York.

Robins, L. N. 1966. *Deviant Children Grown Up*. Williams & Wilkins, Baltimore.

Robins, L. and P. O'Neal. 1958. Mortality, mobility, and crime: Problem children thirty years later. *Am. Sociol. Rev.* 23: 162–171.

Wolfgang, M. E., R. M. Figlio, and T. Sellin. 1972. *Delinquency in a Birth Cohort*. The University of Chicago Press, Chicago.

CHAPTER FOURTEEN

The Cycle of Crime and Socialization Practices*

S TUDIES OF DELINQUENCY are peppered with reports that crime runs in families. Aggressiveness and criminality among the parents of delinquents have been reported in Canada, the United States, Great Britain, and Finland.[1] Evidence from these studies suggests that criminality has both biological and social links. Both linkages also can be inferred from studies of domestic abuse that reveal that abused children have a relatively high probability of becoming violent adults.[2] Over the last two decades, studies of twins and of adoption have implicated genetic factors in the transmission of behaviors related to crime. For example, Goodman and Stevenson[3] found a considerable amount of heritability for hyperactivity among the twins they studied—whether hyperactivity was rated by fathers, by mothers, or by teachers. Several studies have also found evidence for heritability for such related concepts as activity level, impulsivity, and desire for excitement.[4]

Studies comparing biological with sociological father-son pairs in terms of crime show more similarities within the biological pairs.[5] In addition, the longitudinal studies carried out by Eron and Huesmann have tied aggression at age eight to aggression in offspring twenty-two years later.[6]

Despite the wealth of evidence revealing continuities, biological explanations have moved little beyond the speculations of geneticists that gave rise to the Eugenics Movement during the first third of the twentieth century.[7] Suggestions about biological ties have focused on relationships between aggression and hormones,[8] criminality and low autonomic arousal,[9] prevalence of sinistrality among some types of criminals,[10] and difficulties in learning found among hyperactive and conduct disordered children.[11] Disconcertingly, evidence contradicting the suggested relationships as links appears as credible as supporting evidence.[12]

*Reprinted from McCord, J. 1991. The cycle of crime and socialization practices. In *The Journal of Criminal Law and Criminology* 82 (1): 211–228; by special permission of Northwestern University School of Law, *Journal of Criminal Law and Criminology*.

Unfortunately, efforts to understand how the environment interacts with biological differences in the production of crime have received little more than lip service.[13] Genetic studies rarely include direct measures of environmental effects. Furthermore, the most commonly used measure of heritability, h^2, devised by Falconer,[14] assumes the equivalence of environmental variance for monozygotic and dizygotic twins and additive effects. Both assumptions are dubious.

Several studies show that differential attractiveness influences interactions.[15] Dizygotic twins will be differently attractive in larger measure than are monozygotic twins and therefore, dizygotic twins are likely to be exposed to greater variation in environment.

A study of 300 children of unwed mothers[16] offers data suggesting an interactive effect between environment and heredity. In this study, the children were adopted within days of birth, and the adopting mothers did not know the psychological status of the biological mothers. The researchers correlated the scores for the biological mothers' emotional stability, based on an MMPI administered prior to giving birth, with the behavior evaluations of their children provided by their adopting mothers several years later.

Loehlin et al. found that the children of the least emotionally stable mothers were the most emotionally stable. Their explanation of the obtained negative correlations included biological-environmental interactions, suggesting that characteristics that would lead to poor mental health in one environment could promote good mental health in another.

Rather than address issues about how biological factors influence behavior, socio-biological research has typically attempted to answer the question "how much is inherited?" Answers to that quantitative question will vary under different circumstances. Understanding how the interactions occur, however, should transcend particular circumstances.

A common genetic approach to assessing environmental impact can be described (albeit crudely) as one which assigns to environment what remains after identifying biological impact. Such an approach, however, ignores the role of environment in realizing genetically determined characteristics. Thus, for example, the most elegant Rex Begonia will not grow without sufficient shade, warmth, and moisture. These environmental requirements for Rex Begonia, though critical, could not be detected through strategies based on "subtracting out" genetic effects from studies of healthy plants. Further, the genetic approach to assessing environmental impact overlooks the fact that some types of environments have more impact than others. For example, Peperomias are practically immune to differences in light but can be quickly killed through too much watering, whereas sunlight is crucial for the growth of Gladiolus. Hybridizers who popularized rhododendrons and azaleas in the United States combined manipulation of genetic differences with knowledge of appropriate environments to produce at least 1,400 varieties of hardy blooming plants.[17] It seems unlikely that the interplay between genetics and environment would be less complex for human behavior.

Criminality within families could be a function of socialization practices more commonly found among families with a criminal heritage than among those without such heritage. Some differences in socialization practices could be produced

through biological differences. Impatience, high activity level, and ready boredom are likely to have an impact on how a parent reacts to child rearing. Furthermore, no *a priori* grounds exist for assuming that similar socialization techniques will have similar results with children who have inherited different
potentialities for aggressiveness. Regardless of the theoretical grounds for expecting differences, it would be wise to look for interactions between inherited and
environmental conditions to understand the production of criminal behavior.

The present investigation assumes the possibility that some form of criminal
diathesis can be genetically transmitted. As a preliminary approach to understanding the transmission, socialization practices of families in which fathers have
criminal records are compared with families in which the fathers are not criminal. The analyses then turn to two questions: What child-rearing characteristics—
added to or interacting with a transmitted potentiality—promote the criminal
behavior? And conversely, are there particular practices that serve as protective
factors?

Method

Subjects for the study came from a larger longitudinal investigation of males who
had been in a program designed to prevent delinquency. The delinquency prevention program included both "difficult" and "average" youngsters living in deteriorated urban areas of eastern Massachusetts. To permit evaluation of the program, boys in the treatment group had been matched to others from similar
neighborhoods and families prior to intervention. At the time of their introduction to the prevention program, the boys ranged in age from five to thirteen
($M=10.5$, $SD=1.6$). Although the treatment program failed to better the lives of
its charges, it left a legacy of carefully documented case materials.[18]

Approximately twice a month between 1939 and 1945, counselors visited the
homes of 253 boys from 232 families. The counselors appeared at various times
of day and throughout the week to help the boys and their families. After each
encounter, the counselors filed a detailed report that included conversations and
described behavior. Covering a span of more than five years, these running records
reveal the texture of family life. To avoid counting particular constellations of families more than once, this study used only one child per family in the analyses.
Additionally, 18 families in which the biological father could not be rated were
dropped from the analyses.

In 1957, coders—who had no access to information about the subjects other
than what was in the treatment records—transcribed information from the case
records into categorical scales describing the parents, the boys, and family interaction.[19] The present study used these categorical scales, dichotomized, to investigate the impact of socialization practices.

To estimate reliability of the coding, a second rater independently read a 10
percent random sample of the cases. The Scott Interrater Reliability Coefficient,
Pi,[20] was computed to indicate relative improvement over chance agreement
between two raters.[21] Inter-rater agreement as reflected in Scott's estimate of

improvement over chance ranged from 0.55 with 80 percent agreement on parental conflict to 0.92 with 96 percent agreement regarding family structure.

As part of the selection process in 1938, *neighborhoods* were rated in terms of delinquency rates, availability of recreational facilities, and proximity to bars, railroads, and junk yards. The variable describing neighborhood contexts was dichotomized to differentiate between those in the "worst" areas, those dominated by bars and debris, and the rest.

To identify *alcoholic fathers*, information from the case records was combined with information from the fathers' criminal records (which had been gathered in the late 1930s and again a decade later). A father was considered an alcoholic if he lost jobs because of drinking, had marital problems attributed primarily to excessive drinking, received treatment for alcoholism, had been convicted at least three times for public drunkenness, or if welfare agencies repeatedly noted that heavy drinking was the source of his problems. By these criteria, almost one-third of the fathers were alcoholics.

Fathers were coded as *absent* if for at least six months prior to the boy's seventeenth birthday, the boy's domicile was not the same as that of the father. This criterion resulted in identifying the fathers of 74 boys in the study as absent.

A rating of *parental conflict* was based on counselors' reports of disagreements about the child, values, money, alcohol, or religion. Ratings could be "no indication," "apparently none," "some," or "considerable." Parents were classified as evidencing or not evidencing considerable conflict.

If frequent, noncritical interaction occurred between the mother and her son, then the *mother's attitude toward her son* was classified as "affectionate." Alternative classifications were "passively affectionate" (concerned for the boy's welfare, but little interaction); "passively rejecting" (unconcerned for the boy's welfare and interacted little); "actively rejecting" (almost constantly critical of the boy); "ambivalent" (marked alternation between affection and rejection of the child); and "no indication."

How a mother reacted when faced with problems determined the *mother's self-confidence* rating. If she showed signs of believing in her ability to handle the difficulties, then she was rated as self-confident. Alternative ratings were "no indication," "victim or pawn," and "neutral."

Maternal restrictiveness was rated as "subnormal" if a mother permitted her son to make virtually all his choices without her guidance. Alternative ratings were "no indication," "normal" and "overly restrictive."

Supervision described the degree to which a boy's activities after school were governed by an adult. Supervision could be rated "present," or alternatively, "sporadic," "absent," or "no information."

The mother's discipline was classified both by type and by consistency. *Punitive discipline* included very harsh verbal abuse as well as the use of physical force to control the boy. A parent was classified as punitive for either erratic or consistent use of such techniques. *Consistent, nonpunitive discipline* identified a parent who used praise, rewards, or reasoning to control the boy. Alternative categories were "inconsistent, nonpunitive," "extremely lax, with almost no use of discipline," and "no information." Codes showing the mother's discipline as punitive and as consistent, nonpunitive were considered.[22]

The *aggressiveness of each parent* was rated as "unrestrained" if that parent regularly expressed anger by such activities as shouting abuses, yelling, throwing or breaking things, or hitting people. Alternative classifications were "no indication," "moderately aggressive," or "greatly inhibited." About 10 percent of the mothers were rated as highly aggressive and 16 percent of the fathers were so rated. In addition to the ratings of each parent separately, a combined rating identified a boy as exposed or not exposed to at least one highly aggressive parent.

Criminal records for fathers were gathered in 1948, when the fathers averaged fifty-two years in age (SD=7.2 years). Criminal records for the sons were collected in 1978, when they averaged fifty years in age (SD=1.6 years). Both fathers and sons were considered criminals if the record showed a conviction for a Type-1 Index crime: theft, breaking and entering, assault, murder, rape, attempted murder, or attempted rape.

Forty-nine fathers and 69 sons were criminals. Criminal sons constituted 45 percent of the 49 biological father-son pairs among which fathers were criminals, and 28 percent of the biological father-son pairs among which fathers were not criminals. Alternatively, of the 69 sons with criminal records, 32 percent had criminal fathers; of the 145 noncriminal sons, 18 percent had criminal fathers, $\chi^2_{(2)}$=4.659, Phi=0.148, p=0.031.

Results

Comparison between families in which fathers were criminals and those in which the fathers were not criminals revealed differences that might help to explain antisocial behavior among some sons of criminals. As compared with noncriminal fathers, those who had criminal records were more likely to be alcoholics and to be absent from the homes in which their sons were reared. The criminal fathers were also more likely to be highly aggressive and punitive. Parental conflict was more likely present in their families. Furthermore, the mothers of their sons were more likely to be aggressive (Table 14.1).

On the other hand, families of fathers with criminal records were not more likely than families of noncriminal fathers to live in the worst neighborhoods. Nor were their sons reliably less likely to have affectionate, self-confident mothers, to have consistent and nonpunitive discipline, to be supervised or to be subject to normal control (Table 14.2).

Collinearity among variables linked with a father's criminality may account for some of the cross-generational concordance in criminal behavior. For example, parental alcoholism and conflict are more prevalent among families in which fathers have been criminals; these variables, rather than paternal criminality, might cause delinquency. Possibly, however, parental alcoholism and conflict may be spuriously linked with delinquency; they are more prevalent among families in which fathers have been criminals, and criminality might have heritable components. To account for such covariations, criminogenic and protective factors were assessed among families with criminal fathers and separately in

TABLE 14.1   Differences Between Criminal and Noncriminal Fathers (percent of each group)

	Father criminal (N=49)	Father noncriminal (N=165)	p
Father alcoholic	57	24	.000
Father absent	53	29	.002
Parental conflict	55	25	.000
Father aggressive	31	13	.003
Mother aggressive	20	7	.008
Either parent aggressive	45	20	.000

TABLE 14.2   Comparisons Between Criminal and Noncriminal Fathers (percent of each group)

	Father criminal (N=49)	Father noncriminal (N=165)	p
Worst neighborhoods	29	32	>.05
Mother affectionate to son	45	48	>.05
Mother self-confident	27	30	>.05
Mother not restrictive	43	33	>.05
Boy supervised	49	60	>.05
Mother's discipline punitive	43	48	>.05
Mother consistently nonpunitive	31	30	>.05

families without them. In this manner, proclivities toward crime that might be transmitted biologically were controlled. Table 14.3 shows the relationships to criminality of the variables found more frequently in families with criminal than with noncriminal fathers.

Except through a relation to paternal criminality, neither paternal alcoholism nor a father's absence reliably increased the probability for the sons to be criminals. The top half of Table 14.3 compares sons who had criminal fathers. Among them, a majority of fathers of both criminal and noncriminal sons also were alcoholics. Viewed from the alternative perspective, 50 percent of the 28 sons whose fathers were both alcoholics and criminals had been convicted for Index crimes; 38 percent of the 21 sons whose fathers were criminals but not alcoholics had been convicted for Index crimes. Parallel differences appeared between sons of the noncriminals: 40 percent of the sons of alcoholics (N=40) and 25 percent of the sons of nonalcoholics (N=125) were convicted.

The relationship between paternal criminality and paternal absence may account for an apparent relationship between paternal absence and criminal behavior. At least in this sample, a slightly higher proportion of noncriminals than of criminals came from homes without fathers. Viewing the proportions from the direction opposite to that shown in Table 14.3 indicates that sons of criminals who were present in the home were more, rather than less, likely to become criminals: 48 percent (N=23) versus 42 percent (N=26) for father being present or absent,

TABLE 14.3   Differences Between Criminals and NonCriminals (percent of each group)

	Sons criminal (N=22)	Sons noncriminal (N=27)	p
A. CRIMINAL FATHERS			
Father alcoholic	64	52	NS
Father absent	50	56	NS
Parental conflict	77	37	.005
Father aggressive	45	19	.042
Mother aggressive	36	7	.012
Either parent aggressive	73	22	.000

	Sons criminal (N=47)	Sons noncriminal (N=118)	p
B. NONCRIMINAL FATHERS			
Father alcoholic	34	20	NS
Father absent	34	27	NS
Parental conflict	36	21	.046
Father aggressive	19	10	NS
Mother aggressive	13	5	NS
Either parent aggressive	32	15	.016

respectively. Among the sons of noncriminals, 33 percent of the 48 sons whose fathers were absent and 27 percent of the 117 sons whose fathers were present became criminals.

The data suggest that aggressive parental models, however, are criminogenic above and beyond their relationship to paternal criminality. Table 14.3 shows that approximately three-out-of-four of the criminals who had criminal fathers also had been exposed to parental conflict and aggression. These proportions more than double those found among noncriminal sons of criminals and criminal sons of noncriminals. Computed in the opposite direction, the proportions evidence the degree to which parental conflict and aggressiveness increased probabilities that sons of criminals and of noncriminals would be criminals. In 27 families with criminal fathers, a considerable amount of parental conflict occurred, and 63 percent of their sons were convicted for Index crimes. In contrast, a significantly smaller proportion, 23 percent of sons from criminal but nonconflictful family backgrounds, were convicted, $\chi^2_{(1)}=7.933$, $p < 0.005$. In 42 families with noncriminal fathers, a considerable amount of parental conflict also occurred, and 40 percent of their sons were convicted for Index crimes. In comparison, only 24 percent from nonconflictful backgrounds had been convicted, $\chi^2_{(1)}=3.977$, $p < 0.05$. In families with criminal fathers, 22 contained at least one parent exhibiting unrestrained aggressiveness. More than two-thirds (73%) of their sons, compared with 22 percent of the remaining sons of criminal fathers, were convicted for Index crimes, $\chi^2_{(1)}=12.499$, $p < 0.000$. Among the 33 sons of noncriminals having a parent who exhibited unrestrained aggressiveness, 45 percent were convicted for Index crimes; this proportion was reliably greater than the 24 percent of the remaining sons of

TABLE 14.4   Instigating Conditions and Crime (percent of sons who were criminals)

Number of instigating conditions	Fathers criminal	Fathers noncriminal
None	(N: 18) 17	(N: 104) 21
One	(N: 13) 38	(N: 18) 38
Two	(N: 18) 78	(N: 14) 50

$\chi^2(6)=55.159$; $p < .000$.

noncriminal fathers who were convicted, $\chi^2_{(1)}=5.831$, $p < 0.016$. The instigating impact of parental aggressiveness and conflict appears to accumulate. Table 14.4 shows the criminogenic effects of combining aggressive models with criminogenic heritage.

As Table 14.4 indicates, sons of criminal fathers were more likely to be exposed to socializing conditions conducive to crime. Furthermore, instigating conditions interact with criminogenic heritage in such a way as to increase the potentiality for crime when aggressive parents were in open conflict.

Although criminal fathers were not more likely than noncriminal fathers to live in the worst neighborhoods or to be married to women who showed signs of being poor mothers, effects of neighborhood or family socialization practices might depend on whether the child had inherited conditions that promote criminality. To inspect the possibility, criminality among sons of criminals and among sons of

TABLE 14.5   Differences Between Criminals and Noncriminals (percent of each group)

	Sons criminal (N=22)	Sons noncriminal (N=27)	p
A. CRIMINAL FATHERS			
Worst neighborhoods	45	15	.018
Mother affectionate to son	23	63	.005
Mother self-confident	5	44	.002
Mother not restrictive	64	26	.008
Boy supervised	36	59	NS
Mother's discipline punitive	64	26	.008
Mother consistently nonpunitive	9	48	.003
	Sons criminal (N=47)	Sons noncriminal (N=118)	p
B. NONCRIMINAL FATHERS			
Worst neighborhoods	34	31	NS
Mother affectionate to son	36	53	.046
Mother self-confident	17	35	.025
Mother not restrictive	43	29	NS
Boy supervised	45	66	.011
Mother's discipline punitive	53	46	NS
Mother consistently nonpunitive	21	33	NS

noncriminals were examined. Table 14.5 displays the results. Living in unstable neighborhoods appeared to have a criminogenic effect only on sons who had a criminogenic heritage. The relationship can be brought out by examining proportions from the alternative perspective. Fourteen of the families with criminal fathers lived in the worst neighborhoods, and 71 percent of the sons in these families were convicted for Index crimes. In comparison, 34 percent of the sons of criminals living in better neighborhoods were likewise convicted, $\chi^2_{(1)}=5.576$, $p < 0.02$. Only 30 percent of the 53 sons from the worst neighborhoods whose fathers were not criminal were convicted, as were 28 percent of the sons of noncriminal fathers reared in better neighborhoods.

Reliably lower proportions of criminals than of noncriminals had mothers who were affectionate or self-confident. Mothers appeared to be particularly influential in determining whether sons of criminal men became criminal. Maternal affection, self-confidence, and consistently nonpunitive discipline or supervision apparently helped to protect their sons from criminogenic influences. These protective effects are brought out through examining the proportions who became criminals from various types of backgrounds.

Among the sons of criminals, for example, there were 22 men who had affectionate mothers. Although only 23 percent of these were convicted for Index crimes, 63 percent of the 27 sons of criminals whose mothers were not affectionate were convicted, $\chi^2_{(1)}=7.933$, $p < 0.005$. Differences in crime rates related to maternal affection were less dramatic among sons of noncriminal fathers: 21 percent of the men with affectionate mothers ($N=80$) and 35 percent of the remaining men ($N=85$) were convicted, $\chi^2_{(1)}=3.990$, $p < 0.05$.

Maternal self-confidence appeared to be an antidote to whatever criminogenic influences were transmitted from father to son. Only 1 of the 13 men who had criminal fathers and self-confident mothers was convicted for an Index crime; that 8 percent was reliably lower than the 58 percent who became criminals among the remaining 36 sons of criminals, $\chi^2_{(1)}=9.901$, $p < 0.002$.

Among sons of noncriminals, those whose mothers were self-confident ($N=49$) were less likely to be convicted than those whose mothers were not self-confident ($N=116$): 16 percent versus 34 percent, $\chi^2_{(1)}=5.058$, $p < 0.03$.

Among sons of criminals who had received little direction from their mothers ($N=21$), 67 percent became criminals; the proportion was reliably greater than the 29 percent ($N=28$) who became criminals despite more directive mothers, $\chi^2_{(1)}=7.039$, $p < 0.008$. Differences related to maternal restrictions among sons of noncriminals were not reliable.

The mother's consistent, nonpunitive discipline seemed also to be protective. Although only 13 percent of the sons of criminals whose mothers used consistent, nonpunitive discipline ($N=15$) were convicted for Index crimes, 59 percent of the remaining sons of criminals ($N=34$) were convicted, $\chi^2_{(1)}=8.706$, $p < 0.003$. On the other hand, 67 percent of the sons of criminals whose mothers used punitive discipline ($N=21$) were convicted for Index crimes, although only 29 percent of the remaining sons of criminal fathers ($N=28$) were convicted, $\chi^2_{(1)}=7.039$, $p < 0.008$. Neither comparison among the sons of noncriminals yielded a statistically reliable difference.

TABLE 14.6 Protective Factors and Crime (percent of sons who were criminals)

Number of protective factors	Fathers criminal	Fathers noncriminal
None	(N: 25) 64	(N: 39) 44
One	(N: 8) 50	(N: 46) 35
Two	(N: 6) 33	(N: 58) 21
Three	(N: 10) 0	(N: 22) 9

$\chi^2(9)=47.060$; $p < .000$.

Supervision had only a slight effect on sons of criminals. Among sons of non-criminals, however, supervision seemed to be protective. Only 21 percent of the 99 supervised sons compared with 39 percent of the 66 unsupervised sons were convicted, $\chi^2_{(1)}=6.426$, $p < 0.02$.

Maternal affection, self-confidence, and consistently nonpunitive discipline or supervision served as protections against criminogenic influences. The joint effects of these variables were analyzed by defining a scale in which affection, self-confidence, and having either consistently nonpunitive discipline (among sons of criminals) or supervision (among sons of noncriminals) were given equal weights. Table 14.6 shows the cumulative impact of protective factors.

Stepwise discriminant analyses indicated that instigating and protective factors contributed to criminal rates among sons both with and without heritable risk for criminality. The instigating and protective measures were more discriminating among the sons of criminals, accounting for only 9 percent of the variance among sons of noncriminals but accounting for 37.8 percent of the variance among sons of criminals (Table 14.7).

Pairs of discriminant functions were built from the two scales representing protective and instigating conditions. These functions maximized discrimination between criminal and noncriminal sons. The functions correctly identified 18 of the 22 criminals (82%) and 21 of the 27 noncriminals (78%) whose fathers were criminals, together correctly discriminating 79.5 percent of the sons of criminals. Among the sons of noncriminals, the functions correctly identified 26 of the 47 criminals (55%) and 82 of the 118 noncriminals (69%), together correctly

TABLE 14.7 Stepwise Discriminant Analysis (criminals distinguished from noncriminals)

	Partial R^2	Prob. $> F$	Mean R^2
A. SONS OF CRIMINALS			
Instigation	.277	.0001	.277
Protection	.140	.0088	.378
B. SONS OF NONCRIMINALS			
Protection	.066	.0008	.066
Instigation	.025	.0433	.090

identifying 65 percent of the sons of noncriminals. Knowledge about socialization practices clearly provided more accurate classification than would have knowledge of biological risk alone.

Summary and Discussion

A century ago, Havelock Ellis reminded his readers of two factors in criminal heredity: "There is the element of innate disposition, and there is the element of contagion from social environment.... Frequently the one element alone, whether the heredity or the contagion, is not sufficient to determine the child in the direction of crime."[23]

Nevertheless, during most of the twentieth century, social scientists have spent their energies disputing the case for nature *or* nurture, thus making little progress toward understanding how the interactions influence behavior. This study attempted to focus attention on how environmental conditions affect those who inherit different biologically based predispositions toward crime.

This study controlled for unknown factors that can be attributed to heritage. Admittedly, the control was incomplete, because no convincing evidence exists that all criminals are criminals through heritable characteristics. By comparing effects of socialization among sons of men who were and who were not criminals, however, heritable qualities related to crime were included in the analyses.

To gain understanding of the processes accounting for intergenerational transmission of aggression, families in which fathers had been convicted for serious crimes were compared with families in which the fathers were not known to be criminals. This comparison suggests that criminal fathers had a greater likelihood of being alcoholic, aggressive, punitive, and absent. They were also more likely than their noncriminal counterparts to be in conflict with probably aggressive wives.

On the other hand, sons of criminals were not more likely than their peers to live in the worst neighborhoods, to be rejected or subjected to maternal punitiveness, or to be deprived of competent maternal guidance.

Socialization variables fell into two sets. One set promoted crime. These "instigating conditions" were more common in families of criminal fathers than in families of noncriminal fathers. The set included parental conflict and aggression.

The second set was found with approximately equal frequency among families of both criminal and noncriminal fathers. These variables described socialization practices that seemed to reduce the likelihood of crime. The protective factors included having a self-confident mother and maternal affection. Effects of discipline as protection against criminogenic influences depended on whether the family was at genetic risk for criminality. In families having criminal fathers, nonpunitive and consistent discipline had beneficial effects. Although discipline made little difference in families without criminal fathers, supervision seemed beneficial. One may view these differences as indicating that genetically related potentialities require "fertilizer" to develop into antisocial behavior—fertilizer not available when parents provide the protections of affection and clearly specified directives.

Outcome of genetic risk depended on accompanying instigating conditions. That is, unless there was parental conflict and at least one aggressive parent, sons

TABLE 14.8   Heritable Risk, Instigating Conditions, Protective Factors and Crime (percent criminal in each group)

	Father criminal	Father noncriminal
Instigation low and protection high	(N: 10) 0	(N: 61) 11
Instigation low and protection low	(N: 8) 38	(N: 43) 35
Instigation high and protection high	(N: 6) 33	(N: 19) 37
Instigation high and protection low	(N: 25) 68	(N: 42) 43

Source	Categorical analysis of variance table		
	df	Chi-square	Prob.
Father's criminality	1	12.11	.0005
Instigation	1	11.24	.0008
Protection	1	5.39	.0203
Instigation × protection	1	4.86	.0275

of criminals were not more likely to become criminals than were sons of noncriminals.

To examine joint effects of instigating and protecting factors, the scales measuring these influences were divided as close to the mean as possible. Crime rates within categories also were computed. Table 14.8 shows the results.

A categorical analysis of variance[24] evaluating the impact of paternal criminality, instigating conditions, protective factors, and their interactions indicated that each main effect was significant, and that the interaction between instigation and protection was also significant. None of the interactions with paternal criminality was significant, though the distributions show that heritable risk covaried with high instigating and low protective conditions.

Alternative explanations may account for these results. An emphasis on the social interpretation could call upon studies showing that children imitate aggression.[25] An emphasis on the biological interpretation might suggest that parental aggressiveness signifies particularly strong genetic loading on criminogenic factors.

Rather than try to decide which is more cogent, it is worth noting that biological potentialities *must* provide necessary conditions for crime. These conditions may well vary according to dimensions of criminal acts, some requiring speed and some requiring brawn, for example. Beyond these essentials, the present study indicates that biological conditions may promote or retard criminal behavior. Perhaps more importantly, the data suggest that socialization practices have a considerable effect on how the biological potentialities develop into antisocial behavior.

Evidence from the present study indicates that the protective nature of maternal warmth and competence are particularly salient in reducing genetically transmitted characteristics that promote antisocial behavior. This discovery leads to a tentative conclusion that intervention techniques designed to develop competence among parents may be particularly effective when the targets are children at high genetic risk.

Notes

This study was partially supported by United States Public Health Service Research Grant MH26779, National Institute of Mental Health (Center for Studies of Crime and Delinquency). The author wishes to express appreciation to the Department of Probation of the Commonwealth of Massachusetts, the Division of Criminal Justice Services of the State of New York, the Maine State Bureau of Identification, and the states of California, Florida, Michigan, New Jersey, Pennsylvania, Virginia, and Washington for supplemental data about the men. Only the author is responsible for the statistical analyses and for the conclusions drawn from this research. The author thanks Richard Parente, Robert Staib, Ellen Myers, and Ann Cronin for their work in tracing the men and their records and Joan Immel, Tom Smedile, Harriet Sayre, Mary Duell, Elise Goldman, Abby Brodkin, and Laura Otten for their careful coding.

1. See, e.g., S. GLUECK & E. GLUECK, UNRAVELING JUVENILE DELINQUENCY (1950); L. ROBINS, DEVIANT CHILDREN GROWN UP (1966); Farrington, *Environmental Stress, Delinquent Behavior, and Convictions*, in 6 STRESS and ANXIETY 93 (I. Sarason & C. Spielberger eds. 1979); Lewis, Pincus, Lovely, Spitzer & Moy, *Biopsychosocial Characteristics of Matched Samples of Delinquents and Nondelinquents*, 26 J. AM. ACAD. CHILD AND ADOLESCENT PSYCHIATRY 744 (1987); McCord, *Some Child-Rearing Antecedents of Criminal Behavior in Adult Men*, 37 J. PERSONALITY AND SOC. PSYCHOLOGY 1477 (1979); Offord, *Family Backgrounds of Male and Female Delinquents*, in ABNORMAL OFFENDERS, DELINQUENCY, AND THE CRIMINAL JUSTICE SYSTEM 129 (J. Gunn & D.P. Farrington eds. 1982); Pulkkinen, *Search for Alternatives to Aggression in Finland*, in AGGRESSION IN GLOBAL PERSPECTIVE 104 (A. Goldstein & M. Segall eds. 1983).

2. CALL, *Child Abuse and Neglect in Infancy: Sources of Hostility Within the Parent-Infant Dyad and Disorders of Attachment in Infancy*, 8 CHILD ABUSE AND NEGLECT 185 (1984); Gelles, *Violence in the Family: A Review of Research in the Seventies*, 42 J. MARRIAGE & FAM. 873 (1980); Egeland & Sroufe, *Developmental Sequelae of Maltreatment in Infancy*, in DEVELOPMENTAL PERSPECTIVES ON CHILD MALTREATMENT 77 (R. Rizley & D. Cicchetti eds. 1981) [herein after DEVELOPMENTAL PERSPECTIVES]; Herrenkohl & Herrenkohl, *Some Antecedents and Developmental Consequences of Child Maltreatment*, in DEVELOPMENTAL PERSPECTIVES, this note, at 57; Jouriles, Barling & O'Leary, *Predicting Child Behavior Problems in Maritally Violent Families*, 15 J. ABNORMAL CHILD PSYCHOLOGY 165 (1987); Main & Goldwyn, *Predicting Rejection of Her Infant From Mother's Representation of Her Own Experience: Implications for the Abused-Abusing Intergenerational Cycle*, 8 CHILD ABUSE AND NEGLECT 203 (1984); McCord, *A Forty Year Perspective on Effects of Child Abuse and Neglect*, 7 CHILD ABUSE AND NEGLECT 265 (1983); Widom, *Child Abuse, Neglect, and Violent Criminal Behavior*, 27 CRIMINOLOGY 251 (1989).

3. GOODMAN & STEVENSON, *A Twin Study of Hyperactivity. 1. An Examination of Hyperactivity Scores and Categories Derived from Rutter Teacher and Parent Questionnaires*, 30 J. CHILD PSYCHOLOGY, PSYCHIATRY AND ALLIED DISCIPLINES 671 (1989).

4. See, e.g., GOLDSMITH & GOTTESMAN, *Origins of Variation in Behavioral Style: A Longitudinal Study of Temperament in Young Twins*, 52 CHILD DEV. 91 (1981); Pedersen, Plomin, McClearn & Friberg, *Neuroticism, Extraversion, and Related Traits in Adult Twins Reared Apart and Reared Together*, 55 J. PERSONALITY AND SOC. PSYCHOLOGY 950 (1988).

5. BOHMAN, CLONINGER, SIGVARDSSON & VON KNORRING, *Predisposition to Petty Criminality in Swedish Adoptees*, 39 ARCHIVES GEN. PSYCHIATRY 1233 (1982); Crowe, *An Adoptive Study of Psychopathy: Preliminary Results from Arrest Records and Psychiatric Hospital Records*, in GENETIC RESEARCH IN PSYCHIATRY 95 (R. Fieve, D. Rosenthal & H. Brill eds. 1975); Mednick, Gabrielli & Hutchings, *Genetic Factors in the Etiology of Criminal Behavior*, in THE CAUSES OF CRIME: NEW BIOLOGICAL APPROACHES 74 (S. Mednick, T. Moffitt & S. Stack eds. 1987) [hereinafter THE CAUSES OF CRIME]; Schulsinger, *Psychopathy: Heredity and Environment*, in BIOSOCIAL BASES OF CRIMINAL BEHAVIOR 109 (S. Mednick & K. Christiansen eds. 1977) [hereinafter BIOSOCIAL BASES].

6. HUESMANN & ERON, *Cognitive Processes and the repsistence of Aggressive Behavior*, 10 AGGRESSIVE BEHAV. 243 (1984); Eron, Huesmann, Dubow, Romanoff & Yarmel, *Aggression and Its Correlates Over 22 Years*, in CHILDHOOD AGGRESSION AND VIOLENCE: SOURCES OF INFLUENCE, PREVENTION, AND CONTROL 249 (D. Crowell, I. Evans & C. O'Donnell eds. 1987).

7. H. EYSENCK & G. GUDJONSSON, THE CAUSES AND CURES OF CRIMINALITY (1989); M. Haller, EUGENICS: HEREDITARIAN ATTITUDES IN AMERICAN THOUGHT (1963); *id.* (paperback ed. 1984).

8. E. MACCOBY & C. JACKLIN, THE PSYCHOLOGY OF SEX DIFFERENCES (1974); Maccoby & Jacklin, *Sex Differences in Aggression: A Rejoinder and Reprise*, 51 CHILD DEV. 964 (1980); Mednick & Volavka, *Biology and Crime*, in 2 CRIME AND JUST.: AN ANNUAL REVIEW OF RES. 85 (N. Morris & M. Tonry eds. 1980); Olweus, *Aggression and Hormones: Behavioral Relationship With Testosterone and Adrenaline*, in DEVELOPMENT OF ANTISOCIAL AND PROSOCIAL BEHAVIOR 51 (D. Olweus, J. Block & M. Yarrow eds. 1986); Olweus, *Testosterone and Adrenaline: Aggressive Antisocial Behavior in Normal Adolescent Males*, in THE CAUSES OF CRIME, *supra* note 5, at 263.

9. FARRINGTON, *Implications of Biological Findings for Criminological Research*, in THE CAUSES OF CRIME, *supra* note 5, at 42; Hare, *Electrodermal and Cardiovascular Correlates of Psychopathy*, in PSYCHOPATHIC BEHAVIOUR 107 (R. Hare & D. Schalling eds. 1978); Mednick, *A Bio-Social Theory of the Learning of Law-Abiding Behavior*, in BIOSOCIAL BASES, *supra* note 5, at 1; Satterfield, *Childhood Diagnostic and Neurophysiological Predictors of Teenage Arrest Rates: An Eight-Year Prospective Study*, in THE CAUSES OF CRIME, *supra* note 5, at 146; Siddle, *Electrodermal Activity and Psychopathy*, in BIOSOCIAL BASES, *supra* note 5, at 199; Wadsworth, *Delinquency, Pulse Rates and Early Emotional Deprivation*, 16 BRIT. J. CRIMINOLOGY 245 (1976).

10. GABRIELLI & MEDNICK, *Sinistrality and Delinquency*, 89 J. ABNORMAL PSYCHOLOGY 654 (1980).

11. BUIKHUISEN, *Cerebral Dysfunctions and Persistent Juvenile Delinquency*, in THE CAUSES OF CRIME, *supra* note 5, at 168; H. Ellis, THE CRIMINAL (1890); *id.* (reprinted 1972); Goodman & Stevenson, *A Twin Study of Hyperactivity. 2. The Aetiological Role of Genes, Family Relationships & Perinatal Adversity*, 30 J. CHILD PSYCHOLOGY, PSYCHIATRY AND ALLIED DISCIPLINES 691 (1989); Moffitt & Silva, *Self-Reported Delinquency, Neuropsychological Deficit, and History of Attention Deficit Disorder*, 16 J. ABNORMAL CHILD PSYCHOLOGY 553 (1988); Schalling, *Psychopathy-Related Personality Variables and the Psychophysiology of Socialization*, in PSYCHOPATHIC BEHAV. 85 (R. Hare & D. Schalling eds. 1978).

12. *See, e.g.*, BOHMAN, *Some Genetic Aspects of Alcoholism and Criminality: A Population of Adoptees*, 35 ARCHIVES GEN. PSYCHIATRY 269 (1978); Feehan, Stanton, McGee, Silva & Moffitt, *Is There an Association Between Lateral Preference and Delinquent Behavior?*, 99 J. ABNORMAL PSYCHOLOGY 198 (1990); Frost, Moffitt & McGee, *Neuropsychological Correlates of Psychopathology in an Unselected Cohort of Young Adolescents*, 98 J. ABNORMAL PSYCHOLOGY 307 (1989); Mawson & Mawson, *Psychopathy and Arousal: A New Interpretation of the Psychophysiological Literature*, 12 BIOLOGICAL PSYCHIATRY 49 (1977); Nachshon & Denno, *Violent Behavior and Cerebral Hemisphere Function*, in THE CAUSES OF CRIME, *supra* note 5, at 185; Plomin, Foch & Rowe, *Bobo Clown Aggression in Childhood: Environment, Not Genes*, 15 J. RESEARCH IN PERSONALITY 331 (1981); Riese, *Neonatal Temperament in Monozygotic and Dizygotic Twin Pairs*, 61 Child Dev. 1230 (1990); Schalling, *Personality Correlates of Plasma Testosterone Levels in Young Delinquents: An Example of Person-Situation Interaction?*, in THE CAUSES OF CRIME, *supra* note 5, at 283; Schmauk, *Punishment, Arousal, and Avoidance Learning in Sociopaths*, 76 J. ABNORMAL PSYCHOLOGY 325 (1970); Siddle & Trasler, *The Psychophysiology of Psychopathic Behaviour*, in FOUNDATIONS OF PSYCHOSOMATICS 283 (M. Christie & P. Mellett eds. 1981); Venables, *Autonomic Nervous System Factors in Criminal Behavior*, in THE CAUSES OF CRIME, *supra* note 5, at 110.

13. For exceptions, see H. STÅTTIN & D. MAGNUSSON, PUBERTAL MATURATION IN FEMALE DEVELOPMENT (1990), and Udry, *Biological Predispositions and Social Control in Adolescent Sex-*

ual Behavior, 53 AM. SOC. REV. 709 (1988), on the contribution of interaction between physical maturity and peers to adolescent deviant behavior among girls.

14. D. FALCONER, INTRODUCTION TO QUANTITATIVE GENETICS (1960).

15. For evidence and a review of such studies, see Webster & Driskell, *Beauty as Status*, 89 AM. J. SOC. 140 (1983).

16. LOEHLIN, WILLERMAN & HORN, *Personality Resemblances Between Unwed Mothers and Their Adopted-Away Offspring*, 42 J. PERSONALITY AND SOC. PSYCHOLOGY 1089 (1982).

17. P. Livingston & F. West, HYBRIDS AND HYBRIDIZERS: RHODODENDRONS AND AZALEAS FOR EASTERN NORTH AMERICA (1978).

18. Results of the treatment program have been reported in McCord, *A Thirty-Year Follow-Up of Treatment Effects*, 33 AM. PSYCHOLOGIST 284 (1978); McCord, *Consideration of Some Effects of a Counseling Program*, in NEW DIRECTIONS IN THE REHABILITATION OF CRIMINAL OFFENDERS 394 (S. Martin, L. Sechrest & R. Redner eds. 1981); McCord, *Crime in Moral and Social Contexts*, 28 CRIMINOLOGY 1 (1990).

19. *See* W. McCORD & J. McCORD, ORIGINS OF ALCOHOLISM (1960).

20. Scott, *Reliability of Content Analysis: The Case of Nominal Scale Coding*, 3 PUB. OPINION Q. 321 (1955).

21. Pi=(Po-Pe)/(1-Pe), where Po represents observed agreement between raters and Pe represents percent of agreement expected by chance, computed by summing the squared proportions of the cases in each category.

22. These were not, of course, independent ratings.

23. H. ELLIS, THE CRIMINAL 92 (1890).

24. SAS, SAS USER'S GUIDE (1985).

25. BANDURA & HUSTON, *Identification as a Process of Incidental Learning*, 63 J. ABNORMAL AND SOC. PSYCHOLOGY 311 (1961); Bandura, Ross & Ross, *Transmission of Aggression Through Imitation of Aggressive Models*, 63 J. ABNORMAL AND SOC. PSYCHOLOGY 575 (1961); Hall & Cairns, *Aggressive Behavior in Children: An Outcome of Modeling or Social Reciprocity?*, 20 DEVELOPMENTAL PSYCHOLOGY 739 (1984); McCord, *Parental Behavior in the Cycle of Aggression*, 51 PSYCHIATRY 14 (1988).

CHAPTER FIFTEEN

Family Socialization and Antisocial Behavior

Searching for Causal Relationships in Longitudinal Research*

FOR MANY OF US, longitudinal research has involved a deep commitment, a commitment that has seemed justified by the promise of answers to profound questions. We have, in effect, accepted the credo expressed by John Stuart Mill (1843/1973) who wrote: "Of all truths relating to phenomena the most valuable to us are those which relate to the order of their succession. On a knowledge of these is founded every reasonable anticipation of future facts, and whatever power we possess of influencing those facts to our advantage" (p. 324).

Despite the social benefits which success in predictions seemed to promise, interventions to prevent crime have largely failed. Some have explained the failures in terms of implementation, suggesting that the programs have been inconsistent or inadequate. Some have explained failure in terms of dosage, arguing that too little treatment has been given. I suggest that failure may be due to wrong theories about the causes of crime.

Studies of causes of crime run into difficulty, in part, because criminals—serious street criminals, at least—differ in so many ways from law abiding citizens. Almost any reasonable theory about crime seems to be supported by *some* evidence. Studies of crime causation run into trouble, too, because we do not have a meaningful typology in relation to developmental issues. Such studies typically assume that similar environmental conditions have similar effects, ignoring individual differences in the process.

To do research, we identify particular descriptions of complex events and then err in believing that these descriptions necessarily identify causally relevant

---

*Reprinted from McCord, J. 1994. Family socialization and antisocial behavior: Searching for causal relationships in longitudinal research. In *Cross-National Longitudinal Research on Human Development and Criminal Behavior*, edited by I. Gm. M. Weitekamp and H-J. Kerner, 177–188. Dordrecht, Netherlands: Kluwer; with kind permission of Springer Science and Business Media of Springer Science and Business Media.

TABLE 15.1   Hypothetical Study: Convictions in Two Generations

	Father	Father not convicted	Convicted
Son convicted	1100	1500	2600
Son not convicted	1500	7500	9000
TOTAL	2600	9000	11600

$\chi^2(1)=762.66$; Phi$=+.26$; $p=.0000$.

variables. Poverty, lack of education, and diseases seem to accompany crime. Attempts to learn which, if any of these, play a causal role may be fruitless. Environments always interact with genetically determined effects. Empirical attempts to identify relative contributions run into problems because measured relations reflect unreliability, random error, and the amount of variation in the sample.

The social environments in which crimes occur contain potentially active causal influences. We ought not assume that the background variables play no role in the outcome events. A case in point may be the role of attachment in producing crime. Delinquents appear to lack attachment to adults, but close relations introduced through intervention programs fail to reduce the probability of crime. Relevant background conditions may include the competence of a parent (if parental competence leads to close relations in the natural environment), children's compliance (if parents are more likely to have close relations with compliant children), or spontaneity of attraction (if close relations are effective insulators only when they appear spontaneously).

Although crime is an intentional event, motives have typically been treated as peripheral. Yet whatever may be true regarding causes of crime, an adequate theory must allow room for convicted people to be responsible for their actions.

The psychologist Paul Meehl (1978) suggested that theories rise and fall because of baffled boredom. He warned that a criterion of statistical significance ought not be used as a measure of truth, cautioning that the null hypothesis will always be falsified with enough cases unless measures are totally unreliable.

Criminologists, however, have tended to assume that large numbers are advantageous to discovering how events relate to one another. We seem to have forgotten, if ever we knew, the paradox Simpson presented to the *Royal Statistical Society* in 1951 (reported in Kendall, 1975). The paradox arises because relationships found among heterogeneous samples may lead to conclusions true for none

TABLE 15.2   Hypothetical Study: West German Socialization

	Father	Father not convicted	Convicted
Son convicted	100	1000	1100
Son not convicted	1000	7300	8300
TOTAL	1100	8300	9400

$\chi^2(1)=8.22$; Phi$=-.03$; $p=.0041$.

TABLE 15.3 Interrater Reliability: Dichotomous Variables (2 raters on 10 percent random sample)

Characteristic	Percent agreement	Scott Pi[a]
Mother's affection for son	84	.68
Mother's self-confidence	84	.60
Mother's disciplinary consistency	84	.62
Mother's role in family	96	.91
Mother's restrictiveness	84	.65
Mother's aggressiveness	92	.56
Mother's esteem for father	88	.76
Father's affection for son	84	.57
Father's esteem for mother	84	.68
Father's aggressiveness	84	.41
Father's discipline	88	.52
Family conflict	80	.55
Supervision of boy	88	.76
Demands for boy	76	.35

[a]$Pi=(P_o -: P_e)/(1 - P_e)$. P_o=percent agreement observed. P_e=percent agreement expected: $P_e=(p)^2 + (q)^2$, where p=proportion having the characteristic and $q=1$.

or only some of the subsamples. The paradox is profound because, unfortunately, heterogeneity might not be known in advance.

Other problems are more familiar. They include questions about the direction of causality. If measures are gathered longitudinally, it is tempting to assume that the temporal order in which they are gathered represents the order of occurrence. That mistake can be critical when sequences serve to identify causes. The problem of temporal order is particularly difficult because of ignorance about duration and developmental patterns. A first arrest may follow breakup of a marriage; yet unofficial criminality might have preceded—perhaps caused—the marital breakup. Poor socialization practices may precede criminal behavior; yet children's disruptive behavior might produce rejection and inappropriate discipline.

The argument that bad children induce poor parental interactions has gained credence in recent years. Credibility has rested, in part, on experimental evidence showing that when children's behavior is altered through administration of methylphenidate, mothers blind to whether their children have been given drugs or a placebo are more responsive to their hyperactive sons (Dupaul and Barkley, 1992). Credibility has gained support, too, from the degree of constancy found in studies testing continuity of aggression. In their longitudinal study of a New Zealand birth cohort, for example, White, Moffitt, Earls, Robins, and Silva (1990) found that antisocial behavior at age eleven was related to police contacts at age fifteen. The authors concluded that "behavioral problems are the best preschool predictors of antisocial behavior at age 11" (1990, p. 519).

Halfway around the world, in London, Farrington (1986) had discovered similar continuities. After tracing a cohort of boys living in impoverished areas of

TABLE 15.4 Cluster Analysis

Group variable	R-square		Scoring coefficient
	Highest	Second	
Mother's competence			
Disciplinary consistency	.553	.104	.386
Self-confidence	.479	.087	.359
Affection for son	.472	.084	.357
Role in family	.422	.054	.337
Father's interaction			
Father's esteem for mother	.669	.053	.320
Mother's esteem for father	.720	.058	.332
Parental conflict	.532	.049	−.286
Father's affection for son	.323	.045	.222
Father's aggressiveness	.312	.050	−.219
Family monitoring			
Mother's restrictiveness	.710	.096	−.478
Supervision	.692	.154	.472
Demands	.360	.054	.341

	Correlations		
	A	B	C
A Mother's competence	—		
B Father's interaction	0.29	—	
C Family monitoring	0.41	0.31	—

London between the ages of 8 and 24 years, Farrington concluded: "the continuity of troublesome, delinquent, deviant, and criminal behavior from childhood to adulthood seems striking" (p. 373).

Other research has shown high correspondence between aggression or disruptive behavior in childhood and antisocial behavior as adults (e.g., Eron, 1986; Eron, Walder, and Lefkowitz, 1971; Farrington, 1978; McCord, 1983; Patterson, Crosby, & Vuchinich, 1992; Robins & Ratcliff, 1979; Robins, 1966; Satterfield, 1987; Stattin & Magnusson, 1989).

As a consequence of such continuities, Eron, Huesmann, and Zelli (1991) plausibly hypothesized: "Perhaps parental rejection and punishment are reactions to the aggressive behavior that the youngster originally displays and lack of identification then results from the aversive nature of the interactions between parent and child" (p. 179). If Eron and others who share this view are correct, socialization practices would be only accidentally related to the behaviors they predict.

To test the hypothesis about causal direction in relation to parental socialization practices, I turned to evidence from a longitudinal study of males reared in Cambridge and Somerville, Massachusetts.

Methods

Overview

The Cambridge-Somerville Youth Study was designed to assist families living in pockets of poverty in the greater Boston area (Powers and Witmer, 1951). To avoid stigmatizing participants, both "difficult" and "average" boys were included. As a result, about half the boys were considered to be at high risk for delinquency.

The boys were born between 1926 and 1934, with the mean and mode in 1928. Between 1936 and 1939, a selection committee identified pairs they considered similar in terms of conditions thought to cause delinquency. Selection included teachers' reports collected between 1933 and 1938. By tossing a coin, one member of each pair was selected for treatment.

The larger study included 253 pairs of boys. Records for the control group had been based largely on interviews with the mothers and the boys. In order to use strong measures of family interaction, the control families are not included in the present study.

To justify treating each case as independent, only one son from a family was included. Eliminating siblings resulted in dropping 21 boys. To incorporate a clear temporal order for the measured variables, boys who had reached the age of ten prior to having their teachers describe their behavior ($N=17$) and those whose arrest records began prior to the age of ten ($N=9$) were eliminated. After these eliminations 207 cases remained.

Family life was coded from the records describing what went on over a period of approximately 5.5 years between 1939 and 1945, when social workers visited the homes in order to provide a variety of types of assistance to the boys and their families. These records were coded in 1957. Criminal records for the sons were collected between 1978 and 1982, when the men were middle-aged.

Measures

The boys were between the ages of 4 and 9 years in age (mean=7.5), when their teachers described them by checking descriptive phrases on a "Trait Record Card." Boys were considered to have been aggressive if their teachers checked "fights" as part of the description ($N=50$). They were classified as being conduct disordered if their teachers checked more than three of the following: blames others for his difficulties; secretive, crafty, sly; rude, saucy, impudent; disobeys; refuses to cooperate; cruel; cheats; lies; steals; destroys property. Among the 30 boys so classified, 18 had also been considered aggressive. Combined, these measures of disruptive behavior identified 62 of the boys.

Evaluations of family interactions were derived from case records written when the boys ranged from 10.5 to 16 years in age. The records were coded 35 years ago by researchers unaware of information about the boys other than that contained in the case records. Interrater agreement was tested through having a 10 percent random sample of the cases read by a second rater. For variables used in the present study, agreement on classifications ranged from 76 percent (for whether demands placed on the child were high) to 96 percent (for whether the mother showed leadership in the family).

A clustering procedure employed to reduce collinearity identified three meaningful clusters (Varclus, SAS, 1985). This procedure searches for unidimensional factors in terms of combinations of variables that maximize variance among cluster centroids. The first cluster, one that represented the mother's competence, included her discipline, self-confidence, affection for her son, and role. A second dimension, representing the father's interaction, included the parents' esteem for each other, parental conflict, the father's affection for his son, and his aggressiveness. A third dimension, representing monitoring, included maternal restrictiveness, supervision, and demands.

The Varclus procedure reduced collinearity to acceptable levels. To stabilize and simplify the scales, items in each cluster were given equal weights and scored so that higher values represent more socially desirable behaviors: greater mother's competence; more approving, less aggressive father's interaction; and higher degrees of monitoring. Scales were dichotomized as close to the median as possible, permitting description of a family as better or worse on each dimension. Criminality was evaluated through official records gathered in Massachusetts, where approximately 80 percent of the men continued to reside, and in the states to which they had migrated. These records were collected when the men averaged 50 years in age. A man was considered to be a criminal if he had been convicted for a serious crime, that is, one indexed by the Federal Bureau of Investigation (e.g., auto theft, breaking and entering, assault, rape, or attempted murder). The sample included 65 men who had such convictions.

Results

Disruptive Behavior and Criminality

Children who had been disruptive during primary school were, as anticipated, more likely than their nondisruptive peers to be convicted, $\chi^2(1)=4.56$, $p=.033$. Among the disruptive children, 42 percent had been convicted for an Index crime. This figure was reliably larger than the 27 percent among the 145 nondisruptive children who had been convicted.

To test whether this relationship could be attributed to a general tendency of the disruptive children to be troublesome later in life, I compared the rates of alcoholism of those who had been disruptive with alcoholism rates among the nondisruptive group. The results suggested specificity in the relationship between early disruptive behavior and later deviance. Although the disruptive children were slightly more likely than the nondisruptive group to become alcoholics 34% compared with 28%), the difference was unreliable.

Early disruptive behavior seems to influence whether a person becomes a criminal more than the length of a criminal career. The 26 convicted disruptive boys were convicted for 55 Index crimes, an average of 2.1. Their mean age at first conviction was just under 18 years (SD=7.3).

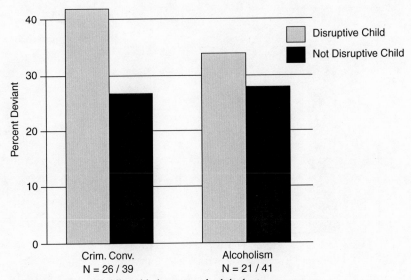

FIGURE 15.1   Childhood behavior and adult deviance

The 39 convicted nondisruptive boys were convicted for 95 Index crimes, an average of 2.4. Their mean age at the time of first conviction for an Index crime was just over age 20 ($SD=8.87$). These differences are not statistically reliable.

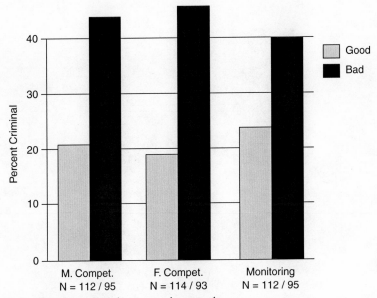

FIGURE 15.2   Socialization and criminality

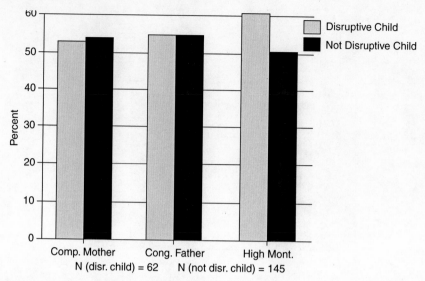

FIGURE 15.3   Childhood behavior and socialization

Socialization and Criminality

Mother's competence ($\chi^2(1)=13.375$ $p=.0003$), father's congeniality ($\chi^2(1)=17.254$, $p=.0000$), and monitoring ($\chi^2(1)=6.027$, $p=.014$) appeared to influence the probability for subsequent criminal behavior.

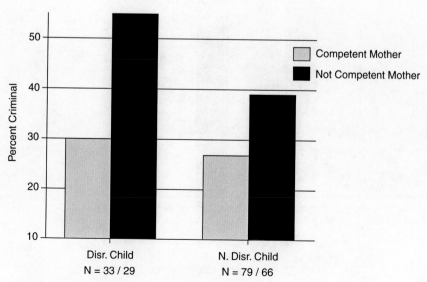

FIGURE 15.4   Mother's competence and criminality

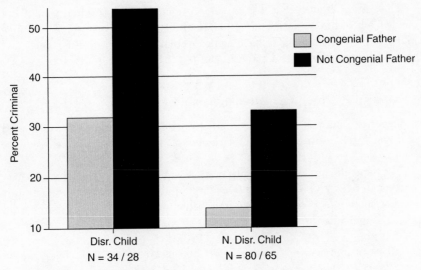

FIGURE 15.5   Father's interaction and criminality

Disruptive Behavior as a Source of Poor Family Life

Unfortunately, I have no evidence about parental socialization prior to the ratings showing which children were disruptive. The teachers' ratings of the children, however, preceded observations of family life. If misbehaving children generated poor family environments, their families should look worse than those of their nondisruptive peers. The two groups were compared.

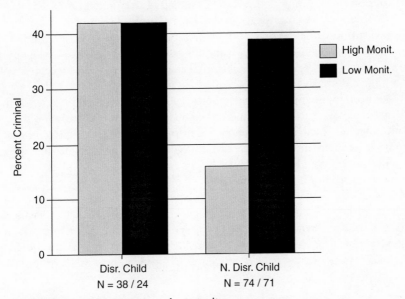

FIGURE 15.6   Monitoring and criminality

The results showed that disruptive and nondisruptive children were about equally likely to have competent mothers. Fathers of disruptive and nondisruptive children were equally likely to have had congenial relations with the family. And the families of disruptive children were not less likely to monitor their behavior.

Socialization Practices as Intervening Variables

A categorical analysis of variance, based on logit transformations, estimated main and interaction effects of early behavior and dimensions of subsequent socialization.

The main effects of early disruptive behavior ($\chi^2(1)=4.67$, $p=.03$) and maternal competence ($\chi^2(1)=11.39$, $p=.0007$) are significant, but their interaction is not. The main effects of early disruptive behavior ($\chi^2(1)=5.18$, $p=.03$) and the father's congeniality ($\chi^2(1)=13.33$, $p=.0003$), too, are significant, but their interaction is not.

Effects of monitoring, however, partially reflected Simpson's paradox. Disruptive children who were monitored were as likely to become criminals as those who were not. Monitoring appeared to decrease the probability of crime only among nondisruptive children. After controlling main effects, the interaction between child behavior and monitoring was statistically reliable, ($\chi^2(1)=4.00$, $p=.045$).

Summary and Discussion

Among the boys reared in poverty pockets of Massachusetts, teachers had identified some as disruptive. That identification, given prior to the time when a boy reached his tenth birthday, proved to be predictive of criminality.

Socialization practices, too, proved to be predictive of criminality. The analyses provided no evidence that poor socialization practices found in families of delinquents had been caused by disruptive behavior on the part of the child. Rather, the evidence suggests that maternal competence and paternal congeniality can tame disruptive children.

Monitoring presented a more complex picture. Although almost twice the proportion of boys who were not monitored had been convicted for Index crimes, monitoring had apparently no effect with disruptive boys. If disruptive boys are the targets for intervention, these analyses suggest that a strategy aimed at improving monitoring would be ineffective.

In many studies of human behavior, differences among people have been overlooked. This oversight may be particularly critical in studies of crime. Treatments that are effective for some people may be ineffective or damaging to others, but if each individual is to be considered as relevantly different from all others, there will be no possibility for learning what interventions are effective. To avoid leaving judgments of effectiveness to political, pragmatic, or intuitive evaluations, people must be classified.

The search for homogeneous subgroups is a tricky business. Chance relationships can easily appear to be real similarities. Improvements in social policies, however, require taking the risk and relying on replications to substantiate theories.

References

DuPaul, G. J. and R. A. Barkley. 1992. Social interactions of children with attention deficit hyperactivity disorder: Effects of Methylphenidate. In *Preventing Antisocial Behavior: Interventions from Birth through Adolescence*, edited by J. McCord and R. E. Tremblay, 89–116. New York: Guilford Press.

Eron, L. D. 1986. *The development of aggressive behavior from the perspective of a developing behaviorist*. Presidential Address: Midwestern Psychological Association, Palmer House, Chicago, IL, May 9.

Eron, L., R. L. Huesmann, and A. Zelli. 1991. The role of parental variables in the learning of aggression. In *The Development and Treatment of Childhood Aggression*, edited by D. J. Pepler and K. H. Rubin, 169–188. Hillsdale, NJ: Lawrence Erlbaum.

Eron, L., L. O. Walder, and M. M. Lefkowitz. 1971. *Learning Aggression in Children*. Boston: Little, Brown & Co.

Farrington, D. P. 1978. The family backgrounds of aggressive youths. In *Aggression and Anti-social Behaviour in Childhood and Adolescence*, edited by L. A. Hersov and M. Berger, 73–93. Oxford: Pergamon.

Farrington, D. P. 1986. Stepping stones to adult criminal careers. In *Development of Antisocial and Prosocial Behavior*, edited by D. Olweus, J. Block, and M. Radke-Yarrow, 359–384. New York: Academic Press.

Kendall, Sir M. 1975. *Multivariate Analysis*. London: Charles Griffin.

McCord, J. 1983. A longitudinal study of aggression and antisocial behavior. In *Prospective Studies of Crime and Delinquency*, edited by K. T. Van Dusen and S. A. Mednick, 269–275. Boston: Kluwer-Nijhoff.

Meehl, P. E. 1978. Theoretical risks and tabular asterisks: Sir Karl, Sir Ronald, and the slow progress of soft psychology. *Journal of Consulting and Clinical Psychology* 46(4): 806–834.

Mill, J. S. 1843/1973. *A System of Logic Ratiocinative and Inductive*. London: Longmans.

Patterson, G. R., L. Crosby, and S. Vuchinich. (1992). Predicting risk for early police arrest. *Journal of Quantitative Criminology* 8(4): 335–355.

Powers, E. and H. Witmer. 1951. *An Experiment in the Prevention of Delinquency: The Cambridge-Somerville Youth Study*. New York: Columbia University Press.

Robins, L. N. 1966. *Deviant Children Grown Up*. Baltimore: Williams & Wilkins.

Robins, L. N. and K. S. Ratcliff. 1979. Risk factors in the continuation of childhood antisocial behavior into adulthood. *International Journal of Mental Health* 7: 96–116.

SAS Institute. 1985. *SAS User's Guide; Statistics* (1985 ed.). Cary, NC: Author.

Satterfield, J. H. 1987. Childhood diagnostic and neurophysiological predictors of teenage arrest rates: An eight-year prospective study. In *The Causes of Crime: New Biological Approaches*, edited by S. A. Mednick, T. E Moffitt, and S. A. Stack, 146–167. Cambridge: Cambridge University Press.

Simpson, C. H. 1951. The interpretation of interactions in contingency tables. *Journal of the Royal Statistical Society* B, 13.

Stattin, H. and D. Magnusson. 1989. The role of early aggressive behavior in the frequency, seriousness, and type of later crime. *Journal of Consulting and Clinical Psychology* 57(6): 710–718.

White, J. L., T. E. Moffitt, F. Earls, L. Robins, and P. A. Silva. 1990. How early can we tell?: Predictors of childhood conduct disorder and adolescent delinquency. *Criminology* 28: 4 (Nov.), 507–533.

CHAPTER SIXTEEN

Family as Crucible for Violence

*Comment on Gorman-Smith et al. (1996)**

ORMAN-SMITH, TOLAN, ZELLI, and Huesmann (1996) studied African American and Latino boys in the fifth and seventh grades. The boys lived in "disadvantaged inner-city neighborhoods in Chicago" (p. 119). Using information supplied by the boys and their caretakers, the researchers developed scales to describe family processes known to be related to serious antisocial behavior. The boys' responses to questions about their delinquency led to their classification as nondelinquent (N=200), nonviolent delinquent (N=65), or violent (N=71). The analyses indicated that "the violent delinquent group reported poorer discipline, less cohesion, and less involvement than mothers and boys in the other two groups" (p. 125). The authors conclude that intervention programs should target family cohesion as well as discipline practices and monitoring.

Gorman-Smith et al.'s (1996) research is noteworthy both because it marks the start of a longitudinal study that may disentangle direction of influence for some of the variables and because the participants were members of ethnic groups at high risk for antisocial behavior. In their article, Gorman-Smith et al. raise three important issues:

1. Should violence be studied apart from embeddedness in other forms of deviance?

2. Can family interaction and socialization practices cause violence, and can conclusion drawn from the studied population be generalized to other times, places, or ethnic groups?

3. Should intervention programs for at-risk youngsters target conditions that predict violent behavior?

*Reprinted from McCord, J. 1996. Family as crucible for violence. In *Journal of Family Psychology* 10 (2): 147–152; Copyright © 1996 by the American Psychological Association; with permission.

Studying Violence

Criminal recidivists typically commit a variety of types of crime. This lack of specialization was demonstrated by Wolfgang, Figlio, and Sellin (1972), who used a Markov process model to describe arrest data for juveniles in Philadelphia. Although there was a small degree of specialization in injury offenses, knowledge of prior criminal behavior gave only a slight predictive advantage regarding type of future crime. Farrington (1991), too, found that criminal specialization was rare among violent males in the London sample he studied from childhood to age 32. His data led him to conclude that "there was no detectable tendency for offenders to specialize in violent or nonviolent offending" (Farrington, 1991, p. 16).

The argument has been made that if criminals do not specialize, predictors of violence must also be predictors of general antisocial behavior. Yet this reasoning is spurious and the conclusion may be in error. Even if violent criminals commit nonviolent crimes as frequently as other criminals do, not all criminals commit violent crimes. Predicting which criminals will commit violent crimes therefore remains a problem.

Violence can be considered from at least two perspectives—perspectives that have been confounded in the literature (Farrington, 1992). The first considers conditions that might lead an individual ever to commit violence against another. The second looks for conditions that increase the probability for violence by someone. The perspectives differ regarding the nature of appropriate evidence. The first perspective focuses on people and rates of participation in violent crime among different groups. The second focuses on behavior, looking for conditions that increase the probability that a violent act will occur.

Both approaches have shown links between violence and family backgrounds. Wadsworth (1980), for example, used the 1946 birth cohort of the British National Survey of Health and Development to discover early life events that were predictive of violent criminal behavior. He found that boys who were subjected to emotional stress, either through separation or divorce of their parents when the boys were very young or through family position as not being an only child for at least 2 years, were more likely than others to commit violent crimes. Farrington (1991) showed that both violent and nonviolent offenders were more likely than nonoffenders to have been exposed to harsh parental discipline and parental conflict. Violent offenders (though not nonviolent offenders) were also more likely to have been reared by authoritarian parents.

In a longitudinal study of men reared in Boston's satellite communities of Cambridge and Somerville, I (McCord, 1980) discovered age differences for first offending between offenders convicted for serious nonviolent and violent crimes and those convicted only for violent crimes. Furthermore, the former had been convicted of more crimes and more typically began their criminal careers with minor crimes. Additional differences between those who committed violent crimes and those who did not were suggested by the different family predictors for property crimes and personal crimes (McCord, 1979).

Violence occurs in many contexts and, seemingly, with different motivations. Some violence can best be described as hostile aggression (Berkowitz, 1978). In this type of violence, the perpetrator wants to injure his victim: Injuring is the goal. Violence can also occur in the course of other types of action in which injuring is not the goal; perhaps the perpetrator even wishes to avoid injuring.

Different types of violence may have different etiologies. Criminologists have tended to look for typologies in relation to crime labels, such as burglary, robbery, assault, or murder. Though these are certainly helpful for some purposes, they may miscue researchers who want to understand why some people are sometimes willing to be violent.

Before researchers can reasonably answer the question of whether violence can best be understood apart from its embeddedness in other forms of deviance, a taxonomy of violence must be developed.

Socialization, Family Interaction, and Violence

Although radical empiricists have claimed that knowledge comes through perceptions that imprint impressions on a clean slate, one would be hard-pressed to find a parent of more than one child who did not recognize inborn differences in early temperament or infant behavior among them. Researchers have plausibly suggested that dysfunctional family styles may be results, rather than causes, of a child's aversive behavior (e.g., Eron, Huesmann, and Zelli, 1991; Lytton, 1990; Rutter and Garmezy, 1983).

To some extent, differences in child rearing seem to be responses to the differences among infants (Anderson, Lytton, and Romney, 1986; Barkley and Cunningham, 1979; Maccoby and Jacklin, 1982). Yet, there is little evidence to show that these responses are more than perturbations in general styles of child rearing that differentiate one family from another.

In a longitudinal study, I (McCord, 1994a) tested the hypothesis that misbehavior of young children leads to parental conflict. Misbehavior among children under the age of 10 was evaluated by teachers, parental conflict was evaluated by scales that were based on descriptions produced by home observers who visited the families when the children were between the ages of 10 and 16, and delinquency as well as adult criminality were measured using court records for convictions. As expected, children who misbehaved early had a tendency to become juvenile delinquents. Parental conflict and juvenile delinquency were significantly correlated, and both predicted adult serious criminality. The child's earlier misbehavior, however, was not significantly related to subsequent parental conflict.

In another test of the hypothesis that misbehavior of children generates dysfunctional family environments, I (McCord, 1994b) compared the family lives of disruptive and nondisruptive children in relation to their mothers' competence, fathers' interactions with the family, and monitoring. That work showed "that disruptive and nondisruptive children were equally likely to have competent mothers. Fathers of disruptive and nondisruptive children were equally likely to have had congenial relations with the family. And the families of disruptive children were not less likely to monitor their behavior" (McCord, 1994b, p. 182).

Data from the longitudinal Cambridge-Somerville Youth Study have shown that home atmosphere measured during childhood provides a better prediction of adult criminality than does an individual's juvenile record (McCord, 1979). Analyses have also shown that child-rearing variables can be strong predictors of both juvenile and adult criminality (McCord, 1991). These studies did not, however, test predictions specifically to violence.

Gorman-Smith et al. (1996) rightly question the degree to which their results from a cross-sectional design can be generalized to other populations. Data from the Cambridge-Somerville Youth Study can be used to test the generalizability of their approach. Participants for the Cambridge-Somerville study were selected from congested urban neighborhoods composed almost exclusively of Caucasians. The participants were part of a project designed to prevent delinquency by providing consistent guidance, alternative activities, and general assistance over a period of many years. Both troubled and well-adjusted children were included in order to avoid stigmatizing participants.

Case records that were coded in 1957 provided information about the families. The scales used in the present article show high interrater agreement (on the basis of independent coding of a 10% random sample). Only one boy from any one family was included in the analyses. A more complete description of the sample and the family scales can be found in McCord, (1991).

Criminal records tracked the participants for 30 years after the last home visit and more than 20 years after the case records had been coded. A man was classified as a violent criminal if he had been convicted for assault, attempted assault, kidnapping, robbery, rape, abuse of a female child, weapons charges, manslaughter, intent to murder, or murder (N=35). If he had not been convicted for a violent crime but had been convicted for burglary, larceny, larceny of auto, breaking and entering, or receiving stolen property, he was considered a nonviolent criminal (N=42). The remaining 155 men were classified as noncriminal, although 57 had been convicted for offenses against order or ordinances.

All dimensions of the scales used to test the impact of family socialization were derived from the case records. These case records reported what the counselors saw and heard during their visits with the boys. The counselors visited the families, without appointments, an average of twice a month. In general, the records supplied information covering a period of 5.5 years, when the boys were between 10 and 16 years of age.

Four categorical variables were used to indicate family cohesion: parental affection for one another, mother's warmth toward her son, absence of parental conflict, and father's moderate or high esteem for the mother. Each dimension differentiated among the three types of groups, with violent criminals least likely to have been reared in cohesive households. The relations between each of these variables and criminality are shown in Table 16.1.

The cohesion dimension was a sum of the number of variables for which the scores were favorable. The scale of family cohesion, with a range of 0 to 4, had a median of 2 and a mean of 1.9 (SD=1.3).

Four variables were used to indicate parenting practices. The mothers' discipline was considered good if she used consistent, nonpunitive techniques. The

TABLE 16.1   Relation Between Family Cohesiveness and Criminal Status

Family cohesiveness variables	Criminal status			$\chi^2(2)$	p
	Noncriminal (N=155) %	Nonviolent (N=42) %	Violent (N=35) %		
Parental affection	33.6	11.9	5.7	16.61	.000
Maternal warmth	55.5	33.3	28.6	12.37	.002
Parental conflict absent	76.1	52.4	48.6	15.39	.000
Father's esteem for mother	55.5	26.2	25.7	18.06	.000

child was considered supervised if any responsible adult generally knew where he was when he was not in school. Expectations were considered high if the boy had responsibilities, such as caring for a sibling or picking up groceries. Mothers were considered to have control if they placed restrictions on the activities of their sons. With these variables, too, violent criminals were least likely to have been reared with good parenting practices. The relations between each of these variables and criminality are shown in Table 16.2.

The parenting practices dimension was a sum of the number of variables for which the scores were favorable. The scale of parenting practices, with a range of 0 to 4, had a median of 2 and a mean of 1.8 (SD=1.3).

Family influences are certainly not restricted to those that derive from cohesiveness and discipline. To introduce effects of values, four variables indicating parental models were included in the analyses. Fathers were considered deviant if they had been convicted of a serious crime or if they were known to be alcoholics (on the basis of frequent arrests for public drunkenness, loss of jobs, and so forth). Mothers were considered to lack confidence if they persistently failed to meet challenges posed by daily living. Throwing things and similar overt expressions of anger marked a parent as aggressive. Each of these variables, too, predicted violence (see Table 16.3).

Again, a summary score was composed by adding the scores on the four variables. In this case, however, the parental model dimension was a sum of the number of variables for which the scores were unfavorable. The parental

TABLE 16.2   Relation Between Parenting Practices and Criminal Status

Parenting practices variables	Criminal status			$\chi^2(2)$	p
	Noncriminal (N=155) %	Nonviolent (N=42) %	Violent (N=35) %		
Good discipline by mother	36.8	23.8	8.6	11.77	.003
Supervised	65.2	47.6	31.4	15.05	.001
High expectations	31.0	16.7	8.6	9.54	.008
Mother in control	72.3	52.4	42.9	13.87	.001

TABLE 16.3   Relation Between Parental Models and Criminal Status

Parental model variables	Criminal status			$\chi^2(2)$	p
	Noncriminal ($N=155$) %	Nonviolent ($N=42$) %	Violent ($N=35$) %		
Father deviant	34.8	52.4	57.1	8.42	.015
Mother lacks confidence	63.2	83.3	94.3	17.03	.000
Father aggressive	11.0	19.1	34.3	11.95	.003
Mother aggressive	5.8	16.7	20.0	9.06	.011

modeling dimension, with a range of 0 to 4, had a median of 1 and a mean of 1.4 ($SD=1.0$).

A stepwise discriminant function analysis showed that the three dimensions together accounted for 11 percent of the variance, $p < .0001$. With prior probabilities equal, the three summary dimensions identified 57 percent of the violent offenders, 38 percent of the nonviolent offenders, and 62 percent of the noncriminals. On the basis of this evidence, it seems fair to conclude that family cohesion, discipline in adolescence, and family values provide at least a partial account of subsequent violence.

Intervention Programs

The evidence indicates that children who will subsequently become violent have not been reared in cohesive families by parents who provide good models and reasonable discipline or monitoring. Nevertheless, the conclusion that intervention strategies should attempt to increase emotional closeness and communication as well as to improve monitoring and disciplinary consistency is unwarranted.

Studies showing relations between family backgrounds and violence have been based on heterogeneous populations. What is effective for a general population may not be so for misbehaving youngsters. In one study, for example, parental monitoring was related to low probabilities that children who were not disruptive before the age of 10 would become criminals: yet among disruptive children, parental monitoring had no relation to subsequent criminality (McCord, 1994b).

Interventions may not be able to undo effects of deficits in backgrounds of people at high risk for violence. A strategy aimed at eliminating the deficiency may be as much a mistake as it would be to cut down trees because broken legs come from falling out of them. Cast and crutches are likely to be more helpful.

A child who is rejected by parents may not be best served by someone else who tries to take the role of parent. Such a strategy might result in an exaggerated sense of loss. Psychologists know that supervision or monitoring is an efficient predictor of socialized behavior. However, absence of supervision is likely to have resulted in a set of expectations, adaptations, and (perhaps) skills. So a child who has not been supervised may become more antisocial if he is placed under close supervision.

The treatment program of the Cambridge-Somerville Youth Study had long-term effects. That treatment program was based on a reasonable reading of evidence showing that criminals had been socialized in families that failed to provide adequate warmth or guidance. The program provided long-term assistance to boys and their families. Its clients thought it was successful. Nevertheless, evaluation using objective criteria found that the program increased risk for criminal recidivism as well as for alcoholism (McCord, 1992).

The Cambridge-Somerville Youth Study is not alone in showing that sensible hunches and adequate implementation may produce interventions that fail to achieve their beneficial goals. One cannot know the degree to which experience has affected individuals at high risk for violence; thus, a strategy that is based on undoing the past may not work. Furthermore, one cannot know whether the tabs placed on disadvantage are the ones that correctly identify causes.

Researchers do not yet know whether effective programs depend on the age of clients, their psychosocial or biological stage of development, the point in their criminal career at which they are caught, or something unmeasured about their backgrounds. Premature closure on issues regarding intervention strategies can result in loss of time for discovering effective strategies as well as a waste of resources and the possibility of doing harm.

Summary

Three issues arising from research reported by Gorman-Smith et al. (1996) have been addressed. Regarding whether violence should be studied apart from its embeddedness in other forms of deviance, I have suggested at least a preliminary affirmative answer. Researchers ought to develop a taxonomy of violence that will permit analyses of the various routes to violence, some of which may incorporate other forms of deviance.

Regarding the second issue—whether conclusions that family interaction and socialization practices cause violence are reasonable for other times or places—I have argued affirmatively. My argument rests on evidence from a longitudinal study in which family behavior that was evaluated while the participants were adolescents predicted their violent criminality as measured 30 years later.

In regard to the third issue—whether the evidence shows appropriate targets for intervention programs—I have urged a negative response. In the absence of research evaluating intervention programs, researchers should not make claims about programs' likely results. Unhealthful experiences leave their residues, and it is a mistake to assume that knowledge about the effectiveness of restorative interventions follows from knowledge about causes.

References

Anderson, K. E., H. Lytton, and D. M. Romney. 1986. Mothers' interactions with normal and conduct-disordered boys: Who affects whom? *Developmental Psychology* 22: 604–609.

Barkley, R. A. and C. E. Cunningham. 1979. The effects of methylphenidate on the mother-child interactions of hyperactive children. *Archives of General Psychiatry* 36: 201–208.

Berkowitz, L. 1978. Is criminal violence normative behavior? *Journal of Research in Crime and Delinquency* 15: 148–161.

Eron, L., R. L. Huesmann, and A. Zelli. 1991. The role of parental variables in the learning of aggression. In *The Development and Treatment of Childhood Aggression*, edited by D. J. Pepler and K. H. Rubin, 169–188. Hillsdale, NJ: Erlbaum.

Farrington, D. P. 1991. Childhood aggression and adult violence: Early precursors and later life outcomes. In *The Development and Treatment of Childhood Aggression*, edited by D. J. Pepler and K. H. Rubin, 5–29. Hillsdale, NJ: Erlbaum.

———. 1992. Explaining the beginning, progress, and ending of antisocial behavior from birth to adulthood. In *Facts, Frameworks, and Forecasts: Advances in Criminological Theory*, edited by J. McCord, vol. 3, 253–286. New Brunswick, NJ: Transaction Press.

Gorman-Smith, D., P. H. Tolan, A. Zelli, and L. R. Huesmann. 1996. The relation of family functioning to violence among inner-city minority youths. *Journal of Family Psychology* 10: 115–129.

Lytton, H. 1990. Child and parent effects in boys' conduct disorder: A reinterpretation. *Developmental Psychology* 26: 683–697.

Maccoby, E. E. and C. N. Jacklin. 1982, June. *The "Person" Characteristics of Children and the Family as Environment*. Paper presented at the Conference on Interaction of Person and Environment, Stockholm.

McCord, J. 1979. Some child-rearing antecedents of criminal behavior in adult men. *Journal of Personality and Social Psychology* 37: 1477–1486.

McCord, J. 1980. Patterns of deviance. In *Human Functioning in Longitudinal Perspective: Studies of Normal and Psychopathological Populations*, edited by S. B. Sells, R. Crandall, M. Roff, J. Strauss, and W. Pollin, 157–162. Baltimore: Williams & Wilkins.

McCord, J. 1991. Family relationships, juvenile delinquency, and adult criminality. *Criminology* 29: 397–417.

McCord, J. 1992. The Cambridge-Somerville Study: A pioneering longitudinal-experimental study of delinquency prevention. In *Preventing Antisocial Behavior: Interventions from Birth through Adolescence*, edited by J. McCord and R. E. Tremblay, 196–206. New York: Guilford Press.

McCord, J. 1994a. Aggression in two generations. In *Aggressive Behavior: Current Perspectives*, edited by L. R. Huesmann, 241–251. New York: Plenum.

McCord, J. 1994b. Family socialization and antisocial behavior: Searching for causal relationships in longitudinal research. In *Cross-national Longitudinal Research on Human Development and Criminal Behavior*, edited by I. G. M. Weitekamp and H.-J. Kerner, 217–227. Dordrecht, Netherlands: Kluwer.

Rutter, M. and N. Garmezy. 1983. Developmental psychopathology. In *Handbook of Child Psychology, vol. IV: Socialization, Personality and Social Development*, edited by E. M. Hetherington, 775–912. New York: Wiley.

Wadsworth, M. E. J. 1980. Early life events and later behavioral outcomes in a British longitudinal study. In *Human Functioning in Longitudinal Perspective: Studies of Normal and Psychopathological Populations*, edited by S. B. Sells, R. Crandall, M. Roff, J. Strauss, and W. Pollin, 168–177. Baltimore: Williams & Wilkins.

Wolfgang, M. E., R. M. Figlio, and T. Sellin. 1972. *Delinquency In a Birth Cohort*. Chicago: University of Chicago Press.

PART V

Alcoholism and Drunk Driving

CHAPTER SEVENTEEN

Drunken Drivers in Longitudinal Perspective*

POPULAR OPINION LENDS credence to a view that men convicted for driving while intoxicated (DWI) are simply men whose friends have failed to note their presumably exceptional inebriety. The implication of this view is that drunken drivers could be any of us. In his careful review of the evidence, however, Waller (1976) suggests a different picture. Men convicted for DWI appear to have a history of violent behavior. This view implies a marked difference between drunken drivers and other people.

The present study has been designed to shed light on the question of which view is more valid. In addition, the study reports on personality differences between men convicted for drunken driving and nonoffenders. It also shows some relationships between childhood and subsequent convictions for DWI. Data for the analyses were drawn from case histories in a study of personality development.

Method

Subjects for the study had been included in a youth program, begun in 1936 as an attempt to prevent delinquency (Powers and Witmer, 1951). The youth program included both "difficult" and "average" youngsters who were born between 1925 and 1932. They were living in congested areas of Cambridge and Somerville, Massachusetts.

Seven hundred boys, divided into 350 matched pairs, had been included in the original design. The intervention of World War II produced problems of staffing and travel. By 1942, the program had been reduced to 506 boys (in 253 matched pairs) from 466 families. To justify statistical analyses for which an

*Reprinted from McCord, J. 1984. Drunken drivers in longitudinal perspective. In *Journal of Studies on Alcohol* 45 (4): 316–320; with permission. Copyright Alcohol Research Documentation, Inc., Rutgers Center of Alcohol Studies, Pitscataway, NJ 08854.

assumption of independence was required, only one boy from a family was included in the present study, leaving 466 subjects.

As part of the procedures for selecting boys for the study, elementary school teachers had described children by marking characteristics on "Trait Record Cards." These cards contained words and phrases that were to be checked if true of a particular boy. At the time of these ratings, the mean ($\pm SD$) age of the boys was 7.6 ± 1.56 yr.

Twenty characteristics had been used as descriptions of at least 8 percent of the boys. A cluster analysis of these variables (SAS Institute, 1981) revealed five unidimensional components. Together, the clusters accounted for 42.2 percent of the variance in teachers' descriptions of the children.

One cluster appears to be descriptive of the degree to which a child used verbal aggression. Children with high scores on this dimension had been described as argumentative, tattlers, blaming other children for their own mistakes, and showing off. A second cluster seems to describe the degree to which a child was insecure and dependent. Children with high scores on this dimension had been described as depending on constant direction, being easily led, having poor work habits, stuttering, thumb-sucking or nailbiting, and lacking in self-confidence.

A third cluster identifies the degree to which a child was temperamental. Children with high scores on this dimension had been described as easily hurt, moody, having few friends, having temper tantrums, being uncooperative, and resentful of criticism. Another cluster identifies the degree to which a child was asocial and aggressive. Children with high scores on this dimension had been described as fighters, cheaters, and bullies, and had not been described as shy or easily embarrassed. The last cluster consists of a single description: truant.

By random process, half of the boys had been selected to receive help through a program that included assigning a counselor to assist the boy and his family. Counselors visited 232 families approximately twice a month between 1939 and 1945. After each encounter with one of the boys or with a member of his family, the staff filed a report. Counselors recorded conversations, described behavior in detail and tried to convey a picture of the families they assisted. To prepare for a longitudinal study, in 1957, coders read these case records thoroughly. Transcribing the information into categorical scales, coders provided descriptions of the parents and of family interaction. A second coder read and rated 25 randomly selected cases to estimate reliability. Agreement between the two raters ranged between .80 and .96 for the variables used in the present research. The validity of the scales is attested by their ability successfully to predict which youngsters would subsequently be convicted as criminals (McCord, 1979). Uncontaminated by retrospective bias, these scales contain descriptions of family life prior to the subjects' arrests for DWI and prior to their alcoholism and criminal convictions.

Cluster analysis of the scales resulted in identification of three principal, unidimensional components, each having only a single eigenvalue greater than one. The clusters represented maternal leadership, paternal interaction, and parental control. A high score on the first dimension described mothers who used consistent, nonpunitive discipline, appeared to be self-confident, and were generally affectionate to their sons. A high score on the second dimension described families in which considerable conflict between the parents marked their inter-action, at least one of the parents was highly aggressive, the father had been either an alcoholic or a criminal, and the father showed little esteem for his wife and little affection for his son. A high score on the third dimension described fam-ilies that supervised the boy, held high expectations for his behavior, and had not been permissive.

In a follow-up project started in 1975, 98 percent of the men were located. Approximately 75 percent of them responded either to a mailed questionnaire or to an interviewer's questions. Records revealed treatment for alcoholism and crim-inal convictions. Information from these sources was coded by researchers unfa-miliar with the material on childhood.

Several criteria were used in the identification of alcoholics. Being diagnosed as an alcoholic in a treatment clinic or mental hospital or by a coroner qualified a man as an alcoholic. If a man gave at least three affirmative answers to the four questions in an alcoholism screening test, the CAGE Questionnaire (Mayfield et al., 1974), he was considered an alcoholic. The CAGE questions asked whether the person had ever taken a morning eye opener, felt the need to cut down on drinking, felt annoyed by criticism of his drinking, or felt guilty about his drink-ing. The CAGE test appeared on the mailed questionnaire and also in the inter-view. Having been convicted at least three times for public drunkenness or DWI led to classification as an alcoholic. Finally, if a respondent had been convicted for drunkenness and also had given affirmative answers to two of the CAGE ques-tions, he was classified as an alcoholic.

Information from criminal records in Massachusetts and nine states to which the men had migrated was coded to show whether the men had ever been con-victed for a crime and, if so, their age at the time of conviction. Convictions for crimes indexed by the Federal Bureau of Investigation (i.e., larceny, burglary, motor-vehicle theft, assault, robbery, forcible rape, murder, and nonnegligent manslaughter) were considered serious crimes.

Some of the information from the interviews was used to depict the current lives of the men. Fifteen dichotomous variables described the men's responses to anger, their recall of parental attitudes and behavior during childhood, their wor-ries related to interpersonal interaction, and whether they had encountered spe-cific difficulties associated with drinking. Cluster analysis showed that these vari-ables comprised five unidimensional factors.

One cluster identifies the degree to which a man had experienced trouble from drinking. Men scoring high on this dimension reported having gotten in fights or arguments, having failed to keep an appointment, and having hurt a friend-ship or marriage, all due to drinking.

A second cluster represents expression of aggression. The men were asked what made them really angry and then, "What do you generally do?" They also described the last time they were angry, with probes (if necessary) to learn what they had done that time. Negative values on this dimension indicate physical expressions of anger. Positive values indicate verbal expressions of anger.

A third dimension represents parental warmth. The interviewer asked: "Look-ing back to the time when you were 12 or 13, how would you describe your mother?" They later asked: "What was your father like?" Coders identified responses that included affection and those that included being strict or firm. Three of these variables formed a unidimensional cluster: recall of an affectionate mother and of an affectionate father (given positive weights) and recall of a strict mother (given negative weight).

The fourth variable appears to represent ego strength. This dimension had men at one end who recalled their fathers as being strict and who agreed with the statement: "When people disagree with you, you generally tend to wonder if your opinion was right." At the other end were men who did not describe their fathers as strict and who disagreed with the statement that they doubted their own opinions when others disagreed with it.

A fifth cluster represents self-confidence. Men scoring at the high end of this dimension had agreed with the statement, "You take a positive attitude toward yourself." They had disagreed with statements that they had trouble getting criticism off their minds and that they worried about what new people might think of them.

Among the 466 subjects in the study, 36 had been convicted for DWI. Teachers' descriptions during the subjects' childhoods, records of treatment for alcoholism, and histories of criminal convictions through five decades were available for all the men. Descriptions of families during the subjects' childhoods were available for 232 men, facilitating comparisons of family background between 19 men who were convicted for DWI and 213 nonoffenders. Although 293 men had been interviewed, missing data reduced the number to 244: 18 men convicted for DWI could be compared with 226 nonoffenders.

Results

Results of comparisons between drunken drivers and their peers have been divided into three sections: deviant behavior, adult personality, and childhood. As noted above, the data came from different sources for these comparisons. Because of incomplete information about adult personality (for some) and childhood (for others), comparisons use the entire group of subjects only in analyses of deviant behavior in relation to DWI.

Deviant Behavior

If convicted drunken drivers are distinguishable from their unconvicted peers merely incidentally, convicted drunken drivers would not be expected to display other signs of alcoholism. Among the 430 nonoffenders, 24 percent showed histories of alcoholism. By contrast, 86 percent of the 36 men convicted for driving under the influence of alcohol had similar histories (χ^2=61.17, 1 df, $p < .0001$). A higher proportion of the drunken drivers had shown evidence of alcoholism using each of the criteria for identifying alcoholics. Twenty-two percent of the nonoffenders, compared with 48 percent of those convicted for drunken driving, answered at least three of the CAGE questions affirmatively (χ^2=7.85, 1 df, p=.0051). Six percent of the nonoffenders, compared with 33 percent of those convicted for drunken driving, had received treatment for alcoholism either in mental hospitals or in clinics (χ^2=33.02, 1 df, $p < .0001$). Of the men convicted for DWI, 69 percent had been convicted at least three times for alcohol-related behavior, compared with 8 percent of the comparison group (χ^2=111.294, 1 df, $p < .0001$).

If drunken drivers have a history of violent behavior, their criminal histories should distinguish them from their peers on grounds other than convictions for DWI. To check this possibility, criminal records of the two groups were compared. Comparison of the age at first conviction shows that men convicted for DWI were only slightly younger. The 309 men with criminal records who had not been convicted for DWI had a mean age of 21.1 ± 7.7 yr when first convicted. The 36 drunken drivers had a mean age of 19.3 ± 8.7 yr at the time of their first convictions.

Despite similarity in age at first conviction, drunken drivers differed from their peers in the proportions convicted for serious crimes indexed by the FBI. Whereas 69 percent of the drunken drivers had been convicted for Index crimes, only 27 percent of the remaining men had been convicted for similar crimes (χ^2=28.82, 1 df, $p < .0001$). Of the men convicted for DWI, 64 percent had been convicted for Index crimes against property and 31 percent had been convicted for Index crimes against persons. Comparable figures among the nonoffenders were 21 and 13 percent, respectively.

Adult Personality

A stepwise discriminant analysis indicated that three of the five clusters distinguished between men convicted for DWI and those not convicted for DWI. In order of their importance, the groups were distinguishable by (1) the degree to which they had been in trouble from drinking, (2) their self-confidence and (3) the way in which they expressed aggression.

The men who had been convicted for DWI were more likely to have reported getting into fights, missing appointments, and hurting friendships or marriages due to drinking. This variable accounted for 5.2 percent of the variance (F=10.77, p=.0012).

High scores on the self-confidence dimension represented people likely to trust their own judgment and those who worry little about what others might think. Men convicted for DWI reported greater confidence in their own judgment. This difference between groups was significant after controlling scores on the trouble from drinking scale (F=10.73, p=.0012). The self-confidence dimension accounted for 5.2 percent additional variance.

Men convicted for DWI tended to be actors rather than talkers when angry. The drunken drivers reported themselves as more likely to act, whereas the other men reported themselves as being more likely to talk. After controlling the first two variables, the style for expressing aggression was marginally significant (F=3.23, p=.0739), accounting for an additional 1.6 percent of the variance.

Eighteen men convicted for DWI and 226 of the comparison group had provided codable answers to questions in the interviews used for each of the three dimensions. A discriminant function based on having been in trouble through drinking, having self-confidence, and acting out of anger correctly identified 72 percent of these drunken drivers and 74 percent of the nonoffenders.

Of the 20 drunken drivers who answered questions about social complications from drinking, 15 (75%) reported getting into fights, missing appointments, or hurting friendships due to drinking. This is considerably higher than the 92 of 273 (34%) reporting problems due to drinking among the men not convicted for drunken driving (χ^2=13.71, 1 df, p=.0002). Of the 21 drunken drivers who responded to the questions about confidence in their own judgment, 16 (76%) gave answers indicating self-confidence in response to all three questions. Among the 269 men who had not been convicted, 143 (53%) gave self-confidence answers to all three questions (χ^2=4.17, 1 df, p=.0414). Among the 18 drunken drivers who described their responses to being angered, 5 (28%) mentioned verbal reactions. In contrast, of the 227 men not convicted for drunken driving who described their responses to being angered, 143 (63%) mentioned verbal reactions (χ^2=8.65, 1 df, p=.0033).

Childhood

Ratings describing the subjects when they were young children had identified those who were aggressive, truants, temperamental, and insecure or dependent. Neither truancy nor aggressiveness, each of which was predictive of subsequent conviction for Index crimes, characterized future drunken drivers. The stepwise discriminant analysis identified only the scale measuring insecurity and dependency as one that discriminated between the 36 DWI offenders and the 430 nonoffenders. This latter scale showed that children who were insecure and dependent were unlikely to become drunken drivers.

Although each of the three dimensions depicting family life during adolescence distinguished between men who later had been convicted for Index crimes and those without serious criminal records, only the scale showing paternal interaction proved predictive of subsequent drunken driving.

The 19 men convicted for DWI had been reared in families characterized by conflict, aggression, paternal rejection, and paternal alcoholism or criminality. The fathers of 10 (53%) were in open conflict with the boys' mothers; the fathers of 11 (58%) were alcoholics; and only 4 (21%) of the fathers exhibited moderate or high esteem for the boy's mother. By comparison, among the remaining 213, the fathers of 65 (31%) were in open conflict with the boy's mother; the fathers of 62 (29%) were alcoholics; and 102 (48%) showed moderate or high esteem for the boy's mother. The two groups did not differ in the proportions whose fathers had been convicted for serious crimes. Nor were there significant differences in any of the variables incorporated in the scales describing mothers or discipline.

Among these 232 men for whom the records provided data about family life as well as childhood behavior, the two cluster scores representing dependency and paternal aggressiveness accounted for 5 percent of the variance discriminating between those who would subsequently be convicted and those who would not be convicted for DWI. Paternal interaction accounted for 3.3 percent of the variance (F=7.95, p=.0052). The cluster representing the degree to which a child was insecure and dependent accounted for an additional 1.7 percent of the variance ($F=3.95$, $p=.0481$).

A prediction from the discriminant function based on the two clusters, one describing the parental environment and one describing the childhood personality, correctly identified 68 percent of those later convicted for DWI. It also correctly identified 65 percent of those who were not convicted for DWI.

Discussion

Comparisons of the men convicted for DWI with those who were not convicted suggest deeper differences related to aggression and antisocial behavior. Although not distinguishable by their age at first conviction, the men convicted for DWI were more likely to have been convicted for serious crimes against property and for crimes against persons. Men convicted for DWI were also more likely to be alcoholics. As children, they were less likely than others in their schools to have appeared to be insecure or dependent. During adolescence, those who would later be convicted for DWI tended to have been exposed to parental conflict and aggression. As adults, these men were likely to get in trouble through their drinking and to express anger physically. Perhaps self-confidence contributed to misjudgments regarding their capabilities when drunk. Perhaps those convicted for DWI had learned to act out their frustrations, hiding feelings of inadequacy.

Although the psychological dynamics remain obscure, the evidence from this longitudinal study suggests a picture of the development of men who drive while intoxicated. As children, their teachers considered them self-reliant. They were raised by inconsiderate parents. The men themselves appear to have been independent and relatively self-confident, both during early childhood and in middle age. Their history of antisocial behavior belies a view that these men have inadvertently risked the safety of others during an unaccustomed lapse in self-control.

Note

This study was partly supported by U.S. Public Health Service research grant RO1 MH26779, National Institute of Mental Health (Center for Studies of Crime and Delinquency).

Acknowledgment

The author thanks Richard Parente, Robert Staib, Ellen Myers, and Ann Cronin for their work in tracing the men and their records, and Joan Immel, Tom Smedile, Mary Duell, Elise Goldman, Abby Brodkin, and Laura Otton for their careful and thoughtful coding.

References

Mayfield, D., G. McLeod, and P. Hall. 1974. The CAGE questionnaire: Validation of a new alcoholism screening instrument. *American Journal of Psychiatry*, 131: 1121–1123.

McCord, J. 1979. Some child-rearing antecedents of criminal behavior in adult men. *Journal of Personality and Social Psychology*, 37: 1477-1486.

Powers, E. and H. Witmer. 1951. *An Experiment in the Prevention Delinquency*. New York: Columbia University Press.

SAS Institute. 1981. *SAS 79.5 Changes and Enhancements*. Raleigh, N.C.

Waller, J. A. 1976. Alcohol and unintentional injury. In *The Biology of Alcoholism*, edited by B. Kissin and H. Begleiter, vol. 4, 307–334. *Social Aspects of Alcoholism*. New York: Plenum Press.

CHAPTER EIGHTEEN

Alcoholism and Crime
Across Generations*

BOTH ALCOHOLISM AND CRIMINALITY tend to run in families. Because a higher proportion of alcoholics than of the general population have alcoholic parents and a higher proportion of criminals than of the general population have criminal parents, the children of alcoholics and criminals are considered to be at high risk for developing problems (e.g. Farrington et al., 1975; Kaij and Dock, 1975; Knop et al., 1985; Mednick et al., 1986; Zucker, 1987; Dodge et al., 1990; Knowles and Schroeder, 1990; Pihl et al., 1990; McCord, 1991a; Bates and Labouvie, 1994; Goodwin et al., 1994; Bush et al., 1995; Simons et al., 1995). A variety of studies have been designed to identify differentiating factors that might account for the heightened risk. In general, these studies fall into two groups. One group focuses on biogenetic factors (e.g. Schuckit et al., 1972; Goodwin et al., 1974; Templer et al., 1974; Kaij and Dock, 1975; Goodwin, 1976, 1991; Schulsinger, 1977; Bohman, 1978; Cadoret and Gath, 1978; Schuckit and Rayses, 1979; McKenna and Pickens, 1981; Schuckit, 1984; Tarter et al., 1985; Hill et al., 1987; Mednick et al., 1987; Vaillant and Milofsky, 1991). A second emphasizes social conditions or personality variables that seem to be productive of aggression, alcoholism, and crime (Fox, 1962; Farrington, 1979; Jacob, 1986; Wahler and Dumas, 1986). In addition, a handful of studies have looked at interactions between genetic risk and social or personality conditions to understand mediating factors for becoming alcoholic or criminal (e.g. Cloninger et al., 1978; Jacob and Leonard, 1986; Bennett et al., 1987; Lahey et al., 1988; McCord, 1988; Pihl and Peterson, 1991; Sher et al., 1991; Wu and Kandel, 1995). These latter studies show particular promise for uncovering mechanisms by which the processes of transmittal can be understood.

In line with the thrust toward understanding mechanisms of transmittal, this paper considers two issues:

*Reprinted from McCord, J. 1999. Alcoholism and crime across generations. In *Criminal Behavior and Mental Health* 9: 107–117. Copyright © 1999 John Wiley & Sons Ltd; with permission.

1. whether the fact that alcoholism and crime tend to run in families should be at least partly attributed to a general tendency of alcoholic or criminal parents to provide poor socializing environments;
2. whether good socializing conditions retard and bad socializing conditions promote the likelihood that alcoholism and criminality will be transmitted from one generation to the next.

Methods and Background

Information for the analyses comes from the Cambridge-Somerville Youth Study. These data include 214 pairs of natural fathers and their sons. Both generations were traced into their fourth decades in age. The data also include socializing information about the fathers in their roles as parents and husbands. In addition, the data describe, in their roles as mothers, the women these men married.

A father was considered to be an alcoholic if the case records indicated that he was a habitual or excessive drinker, if he had lost jobs or had family problems due to drinking, if he had been arrested at least three times for driving under the influence of alcohol or public drunkenness, or if his son described him during the adult interview (between 1977 and 1980) as having been regularly drunk or making trouble when he drank. Among the 68 biological fathers recognized as alcoholic (32%), about half were so identified by more than one criterion.

A son was considered an alcoholic if he responded affirmatively, as do alcoholics (Mayfield et al., 1974), to at least three of the four questions on the CAGE test. A son was considered to be alcoholic also if he had received treatment for alcoholism, if he had been arrested at least three times for public drunkenness or driving while intoxicated, or if he described himself as an alcoholic. Additionally, a son was considered an alcoholic if he had been arrested twice for alcoholism and answered affirmatively to two of the CAGE questions.

Ten men had been arrested one or two times for public drunkenness or driving while intoxicated but showed no other signs of alcoholism in our records. These ten men were dropped from analyses of sons' problem behaviors (four were sons of alcoholics, one was a son of an alcoholic criminal, and five were sons of men who were neither alcoholic nor criminal). Among the 67 sons recognized as alcoholic (28%) in this study, about a quarter were so identified by more than one criterion.

For both generations, men were considered as criminals if they had been convicted for an Index crime. Among the fathers, 49 had been convicted, and among the sons, 71 had been convicted for Index crimes.

For both generations, analyses were carried out using four categories regarding deviant behavior: neither alcoholic nor criminal; alcoholic but not criminal, criminal but not alcoholic, and both criminal and alcoholic. The division for comorbidity avoids confusing descriptions that are true regarding alcoholic criminals with those of alcoholics who are not criminals or criminals who are not alcoholics. Nevertheless, for some purposes, all alcoholics are compared with nonalcoholics, and all criminals are compared with noncriminals.

TABLE 18.1   Father's Deviance and Son's Deviance (%)

	Father's deviance			
Son's deviance	Neither (N=120)	Alcoholic (N=36)	Criminal (N=21)	Both (N=27)
Neither	61	31	43	33
Alcoholic	12	25	19	15
Criminal	13	19	29	22
Both	14	25	10	30
TOTAL	100	100	101	100

$\chi^2(9)=18.76$; $p=0.027$.

Note: Not all columns total 100 percent due to rounding.

Table 18.1 shows the relation between generations of these two types of deviance and their combination.

Among the four groups of fathers, a majority (61%) of only those who themselves were neither alcoholic nor criminal had sons who were neither alcoholic nor criminal. The distribution of alcoholism and criminality among the remaining three groups indicates an intergenerational influence:

1. The highest proportion of alcoholic noncriminal sons appeared among alcoholic noncriminal fathers.
2. The highest proportion of criminal nonalcoholic sons appeared among criminal nonalcoholic fathers.
3. The highest proportion of alcoholic and criminal sons appeared among alcoholic and criminal fathers. The relationships between generations were statistically reliable, $\chi^2(9)=18.76$, $p=0.027$.

All family variables in this study relied on contemporaneous records written by social workers who repeatedly visited the homes of the sons between 1939 and 1945. These records were coded a decade later, in the late 1950s—long before information about the sons' deviance was gathered. Thus, no possible retrospective biases infused the analyses. Furthermore, because the information relied on reports from repeated home visits (rather than responses to specific questions), the biases of self-reported behaviors, too, were avoided. Reliability for the variables, measured by agreement between two coders independently rating a 10 percent random sample of case histories, ranged from 0.80 to 0.88. See McCord and McCord (1960) for detailed descriptions of the coding. Two potentially confounding variables were considered in order to look at how socialization might affect the transmission of alcoholism and criminality between generations. The first was the father's aggression in the family. This variable was viewed as promoting crime and alcoholism (Farrington, 1978; Pollock et al., 1990; Eron et al., 1991; McCord, 1991b; Pakaslahti et al., 1996). The second was maternal competence. This vari-

TABLE 18.2   Paternal Deviance and Father's Aggression in Family (%)

	Father's deviance			
Father's aggression	Neither (N=125)	Alcoholic (N=40)	Criminal (N=21)	Both (N=28)
High	10	10	19	43
Moderate	24	60	24	39
Low	66	30	57	18
TOTAL	100	100	100	100

$\chi^2(6)=44.13$; $p=0.001$.

able was considered to be a protecting factor against the development of criminal or alcoholic tendencies (Rutter, 1987; Hawkins et al., 1992; Newcomb and Felix-Ortiz, 1992; Werner, 1993; Smith et al., 1995; Fitzpatrick, 1997).

Three descriptive categories were involved in measurement of the father's aggression in the family: family conflict rated as considerable, father's aggressiveness rated as unrestrained, and father's discipline rated as consistently punitive (reliabilities: 0.80, 0.84, 0.88). If none of these descriptions had been given to a father, his aggression in the family was considered low; if one, moderate; and if more than one, his aggression in the family was considered high. Four descriptive categories were involved in measurement of the mother's competence: ratings of the mother as self-confident, as a consistent nonpunitive disciplinarian, as being actively affectionate, and as not displaying unrestrained aggressiveness (reliabilities: 0.84, 0.84, 0.84, 0.92). A mother's competence was rated as high if the mother was coded favorably on all four variables, moderate if coded favorably on at least two, and low if described unfavorably on at least three of the four descriptions.

Paternal Deviance, Father's Aggression, and Mother's Competence

As hypothesized, paternal alcoholism and criminality were reliably related to the father's aggression in the family, $\chi^2(6)=44.127$, $p=0.001$. A minority of the nonalcoholic fathers (52 of 146=36%) had been rated as aggressive by any of the criteria. On the other hand, a majority of the alcoholic fathers (51 of 68=75%) had ratings as aggressive in at least one category. Similarly, as compared with just 10 percent of the noncriminal fathers (17 of 165), 33 percent of the criminal fathers (16 of 49) were highly aggressive. Table 18.2 shows the relationship.

As hypothesized, paternal alcoholism and criminality were also reliably related to the mother's competence, $\chi^2(6)=15.994$, $p=0.014$. More than half the mothers of sons of men who were both alcoholic and criminal were low in competence, and almost half of the mothers of sons of men who were either alcoholic or criminal were low in competence. Table 18.3 indicates the relationship.

TABLE 18.3   Paternal Deviance and Mother's Competence (%)

| | Father's deviance | | | |
Mother's competence	Neither (N=125)	Alcoholic (N=40)	Criminal (N=21)	Both (N=28)
High	11	8	24	18
Moderate	55	45	29	21
Low	34	48	48	61
TOTAL	100	101	101	100

$\chi^2(6)=15.99$; $p=0.01$.

Note: Not all columns total 100 percent due to rounding.

Sons' Deviance in Relation to Paternal Alcoholism, Crime, and Aggression in the Family

To see whether a father's aggression in the family influenced transmission of alcoholism or criminality from one generation to the next, paternal aggression was examined in a context of paternal deviance.

Table 18.4a shows alcoholism and criminality of sons in relation to their fathers' aggression in the family, modified by presence or absence of paternal alcoholism. It shows that at each level of paternal aggression in the family, sons of alcoholics were more likely to be alcoholics than were sons of nonalcoholics. It shows also that if the father was aggressive, sons were more likely to be criminals than alcoholics—whether or not the father was an alcoholic.

Table 18.4b shows alcoholism and criminality of sons in relation to their fathers' aggression in the family, modified by presence or absence of paternal criminality. It shows that a majority of the sons of highly aggressive men became criminals (combining those who were only criminals with those who were both criminal and alcoholic)—regardless of whether or not their fathers were criminals. On the other hand, a minority of sons of nonaggressive men became criminals whether or not their fathers were criminals.

Recalling the strong relation between paternal deviance and paternal aggression in the family, it seems likely that at least some of the transmission of criminality from father to son is brought about through the greater likelihood of criminal fathers being aggressive in their families.

Sons' Deviance in Relation to Paternal Alcoholism, Crime, and Maternal Competence

Recall that alcoholic and criminal men, but especially alcoholic criminal men, tend to father children whose mothers are low in maternal competence. Table 18.5a shows alcoholism and criminality of sons in relation to maternal competence, modified by whether or not the father was an alcoholic. The data suggest an impact of maternal competence on alcoholism and criminality. The greater the

TABLE 18.4a   Paternal Alcoholism and Aggression in Family: Son's Problem Behaviours (%)

Son	Father alcoholic: Father's aggression			Father not alcoholic: Father's aggression		
	High (N=15)	Moderate (N=33)	Low (N=15)	High (N=17)	Moderate (N=32)	Low (N=92)
Neither	33	27	40	35	47	66
Alcoholic	7	24	27	6	16	13
Criminal	20	27	7	35	19	11
Both	40	21	27	24	19	10
TOTAL	100	99	101	100	101	100
	$\chi^2(6)=5.91$, NS[a]			$\chi^2(6)=12.74$, $p < 0.05$[a]		

Note: Not all columns total 100 percent due to rounding.

[a]Low expected values in at least 50 percent of the cells.

TABLE 18.4b   Paternal Criminality and Aggression in Family: Son's Problem Behaviours (%)

Son	Father criminal: Father's aggression			Father not criminal: Father's aggression		
	High (N=15)	Moderate (N=16)	Low (N=17)	High (N=17)	Moderate (N=49)	Low (N=90)
Neither	27	19	65	41	43	62
Alcoholic	7	25	18	6	18	14
Criminal	40	31	6	18	20	11
Both	27	25	12	35	18	12
TOTAL	101	100	101	100	99	99
	$\chi^2(6)=12.04$, NS[a]			$\chi^2(6)=10.79$, NS		

Note: Not all columns total 100 percent due to rounding.

[a]Low expected values in at least 50 percent of the cells.

competence of the mother, the less likely her son became either alcoholic or criminal—whether or not the boy's father was an alcoholic ($\chi^2(6)=13.822$, $p=0.032$ for sons of alcoholics; $\chi^2(6)=15.446$, $p=0.017$ for sons of nonalcoholics). In addition, the data show that at each level of maternal competence, the likelihood of a son being neither alcoholic nor criminal was smaller among sons of alcoholics. Sons of alcoholics reared by mothers who had low or only moderate competence were more likely to become alcoholics than were the sons of nonalcoholics with roughly equivalent mothers. Yet notably, among sons of alcoholics, the eight who had highly competent mothers were not more likely to be alcoholics than were sons of highly competent mothers whose fathers were not alcoholics. In short, maternal competence appears to have a modifying effect on the transmission of alcoholism from one generation to the next—an effect that may

TABLE 18.5a   Paternal Alcoholism and Mother's Competence: Son's Problem Behaviours (%)

Son	Father alcoholic: Mother's competence			Father not alcoholic: Mother's competence		
	High (N=8)	Moderate (N=22)	Low (N=33)	High (N=19)	Moderate (N=73)	Low (N=49)
Neither	63	41	18	79	62	45
Alcoholic	13	32	15	16	15	8
Criminal	25	9	27	0	11	29
Both	0	18	39	5	12	18
TOTAL	101	100	99	100	100	100
	$\chi^2(6)=13.82$, $p=0.03$[a]			$\chi^2(6)=15.45$, $p < 0.02$		

Note: Not all columns total 100 percent due to rounding.

[a]Low expected values in at least 50 percent of the cells.

be tempered by the influence of paternal alcoholism on the ability of women to carry out their maternal role.

The sons' alcoholism and criminality in relation to maternal competence, modified by whether or not the father was a criminal, is presented in Table 18.5b. Again, the data show that maternal competence is positively correlated with the likelihood that sons will be neither alcoholic nor criminal—whether or not the father was criminal ($\chi^2(6)=15.241$, $p=0.02$ for sons of criminals; $\chi^2(6)=14.632$, $p=0.023$ for sons of noncriminals). In fact, sons of criminals who had competent mothers were not more likely to become criminals than were sons of noncriminals who had competent mothers. In short, maternal competence appears to have a modifying effect on the transmission of criminality from one generation to the next.

TABLE 18.5b   Paternal Criminality and Mother's Competence: Son's Problem Behaviours (%)

Son	Father criminal: Mother's competence			Father not criminal: Mother's competence		
	High (N=10)	Moderate (N=12)	Low (N=26)	High (N=17)	Moderate (N=83)	Low (N=56)
Neither	70	50	19	76	58	41
Alcoholic	30	17	12	6	19	11
Criminal	0	17	38	12	10	23
Both	0	17	31	6	13	25
TOTAL	100	101	100	100	100	100
	$\chi^2(6)=15.24$, $p=0.02$[a]			$\chi^2(6)=14.63$, $p < 0.02$		

Note: Not all columns total 100 percent due to rounding.

[a]Low expected values in at least 50 percent of the cells.

TABLE 18.6 Maximum-Likelihood Analysis-of-Variance Table

Source	df	Chi-square	Prob.
A. RESPONSE=SON'S ALCOHOLISM			
Paternal alcoholism	1	4.59	0.03
Paternal criminality	1	1.77	0.18
Maternal competence	1	2.63	0.10
Paternal aggression	1	1.83	0.18
Likelihood ratio	11	8.64	0.66
B. RESPONSE=SON'S CRIMINALITY			
Paternal alcoholism	1	1.59	0.21
Paternal criminality	1	2.46	0.12
Maternal competence	1	12.70	0.00
Paternal aggression	1	5.90	0.02
Likelihood ratio	12	15.64	0.21

Summary and Discussion

The data suggest that alcoholic and criminal men are disproportionately likely to be aggressive in their families and to have fathered sons whose mothers are disproportionately incompetent in their maternal roles. The data indicate, therefore, that alcoholism and crime tend to run in families at least partially because alcoholic and criminal parents tend to provide poor socializing environments.

Although the sample was small and categories unevenly divided, categorical analyses of variance (CATMOD, SAS) using maximum likelihood estimators were used to examine independent contributions of paternal alcoholism, paternal criminality, paternal aggression in the family (dichotomized), and maternal competence (dichotomized) to the sons' alcoholism and criminality. In each case, the deviant category (alcoholism or criminality) was compared with those who were neither alcoholic nor criminal. In predicting alcoholism, only paternal alcoholism was statistically reliably related, $p < 0.05$, to predicting alcoholism. Maternal competence and paternal aggression in the family were reliably related to predicting criminality (see Table 18.6).

The data suggest that alcoholism tends to be transmitted through somewhat different mechanisms than criminality. Although suggestive, the tendency for maternal competence to mitigate the impact of paternal alcoholism requires more evidence. On the other hand, the data show that paternal aggression promotes the transmission of crime and maternal competence tends to impede the likelihood that criminality will be transmitted from one generation to the next.

References

Bates, M. E. and E. W. Labouvie. 1994. Familial alcoholism and personality-environment fit: A developmental study of risk in adolescents. *Types of Alcoholics—Annals of the New York Academy of Sciences* 708: 202–213.

Bennett, L. A., S. J. Wolin, D. Reiss, and M. A. Teitelbaum. 1987. Couples at risk for transmission of alcoholism: Protective influences. *Family Process* 26: 111–129.

Bohman, M. 1978. Some genetic aspects of alcoholism and criminality: A population of adoptees. *Archives of General Psychiatry* 35(2): 269–276.

Bush, S. I., M. E. Ballard, and W. Fremouw. 1995. Attributional style, depressive features, and self-esteem: Adult children of alcoholic and nonalcoholic parents. *Journal of Youth and Adolescence* 24(2): 177–185.

Cadoret, R. and A. Gath. 1978. Inheritance of alcoholism in adoptees. *British Journal of Psychiatry* 132: 252–258.

Cloninger, C. R., T. Reich, and S. B. Guze. 1978. Genetic-environmental interactions and antisocial behaviour. In *Psychopathic Behaviour: Approaches to Research*, edited by R. D. Hare and D. Schalling, 225–237. Chichester: Wiley.

Dodge, K. A., J. E. Bates, and G. A. Petit. 1990. Mechanisms in the cycle of violence. *Science* 250: 1678–1683.

Eron, L., L. R. Huesmann, and A. Zelli. 1991. The role of parental variables in the learning of aggression. In *The Development and Treatment of Childhood Aggression*, edited by D. J. Pepler and K. H. Rubin, 169–188. Hillsdale NJ: Lawrence Erlbaum.

Farrington, D. P. 1978. The family backgrounds of aggressive youths. In *Aggression and Antisocial Behaviour in Childhood and Adolescence*, edited by L. A. Hersov and M. Berger, 73–93. Oxford: Pergamon.

Farrington, D. P. 1979. Longitudinal research on crime and delinquency. In *Crime and Justice: An Annual Review of Criminal Justice Research*, edited by N. Morris and M. Tonry. Chicago: University of Chicago Press.

Farrington, D. P., G. Gundry, and D. J. West. 1975. The familial transmission of criminality. *Medicine, Science and the Law* 15(3): 177–186.

Fitzpatrick, K. M. 1997. Fighting among America's youth: A risk and protective factors approach. *Journal of Health and Social Behaviour* 38: 131–148.

Fox, R. 1962. Children in the alcoholic family. In *Problems in Addiction: Alcohol and Drug Addiction*, edited by W. C. Bier, 71–96. New York: Fordham University Press.

Goodwin, D. W. 1976. *Is Alcoholism Hereditary?* New York: Oxford University Press.

———. 1991. The etiology of alcoholism. In *Society, Culture and Drinking Patterns Reexamined*, edited by D. J. Pittman and H. R. White, 598–608. New Brunswick, NJ: Rutgers Center for Alcohol Studies.

Goodwin, D. W., J. Knop, P. Jensen, W. F. Gabrielli Jr., F. Schulsinger, and E. C. Penick. 1994. Thirty-year follow-up of men at high risk for alcoholism. *Types of Alcoholics—Annals of the New York Academy of Sciences* 708: 97–101.

Goodwin, D. W., F. Schulsinger, N. Moller, L. Hermansen, G. Winokur, and S. Guze. 1974. Drinking problems in adopted and nonadopted sons of alcoholics. *Archives of General Psychiatry* 31(2): 164–169.

Hawkins, J. D., R. F. Catalano, and J. Y. Miller. 1992. Risk and protective factors for alcohol and other drug problems in adolescence and early adulthood: Implications for substance prevention. *Psychological Bulletin* 112: 64–105.

Hill, S. Y., S. R. Steinhauer, and J. Zubin. 1987. Biological markers for alcoholism: A vulnerability model conceptualization. In *Nebraska Symposium on Motivation*, vol. 34: *Alcohol and Addictive Behaviours*, edited by P. C. Rivers. Lincoln: University of Nebraska Press.

Jacob, T. 1986. Alcoholism: A family interaction perspective. In *Nebraska Symposium on Motivation*, vol. 34: *Alcohol and Addictive Behaviours*, edited by C. Rivers. Lincoln: University of Nebraska Press.

Jacob, T. and K. Leonard. 1986. Psychosocial functioning in children of alcoholic fathers, depressed fathers, and control fathers. *Journal of Studies on Alcohol* 47: 373–380.

Kaij, L. and J. Dock. 1975. Grandsons of alcoholics. *Archives of General Psychiatry* 32(11): 1379–1381.

Knop, J., T. W. Teasdale, F. Shulsinger, and D. W. Goodwin. 1985. A prospective study of young men at high risk for alcoholism: School behaviour and achievement. *Journal of Studies on Alcohol* 46: 273–278.

Knowles, E. E. and D. A. Schroeder. 1990. Personality characteristics of sons of alcohol abusers. *Journal of Studies on Alcohol* 51(2): 142–147.

Lahey, B. B., S. E. Hartdagen, P. J. Frick, K. McBurnett, R. Conner, and G. W. Hynd. 1988. Conduct disorder: Parsing the confounded relation to parental divorce and antisocial personality. *Journal of Abnormal Psychology* 97: 334–337.

Mayfield, D., G. McLeod, and P. Hall. 1974. The CAGE questionnaire: Validation of a new alcoholism screening instrument. *American Journal of Psychiatry* 131: 1121–1123.

McCord, J. 1988. Identifying developmental paradigms leading to alcoholism. *Journal of Studies on Alcohol* 49(4): 357–362.

———. 1991a. The cycle of crime and socialization practices. *Journal of Criminal Law and Criminology* 82(1): 211–228.

———. 1991b. Family relationships, juvenile delinquency, and adult criminality. *Criminology* 29(3): 397–417.

McCord, W. and J. McCord. 1960. *Origins of Alcoholism*. Stanford, CA: Stanford University Press.

McKenna, T. and R. Pickens. 1981. Alcoholic children of alcoholics. *Journal of Studies on Alcohol* 42(11): 1021–1029.

Mednick, S. A., W. F. Gabrielli, and B. Hutchings. 1987. Genetic factors in the etiology of criminal behaviour. In *The Causes of Crime: New Biological Approaches*, edited by S. A. Mednick, T. E. Moffitt, and S. A. Stack, 74–91. Cambridge: Cambridge University Press.

Mednick, S. A., T. Moffitt , W. Gabrielli, and B. Hutchings. 1986. Genetic factors in criminal behavior: A review. In *Development of Antisocial and Prosocial Behaviour*, edited by D. Olweus, J. Block, and M. Radke-Yarrow, 33–50. Orlando, FL: Academic Press.

Newcomb, M. D. and M. Felix-Ortiz. 1992. Multiple protective and risk factors for drug use and abuse: Cross-sectional and prospective findings. *Journal of Personality and Social Psychology* 63: 280–296.

Pakaslahti, L., R-L. Asplund-Peltola, and L. Keitikangas-Järvinen. 1996. Parents' social problem-solving strategies in families with aggressive and nonaggressive boys. *Aggressive Behavior* 22(5): 345–356.

Pihl, R. O. and J. B. Peterson. 1991. A biobehavioural model for the inherited predisposition to alcoholism. *Alcohol and Alcoholism* Suppl 1: 151–156.

Pihl, R. O., J. Peterson, and P. Finn. 1990. Inherited predisposition to alcoholism: Characteristics of sons of male alcoholics. *Journal of Abnormal Psychology* 99(3): 291–301.

Pollock, V. E., J. Briere, L. Schneider, J. Knop, S. A. Mednick, and D. Goodwin. 1990. Childhood antecedents of antisocial behavior: Parental alcoholism and physical abusiveness. *American Journal of Psychiatry* 147(10): 1290–1293.

Rutter, M. 1987. Psychosocial resilience and protective mechanisms. *American Journal of Orthopsychiatry* 57(3): 316–331.

Schuckit, M. A. 1984. Relationship between the course of primary alcoholism in men and family history. *Journal of Studies on Alcohol* 45(4): 334–338.

Schuckit, M. A. and V. Rayses. 1979. Ethanol ingestion: Differences in blood acetaldehyde concentrations in relatives of alcoholics and controls. *Science* 203(4375): 54–55.

Schuckit, M. A., D. W. Goodwin, and G. Winokur. 1972. A study of alcoholism in half siblings. *American Journal of Psychiatry* 128, Pt. 2 (9): 122–126.

Schulsinger, F. 1977. Psychopathy: Heredity and environment. In *Biosocial Bases of Criminal Behavior*, edited by S. A. Mednick and K. O. Christiansen, 109–141. New York: Gardner.

Sher, K. J., K. S. Walitzer, P. K. Wood, and E. E. Brent. 1991. Characteristics of children of alcoholics: Putative risk factors, substance use and abuse, and psychopathology. *Journal of Abnormal Psychology* 100(4): 427–449.

Simons, R. L., C. Wu, C. Johnson, and R. D. Conger. 1995. A test of various perspectives on the inter-generational transmission of domestic violence. *Criminology* 33(1): 141–171.

Smith, C., A. J. Lizotte, T. P. Thornberry, and M. D. Krohn. 1995. Resilient youth: Identifying factors that prevent high-risk youth from engaging in serious delinquency and drug use. In *Current Perspectives on Aging and the Life Cycle*, vol. 4: *Delinquency and Disrepute in the Life Course*, edited by Z. S. Blau and J. Hagan, 217–248. Greenwich, CT: JAI Press.

Tarter, R. E., A. I. Alterman, and K. Edwards. 1985. Vulnerability to alcoholism in men: A behavior-genetic perspective. *Journal of Studies on Alcohol* 46(4): 329–356.

Templer, D. I., C. F. Ruff, and J. Ayers. 1974. Essential alcoholism and family history of alcoholism. *Quarterly Journal of Alcohol* 35, Pt. 2 (2): 655–657.

Vaillant, G. E. and E. S. Milofsky. 1991. The etiology of alcoholism: A prospective viewpoint. In *Society, Culture and Drinking Patterns Reexamined*, edited by D. J. Pittman and H. R. White, 492–512. New Brunswick, NJ: Rutgers Center for Alcohol Studies.

Wahler, R. G. and J. E. Dumas. 1986. "A chip off the old block": Some interpersonal characteristics of coercive children across generations. In *Children's Social Behavior: Development Assessment and Modification*, edited by P. S. Strain, M. T. Gunalnick, and H. M. Walker, 49–91. New York: Academic Press.

Werner, E. E. 1993. Risk resilience and recovery: Perspectives from the Kauai Longitudinal Study. *Development and Psychopathology* 5: 503–515.

Wu, P. and D. B. Kandel. 1995. The roles of mothers and fathers in intergenerational behavioral transmission: The case of smoking and delinquency. In *Drugs, Crime and Other Deviant Adaptations: Longitudinal Studies*, edited H. B. Kaplan, 49–81. New York: Plenum Press.

Zucker, R. A. 1987. The four alcoholisms: A developmental account of the etiological process. In *Nebraska Symposium on Motivation*, vol. 34: *Alcohol and Addictive Behavior*, edited by P. C. Rivers, 27–83. Lincoln: University of Nebraska Press.

Identifying Developmental Paradigms Leading to Alcoholism*

ALCOHOLISM, LIKE CRIME and mental illness, seems to run in families. Few who have known an alcoholic are likely to argue that an alcoholic's behavior will have no impact on his or her family. Partly for this reason, the relatively high rate of alcoholism found among children of alcoholics has often been interpreted in social-psychological terms (e.g., Blane and Barry, 1973; Burk, 1972; Fox, 1962; Zucker and Gomberg, 1986).

Over the last two decades, however, evidence has mounted to suggest a genetic component in the development of alcoholism (Bohman, 1978; Cadoret and Gath, 1978; Goodwin, 1976, 1981; Goodwin et al., 1974; Kaij and Dock, 1975; McKenna and Pickens, 1981; Schuckit, 1984; Schuckit et al., 1972; Schuckit and Rayses, 1979; Tarter et al., 1985; Templer et al., 1974).

Whether genetic factors placing a person at risk for alcoholism will produce alcoholism seems to depend, at least in part, on the environment. Various authors suggest that poverty contributes to the risk (El-Guebaly and Offord, 1977), that affection reduces it (Werner, 1986), and that attitudes toward drinking and drunkenness probably have an important impact (Cahalan, 1970; Robins et al., 1962).

A prospective approach is particularly important for studying the impact of childhood on alcoholism. Alcoholics asked to recall their childhood may well have distorting memories that either justify their behavior or serve its self-punitive formula. The present study uses data collected as part of case materials when the subjects of interest were children.

*Reprinted from McCord, J. 1988. Identifying developmental paradigms leading to alcoholism. In *Journal of Studies on Alcohol* 49: 357–362; with permission. Copyright © 1988 by Alcohol Research Documentation, Inc., Rutgers Center of Alcohol Studies, Piscataway, NJ 08854.

Method

Subjects for this study were drawn from cases in a project designed as a treatment program to prevent delinquency. The boys, born between 1926 and 1933, typically received help between their tenth and sixteenth birthdays. All lived in congested, urban areas near Boston, Massachusetts. Counselors visited their homes about twice a month, over a period of more than 5 years, recording what they saw and heard (see Powers and Witmer, 1951).

Intake records had included reports of the children's teachers in elementary school. These, plus the counselors' records, provided data upon which to classify children and their families along many dimensions.

In 1957, records describing the families of those 253 boys who had remained in the program after an initial cut in 1941 were coded (see McCord and McCord, 1960). The codes included ratings of parental alcoholism, family structure and conflict, esteem of each parent for the other, parental supervision and disciplinary characteristics, parental warmth and aggressiveness. To estimate reliability of the coding, two raters independently read a 10 percent random sample of the cases. Agreement for these ratings ranged from 76 percent to 96 percent (see Table 19.1).

The coded records, uncontaminated by retrospective bias, contain the information about family life used in the present study. The predictive validity of the

TABLE 19.1 Interrater Reliability: Dichotomous Variables (2 raters on 10 percent random sample)

	Percent agreement	Scott[a] π
Father's alcoholism	96	91
Family structure	96	92
Family conflict	80	55
Father's esteem for mother	84	68
Mother's esteem for father	88	76
Mother's self-confidence	84	60
Mother's control over boy	84	65
Boy's supervision	88	76
Expectations for boy	76	35
Father's discipline	88	52
Mother's discipline	84	62
Mother's leadership	96	91
Mother's "martyrdom"	88	25
Mother's attitude to son	84	68
Father's attitude to son	84	57
Mother's aggressiveness	92	56
Father's aggressiveness	84	41

[a]This measure provides a ratio of actual to possible improvement over chance, where chance equals the square of the proportion of the population with the characteristic plus the square of the proportion without the characteristic (Scott, 1955).

TABLE 19.2 Families of Alcoholic and Nonalcoholic Men (percent)

	Father not alcoholic (N=138)	Father alcoholic (N=65)
Father had criminal record****	14	43
Intact family***	72	46
Considerable family conflict****	20	57
Father had high esteem for mother****	59	26
Mother had high esteem for father****	61	26
Mother was self-confident*	32	18
Mother had little control over boy*	30	48
Boy was supervised**	66	43
High expectations for boy	28	18
Father was consistently punitive	20	14
Mother was consistently nonpunitive	30	26
Mother was a leader	64	54
Mother acted as a martyr	7	14
Mother was affectionate to son	50	40
Father was affectionate to son*	33	18
Mother was aggressive	9	14
Father was aggressive****	9	34

*$p < .05$. **$p < .01$. ***$p < .001$. ****$p < .0001$.

scales has been demonstrated in relation to adult criminal behavior (McCord, 1979).

The 253 boys in the follow-up study included 21 boys whose brothers were also in the study. To avoid counting particular constellations of families more than once, only one child per family was used in analyses. The study also had included 29 boys whose acting parents were not their biological parents. Information about their biological parents was unavailable. They, too, were dropped from the present analyses.

Among the remaining 203 families, 65 fathers (32%) had been classified as alcoholics. The designation of alcoholic was given a father if he had lost jobs because of drinking or had marital problems attributed primarily to excessive drinking, if welfare agencies repeatedly noted that his heavy drinking was the source of problems, if he had received treatment for alcoholism, or if he had been convicted at least three times for public drunkenness. Using the same criteria to identify alcoholic mothers, 14 women were classified as alcoholics; eight were mothers of men whose fathers also were alcoholics.

The alcoholic fathers and their families differed from nonalcoholic fathers and their families in many ways (see Table 19.2). Alcoholic fathers were more likely to have been convicted for serious crimes, $\chi^2=21.334$, 1 df, $p=.0001$; to be living apart from the mothers of their children, $\chi^2=12.487$, 1 df, $p=.0004$; and to be highly aggressive, $\chi^2=18.476$, 1 df, $p=.0001$. They were less likely to be affectionate toward their sons, $\chi^2=4.379$, 1 df, $p=.0364$; and less likely to show respect for their wives, $\chi^2=18.739$, 1 df, $p=.0001$. Families in which the father was alcoholic were more likely to exhibit considerable conflict, $\chi^2=28.567$, 1 df,

p=.0001; and less likely to provide supervision for the child, χ^2=9.524, 1 df, p=.0020. Mothers in such families were less likely to be self-confident, χ^2=3.985, 1 df, p=.0459; to exert control over the child, χ^2=5.715, 1 df, p=.0168; or to hold the boy's father in high regard, χ^2=21.302, 1 df, p=.0001.

Between 1975 and 1980, the men were traced through courts, clinics for treatment of alcoholism, and public records. Once found, they were asked to respond to questionnaires and to participate in interviews. Information from these sources as well as from the records helped identify some of the men as alcoholics.

Sons were considered alcoholics on the basis of the follow-up, when they were 45–53 years of age. Both the questionnaire and the interview included the CAGE test for alcoholism (Ewing, J. A. and Rouse, B. A. Identifying the Hidden Alcoholic. Presented at the 29th International Congress on Alcoholism and Drug Dependence, Sydney, NSW, Australia, 2–6 February 1970). In this test, respondents are asked if they have ever taken a morning eye-opener, felt the need to cut down on drinking, felt annoyed by criticism of their drinking, or felt guilty about drinking. A man was considered an alcoholic if he responded affirmatively, as do alcoholics (Mayfield et al., 1974), to at least three of these questions.

There were 38 men who met the criteria for alcoholics used in the CAGE test. A man was also considered an alcoholic if he had received treatment for alcoholism (17 met this criterion), if he had been arrested at least three times for public drunkenness or driving while intoxicated (28 met this criterion), if he described himself as an alcoholic (true for one man), or if he was arrested twice for alcoholism and answered affirmatively to two of the CAGE questions (true for two). Altogether, 61 men (32%) met at least one of the criteria for alcoholism.

To qualify as nonalcoholic, a man had not been arrested for public drunkenness or driving while intoxicated, had not been treated for alcoholism, had scored less than three on the CAGE test, and had not described himself as an alcoholic. There were 132 nonalcoholics.

Ten men could not be classified. These men had been arrested for public drunkenness, but they met none of the criteria for classification as alcoholics. Two had been arrested twice and eight had been arrested once for public drunkenness. Of these ten, two had died in California, five were living in Massachusetts, two were found elsewhere, and one was not found. Analyses used the sample of 193 men who could be classified for alcoholism.

About two-thirds of the alcoholics were identified through records and about two-thirds were identified through self-descriptions. Sources for the diagnoses of alcoholism among sons of alcoholics (n=28) and sons of nonalcoholics (n=33) differed little: 9 (32%) sons of alcoholics were identified from records only, 11 (39%) from self-description only, and 8 (29%) from records and self-description; 11 (33%) sons of nonalcoholics were identified from records only, 13 (39%) from self-description only, and 9 (27%) from records and self-description.

Criminal records had been searched in 1948, as part of treatment evaluation. In 1975, criminal records were searched again. These records showed the age of conviction as well as the charge for each of the men who had appeared in court. Sons could be classified by their juvenile records as well as by whether they had been convicted for the more serious street crimes that appear on the Federal Bureau of Investigation Index.

Results

Like other studies, this one shows that sons of alcoholics were at increased risk for alcoholism. Whereas 25 percent of the 133 men whose fathers were not alcoholic had become alcoholics, 47 percent of the 60 men with alcoholic fathers were alcoholics. Additionally, alcoholic fathers and their sons were at increased risk for serious criminal behavior: In the alcoholic father group, 45 percent of the fathers and 47 percent of the sons were convicted for an Index crime; and in the nonalcoholic father group, 19 percent of the fathers and 28 percent of the sons were convicted for an Index crime.

Cross-classification of criminal histories for the sons and alcoholism in two generations suggests that both the father's alcoholism and that of the son are related to criminality. The relationships are shown in Table 19.3.

Juvenile delinquency was tied to paternal alcoholism. Boys whose fathers were alcoholics were more likely than their peers to have a record for juvenile delinquencies. Subsequent serious crimes, however, appeared to be more closely tied to the subject's own alcoholism.

As part of the selection process, teachers had completed "Trait Record Cards," describing the boys. Gathered in 1936 and 1937, these records were used to classify the boys as aggressive (if their teachers had checked the description "fights") or as shy (if their teachers checked "shy," "easily hurt," or "easily moved to tears"). Eighteen boys were classified as both shy and aggressive. These teachers' ratings of the boys in elementary school proved to be predictive of behavior decades later (see Table 19.4).

Shy children were least likely to become alcoholics or criminals. Boys rated as both aggressive and shy, however, were most likely to become alcoholics or criminals. Six of the eight shy-aggressive boys who had alcoholic fathers had become alcoholics as had three of the ten whose fathers were not alcoholic.

TABLE 19.3   Father's Alcoholism and Son's Criminal History (percent convicted, by record type)

	Father alcoholic		Father not alcoholic	
	Son alcoholic (N=28)	Son not alcoholic (N=32)	Son alcoholic (N=33)	Son not alcoholic (N=100)
Son convicted as juvenile*	46	41	27	22
Son convicted for index crime as a juvenile**	39	31	24	13
Son ever convicted for an Index crime**	57	38	45	22

df=3. *p < .05. **p < .01.

TABLE 19.4 Boys According to Teachers' Descriptions (1936–37) and Type of Deviance (percent of each category of boys)

Deviance type	Aggressive (N=33)	Shy (N=57)	Aggressive and shy (N=18)	Neither (N=85)
Neither	45	63	28	49
Alcoholic only	12	19	17	14
Criminal only	30	12	22	15
Alcoholic and criminal	12	5	33	21
TOTAL	99[a]	99[a]	100	99[a]

χ^2=18.300; 9 df; p=.032.

[a]Deviation from 100 percent due to rounding.

To identify parental behaviors related to alcoholism of the son, 18 variables were entered into a stepwise logistic regression analysis, using BMDPLR (Dixon, 1985). These variables described the father in terms of alcoholism, criminality, affection for his son, esteem for the boy's mother, disciplinary techniques, and aggressiveness. They described the mother in terms of role, affection for her son, self-confidence, esteem for the boy's father, disciplinary techniques, and aggressiveness. The families were further described as being intact or broken, whether or not the parents were in considerable conflict, whether anyone supervised the boy after school, and whether the boy was expected to perform well.

Using remove and enter limits of .15 to .10, the analysis identified four variables as predictors of subsequent alcoholism of the sons. The father's alcoholism accounted for the greatest amount of variance, F=8.32, 1/187 df, p=.0044. The mother's esteem for the boy's father accounted for an additional significant proportion of the variance, F=7.64, 1/187 df, p=.0063. The mother's control over the

TABLE 19.5 Stepwise Logistic Regression

Term	Coefficient	Standard error	Coeff./SE
Alcoholic father	0.568	0.194	2.929
Mother's esteem	0.669	0.238	2.808
Mother's control	0.336	0.173	1.948
Parental conflict	0.366	0.245	1.495
Constant	−0.406	0.184	−2.201

	Correlation coefficients				
	Alcoholic father	Mother's esteem	Mother's control	Conflict	Constant
Alcoholic father	1.000				
Mother's esteem	0.236	1.000			
Mother's control	−0.007	0.178	1.000		
Parental conflict	−0.187	0.612	0.037	1.000	
Constant	0.167	0.273	0.215	0.335	1.000

TABLE 19.6   Family Backgrounds for Alcoholism (log-linear analysis)

Source (effect)	df	χ^2	Probability
SATURATED MODEL			
Father's alcoholism	1	19.78	.0001
Mother's esteem for father	1	12.58	.0004
Mother's control of boy	1	4.84	.0278
Father's alcoholism × mother's esteem	1	6.37	.0116
Father's alcoholism × mother's control	1	0.06	.8075
Mother's esteem × mother's control	1	0.22	.6395
Father's alcoholism × mother's esteem × control	1	0.71	.3992
Residual	1	3.16	.0755
FULLY SPECIFIED MODEL			
Father's alcoholism	1	20.75	.0001
Mother's esteem for father	1	12.15	.0005
Mother's control of boy	1	5.23	.0222
Father's alcoholism × mother's esteem	1	6.70	.0096
Residual	4	4.38	.3569

boy improved the fit, $F=3.68$, 1/187 df, $p=.0568$. And parental conflict, with $F=2.17$, 1/187 df, $p=.1428$, provided the next best predictor. Regression coefficients, standard errors, their ratios, and associated probabilities are shown in Table 19.5, along with correlations among the four variables. Together, the linear function based on these four variables provided a logistic model having a reasonable fit to the data, $\chi^2=0.327$, 2 df, $p=.849$.

Log linear analyses were used to inspect the interaction terms and main effects of the three most important predictors: father's alcoholism, mother's esteem for the father, and mother's control of the boy during childhood (see Table 19.6). As can be seen, father's alcoholism, mother's esteem for the father, and mother's control of the boy each significantly differentiated alcoholic from nonalcoholic sons. In addition, the interaction between father's alcoholism and mother's esteem contributed reliably to prediction of the son's alcoholism.

TABLE 19.7   Family Type and Alcoholism

Father's alcoholism?	Mother's high esteem?	Mother's little control?	% Alcoholic	N
No	No	No	12	33
No	No	Yes	32	19
No	Yes	No	25	61
No	Yes	Yes	40	20
Yes	No	No	35	23
Yes	No	Yes	41	22
Yes	Yes	No	70	10
Yes	Yes	Yes	80	5

Maternal control and the mother's esteem for her husband differed in their effects depending on whether or not the father was alcoholic (Table 19.7). Maternal control over the boy had a stronger effect among sons of nonalcoholics than among sons of alcoholics. Maternal esteem for the boy's father, on the other hand, had a particularly strong effect on alcoholism among boys whose fathers were alcoholics. Among the sons of alcoholics, 73 percent of the 15 whose mothers showed high esteem for their fathers had become alcoholics compared with 38 percent of the 45 whose mothers had not shown high esteem for their fathers.

These analyses suggest two paths toward alcoholism. One path appears to be imitative and the other to represent uninhibited behavior. Additional differences between sons of alcoholics and sons of nonalcoholics were sought in responses to interview questions about behavior related to drinking.

During the interviews, men were asked whether they had ever had an accident due to drinking, hurt a friendship or marriage due to drinking, missed an appointment, or been involved in a fight due to drinking. A majority of the alcoholics (85%) answered affirmatively, whether or not their fathers had been alcoholics: 87 percent of the alcoholic sons of alcoholics ($n=23$), and 83 percent of the alcoholic sons of nonalcoholics ($n=23$). Among nonalcoholics, however, men whose fathers had been alcoholics were more likely to have been in these types of trouble: 47 percent of the nonalcoholic sons of alcoholics ($n=19$) and only 14 percent of the nonalcoholic sons of nonalcoholics ($n=65$) had gotten into trouble due to drinking ($\chi^2=9.813$, 1 df, $p=.0017$).

During the interviews, the men were asked about their drinking patterns. Alcoholics from families in which the father was also alcoholic were almost twice as likely as other alcoholics to report daily drinking. Whereas 83 percent of the alcoholic sons of alcoholics reported daily drinking, 48 percent of the alcoholic sons of nonalcoholic men reported daily drinking ($\chi^2=6.133$, 1 df, $p=.0133$). The proportions of nonalcoholics from alcoholic families approximated those from nonalcoholic families regarding daily drinking: 21 percent of the former and 23 percent of the latter said they drank every day.

Drinking and trouble seemed linked for sons of alcoholics. Drinking and companionship seemed linked for alcoholics from nonalcoholic families. These latter tended to be active in social clubs. Among alcoholics whose fathers were not alcoholic, 87 percent reported being active in clubs, compared with 41 percent of the alcoholic sons of alcoholic men ($\chi^2=10.405$, 1 df, $p=.0013$). The proportions of nonalcoholics from alcoholic families approximated those from nonalcoholic families regarding the proportions who were active in clubs: 61 percent of the former and 63 percent of the latter described at least one club in which they were active.

Discussion

This study has considered development of alcoholism using a prospective design. Subjects were drawn from youths who participated in a program designed to prevent delinquency. Their case material dated from the 1930s. The case records, uncontaminated by retrospective bias, included descriptions of their behavior in elementary school and observations of family interactions over several years.

The records indicate that shy-aggressive children tend to be at risk for criminal and alcoholic behavior. The records also indicate that alcoholic fathers and their families differ from nonalcoholic fathers and their families in many ways. Although having an alcoholic father increased exposure to conflict and rejection, these conditions appeared not to increase the risk of alcoholism.

Two developmental paradigms seemed to emerge from the analyses. In one, men with alcoholic fathers seem to be imitating a respected father. Sons of alcoholic men were more likely to become alcoholics if their mothers showed high esteem for their fathers. These alcoholics were likely to drink on a daily basis. Even if not alcoholic themselves, sons of alcoholics tended to report getting into trouble while drinking. Men whose fathers were alcoholics may have been taught that their fathers' behavior was acceptable—or, at least, forgivable. They may have accepted drinking as part of the masculine role. In the other developmental paradigm, lack of maternal control increased the probability that sons would become alcoholics. These alcoholics, especially those whose fathers were not alcoholics, apparently associate drinking with uninhibited, often antisocial behavior.

The models built on paternal alcoholism, mother's approval of her husband, and maternal control clearly provide only a partial explanation for the development of alcoholism. Other variables, both biological and social, could undoubtedly improve both specificity and sensitivity of the predictions. It seems reasonable to suggest that better measures of genetic loading might improve predictions as might the addition of such social variables as approval of heavy drinking.

Note

This study was partly supported by U.S. Public Health Service research grant MH26779 (Center for Studies of Crime and Delinquency, National Institute of Mental Health). An earlier version of this article was presented at the joint meeting of the Research Society on Alcoholism and the Committee on Problems of Drug Dependence, Philadelphia, PA, 14–19 June 1987.

References

Blane, H. T. and H. Barry, III. 1973. Birth order and alcoholism: A review. Q. J. Stud. Alcohol 34: 837–852.

Bohman, M. 1978. Some genetic aspects of alcoholism and criminality: A population of adoptees. Arch. Gen. Psychiat. 35: 269–276.

Burk, E. D. 1972. Some contemporary issues in child development and the children of alcoholic parents. Ann. N.Y. Acad. Sci. 197: 189–197.

Cadoret, R. J. and A. Gath. 1978. Inheritance of alcoholism in adoptees. Brit. J. Psychiat. 132: 252–258.

Cahalan, D. 1970. Problem Drinkers. San Francisco: Jossey-Bass.

Dixon, W. J. 1985. BMDP Statistical Software. Berkeley, Calif.: University of California Press.

El-Guebaly, N. and D. R. Offord. 1977. The offspring of alcoholics: A critical review. *Amer. J. Psychiat.* 34: 357–365.

Fox, R. Children in the alcoholic family. 1962. In *Problems in Addiction: Alcohol and Drug Addiction*, edited by W. C. Bier, 71–96. New York: Fordham University Press.

Goodwin, D. W. 1981. *Is Alcoholism Hereditary?* New York: Oxford University Press.

———. Family studies of alcoholism. *J. Stud. Alcohol* 42: 156–162.

Goodwin, D. W., F. Schulsinger, N. Møller, L. Hermansen, G. Winokur, and S. Guze. 1974. Drinking problems in adopted and nonadopted sons of alcoholics. *Arch. Gen. Psychiat.* 31: 164–169.

Kau, L. and J. Dock. 1975. Grandsons of alcoholics: A test of sex-linked transmission of alcohol abuse. *Arch. Gen. Psychiat.* 32: 1379–1381.

McCord, J. 1979. Some child-rearing antecedents of criminal behavior in adult men. *J. Pers. Social Psychol.* 37: 1477–1486.

McCord, W. and J. McCord. 1960. *Origins of Alcoholism*. Stanford, Calif.: Stanford Univeristy Press.

McKenna, T. and R. Pickens. 1981. Alcoholic children of alcoholics. *J. Stud. Alcohol* 42: 1021–1029.

Mayfield, D., G. McLeod, and P. Hall. 1974. The CAGE questionnaire: Validation of a new alcoholism screening instrument. *Amer. J. Psychiat.* 131: 1121–1123.

Powers, E. and H. Witmer. 1951. *An Experiment in the Prevention of Delinquency: The Cambridge-Somerville Youth Study*. New York: Columbia University Press.

Robins, L. N., W. M. Bates, and P. O'Neal. 1962. Adult drinking patterns of former problem children. In *Society, Culture and Drinking Patterns*, edited by D. J. Pittman and C. R. Snyder, 395–412. New York: John Wiley & Sons, Inc.

Schuckit, M. A. 1984. Relationship between the course of primary alcoholism in men and family history. *J. Stud. Alcohol* 45: 334–338.

Schuckit, M. A., D. W. Goodwin, and G. Winokur. 1972. A study of alcoholism in half siblings. *Amer. J. Psychiat.* 128: 122–126.

Schuckit, M. A. and V. Rayses. 1979. Ethanol ingestion: Differences in blood acetaldehyde concentrations in relatives of alcoholics and controls. *Science* 203: 54–55.

Scott, W. A. 1955. Reliability of content analysis: The case of nominal scale coding. *Publ. Opinion Quart.* 19: 321–325.

Tarter, R. E., A. I. Alterman, and K. L. Edwards. 1985. Vulnerability to alcoholism in men: A behavior-genetic perspective. *J. Stud. Alcohol* 46: 329–356.

Templer, D. I., C. F. Ruff, and J. Ayers. 1974. Essential alcoholism and family history of alcoholism. (Notes and Comment). *Q. J. Stud. Alcohol* 35: 655–657.

Werner, E. E. 1986. Resilient offspring of alcoholics: A longitudinal study from birth to age 18. *J. Stud. Alcohol* 47: 34–40.

Zucker, R. A. and E. S. L. Gomberg. 1986. Etiology of alcoholism reconsidered: The case for a biopsychosocial process. *Amer. Psychol.* 41: 783–793.

CHAPTER TWENTY

Another Time, Another Drug*

RECENT RESEARCH has suggested that drinking alcohol is almost a necessary precursor for using illegal drugs and that abusing the legal drug alcohol sets the stage for abusing illegal drugs (Kandel, 1980; Mills and Noyes, 1984; Osgood, Johnston, O'Malley, and Bachman, 1988; Welte and Barnes, 1985). Understanding the etiology of alcohol abuse is therefore a preliminary step toward understanding the transition to other forms of drug abuse. Understanding alcohol abuse is important also because its consequences, like those of illegal drugs, are known to be harmful both physically and socially. In the case of both alcohol abuse and the abuse of illegal substances, the "addict" appears knowingly to choose self-inflicted damage. If we can learn why such choices occur in the one case, we will have information relevant to comprehending the other. And finally, a focus on alcohol is important because the history of its widespread use and condemnation gives a perspective to contemporary problems of substance abuse.

The parallel between alcohol and opium abuse was drawn in 1921 by Edward A. Ross, who noted that what opium was to China, alcohol was to the United States: "Even in small quantities alcohol is an upsetter and deranger of the functions of the mind as well as the body" (p. 187). Citing industrial accidents, as well as physical and mental problems, putatively caused by alcohol, he argued that unless Prohibition were successful, the country would go through a period of self-destruction in which people susceptible to alcohol would annihilate one another or themselves. A geneticist, Ross predicted that by the year 2100 A.D. our descendents might be as constitutionally resistant to alcohol beguilement as are the Portuguese today" (p. 189).

*Reprinted from McCord, J. 1992. Another time, another drug. In *Vulnerability to Drug Abuse* edited by M. Glantz, and R. Pickens, 473–489. Washington, D.C.: American Psychological Association; with permission.

Earlier commentators had noted relationships between drinking and criminal behavior. Enrico Ferri (1897), for example, remarked on the relationship between the "abundance of vintage" and crimes of violence in France between 1850 and 1880. Ferri believed that alcohol was clearly a cause of crime, and he urged an international effort to reduce the use of alcohol. Some estimates of the link between alcohol and crime were gained by surveys of convicts. In one study in the United States, Koren attributed 50 percent of the crimes of more than 13,000 convicts to drinking alcohol (cited in Howard, 1918). Lombroso (1912/1968) made similar claims in England, with even higher estimates of the relationship between alcohol and crime. Other studies presented figures close to 100 percent. In summarizing the evidence, the sociologist George Elliott Howard (1918) indicated the dimensions of the problem: "To master the crime-producing environment which consists in alcohol and the organized alcohol traffic may cost more courage, wisdom, and toil than it cost to abolish human slavery . . . " (p. 63).

Movement toward Prohibition had gained momentum during World War I as social workers, joined by industrialist, backed Prohibition as patriotic. Servicemen were not allowed to drink, and dry zones were created surrounding military bases. Around the same time, according to Timberlake (1966), scientific evidence had been adduced to show that "inebriety in parents was a cause of physical, mental, and moral degeneracy in children . . . " (p. 44).

Local elections revealed resistance to the temperance movement. In 1916, Boston voters rejected almost two to one a bill that would have prohibited the licensing of saloons. Yet by 1917, 26 states had outlawed the sale of liquor. That year, a surprise federal resolution was introduced in congress to prohibit the "manufacture, sale, or transportation of intoxicating liquors within, the importation thereof into, or the exportation thereof from the United States and all territory subject to the jurisdiction thereof for beverage purposes."

Timberlake (1966) traced the success of the movement to enforce Prohibition to a conjunction of scientific discoveries and social changes brought about through the Progressive movement. The Eighteenth Amendment did not take effect until January 16, 1920, although the War Prohibition Act, enacted on November, 21, 1918, and enforced after July 1, 19191, was the effective beginning of national Prohibition in the United States. Restricted liquor sales had been in place since 1917, and by 1919, the voting public seemed overwhelmingly to favor Prohibition. Referring to passage of national Prohibition, the 14th edition of the *Encyclopedia Britannica*, published in 1929, described the process as follows: "It was adopted after full and free public discussion, in the face of determined and powerful opposition, by larger majorities and greater unanimity in Congress and in the forty-six States (out of a total of 48 States) which ratified it than any other amendment" (Lindsay, 1929, p. 566).

Nonetheless, enforcement remained a problem (Catlin, 1932; Gebhart, 1932). Between 1920 and 1930, enforcement was the responsibility of the Treasury Department. Jurisdiction switched to the Department of Justice with passage of the Williamson Act in 1930. In 1929, the Jones Law had increased penalties for violation to maximum of $10,000 or up to 5 years imprisonment. This was modified in 1931 to reduce penalties for offenders who sold or transported less than a gallon of liquor. That year, too, the Supreme Court handed down a unanimous opinion to overturn a year-old District Court decision by Judge William Clark that had raised questions about the constitutionality of the Eighteenth Amendment.

Perception that drinking was a common practice throughout Prohibition, coupled with repeal of the Eighteenth Amendment in 1933, has lead some observers to cite Prohibition as a failed policy of drug control. Nevertheless, there is some evidence that crime decreased during the period (Ferdinand, 1967) and that the incidence of alcohol psychoses may have also decreased (Burnham, 1968; Emerson, 1932). Sinclair (1962) argued that a change in drinking patterns created the mistaken impression that alcohol consumption had increased. During the early years of the 20th century, salons were the social clubs for immigrants, but the middle classes drank little. Sinclair suggested that Prohibition made drinking stylish, becoming fashionable for the middle classes, while making it more difficult for the working classes to find a drink.

A variety of attempts have been made to identify the effects of Prohibition. Hospital admissions for cirrhosis of the liver and deaths from alcoholism fluctuated slightly throughout the years of Prohibition (Brown, 1932). Crime rates in New York City decreased during this period (Willbach, 1938). Yet in Chicago, "the ratios of the population arrested for crimes against the person showed an almost continuous increase up to 1927, which was followed by an almost uninterrupted decrease through 1939" (Willbach, 1941).

Studies of the effects of Prohibition have not examined the impact of changing populations caused by immigration and urbanization. Yet dramatic changes in the population took place between 1920 and 1930 (Lyman, 1932). Without a control for social class, it would be premature to judge whether the prohibition of alcohol had an impact on drinking or on other socially relevant problems. The purpose of the present study was to take a new look at the effects of Prohibition by comparing two cohorts of people whose exposure to the propaganda and to the legal changes would have affected them differently.

Method

Subjects for the study came from a generation of men born between 1872 and 1913. They were selected because their sons were part of a youth study active between 1935 and 1945. Descriptions of the fathers' behavior became available through their participation in the latter study. Of the original 232 families, information was available about the drinking habits of 183 fathers.

All subjects lived in overcrowded, run-down neighborhoods of Cambridge and Somerville, Massachusetts. High crime rates, poverty, and obvious property deterioration were grounds for selecting neighborhoods, and the subjects were selected because of the neighborhood in which they lived and because of the ages of their sons.[1]

Data were gathered between 1939 and 1945 when, approximately twice a month, counselors visited the homes of boys to try to help them and their families.

The councelors appeared at various times of the day and throughout the week. After each encounter, the counselors filed a detailed report that included conversations and described behavior. Covering a span of more than 5 years, these running records provided the information used in the present study. In 1957, coders who had access to no information other than that in the case records transcribed the information into categorical scales describing the parents, the boys, and family interactions.

In terms of occupation,[2] 60 percent (n=108) of the fathers were unskilled workers. Most of the remaining fathers, 32 percent (n=58), were skilled workers. Only 8 percent held white-collar positions, including one professional. The sample included nine Blacks; the remaining subjects were Whites. Almost half had completed the eighth grade, although only 20 had graduated from high school, and 3 had graduated from college.[3] About half (n=96) were born in the United States. Italy (n=33), Canada (n=22), and Portugal (n=15) were the birth places of most of the rest.[4]

Information from criminal records, gathered for the fathers in 1948 and for their sons in 1976, was added to the information gained through the case records. Some additional information about the lives of the subjects was collected through interviews with the adult sons between 1975 and 1980. Questionnaires, interviews, and records of treatment for alcoholism, also collected between 1975 and 1980, added data about the sons.

To justify considering each family as independent, 16 brothers were dropped from the analyses. If one brother had been interviewed and the other had not (n=7), the interviewed brother was included. If both or neither had been interviewed (n=9), the one whose given name came first alphabetically was selected.

Subjects were divided into two groups according to their dates of birth. Those born between 1896 and 1913 (inclusive) would have been exposed to the antiliquor campaign and to Prohibition during their minority; they were less than age 21 in 1917. Those born between 1872 and 1895 had reached majority by 1917. The impact of legal and social changes can be expected to differ for the adolescents, whose average age was 16 in 1917, and the adults, whose average age was 29 in 1917; therefore, these groups provide the basis for assessing effects of Prohibition. Dates of birth were missing for 2 of the 183 subjects for whom drinking problems could be coded; they were dropped from the study.

Ratings analyzed for the present study focus on problems related to alcohol and crime. Paternal behavior was evaluated in terms of drinking problems reported in the case records; these were coded in 1957. At that time, two raters independently read a 10 percent random sample of the cases in order to estimate the reliability of the coding.

One of the codes identified fathers as habitual, excessive drinkers. For this identification, the ratings of the two coders were in agreement on 92 percent of the fathers. A second rating noted whether fathers had lost jobs or had family problems because of their current or prior drinking; ratings indicated 96 percent agreement on this code. Fathers were considered to have problems with alcohol if they were so rated or if they had been arrested at least three times for driving under the influence of alcohol or for public drunkenness. Additional evidence for drinking problems was gathered through interviews. Sons were asked to describe their fathers' attitudes toward drinking; coded for reliability, two raters agreed on 91 percent of the ratings. A father was also considered to have problems with drinking if his son described him as regularly drunk or making trouble when he drank. According to these criteria, among the 181 men in the study, 94 (52%) had drinking problems.

Among the 181 men whose drinking problems, dates of birth, and drinking habits could be rated, 17 were teetotalers, including 9 percent of the 75 men born before 1896 and 9 percent of the 106 men born after 1895. Only 10 fathers had been convicted for the illegal sale of alcohol.

Information about the sons of the subjects was collected between 1975 and 1980, when they ranged in age from 45 to 53 years. Records from courts, clinics for treatment of alcoholism, and mental hospitals were searched for each of the men. Voting records, visits to old home neighborhoods, and a variety of tracing techniques led to the retrieval of addresses for 98 percent of the sons. Once found, they were asked to respond to questionnaires and to participate in interviews. Both the questionnaires and the interviews used the CAGE test (Ewing and Rouse, 1970) to identify alcoholics. In this test, respondents are asked if they have ever taken a morning eye-opener, felt the need to cut down on drinking, felt annoyed by criticism of their drinking, or felt guilty about drinking. A man was considered an alcoholic if he responded affirmatively, as do alcoholics (Mayfield, McLeod, and Hall, 1974), to at least three of these questions. A son was also considered to be alcoholic if he had received treatment for alcoholism, if he had been arrested at least three times for public drunkenness or driving while intoxicated, or if he described himself as an alcoholic. Additionally, a son was considered an alcoholic if he had been arrested twice for alcoholism and answered affirmatively to two of the CAGE questions. By these criteria, the sons of 57 of the subjects were classified as alcoholics.

Criminal records of the fathers had been searched in 1948, and those of the sons were checked in 1975. These records showed the age of conviction as well as the charge for each of the men who had appeared in court. Ninety-six of the fathers and 134 of the sons had been convicted for at least one nontraffic crime. Street crimes that appear on the Federal Bureau of Investigation Index are considered "serious"; 46 fathers and 59 sons had been convicted for crimes in the Federal Bureau of Investigation Index.

Results

Men exposed to Prohibition as adolescents had a higher probability of manifesting problems with alcohol than did those men who were already adults in 1917. Whereas 41 percent of the men who were over 21 in 1917 had problems with alcohol, 58 percent of those between 17 and 21 in 1917 had problems with alcohol ($\chi^2_{(1)}$=5.176, p < .023).

Age at exposure to Prohibition appeared to have little direct impact on whether a person became a criminal. Comparisons of the proportions convicted for nontraffic crimes and for serious crimes revealed no significant difference in

TABLE 20.1   Exposure to Prohibition, Alcohol Problems, and Criminal Behavior

| | Father's age at exposure to prohibition | | | |
| | 17–21 | | Over 21 | |
Criminal activity	Drinking problem (%)	No problem (%)	Drinking problem (%)	No problem (%)
Not convicted	21	80	26	66
Minor crimes	37	11	39	23
Serious crimes	42	9	35	11
N	62	44	31	44

$\chi^2(1)=49.10$; $p=.000$.

relation to age at exposure. In both cohorts, however, criminal behavior was strongly related to having problems with alcohol (Table 20.1).

Although there was little difference in the proportions who committed at least one nontraffic crime, men who were exposed to Prohibition during adolescence differed from those who were already adults by 1917 in terms of the number of crimes they committed, with the younger cohort more actively criminal. The 75 men who were over 21 in 1917 committed an average of 2.15 nontraffic crimes ($SD=5.8$); the 106 who were under 21 in 1917 committed an average of 5.24 crimes ($SD=11.93$), $t_{(161.6)}=2.306$, $p < .022$. In terms of the probability of committing at least one more crime, those exposed to Prohibition as adolescents were more likely to be recidivists. For the men exposed to Prohibition as adolescents, the probability of recidivism was higher following the first through the fifth crime, and convicted men who had been older during Prohibition were more likely to be recidivists after convictions for at least seven crimes. Figure 20.1 shows the probability for recidivism after each crime number to the ninth crime.

The older men also committed fewer serious crimes. Those exposed to Prohibition as adolescents committed an average of 0.73 ($SD=1.54$) serious crimes, compared with an average of 0.28 ($SD=0.61$) for the older men, $t_{(145.7)}=2.69$, $p < .007$.

The group exposed to Prohibition as adolescents began committing crimes at younger ages. The mean age for the 57 convicted men who were under 21 in 1917 was 27.2 ($SD=7.8$), whereas the mean age for the 38 convicted men who were at least 21 in 1917 was 39.7 ($SD=9.8$), $t_{(93)}=6.913$, $p < .0001$. For serious crimes, the average age at first conviction among the 30 men exposed to Prohibition as adolescents was 26.33 years ($SD=8.17$), whereas the mean age for the 15 convicted men who were at least 21 in 1917 was 38.73 years ($SD=6.66$), $t_{(43)}=5.09$, $p < .0001$.

Figure 20.2 shows hazard rates for ages at first convictions, both for all nontraffic crimes and for only serious crimes (SAS Institute, 1985). The distributions indicate peak hazard rates in the early twenties for those exposed to Prohibition as adolescents and in the mid-forties for those exposed to Prohibition as adults. For nontraffic crimes, the Wilcoxon test for differences had a chi-square value of

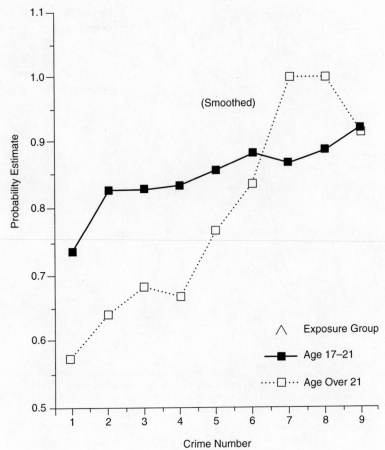

FIGURE 20.1   Age at exposure to prohibition: conditional probability for committing at least one more nontraffic crime.

9.612, $p < .0019$. For serious crimes, the Wilcoxon test for differences had a chi-square value of 4.206, $p < .0403$.

Age differences between those exposed to Prohibition as adolescents and those exposed as adults are evidenced among both the men who had problems with alcohol and those who did not. Figure 20.3 shows the distribution for the ages at first conviction for all nontraffic crimes. As can be seen, in both groups, men who had problems with alcohol were also at greater risk for being convicted—well into their mid-fifties. The Wilcoxon test of equality over strata had a chi-square value of 8.587, $p < .0034$.

Figure 20.4 shows age-related hazard rates for the first serious crime. Within both the younger and the older cohorts, men who had problems with alcohol were

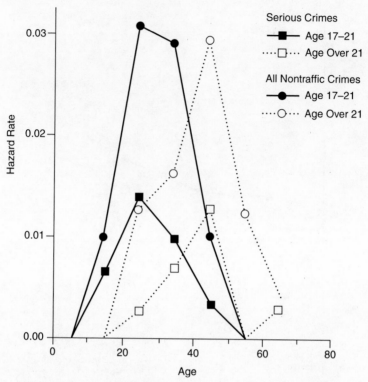

FIGURE 20.2   Age at exposure to prohibition: age at first conviction.

at greater risk for committing a first serious crime. The Wilcoxon test of equality over strata had a chi-square value of 26.267, $p < .0001$.

Hazard rates for age at first conviction, adjusted for year of birth, show similar patterns for the two cohorts. Among both the older and the younger men, hazard rates rose between 1915 and 1935, falling thereafter (Figure 20.5).

The evidence suggests that men exposed to Prohibition as adolescents were more likely than older cohorts to have problems with alcohol and to commit crimes. If biological or cultural differences between cohorts accounted for the observed differences in patterns of crime, one would expect that sons as well as fathers in the two cohorts would differ in their crime rates. This was not the case. Sons of the two cohorts differed little in their ages at first conviction for nontraffic crimes or for serious crimes. Nor did they differ reliably in terms of the number of nontraffic crimes or serious crimes for which they were convicted (Table 20.2).

Almost equal proportions of the sons of the two cohorts were alcoholic: 31 percent of the younger men and 32 percent of the older ones. For both cohorts, sons of alcoholics were more likely to be alcoholics, with the stronger relationship among older men (Table 20.3).

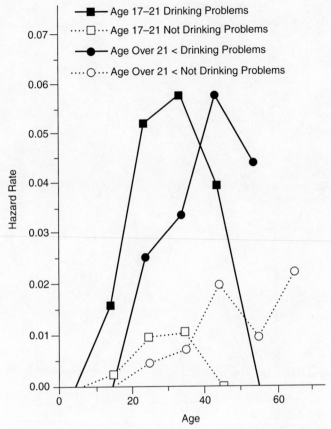

FIGURE 20.3 Prohibition exposure and drinking problems: age of conviction for nontraffic crimes.

Summary and Discussion

This chapter has compared two cohorts of men exposed to Prohibition at different periods in their lives. Members of the younger cohort were adolescents as the issues were argued and the legislation passed to make the sale and purchase of liquor an offense. Members of the older cohort had already reached majority when the Eighteenth Amendment became law. The first group was expected to be more responsive to the changes. They might have shown responsiveness by exhibiting greater control over drinking; such was the optimistic perception of those who have argued the case for Prohibition. They might have shown a greater disrespect for the law; such was the pessimistic perception of those who consider Prohibition to have been a failure. This study suggests that the pessimists were more nearly correct than the optimists. At least for these men, Prohibition seems to

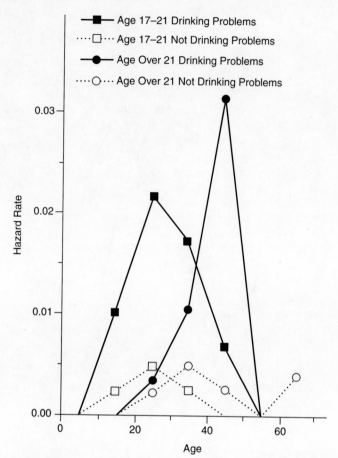

FIGURE 20.4 Prohibition exposure and drinking problems: age of first conviction for serious crimes.

have introduced factors that increased criminal behavior. The data also suggest that age at first crime, a variable known to predict subsequent criminality (Blumstein, Cohen, Roth, and Visher, 1986; Farrington, 1983; McCord, 1981), was influenced by Prohibition.

Crime rates can change because a population base shifts (Greenberg, 1979), as well as because of increases in criminal behavior. Increases in criminal behavior occur either when more people become criminals or when criminals commit more crimes (Barnett, Blumstein, and Farrington, 1989; Blumstein et al., 1986; Willbach, 1938). The data presented here indicate that Prohibition influenced criminal behavior by increasing the amount of crime committed by criminals rather than by increasing the number of criminals.

There are several ways to interpret a relationship between Prohibition and increased crime. One argument would rest on the view that Prohibition was an illegitimate attempt to legislate morality that might have created resistance to a

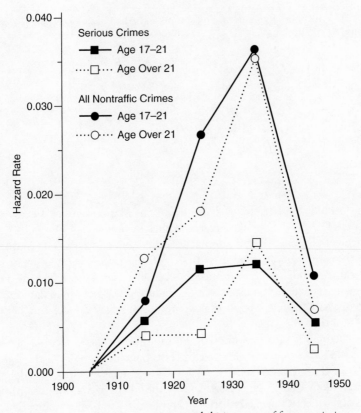

FIGURE 20.5   Age at exposure to prohibition: year of first conviction.

broad range of legal restrictions. A variant of psychological reactance theory (J. W. Brehm, 1966; S. S. Brehm and Brehm, 1981), this argument maintains that the attempt to enforce too much weakened social control. A more sociological argument would note that. Prohibition affected primarily the lower classes. Pro-

TABLE 20.2   Exposure to Prohibition and Son's Criminal Behavior

| | Father's age at exposure to prohibition | | | |
| | 17–21 | | Over 21 | |
Son's criminal behavior	M	SD	M	SD
Age at first conviction				
Nontraffic crime	20.90	8.09	21.53	8.63
Serious crime	16.97	7.13	18.67	9.45
Number of crimes				
Minor	2.58	4.89	2.09	3.56
Serious	0.78	1.64	0.63	1.54

TABLE 20.3   Father's Exposure to Prohibition and Alcohol Problems, and Percent of Sons with Alcoholism

| | Father's age at exposure to prohibition | | | |
| | 17–21 | | Over 21 | |
Father's experience	N	Alcoholic sons (%)	N	Alcoholic sons (%)
Drinking problems	62	40	31	45
No drinking problems	44	18	44	23

$\chi^2(2)=10.11$; $p=.018$.

hibitions would thus be perceived as unfair, as legislation serving the interests of the powerful. Affected populations could thus have reduced their beliefs in the legitimacy of all laws. A third alternative would emphasize the fact that in Boston, anti-Prohibition sentiment had been strong prior to endorsement of the Eighteenth Amendment. If resistance to Prohibition was perceived in a favorable light, teenagers may have judged that obedience to the law was of dubious value. Another possibility, of course, is that the results are due to unmeasured or unanalyzed conditions.

On balance, it seems to me that Prohibition increased alcohol abuse and antisocial behavior among some groups. This conclusion rests on the following summary of the present results: (a) Men exposed to Prohibition as adolescents were more likely than older cohorts to have problems with drinking. (b) Criminal activity, which was linked to drinking problems, was higher among those who had been exposed to Prohibition as adolescents. (c) The cohorts were apparently similar in terms of variables affecting their sons' criminal behavior and alcoholism. (d) Across age groups, rates for first offenses rose sharply at the beginning of Prohibition.

Recognizing that any set of data is subject to multiple interpretations, a plausible conclusion seems to be that Prohibition may be counterproductive. Those least attached to social consensus about the legitimacy of drug use may perceive failed attempts at enforcement as evidence that the law more broadly interpreted can be ignored. If this conclusion is correct, then a government that seeks to change behavior would be wise to do so by persuasion rather than through Prohibition.

Notes

This study was partially supported by U.S. Public Health Service Research Grant MH26779, National Institute of Mental Health (Center for Studies of Crime and Delinquency). I wish to express appreciation to the Department of Probation of the Commonwealth of Massachusetts, to the Division of Criminal Justice Services of the State of New York, to the Maine State Bureau of Identification, and to the states of California, Florida, Michigan, New Jersey, Pennsylvania, Virginia, and Washington for supplemental data about the men. I thank Richard Parente, Robert Staib, Ellen Myers, and Ann Cronin for their work in tracing the men and their records; Joan Immel, Tom Smedile, Harriet Sayre, Mary Duell, Elise Goldman, Abby Brodkin, and Laura Otten for their careful coding; and Daniel Glaser for his helpful comments on an earlier version of the manuscript. The author is responsible for statistical analyses and for the conclusions drawn from this research.

1. An additional criterion for selection was that the son could be matched to a boy with a similar character and background. See Powers and Witmer (1951) for details.
2. The occupations of three fathers were unknown.
3. The education of 24 fathers was unknown.
4. The birth places of two fathers were unknown. No other country was the birth place for as many as 5 of the subjects.

References

Barnett, A., A. Blumstein, and D. P. Farrington. 1989. A prospective test of a criminal career model. *Criminology* 27(2): 373–388.

Blumstein, A., J. Cohen, J. A. Roth, and C. A. Visher, eds. 1986. *Criminal Careers and "Career Criminals."* Washington, DC: National Academy Press.

Brehm, J. W. 1966. *A Theory of Psychological Reactance.* San Diego, CA: Academic Press.

Brehm, S. S. and J. W. Brehm. 1981. *Psychological reactance: A theory of freedom and control.* San Diego, CA: Academic Press.

Brown, F. W. 1932. Prohibition and mental hygiene: Effects on mental health-specific disorders. *Annals of the American Academy of Political Science and Social Science* 163: 61–68.

Burnham, J. C. 1968. New perspectives on the prohibition "experiment" of the 1920's. *Journal of Social History* 2(1): 51–68.

Catlin, G. E. G. 1932. Alternatives to prohibition. *Annals of the American Academy of Political and Social Science* 163: 181–187.

Emerson, H. 1932. Prohibition and mortality and morbidity. *Annals of the American Academy of Political and Social Science* 163: 53–60.

Ewing, J. and B. A. Rouse. 1970. *Identifying the hidden alcoholic.* Paper presented at the 29th International Congress on Alcohol and Drug Dependence, Sydney, Australia.

Farrington, D. P. 1983. Offending from 10 to 25 years of age. In *Prospective Studies of Crime and Delinquency,* edited by K. T. Van Dusen and S. A. Mednick, 73–97. Boston: Kluwer-Nijhoff.

Ferdinand, T. N. 1967. The criminal patterns of Boston since 1848. *American Journal of Sociology* 79(1): 84–99.

Ferri, E. 1897. *Criminal Sociology.* New York: Appleton.

Gebhart, J. C. 1932. Movement against prohibition. *Annals of the American Academy of Political and Social Science* 163: 172–180.

Greenberg, D. 1979. Delinquency and the age structure. In *Criminology Review Yearbook,* edited by S. Messinger and E. Bittner, 586–620. Beverly Hills, CA: Sage.

Howard, G. E. 1918. Alcohol and crime: A study in social causation. *American Journal of Sociology* 24: 61–80.

Kandel, D. B. 1980. Drug and drinking behavior among youth. *Annual Review of Sociology* 6: 235–285.

Lindsay, S. M. 1929. Prohibition. In *Encyclopedia Britannica,* 14th ed., vol. 18, 566–572. New York: Encyclopedia Britannica.

Lombroso, C. 1968. *Crime: Its causes and remedies.* Montclair, NJ: Patterson Smith. (Original work published 1912)

Lyman, R. H. 1932. *The world almanac and book of facts for 1932.* New York: New York World-Telegram.

Mayfield, D., G. McLeod, and P. Hall. 1974. The CAGE questionnaire: Validation of new alcoholism screening instrument. *American Journal of Psychiatry* 131: 1121–1123.

McCord, J. 1981. A longitudinal perspective on patterns of crime. *Criminology* 19(2): 211–218.

Mills, C. J. and H. L. Noyes. 1984. Patterns and correlates of initial and subsequent drug use among adolescents. *Journal of Consulting and Clinical Psychology* 52: 231–243.

Osgood, D. W., L. D. Johnston, P. M. O'Malley, and J. G. Bachman. 1988. The generality of deviance in late adolescence and early adulthood. *American Sociological Review* 53(1): 81–93.

Powers, E. and H. Witmer. 1951. *An experiment in the prevention of delinquency: The Cambridge-Somerville Youth Study*. New York: Columbia University Press.

Ross, E. A. 1921. Prohibition as the sociologist sees it. *Harper's Magazine* 186–192.

SAS Institute. 1985. *SAS user's guide: Statistics*, revised edition. Cary, NC: Author.

Sinclair, A. 1962. *Prohibition, the era of excess*. Boston: Little Brown.

Timberlake, J. H. 1966. *Prohibition and the progressive movement, 1900–1920*. Cambridge, MA: Harvard University Press.

Welte, J. W. and G. M. Barnes. 1985. Alcohol: The gateway to other drug use among secondary school students. *Journal of Youth and Adolescence* 14: 487–498.

Willbach, H. 1938. The trend of crime in New York City. *Journal of Criminal Law, Criminology, and Police Science* 29: 62–75.

———. 1941. The trend of crime in Chicago. *Journal of Criminal Law, Criminology, and Police Science* 31: 720–727.

PART VI

Miscellany

CHAPTER TWENTY-ONE

Competence in Long-Term Perspective*

DESPITE THEIR SEPARATION, the two views have converged in studies of young children that suggest a link between learning disabilities and conduct disorders (e.g., Coie and Krehbiel, 1984; Dodge, 1983; Farrington and Loeber, 1987; Green et al., 1980; McGee and Share, 1988) and in studies indicating that delinquents tend to lack interest in school (Bachman et al., 1971; Elliott and Voss, 1974; Farrington et al., 1986; Reiss and Rhodes, 1959).

The two views converge also in terms of family backgrounds. Studies of achievement have shown that children who do well in school tend to have warm, supportive parents with democratic interaction patterns (Amato and Ochiltree, 1986; Bachman et al., 1971; Barton et al., 1974; McClelland, 1961; McClelland et al., 1953; Rosen and D'Andrade, 1959; Strodtbeck, 1958). And studies of crime indicate that delinquents are more likely than nondelinquents to have rejecting parents and to be reared in conflictful households (Farrington, 1986; Hirschi, 1969; Loeber and Stouthamer-Loeber, 1986; McCord, 1979).

Despite congruence between pathways seeming to lead to delinquency and those leading to academic difficulties, there are grounds for doubting whether achievement orientation and social conformity should be treated as two forms of the same phenomenon. Studies of delinquent friendships provide some evidence favoring a view of social competence among delinquents (e.g., Giordano et al., 1986). Furthermore, stress theories (e.g., Cohen, 1955; Cloward and Ohlin, 1960) and data supporting them (e.g., Gould, 1969) suggest that motivationally, delinquents share achievement orientations with more conforming peers.

In sum, despite a degree of congruence between results from studies of achievement and from studies of crime, the relationship between competence as social conformity and competence as achievement remains problematic.

*Reprinted from McCord, J. 1991. Competence in long-term perspective. *Psychiatry* 54 (3): 227–237: with permission of Guilford Press.

Method

Overview

The 225 male subjects in the study were raised in urban neighborhoods that had high rates of crime. Although they were part of a delinquency prevention program, well-behaved boys had been included in order to avoid stigmatizing participants. The original study, launched in the mid-1930s, called for matching cases in order to assign a randomly selected half to a treatment program. Initially, 325 cases were matched and half placed in the treatment program. Due to the exigencies of World War II, the case load was reduced. By the end of 1941, 253 cases from 232 families remained in the program. Because analyses involve family data, only one boy per family has been used for the present study. At follow-up 40 years after the program began, the occupations of 225 of these men could be ascertained.

The data come from three waves of investigation: screening material collected between 1936 and 1939; material from case records written during the prevention program between 1939 and 1945; and follow-up material gathered between 1976 and 1980.

Screening Material

In 1936 and 1937, approximately 200 teachers had described boys being considered for the study. The teachers checked descriptive phrases on a "Trait Record Card." To reduce collinearity, a cluster procedure (Sarle, 1985) was used to identify groups of variables that referenced the same behaviors. Clusters that remained stable when tested against a validation group were substituted for the descriptive terms.

Twelve types of behavior based on teachers' descriptions were used in identifying predictors of competence. These were: refuses to take responsibility (blames others for his difficulties, makes excuses, or tattles); inattentive (daydreams, dawdles, lacks ambition, indifferent, poor work habits); antisocial (swears, lies, steals); seclusive (seclusive or holds himself apart); demands attention (meddles, boasts, or acts silly); fights; restless or nervous; depends on constant direction; few friends; easily led; poor work habits or careless, untidy, slovenly, or irresponsible; dull, slow, retarded.

At the time of these descriptions, the boys ranged from 4 to 11 years, with a mean of 7.6 years, and standard deviation of 1.5 years in age. Table 21.1 shows their class placements when the teachers completed descriptions of them in 1936 or 1937.

As part of the selection process, too, the neighborhoods where the boys lived were given ratings ranging from +5 for residential areas to −5 for the most run-down, crime-infested, dirty sections of the city. Neighborhood ratings were combined with the fathers' occupational status, using Hollingshead's Occupational Scale (Hollingshead and Redlich, 1958), to evaluate the social status of the boys' families. Families were considered "high status" if the father had a profession or

TABLE 21.1   School Grade at Time of Teachers' Descriptions (1936–1937)

Grade	Number	Percent
Kindergarten	21	9.3
First grade	49	21.8
Second grade	66	29.3
Third grade	51	22.7
Fourth grade	25	11.1
Fifth grade	7	3.1
Ungraded	6	2.7
	225	100.0

was a white collar worker and the family lived in a neighborhood ranked at least +3. Families were given a "moderate" status ranking if the father's occupation was professional or white collar but the family lived in a poor neighborhood, if the father was a skilled worker, or if the neighborhood was ranked as least +3 although the father's occupation was ranked as semiskilled or unskilled. Families were rated as "low status" if the father was a semiskilled or unskilled worker, unless the family lived in a good neighborhood.

Material from Case Records

Case records described details of family interactions between 1939 and 1945. After each home visit, counselors reported their conversations and observations. These reports included conversations with the parents, friends, neighbors, and teachers as well as with the boys. In 1957, researchers who had no access to follow-up information read and coded the records. (See McCord and McCord, 1960, for a complete description of the coding.)

Family interaction codes were dichotomized. Parental conflict reflected reports of disagreements about the child, values, money, alcohol, or religion. A rating of each parent's esteem for the other was based on evidence indicating whether or not a parent showed respect for the judgment of the other. Ratings for the mother's self-confidence were based on how she reacted when faced with problems. If she showed signs of believing in her ability to handle the problems, she was rated as self-confident. Maternal restrictiveness was rated as "subnormal" if a mother permitted her son to make virtually all his choices without her guidance. Supervision described the degree to which the boy's activities after school were governed by an adult; it was rated as "present," if there generally was an adult in charge of the boy's activities. The level of expectations placed upon a child was considered "high" if they involved doing well at school and performing tasks at home or included unusually high standards for school or home. A parent's discipline was classified as "consistent, nonpunitive" if the parent used praise, rewards, or reasoning to control the boy. It was considered "punitive" if power-methods were used for punishment. A mother's role in the family was classified as "leader" if she was an active participant in family decisions. The attitude of a parent toward the boy

TABLE 21.2 Interrater Reliability Dichotomous Variables (2 raters on 10 percent random sample)

Characteristic	Percent agreement	Scott Pi[a]
Family conflict	80	.55
Father's esteem for mother	84	.68
Mother's esteem for father	88	.76
Mother's self-confidence	84	.60
Mother's restrictiveness	84	.65
Boy's supervision	88	.76
Expectations for boy	76	.35
Father's discipline	88	.52
Mother's discipline	84	.62
Mother's leadership	96	.91
Mother's attitude to son	84	.68
Father's attitude to son	84	.57
Mother's aggressiveness	92	.56
Father's aggressiveness	84	.41

[a]$Pi = (P_o - P_e)/(1 - P_e)$. P_o=percent agreement observed. P_e=percent agreement expected: $P_e = (p)^2 + (q)^2$, where p=proportion having the characteristic and $q = 1 - p$.

was classified as "affectionate" if that parent interacted frequently with the child, without being generally critical. The aggressiveness of each parent was rated as "unrestrained" if that parent regularly expressed anger by such activities as shouting abuses, yelling, throwing things, breaking things, or hitting people.

To estimate reliability of the coding, two raters independently read a 10 percent random sample of the cases. Agreement for these ratings ranged from 76 percent to 96 percent. Since chance agreement between raters varies in relation to distribution, the Scott (1955) Interrater Reliability Coefficient, Pi, was computed to indicate improvement over chance. (See Table 21.2.)

The 14 variables describing family interactions were introduced into a clustering procedure that searches for combinations of variables to identify unidimensional factors in such a way as to maximize variance among cluster centroids (Sarle, 1985). The first cluster included (in order of contribution) mother's discipline, self-confidence, affection for her son, and role. The factor appeared to represent Mother's Competence. A second dimension included (in order of contribution) mother's esteem for the father, father's esteem for the mother, parental conflict, father's affection for his son, and father's aggressiveness. The factor appeared to represent Father's Interaction with the family. A third dimension included (in order of contribution) maternal restrictiveness, supervision, and demands. The factor represented Family Expectations. A fourth dimension included father's punitiveness and mother's aggressiveness, weighted in opposite directions. The factor appeared to measure something like Disciplinarian. This factor was dropped, however, because 75 percent of the families scored at the midpoint. Table 21.3 shows descriptive characteristics of the clusters representing Mother's Competence, Father's Interaction, and Family Expectations.

TABLE 21.3   Cluster Analysis

Group variable	R-square		Scoring coefficient
	Highest	Second	
Mother's competence			
Mother's consistent discipline	.553	.104	.386
Mother's self-confidence	.479	.087	.359
Mother's affection	.472	.084	.357
Mother's role	.422	.054	.337
Father's interaction			
Father's esteem for mother	.669	.053	.320
Mother's esteem for father	.720	.058	.332
Parental conflict	.532	.049	−.286
Father's affection for son	.323	.045	.222
Father's aggressiveness	.312	.050	−.219
Family expectations			
Mother's restrictiveness	.710	.096	−.478
Supervision	.692	.154	.472
Demands	.360	.054	.341

	Correlations		
	A	B	C
A Mother's competence	1.00		
B Father's interaction	0.29	1.00	
C Family expectations	0.41	0.31	1.00

To simplify the scales, items in each factor were given equal weights and scored so that the scales would yield higher scores for more socially desirable behaviors: greater mother's competence; more approving, less aggressive father's interaction; and stronger family expectations. Scores on Mother's Competence ranged from 0 to +4; on Father's Interaction, they ranged from −2 to +3; and on Family Expectations, they ranged from −1 to +2. Each factor was divided as close to the median as possible so that a family could be described as high or low in terms of each of the variables.

Family structure was defined in terms of whether or not the child was living with his natural (biological) parents. A parent was coded as absent if for at least 6 months prior to the boy's 17th birthday, the boy's domicile was not the same as that of the parent. If a boy was reared by his two natural parents, with neither absent as long as 6 months, his family was classified as "Intact." If a boy's father was absent a minimum of 6 months prior to the boy's 17th birthday and his mother did not remarry, the family was classified as "Mother-alone." If the mother was absent at least 6 months or the boy had a stepfather, the family was placed into the heterogeneous classification as "Broken."

Information from childhood included criminal records for the families of the boys. These had been gathered in the late 1930s and again a decade later. These records were used to identify which fathers were criminals. A father was considered a criminal if he had been convicted for a Type-1 Index crime (theft, breaking and entering, assault, murder, rape, attempted murder, or attempted rape). The designation of alcoholic was given to a father if he had lost jobs because of drinking or had marital problems attributed primarily to excessive drinking, if welfare agencies repeatedly noted that heavy drinking was the source of his problems, if he had received treatment for alcoholism, or if he had been convicted at least three times for public drunkenness.

The case records also provided information for a second classification of the neighborhoods in which the boys were reared. These were coded as either transitional or residential. Coders agreed in 96 percent of the ratings made to estimate reliability for this variable.

Follow-up Material

Between 1975 and 1980, when they ranged from 45 to 53 years in age, the former youth study participants were retraced. Tracing included searches through records of the voting registries, drivers' licenses, criminal courts, mental hospitals, and clinics for treatment of alcoholism. Almost all the men (98%) were located. Close to 80 percent of those not known to be dead responded to questionnaires or participated in interviews.

Men were considered alcoholics if they described themselves as alcoholics, if their answers on the CAGE test indicated that they were alcoholics (Mayfield et al., 1974), if they had received treatment for alcoholism, or if they had been convicted at least three times for public drunkenness or driving while intoxicated. They were considered as criminal if they had been convicted for crimes on the Federal Bureau of Investigation Part I Index. They were considered manic depressive or schizophrenic if they had been so diagnosed in records from a mental hospital in Massachusetts. And their age at death was determined through death certificates. Information about occupations was determined through interviews or, when these were absent, through records.

The study compares four groups of men. These groups were identified through application of two criteria, one representing social adjustment and the other representing achievement. Adjustment was judged by presence or absence of evidence that a man was alcoholic, criminal, manic depressive, schizophrenic, or had died prior to his thirty-fifth birthday. These marks of failure, it seemed reasonable to assume, would be considered undesirable by the subjects themselves as well as by society. Men evidencing none of these problems were considered adjusted, and those evidencing any were considered maladjusted.

Because the men had been reared in areas with low socioeconomic status and high rates of crime, occupational status appeared to represent a reasonable standard of achievement. The measure of achievement, therefore, was determined by whether or not the man had attained a white collar occupation.

The four groups included high achieving, adjusted men (N=42); high achieving, maladjusted men (N=33); nonachieving, adjusted men (N=66); and nonachieving, maladjusted men (N=84). Among the high achieving, maladjusted men, 18 (55%) were alcoholic, 20 (61%) had been convicted for Index crimes, 1 (3%) had been diagnosed as manic depressive or schizophrenic, and 3 (9%) had

TABLE 21.4 Competence and Family Social Status in Childhood (percent of each type by social status)

	High achieving		Nonachieving	
	Adjusted (N=42)	Maladjusted (N=33)	Adjusted (N=66)	Maladjusted (N=84)
High status	19	12	15	6
Moderate status	40	39	36	37
Low status	40	48	48	57

died prior to having a thirty-fifth birthday. Among the nonachieving, maladjusted men, 52 (62%) were alcoholic, 53 (63%) had been convicted for Index crimes, 7 (8%) had been diagnosed as manic depressive or schizophrenic, and 10 (12%) had died prior to having a thirty-fifth birthday. Although a higher proportion of the nonachieving than of the achieving maladjusted men had more than one symptom of maladjustment, the difference was statistically unreliable. Comparisons of the backgrounds of high achieving, adjusted men; high achieving, maladjusted men; nonachieving, adjusted men; and nonachieving, maladjusted men provide the basis for this study.

Results

The social status of the boys' families appeared to have little influence on outcomes as identified by occupational achievement and social adjustment, $p > .20$. (See Table 21.4.)

On the other hand, the boys' behavior in primary school as rated by their teachers predicted differences among the groups. Those who combined achieving with adjustment were showing signs of success even at early ages. They were least likely to demand attention, to get in fights, to appear restless or nervous, to be easily led, to have poor work habits, or to be dull, slow, or retarded. The high achieving, maladjusted men were most likely to have demanded attention, gotten into fights, and been easily led by their peers. The nonachieving, adjusted men were most likely to have had poor work habits and to have seemed dull, slow, or retarded. These comparisons are shown in Table 21.5.

A look at Table 21.5 suggests that among the high achieving men, the adjusted could have been differentiated from the maladjusted during childhood. The maladjusted men were more likely to demand attention, $\chi^2_{(1)}=8.88$, $p < .01$. They were more likely to get in fights, $\chi^2_{(1)}=7.93$, $p < .01$; and they were more likely to be easily led, $\chi^2_{(1)}=10.29$, $p < .01$. None of these differences appeared in comparisons between adjusted and maladjusted nonachieving men.

Among the nonachieving men, those who had poor work habits during primary school were *less* likely to be maladjusted adults, $\chi^2_{(1)}=10.29$, $p < .01$. The adjusted men who had been boys with poor work habits in primary school were, however, disproportionately nonachieving, $\chi^2_{(1)}=7.29$, $p < .01$, and dull, slow, or retarded, $\chi^2_{(1)}=9.70$, $p < .01$.

TABLE 21.5 Competence and Childhood Behavior (percent of each type given the rating by his teacher)

	High achieving		Nonachieving	
	Adjusted (N=42)	Maladjusted (N=33)	Adjusted (N=66)	Maladjusted (N=84)
Refuses responsibility	45	61	55	49
Inattentive	52	61	67	55
Antisocial*	17	30	14	25
Seclusive	10	6	14	11
Demands attention**	24	58	38	36
Fights**	10	36	26	27
Restless or nervous**	26	36	48	50
Depends on direction	14	27	32	24
Few friends	12	6	18	13
Easily led**	5	30	26	21
Poor work habits**	45	64	71	52
Dull, slow, retarded**	21	36	52	42

*Although differences among the 4 groups were not statistically reliable, the difference between combined adjusted and combined maladjusted groups, $\chi^2(1)=4.64$, is $p < .05$.

**Differences among the 4 groups, $p < .05$, two-tailed.

TABLE 21.6 Competence and Parental Behavior (percent of each type)

	High achieving		Nonachieving	
	Adjusted (N=42)	Maladjusted (N=33)	Adjusted (N=66)	Maladjusted (N=84)
Mother competent**	76	52	50	44
Consistent**	50	30	29	19
Self-confident***	50	42	24	17
Affectionate*	64	45	52	37
Leader role	74	58	64	58
Good father interaction*	67	58	56	42
High esteem for mother**	64	48	53	29
High esteem for father	60	52	48	38
Parental conflict*	19	39	26	40
Father affectionate	29	33	32	18
Father aggressive	12	12	14	21
Strong expectations*	69	55	58	40
Mother permissive***	19	36	27	51
Supervised	71	55	59	46
High demands**	45	21	26	15

*Differences among the 4 groups, $p < .05$, two-tailed.

**Differences among the 4 groups, $p < .01$, two-tailed.

***Differences among the 4 groups, $p < .001$, two-tailed.

TABLE 21.7 Competence and Parental Summary (percent of each type)

Number of dimensions rated positive	High achieving		Nonachieving	
	Adjusted (N=42)	Maladjusted (N=33)	Adjusted (N=66)	Maladjusted (N=84)
Three	48	27	23	17
Two	26	21	32	18
One	17	39	32	40
None	10	12	14	25

$\chi^2(9)=24.6; p < .003.$

Table 21.6 shows the relation between family interaction and adult competence. Each of the three dimensions of socialization during childhood appeared to influence adult competence.

Competent mothers were those most likely to have reared high achieving, adjusted sons. The mother's self-confidence, consistency, and affection—in that order—contributed to the effect. Maternal self-confidence appeared to have a greater impact on achievement whereas maternal affection appeared to have a greater impact on adjustment. Although maternal leadership formed part of the dimension of maternal competence, this variable was not significantly related to the outcome differences.

Fathers with bad family interactions were the most likely to have nonachieving, maladjusted sons. The effect of the father's interaction appeared to be transmitted largely through his expressions of low esteem for the mother and through parental conflict. Neither paternal affection for the boy nor paternal aggressiveness was significantly related to the outcome differences.

Strong family expectations appeared to increase the probability of rearing achieving, adjusted sons. Both maternal permissiveness and the presence of high demands contributed to competence.

The combined influence of maternal competence, paternal interaction, and family expectations can be seen in the fact that almost half the high achieving, adjusted men had been reared in families classified as "good" along all three dimensions—though about a quarter or less of the families of the remaining men had been so classified. A quarter of the nonachieving, maladjusted men had been reared in families classified as "good" along none of these dimensions. (See Table 21.7.)

With few exceptions, fathers of the high achieving, adjusted men were neither alcoholic nor criminal. More than 4 out of 10 of the men whose fathers had been alcoholic, however, showed signs of maladjustment. (See Table 21.8.)

Although childhood behavior and family interaction predicted both achievement and adjustment, family structure appeared to be related only to maladjustment—and that, only among nonachieving sons. Within the nonachieving group, a higher proportion of the maladjusted came from mother-alone families, $\chi^2_{(1)}=4.970, p < .05$. Table 21.9 shows the relationship between family structure and competence.

TABLE 21.8   Competence and Paternal Behavior (percent of each type)

	High achieving		Nonachieving	
	Adjusted (N=42)	Maladjusted (N=33)	Adjusted (N=66)	Maladjusted (N=84)
Father alcoholic	7	33	17	21
Father criminal	12	6	6	13
Father both	5	12	12	19
Father neither	76	48	65	46

$\chi^2(9)=19.554$; $p < .021$.

Neighborhood differences during adolescence appeared to have some impact on developing competence. Among the high achieving, adjusted men, 43 percent were from transitional neighborhoods; among the high achieving, maladjusted men, 52 percent were from transitional neighborhoods; among the nonachieving, adjusted men, 66 percent were from transitional neighborhoods; and among the nonachieving, maladjusted men, 68 percent were from transitional neighborhoods. These differences are statistically reliable, $\chi^2_{(3)}=9.334$, $p < .025$.

To test the degree to which the background conditions could account for variation in competence, 11 dichotomous variables significantly related to the outcome measure were used in stepwise regression. Table 21.10 shows the resulting selection, using $p < .15$ both to enter and to stay.

Paternal alcoholism and maternal competence appeared influential as did appearing dull, demanding attention, being restless, having poor work habits in primary school, and neighborhood during adolescence. Together these seven variables accounted for 8.9 percent of the variance, $p < .0001$.

A discriminant function based on these seven variables correctly classified 48 percent of the 42 high achieving, adjusted men; 51 percent of 65 nonachieving, adjusted men; 58 percent of the 84 nonachieving, maladjusted men; but only 15 percent of the high achieving, maladjusted men. Results of this analysis are shown in Table 21.11.

Random assignment to groups proportionate to their actual distribution would lead to correct assignment of 63 of the 231 men who were classified. By comparison, 107 were correctly classified using the discriminant function based on 7 variables. The improvement of 69.8 percent is statistically reliable, $\chi^2_{(1)}=42.254$, $p < .0001$.

TABLE 21.9   Competence and Family Structure (percent of each type)

	High achieving		Nonachieving	
	Adjusted (N=42)	Maladjusted (N=33)	Adjusted (N=66)	Maladjusted (N=84)
Intact	57	58	62	50
Mother alone	24	24	18	35
Broken	19	18	20	15

TABLE 21.10 Background and Competence

Step	Variable	Partial R^2	F	Prob. > F
1	Father alcoholic	.0597	4.658	.0037
2	Dull, slow, retarded	.0453	3.465	.0170
3	Mother's competence	.0493	3.770	.0115
4	Demands attention	.0398	2.999	.0311
5	Neighborhood	.0307	2.282	.0788
6	Restless or nervous	.0306	2.265	.0805
7	Poor work habits	.0256	1.876	.1328

Summary and Discussion

This study examines the life course of men differentiated along two criteria for competence: achievement and adjustment. Overall, the study indicates that both forms of competence are fostered by good family interactions in childhood. Details of family interaction and behavior during childhood, however, contributed differently to these two types of competence.

Maternal self-confidence appears to influence achievement. Maternal affection, parental conflict, and family expectations appear to have an impact on adjustment.

Paternal alcoholism seems to be more influential in producing maladjustment among high achievers than among nonachievers. On the other hand, only among nonachievers does family structure appear to influence maladjustment. This evidence suggests that some of the apparently contradictory results among studies of the effects of paternal alcoholism and of family structure may be reconciled by taking achievement orientation into account.

Disaggregation of social adjustment and achievement revealed childhood dissimilarities between their predictors. Antisocial behavior in childhood was predictive only of social maladjustment. Restlessness was a better indicator of nonachievement. Well-adjusted achievers were likely to be neither antisocial nor restless, a fact which could misleadingly suggest less tracking of personality than appears to be the case.

TABLE 21.11 Actual and Predicted Classification (number in each category)

	Actual			
	High achieving		Nonachieving	
	Adjusted (N=42)	Maladjusted (N=33)	Adjusted (N=65)[a]	Maladjusted (N=84)
High achieving adjusted	20	6	6	11
High achieving maladjusted	2	5	1	5
Nonachieving adjusted	10	7	33	19
Nonachieving maladjusted	10	15	25	49

[a] 1 case could not be classified due to missing information.

Demanding attention and fighting were predictive of maladjustment among those who would become high achievers. These behaviors, however, were unrelated to adjustment among those who were nonachievers. One interpretation of these results is that prosocial childhood behavior acquires value in relation to social mobility.

Social interactions during childhood seemed to serve different functions for the maladjusted and well-adjusted men. Among the maladjusted, those who demanded attention were the achievers—whereas among the adjusted, demanding attention and fighting signified low achievement. Possibly, the men whose backgrounds tended to produce poor adjustment were signaling a need for help (which they may have received) through dysfunctional childhood behavior.

The men who were both successful and adjusted had shown signs of good adjustment during primary school. They worked well, demanded little attention, and seemed not to get into fights.

Contrary to an easy assumption that bad behavior during childhood predicts problems later, among the nonachieving men those who had poor work habits and appeared dull or retarded had a better chance for adjustment. These results parallel those found by Kellam et al. (1983) in their longitudinal study of teenage drug use. They also lend support to the theory that frustration contributes to maladjustment (e.g., Cohen, 1955; Cloward and Ohlin, 1960). Some children seem to start out trying to do well in school despite adversity. These children may be particularly vulnerable to seeking alternative sources of success if their efforts at conformity fail to bear fruit.

Maladjusted, nonachieving men had backgrounds that reflect parental alcoholism, incompetence, and disharmony. The evidence indicates, however, that failure to achieve should not be viewed merely as a step in the direction of general maladjustment.

The results of this study suggest that conditions of childhood socialization have long-range effects on social adjustment and achievement. They also suggest that some of the marks of success as well as of future trouble can be recognized in childhood.

References

Amato, P. R. and G. Ochiltree. 1986. Family resources and the development of child competence. *Journal of Marriage and the Family* 48 (Feb.): 47–56.

Bachman, J. G., S. Green, and I. Wirtanen. 1971. *Youth in Transition.* vol. 3, *Dropping out: Problem or Symptom?* Ann Arbor, Mich.: Institute for Social Research.

Barton, K., T. E. Dielman, and R. B. Cattell. 1974. Child rearing practices and achievement in school. *Journal of Genetic Psychology* 124: 155–165.

Cloward, R. A. and L. E. Ohlin. 1960. *Delinquency and Opportunity.* Free Press.

Cohen, A. K. 1955. *Delinquent Boys.* Free Press.

Coie, J. D. and G. Krehbiel. 1984. Effects of academic tutoring on the social status of low-achieving, socially rejected children. *Child Development* 55: 1465–1478.

Dodge, K. A. 1983. Behavioral antecedents of peer social status. *Child Development* 54: 1386–1399.

Elliott, D. S. and H. L. Voss. 1974. *Delinquency and Dropout.* Heath.

Farrington, D. P. 1986. Stepping stones to adult criminal careers. In *Development of Antisocial and Prosocial Behavior*, edited by D. Olweus, J. Block, and M. R. Yarrow. Academic Press.

Farrington, D. P. and R. Loeber. 1987. Long-term criminality of conduct disorder boys with or without impulsive-inattentive behavior. Presented at Life History Research Society, St. Louis, October 14–16.

Farrington, D. P., B. Gallagher, L. Morley, et al. 1986. Unemployment, school leaving, and crime. *British Journal of Criminology* 26: 355–356.

Giordano, P. C., S. A. Cernkovich, and M. D. Pugh. 1986. Friendships and delinquency. *American Journal of Sociology* 91: 1170–1202.

Gould, L. C. 1969. Juvenile entrepreneurs. *American Journal of Sociology* 74: 710–719.

Green, K. D., R. Forehand, S. J. Beck, and B. Vosk. 1980. An assessment of the relationship among measures of children's academic achievement. *Child Development* 51: 1149–1156.

Hirschi, T. 1969. *Causes of Delinquency*. University of California Press.

Hollingshead, A. B. and F. C. Redlich. 1958. *Social Class and Mental Illness: A Community Study*. Wiley.

Kellam, S. G., M. B. Simon, and M. E. Ensminger. 1983. Antecedents in first grade of teenage substance use and psychological well-being: A ten-year community-wide prospective study. In *Origins of Psychopathology*, edited by D. F. Ricks and B. S. Dohrenwend. Cambridge University Press.

Loeber, R. and M. Stouthamer-Loeber. 1986. Family factors as correlates and predictors of juvenile conduct problems and delinquency. In *Crime and Justice*, edited by M. Tonry and N. Morris, vol. 7. University of Chicago Press.

Mayfield, D., G. McLeod, and P. Scall. 1974. The CAGE questionnaire: Validation of a new alcoholism screening instrument. *American Journal of Psychiatry* 131: 1121–1123.

McClelland, D. C. 1961. *The Achieving Society*. Van Nostrand.

McClelland, D. C., J. W. Atkinson, R. A. Clark, and E. Lowell. 1953. *The Achievement Motive*. Appleton-Century-Crofts.

McCord, J. 1979. Some child-rearing antecedents of criminal behavior in adult men. *Journal of Personality and Social Psychology* 37: 1477–1486.

McCord, W. and J. McCord. 1960. *Origins of Alcoholism*. Stanford University Press.

McGee, R. and D. L. Share. 1988. Attention deficit disorder-hyperactivity and academic failure: Which comes first and what should be treated? *Journal of American Academy of Child and Adolescent Psychiatry* 27: 318–325.

Reiss, A. J., Jr. and A. L. Rhodes. 1959. Are educational norms and goals of conforming, truant and delinquent adolescents influenced by group position in American society? *Journal of Negro Education* 28: 252–267.

Rosen, B. C. and R. G. D'Andrade. 1959. The psychosocial origins of achievement motivation. *Sociometry* 22: 185–218.

Sarle, W. S. Varclus. 1985. In *SAS, Version 5*. Cary, N.C.: SAS Institute.

Scott, W. A. 1955. Reliability of content analysis: The case of nominal scale coding. *Public Opinion Quarterly* 19: 321–325.

Strodtbeck, F. L. 1958. Family interaction and achievement. In *Talent and Society*, edited by D. C. McClelland, et al. Van Nostrand.

CHAPTER TWENTY-TWO

Understanding Motivations

Considering Altruism and Aggression*

T HE FACT THAT CRIMINAL actions are performed intentionally distinguishes them from accidental actions and from those performed as a consequence of mental illness. Intentional actions require motives, so motivations should play a central role in an adequate theory of crime. This article addresses what appears to be a gap in theories of criminal behavior: a gap between external forces and intentional behavior.

Although several theories of crime rely upon assumptions about underlying motives, the motives implicated by these theories would not qualify as such in a criminal court. For example, Cohen (1955) considered delinquency a response to "a chronic fund of motivation, conscious or repressed, to elevate one's status position" (122). Sutherland and Cressey (1924/1974) argued that delinquency occurs through adopting from the social surroundings beliefs that justify criminal behavior as reasonable. Yet neither desire for increased status nor desire to act reasonably could be considered grounds for distinguishing criminal from irrational or unintended action.

Sykes and Matza (1957) suggested that delinquents prepare the way for delinquency by defining criminal actions as excusable, necessary, or permissible if rightly understood. The set of beliefs which they termed "techniques of neutralization" and which Bandura (1986, 1990) called "disengagement" can be seen as justifying antisocial behavior; but the theory does not explain why such techniques are invoked. Glaser (1978) proposed that expectations created by biological and social conditions influence perception of opportunities and anticipation of consequences for committing crimes. Lurking behind these and other theories of crime is an assumption that people are motivated to do what they believe will benefit themselves. In this vein, Hirschi (1969) argued that criminality requires

---

*Reprinted from McCord, J. 1992. Understanding motivations: Considering altruism and aggression. In *Facts, Frameworks, and Forecasts: Advances in Criminological Theory*, edited by J. McCord 3: 115–135. New Brunswick, N.J.: Transaction.

no explanation; rather, conventional children are rule-abiding because they care what their parents will think and, presumably, want to please their parents because they will be rewarded (88). More recently, Gottfredson and Hirschi (1990) asserted that people are criminals because they lack self-control and their behavior reflects their short-term assessment of personal gain.

Egocentric motivations are assumed also, without critical evaluation, by what has come to be called "rational" theories of crime (Cornish and Clarke, 1986). In this view, crime is caused by desire to maximize the ratio of personal gain to pain. Some evidence indicates that people avoid some types of crimes when they believe that committing them will result in painful consequences to themselves (Erickson, Gibbs, and Jensen, 1977; Farrington, 1979; Grasmick and Bryjak, 1980; Nagin, 1978), but there is also evidence to suggest that most criminals do not consider such consequences before they commit crimes (Carroll, 1982; Erez, 1987).

Freud (1930/1961) linked eogcentrism with aggression: "Civilization has to use its utmost efforts in order to set limits to man's aggressive instincts . . . and hence too the ideal's commandment to love one's neighbor as oneself—a commandment which is really justified by the fact that nothing else runs so strongly counter to the original nature of man" (59).

Aggression has been postulated as a dominant force underlying antisocial behavior. The association has sometimes been so close that studies of criminality have been interpreted as shedding light on aggression (e.g., Bandura and Walters, 1959), as validating measures of aggression (e.g., Lefkowitz et al., 1977), and as support for the thesis that frustration leads to aggression (Dollard et al., 1939).

Longitudinal research has confirmed relationships between childhood aggressiveness and subsequent criminal behavior among blacks (Ensminger et al., 1983) and Caucasians (McCord, 1983) in the United States, and in Great Britain (Farrington, 1991; Farrington and West, 1981), Finland (Pulkkinen, 1988), and Sweden (Magnusson and Bergman, 1988). There are therefore empirical grounds for arguing that aggression could be a motive for criminal behavior.

Aggression implies that an actor has a desire to injure others, so there are conceptual grounds for reasoning that there might be a motivational continuum along which a desire to help others would be at the opposite end of aggressiveness. Nevertheless, aggressiveness has been related to such socialized behaviors as striving and prosociality (Pulkkinen, 1984; Friedrich and Stein, 1973). As Eisenberg and Mussen suggest, "Moderate levels of aggression probably reflect outgoingness, emotional responsiveness, and assertiveness, and such qualities may facilitate young children's tendencies to engage in positive, prosocial interactions with others" (1989, 63).

Although only a handful of studies have embraced both antisocial and prosocial behavior, results of the separate studies provide a fairly coherent picture of etiology. Research into the development of aggression shows with some consistency that children imitate aggressive models—including their parents. Family conflict seems to produce aggression; aggressive fathers tend to have aggressive sons; children tend to imitate television aggression; and abusing parents overrepresent formerly abused children (Bandura, Ross, and Ross, 1961; Berkowitz et al., 1978; Eron and Huesmann, 1984, 1986; Farrington, 1978; Friedrich and Stein,

1973; Goldstein and Arms, 1971; McCord, 1983; Widom, 1989; Wilkens, Scharff, and Schlottman, 1974).

Research into the development of helpful behavior seems to show that children imitate helpful or generous models—including their parents. Altruistic people tend to have altruistic children; children tend to imitate prosocial behavior seen on television or in films; and altruistic children tend to have parents who use principles of moral action in their discipline practices (Bryan and London, 1970; Eisenberg, 1986; Eron and Huesmann, 1986; Rosenhan and White, 1967; Rushton, 1979; Staub, 1979; White, 1972; Zahn-Waxler, Radke-Yarrow, and King, 1979).

Research into the development of aggression also shows that closeness to parents is related to low levels of aggression. Parental neglect is a strong predictor of aggression, and parental warmth seems to decrease the probability for aggression (Eron and Huesmann, 1984; Farrington, Gundry, and West, 1975; Loeber and Stouthamer-Loeber, 1986; McCord, 1977, 1984). Evidence is mixed regarding the impact of parental warmth on altruism, with some studies indicating that closeness to parents and empathic care result in high levels of prosocial behavior (London, 1970; Staub, 1986; Whiting and Whiting, 1975; Zahn-Waxler, Radke-Yarrow, and King, 1979) and others failing to do so (Eisenberg and Mussen, 1989).

To summarize, research about the development of aggression and the development of helpful behavior suggests that imitation influences both. The evidence that parental interaction affects aggressiveness and prosociality may be interpreted in the light of how parents provide models for interaction with others. If a child is exposed to aggressive models, the child's aggression can be anticipated; if a child is exposed to prosocial models, helpful behavior can be anticipated. And if a child is exposed to both types of behavior, it seems reasonable to anticipate that both aggressive and prosocial behavior will result.

Research into situational influences on aggression and on prosocial behavior indicate that opportunities for choice of action influences both. Assuming that restrictions of choice are frustrating and that doing poorly in school reduces opportunities, frustration provides a plausible account of why children who do poorly in school are aggressive (Berkowitz, 1962; Dollard et al., 1939; Feshbach and Price, 1984). Forced choices also seem to reduce voluntary helping (Aderman and Berkowitz, 1983; Berkowitz, 1973; Fabes et al., 1989). In sum: perceived restrictions of freedom appear to reduce altruistic behavior and to increase aggression.

Studies of motivations show that when people are happy, they are more likely to be helpful and generous (Berkowitz, 1987; Eisenberg and Mussen, 1989; Isen and Levin, 1972; Marcus, 1986; Moore, Underwood, and Rosenhan, 1973; Rosenhan, Underwood, and Moore, 1974). Angered subjects tend to become aggressive (Berkowitz, 1965; Donnerstein and Wilson, 1976; Wilkens, Scharff, and Schlottman, 1974; Zillman, 1979). Although aggressive and prosocial behaviors have different motivational links, friendships seem to reinforce helping behavior—and friendships seem to reinforce aggression (Cairns et al., 1988; Maccoby, 1986).

Two hypotheses about the relationship between altruism and aggression are plausible.

1. Altruism and aggressiveness are opposite ends of a continuum. In this view, to the extent that one is aggressive, altruism must be weak. Conversely, to the extent that one is altruistic, little aggression can be expected. To account for failure to detect a negative relationship between altruism and aggression, those persuaded by this view argue that what appears to be aggressiveness or what appears to be altruism is incorrectly viewed to be such.
2. Altruism and aggressiveness are independent dimensions. From this second perspective, the occurrence of altruism even among extremely aggressive youths would be possible. Evidence of negative relationships are particular to circumstances of measurement, individuals, or to the technique for measuring.

In a certain sense, of course, altruistic and aggressive behavior are incompatible. As Plato (*Republic*, 436b) remarked, one cannot at the same time "do or suffer opposites in the same respect in relation to the same thing." This does not preclude the possibility of being altruistic at one time and aggressive at another, nor of being altruistic toward one person and aggressive toward another.

There are prima facie grounds for believing that aggression and altruism coexist as potential responses and as dispositional characteristics of ordinary people. Studies such as those that have randomly assigned people to roles, as in the Stanford Prison experiment where students were assigned to be prison guards (Zimbardo et al., 1974) and the studies of obedience by Stanley Milgram (1963, 1974), where students were assigned to give painful shocks to fellow students, have demonstrated aggressive behavior among people who volunteered to be subjects in laboratory studies and did so, presumably, with prosocial intentions. At the opposite extreme, medical doctors in Nazi prison camps were known to be occasionally kind to inmates (Staub, 1989) and the SS at Auschwitz occasionally showed compassion (Pawelczynska, 1979).

Before continuing an examination of the relationship between altruism and aggression, let us examine the concepts. In the works briefly summarized above, both "aggression" and "altruism" are used sometimes to refer to behaviors, sometimes to motives, and sometimes to actions. For example, a measure of aggression that depends on behavior is involved when peers are asked: "Who gets in fights a lot?" A measure of aggression that depends on motives is involved when subjects are asked: "Do you often want to hurt someone?" A measure of aggression that depends on actions is involved when teachers are asked: "Which children try to destroy the work of others?" Cairns and Cairns (1984) found little agreement between self-ratings of aggression and public ratings by observers, teachers, and peers. As they (Cairns and Cairns, 1986) and Hinde (1986) point out, the criteria for identifying aggression may be different across raters.

The links among behaviors, motives, and actions are not always obvious. A classic example comes from the Kwakiutl Indians who have great potlatches (Benedict, 1934; Boas, 1897). At these ceremonies, the Kwakiutl donate and destroy property competitively; they do so in order to demonstrate status. In these, as in other instances of conspicuous consumption, gifts are inextricably merged with an intention to injure.

Impulsiveness, linked conceptually and empirically with aggressive behavior in some studies, may be altruistic as well as aggressive (Pulkkinen, 1984). Giving aid can be as self-interested as aggression. In viewing human behavior as fundamentally a competitive striving for status, Homans argued that a recipient of services gives up status: "The social approval he gives Other is at the same time an admission of his own inferiority" (1961, 61). Similarly, Gouldner (1960) was persuaded that strong and universal expectations for reciprocal benefits provided incentives for apparently altruistic actions. "Between the time of Ego's provision of a gratification and the time of Alter's repayment," he wrote, "falls the shadow of indebtedness" (174). As Blau (1964) noted, benefits from apparently altruistic behavior are broader than suggested by the norm of reciprocity, so that much that passes for altruistic may be mistakenly so conceived.

Some injuries are accidental, so not all injurious actions should be attributed to aggression. There are actions that injure, people who perform actions that injure, and people who intend to injure through their actions, though they may fail or find that another has done the work for them. For purposes of clarity, let me stipulate: *Aggression refers to injurious actions performed with the intention of injuring.*

In parallel, there are actions that help others; people who perform actions that help others; and people who intend to help others through their actions, though they may fail. For purposes of clarity, again let me stipulate: *Altruism refers to helpful actions that a person performs with the intention of helping someone else.*

Measures of aggression and of conduct disorder have confounded two types of motivation: actions intended to injure others and actions intended to benefit oneself. Some do so by defining a scale on which helpful behavior is at one end and misbehavior at the other (e.g., Klinteberg, Schalling, and Magnusson, 1990). Others have incorporated general misconduct, conduct that disregards the welfare of others, as part of the meaning of aggressiveness (e.g., Kellam, Simon, and Ensminger, 1983; Robins and McEvoy, 1990; Tremblay, Desmarais-Gervais, Gagnon, and Charlebois, 1987). A theory of crime that takes motivations as a starting point would expect differences in behavior related to these seemingly different motives.

Empirical Evidence

I used data from a longitudinal study (McCord, 1983) to look at the relationships of aggression and altruism to criminal behavior. Designed to prevent delinquency and evaluate the intervention, the study included ratings by approximately 200 teachers of boys living in blighted areas of Cambridge and Somerville, Massachusetts. In 1936 and 1937, the teachers had checked descriptive phrases on a "Trait Record Card." Initially, there were 506 males in the study. I used those who were less than age ten at the time data were collected and selected only one boy per family. This resulted in having 468 males for analyses. They ranged in age from four to nine, with a median and mode of eight years at the time of teachers' ratings.

Boys were considered to have been aggressive if their teachers checked "fights" as part of their description (N=95). They were considered conduct disordered if

TABLE 22.1 Behavior of Young Child and Subsequent Criminal Behavior (percent of group)

	Not aggressive or conduct disorder (N=340)	Aggressive (N=62)	Conduct disorder (N=33)	Conduct disorder and aggressive (N=33)
No crimes	30.6	16.1	30.3	12.1
Minor only	43.2	41.9	36.4	45.5
Property	12.1	17.7	24.2	24.2
Person	14.1	24.2	9.1	18.2
	100.0	99.9	100.0	100.0

$\chi^2(9) = 18.114$; $p=.034$.

their teachers checked more than three of the following eleven possibilities: frequent truancy; blames others for his difficulties; secretive, crafty, sly; rude, saucy, impudent; disobeys; refuses to cooperate; cruel; cheats; lies; steals; destroys property.

In 1948, police records were searched for evidence of criminal behavior. In 1978, when the average age of the subjects was fifty years, records were collected from the courts, mental hospitals, vital statistics, and clinics treating alcoholics. Criminal records were used to classify the men according to a scale of seriousness for their criminal histories. Each person was classified according to his most serious conviction. Records from juvenile courts were combined with those from adult courts. Misdemeanor crimes were considered less serious than felony crimes against property, which were considered less serious than felony crimes against persons. As Table 22.1 indicates, boys who were aggressive in primary grades were more likely than other boys to be convicted for crimes against persons.

The subjects were retraced between 1975 and 1980. All but eighteen (4%) were located. Among those located, forty-eight (10%) had died. The remainder were asked to respond to a questionnaire and to consent to an interview. Requests for completing the questionnaire appealed to altruistic motives by using some version of the following: "You were once a member of the Cambridge-Somerville Youth Study, which makes your opinions important for helping other parents and children." No other incentives were used. For the interviews, we offered "$20 for your time." Men were counted as altruistic if they responded to the questionnaire. Some men failed to answer the questionnaires because of poor reading or because the questionnaires had been misplaced; therefore, men were also counted as altruistic if they were interviewed but refused to take the $20 offered to them.

A majority of the men (60.2%) were classified as altruistic. This proportion was composed of 66.4 percent of the noncriminals, and 64.4 percent of those convicted only for minor crimes, but only 49.1 percent of those convicted for crimes against property, and 45.6 percent of those convicted for crimes against persons ($\chi^2_{(3)}=10.998$, p=.012).

As indicated in Table 22.2, neither aggressiveness nor conduct disorder was reliably related to a lack of altruism.

TABLE 22.2 Behavior of Young Child and Subsequent Altruistic Behavior (percent of group)

	Not aggressive or conduct disorder ($N=294$)	Aggressive ($N=50$)	Conduct disorder ($N=28$)	Conduct disorder and aggressive ($N=30$)
Altruistic	61.6	50.0	64.3	60.0
Not	38.4	50.0	35.7	40.0
	100.0	100.0	100.0	100.0

$\chi^2(3) = 2.595$; $p=.458$.

Discussion

Other studies have shown continuity in aggressive behavior (e.g., Huesmann, Eron, Lefkowitz, and Walder, 1984; Olweus, 1979). The longitudinal evidence linking aggression to crimes of violence corroborates these studies. In addition, the evidence suggests that although egocentric behavior (represented by property crimes) is not conducive to altruism, altruism is not merely the inverse of aggression.

Immanual Kant (1785/1959) observed that "the principle of one's own happiness is the most objectionable of all . . . for it puts the motives to virtue and those to vice in the same class, teaching us only to make a better calculation" (61). Many helpful actions are doubtless due to self-interest, so not all helpful actions can be attributed to altruism. Yet there is reason to believe that at least sometimes, some people perform altruistic actions.

Many of the theories used to account for altruism refer only to self-interest. These include Attribution Theory, which in one form considers altruism to be dependent upon attributing socially desirable characteristics to oneself (Berkowitz, 1965; Grusec and Dix, 1986; Heider, 1946) and Reactance Theory, which considers behavior a response to a quest for perceived freedom or control (Brehm and Brehm, 1981). Reciprocity theories of a variety of types, including those that claim self-rewards motivate altruistic acts, make the assumption that giving depends on expectations for receiving (Baumann, Cialdini, and Kenrick, 1981; Cialdini et al., 1987; Hatfield, Walster, and Piliavin, 1978; Hinde, 1979; Rosenhan, 1978).

Hoffman (1963) found negative correlations between the use of power-oriented punishment and consideration of others. Attempting to develop an alternative to altruism as an explanation, Hoffman (1980) favored an empathy-based theory. At the time, Hoffman pointed to physiological arousal from others' pain and assumed that this gave rise to pain in the self which became guilt if the cause of pain was attributed to one's own actions.

Critics noted that Hoffman had provided an explanation involving concealed psychological egoism. If the pain of others gives pain, then relieving one's own pain motivates what appears to be altruistic behavior.

Cialdini and his co-workers (1987) claimed support for the egoistic view of altruism. In their study, they contrived to convince some subjects that a drug they had taken (which really was a placebo) had fixed the mood of the subjects. Only those students who, according to the experimenters, believed they had "labile" moods agreed to help a student described as needing help because of a recent automobile accident. The experimenters do not discuss alternatives to their own explanation, one of which is the possibility that student subjects resented giving the extra time it would take to wait out drug effects. But more importantly, they mistake the issue. It would be foolish to argue that *all* help-giving is altruistic; rather, the issue at stake is whether there can be *any* altruistic behavior.

In a seminal article, Hoffman (1981) asked "Is altruism part of human nature?" Countering critics, Hoffman pointed to the ad hoc nature of egoistic interpretations. After an apparently altruistic act, psychological egoists "invent" plausible stories about the nature of benefits that might be attributed to the actor. Such postulated motivations ought not be mistaken as evidence. Furthermore, research indicates that giving help is reduced when others are present (Clark and Word, 1972; Latané and Dabbs, 1975; Latané and Darley, 1968; Levy et al., 1972)—a finding that runs contrary to at least one basis for converting altruistic acts into covertly hedonistic ones. Had giving help increased, one could argue that desire for approval provided a motive. Hoffman concluded that giving help is "difficult to explain without assuming an independent altruistic motive system" (135).

Experiments designed to test some of the hedonistic accounts of altruistic behavior have been added to the arsenal against psychological hedonism. In one of these, Batson et al. (1988) manipulated subjects so that it looked as though, by giving correct answers, subjects could relieve a partner from the pain of being shocked. Their empathy and mood were measured. Then half were told of a change in plans; the partner would not receive shock. These subjects' help was unnecessary. Empathy and mood were again measured.

The experimenters reasoned that if helping actions provided self-rewarding relief, the subjects would be disappointed by loosing an opportunity to help. On the other hand, if altruism motivated help-giving, the relief should be as great whether or not it was the subject who acted to do the relieving. In fact, the evidence in this study and in others (including one with a Stroop task in which subjects named colors of neutral words and words relevant to altruism, punishment, and rewards) supported the conclusion: "More and more, it appears that the motivation to help evoked by feeling empathy is at least partly altruistic. If it is, then psychologists will have to make some fundamental changes in their conceptions of human motivation and, indeed, of human nature" (75–76).

Altruism appears to be as natural as aggression (Zahn-Waxler and Radke-Yarrow, 1982; Zahn-Waxler, Radke-Yarrow, Wagner, and Pyle, 1988). Rheingold and Emery (1986) found that by eighteen months, children show patterns of nurturance. By the time children are three to four years old, their friendship choices reflect prosocial behavior (Denham, Mckinley, Couchoud, and Holt, 1990). Like curiosity, altruism apparently can be reduced through training. In studying children in primary school, Staub (1970) discovered that eleven year olds were less likely than seven year olds to attempt to help a child in the next room who had apparently fallen off a chair. Staub (1979) suggested that punishment probably reduced altruism by focusing the children's attention on themselves.

Connections between a focus on oneself and reduced altruism have been confirmed through experiments in which randomly selected subjects are induced to focus on themselves, for example by being told they would soon hear how well they have done on a test, and then asked for help (Aderman and Berkowitz, 1983). Those who were waiting to hear test results gave less help than those who had performed a similar task under a different description.

Self-awareness, under some circumstances, also increases helping (Berkowitz, 1987; Duval, Duval, and Neely, 1979; Gibbons and Wicklund, 1982; Wicklund, 1975). The conditions under which these favorable consequences occur seem to depend on absence of anxiety.

Awareness of how others feel is related to both aggression and popularity among very young children (Denham, McKinley, Couchoud, and Holt, 1990). Children may believe that injuring others is permissible or that others do not feel a pain they themselves do not feel. By training delinquents to understand one another, Chandler (1973) reduced their delinquency.

Child-rearing techniques teach children what to expect from others and therefore influence estimates about the consequences of their own actions. Parents who help others, including their children, are teaching that benefiting others is a reasonable thing to do. Use of rewards and punishments, on the other hand, provides demonstrations that instruct children to do things for their own benefit (McCord, 1991).

Continuity that has been attributed to character might well be due to constancy in beliefs. We select (Festinger, 1957, 1964), create (Dodge, 1986; Dodge and Somberg, 1987; Eron and Huesmann, 1986), and recall (Eich, Rachman, and Lopatka, 1990) experiences that tend to confirm the beliefs we already have. As researchers, we've spent far too little time considering how children interpret the lessons we intend.

Criminal behavior ought to be studied with recognition that crime is a consequence of motives to injure others or to benefit oneself without a proper regard to the welfare of others. Practices that foster these motives are likely to promote crime. Claims that all behavior is egoistic, that crime requires no explanation, and that beliefs are irrelevant to criminal action have been a disservice to criminological theory.

References

Aderman, D. and L. Berkowitz. 1983. Self-concern and the unwillingness to be helpful. *Social Psychology Quarterly* 46(4): 293–301.

Bandura, A. 1986. *Social Foundations of Thought and Action.* Englewood Cliffs, N.J.: Prentice-Hall.

Bandura, A. 1990. Selective activation and disengagement of moral control. *Journal of Social Issues* 46(1): 27–46.

Bandura, A., D. Ross, and S. A. Ross. 1961. Transmission of aggression through imitation of aggressive models. *Journal of Abnormal and Social Psychology* 63: 575–582.

Bandura, A. and R. H. Walters. 1959. *Adolescent Aggression.* New York: Ronald.

Batson, C. D., J. L. Dyck, J. R. Brandt, J. G. Batson, A. L. Powell, M. R. McMaster, and C. Griffitt. 1988. Five studies testing two new egoistic alternatives to the Empathy-Altruism Hypothesis. *Journal of Personality and Social Psychology* 55(1): 52–77.

Baumann, D. J., R. B. Cialdini, and D. T. Kenrick, 1981. Altruism as hedonism: Helping and self-gratification as equivalent responses. *Journal of Personality and Social Psychology* 40(6): 1039–1046.

Benedict, R. 1934. *Patterns of Culture.* Boston: Houghton Mifflin Co.

Berkowitz, L. 1962. *Aggression: A Social Psychologist Analysis.* New York: McGraw-Hill.

Berkowitz, L. 1965. The concept of aggressive drive: Some additional considerations. In *Advances in Experimental Social Psychology vol. 2,* edited by L. Berkowitz, 301–329. New York: Academic Press.

Berkowitz, L. 1973. Reactance theory and helping. *Psychological Bulletin* 79(5): 310–317.

Berkowitz, L. 1987. Mood, self-awareness, and willingness to help. *Journal of Personality and Social Psychology* 52(4): 721–729.

Berkowitz, L., R. D. Parke, J. P. Leyens, S. West, and J. Sebastian. 1978. Experiments on the reactions of juvenile delinquents to filmed violence. In *Aggression and Anti-Social Behaviour in Childhood and Adolescence,* edited by L. A. Hersov and M. Berger, 59–71. Oxford: Pergamon Press.

Blau, P. M. 1964. *Exchange and Power in Social Life.* New York: Wiley.

Boas, F. 1897. The Social Organization and the Secret Societies of the Kwakiutl Indians, Based on Personal Observations and on Notes Made by Mr. George Hunt. *Annual Report of the Board of Regents of the Smithsonian Institution for the Year ending June 30th 1895. Report of the United States National Museum, 1895,* 311–738, Washington, D.C.

Brehm, S. S. and J. W. Brehm. 1981. *Psychological Reactance: A Theory of Freedom and Control.* New York: Academic Press.

Bryan, J. H. and P. London. 1970. Altruistic behavior by children. *Psychological Bulletin* 73(3): 200–211.

Cairns, R. B. and B. D. Cairns. 1984. Predicting aggressive patterns in girls and boys: A developmental study. *Aggressive Behavior* 10(3): 227–242.

———. 1986. The developmental-interactional view of social behavior: Four issues of adolescent aggression. In *Development of Antisocial and Prosocial Behavior,* edited by D. Olweus, J. Block, and M. R. Yarrow, 315–342. New York: Academic Press.

Cairns, R. B., B. D. Cairns, H. J. Neckerman, S. D. Gest, and J. Gariépy. 1988. Social networks and aggressive behavior: Peer support or peer rejection? *Developmental Psychology* 24(6): 815–823.

Carroll, J. S. 1982. The decision to commit the crime. In *The Criminal Justice System,* edited by J. Konecni and E. B. Ebbesen, 49–67. San Francisco: W. H. Freeman.

Chandler, M. J. 1973. Egocentrism and antisocial behavior: The assessment and training of social perspective-taking skill. *Developmental Psychology* 9: 326–332.

Cialdini, R. B., M. Schaller, D. Houlihan, K. Arps, J. Fultz, and A. Beaman. 1987. Empathy-based helping: Is it selflessly or selfishly motivated? *Journal of Personality and Social Psychology* 52(4): 749–758.

Clark, R. D., III and L. E. Word. 1972. Why don't bystanders help? Because of ambiguity? *Journal of Personality and Social Psychology* 24(3): 392–400.

Cohen, A. K. 1955. *Delinquent Boys.* Glencoe, Ill.: Free Press.

Cornish, D. and R. Clarke. 1986. Introduction. In *The Reasoning Criminal: Rational Choice Perspectives on Offending,* edited by D. B. Cornish and R. V. Clarke, 1–16. New York: Springer-Verlag.

Denham, S. A., M. McKinley, E. A. Couchoud, and R. Holt. 1990. Emotional and behavioral predictors of preschool peer ratings. *Child Development* 61(4): 1145–1152.

Dodge, K. A. 1986. Social information-processing variables in the development of aggression and altruism in children. In *Altruism and Aggression: Biological and Social Origins,* edited by C. Zahn-Waxler, E. M. Cummings, and R. Iannotti, 280–302. Cambridge: Cambridge University Press.

Dodge, K. A. and D. R. Somberg. 1987. Hostile attributional biases among aggressive boys are exacerbated under conditions of threats to the self. *Child Development* 58: 213–224.

Dollard, J., L. W. Doob, N. E. Miller, O. H. Mowrer, and R. R. Sears. 1939. *Frustration and Aggression*. New Haven: Yale University Press.

Donnerstein, E. and D. W. Wilson. 1976. Effects of noise and perceived control on ongoing and subsequent aggressive behavior. *Journal of Personality and Social Psychology* 34(5): 774–781.

Duval, S., V. H. Duval, and R. Neely. 1979. Self-focus, felt responsibility, and helping behavior. *Journal of Personality and Social Psychology* 37(10): 1769–1778.

Eich, E., S. Rachman, and C. Lopatka. 1990. Affect, pain, and autobiographical memory. *Journal of Abnormal Psychology* 99(2): 174–178.

Eisenberg, N. 1986. *Altruistic Emotion, Cognition, and Behavior*. Hillsdale, N.J.: Lawrence Erlbaum.

Eisenberg, N. and P. H. Mussen. 1989. *The Roots of Prosocial Behavior in Children*. Cambridge: Cambridge University Press.

Ensminger, M. E., S. G. Kellam, and B. R. Rubin. 1983. School and family origins of delinquency: Comparisons by sex. In *Prospective Studies of Crime and Delinquency*, edited by K. T. Van Dusen and S. A. Mednick, 73–97. Boston: Kluwer-Nijhoff.

Erez, E. 1987. Situational or planned crime and the criminal career. In *From Boy to Man, from Delinquency to Crime*, edited by M. E. Wolfgang, T. P. Thornberry, and R. M. Figlio, 122–133. Chicago: University of Chicago Press.

Erickson, M. L., J. P. Gibbs, and G. F. Jensen. 1977. The deterrence doctrine and the perceived certainty of legal punishments. *American Sociological Review* 42(Apr.): 305–317.

Eron, L. D. and L. R. Huesmann. 1984. The relation of prosocial behavior to the development of aggression and psychopathology. *Aggressive Behavior* 10(3): 201–211.

Eron, L. D. and L. R. Huesmann. 1986. The role of television in the development of prosocial and antisocial behavior. In *Development of Antisocial and Prosocial Behavior*, edited by D. Olweus, J. Block, and M. R. Yarrow, 285–314. New York: Academic Press.

Fabes, R. A., J. Fultz, N. Eisenberg, T. May-Plumlee, and F. S. Christopher. 1989. Effects of rewards on children's prosocial motivation: A socialization study. *Developmental Psychology* 25(4): 509–515.

Farrington, D. P. 1978. The family backgrounds of aggressive youths. In *Aggression and Anti-Social Behaviour in Childhood and Adolescence*, edited by L. A. Hersov and M. Berger, 73–93. Oxford: Pergamon.

Farrington, D. P. 1979. Experiments on deviance with special reference to dishonesty. In *Advances in Experimental Social Psychology, vol. 12*, edited by L. Berkowitz, 207–252. New York: Academic Press.

Farrington, D. P. 1991. Childhood aggression and adult violence: Early precursors and later life outcomes. In *The Development and Treatment of Childhood Aggression*, edited by D. J. Pepler and K. H. Rubin, 5–29. Hillsdale, N.J.: Lawrence Erlbaum.

Farrington, D. P., G. Gundry, and D. J. West. 1975. The familial transmission of criminality. *Medical Science Law* 15(3): 177–186.

Farrington, D. P. and D. J. West. 1981. The Cambridge Study in delinquent development (United Kingdom). In *Longitudinal Research: An Empirical Basis for Primary Prevention*, edited by S. A. Mednick and A. E. Baert, 137–145. Oxford: Oxford University Press.

Feshbach, S. and J. Price. 1984. Cognitive competencies and aggressive behavior: A developmental study. *Aggressive Behavior* 10(3): 185–200.

Festinger, L. 1957. *A Theory of Cognitive Dissonance*. Stanford, Calif.: Stanford University Press.

Festinger, L. 1964. *Conflict, Decision and Dissonance*. Stanford, Calif.: Stanford University Press.

Freud, S. 1930/1961. *Civilization and Its Discontents*, translated by J. Strachey. New York: W. W. Norton.

Friedrich, L. K. and A. H. Stein. 1973. Aggressive and prosocial television programs and the natural behavior of preschool children. *Monographs of the Society for Research in Child Development* 38(4, Serial No. 151): 1–64.

Gibbons, F. X. and R. A. Wicklund. 1982. Self-focused attention and helping behavior. *Journal of Personality and Social Psychology* 37(10): 1769–1778.

Glaser, D. 1978. *Crime in Our Changing Society.* New York: Holt, Rinehart & Winston.

Goldstein, J. H. and R. L. Arms. 1971. Effects of observing athletic contests on hostility. *Sociometry* 34(1): 83–90.

Gottfredson, M. R. and T. Hirschi. 1990. *A General Theory of Crime.* Stanford, Calif.: Stanford University Press.

Gouldner, A. W. 1960. The norm of reciprocity. *American Sociological Review* 25(2): 161–178.

Grasmick, H. G. and G. J. Bryjak. 1980. The deterrent effect of perceived severity of punishment. *Social Forces* 59(2): 471–491.

Grusec, J. E. and T. Dix. 1986. The socialization of prosocial behavior: Theory and reality. In *Altruism and Aggression: Biological and Social Origins,* edited by C. Zahn-Waxler, E. M. Cummings, and R. Iannotti, 218–237. Cambridge: Cambridge University Press.

Hatfield, E., G. W. Walster, and J. A. Piliavin. 1978. Equity theory and helping relationships. In *Altruism, Sympathy, and Helping,* edited by L. Wispé, 115–139. New York: Academic Press.

Heider, F. 1946. Attitudes and cognitive organization. *Journal of Psychology* 21: 107–112.

Hinde, R. A. 1979. *Towards Understanding Relationships.* London: Academic Press.

———. 1986. Some implications of evolutionary theory and comparative data for the study of human prosocial and aggressive behavior. In *Development of Antisocial and Prosocial Behavior,* edited by D. Olweus, J. Block, and M. R. Yarrow, 13–32. New York: Academic Press.

Hirshi, T. 1969. *Causes of Delinquency.* Berkeley: University of California Press.

Hoffman, M. L. 1963. Parent discipline and the child's consideration for others. *Child Development* 34: 573–588.

Hoffman, M. L. 1980. Moral development in adolescence. In *Handbook of Adolescent Psychology,* edited by J. Adelson, 295–343. New York: Wiley.

Hoffman, M. L. 1981. Is altruism part of human nature? *Journal of Personality and Social Psychology* 40(1): 121–127.

Homans, G. C. 1961. *Social Behavior: Its Elementary Forms.* New York: Harcourt Brace.

Huesman, L. R., L. D. Eron, M. M. Lefkowitz, and L. O. Walder. 1984. Stability of aggression over time and generations. *Developmental Psychology* 20: 1120–1134.

Isen, A. M. and P. F. Levin. 1972. Effect of feeling good on helping: Cookies and kindness. *Journal of Personality and Social Psychology* 21(3): 384–388.

Kant, I. 1785/1959. *Foundations of the Metaphysics of Morals,* translated by L. W. Beck. Indianapolis: Bobbs-Merrill.

Kellam, S. G., M. B. Simon, and M. E. Ensminger. 1983. Antecedents in first grade of teenage substance use and psychological well-being: A ten-year community-wide prospective study. In *Origins of Psychopathology,* edited by D. F. Ricks and B. S. Dohrenwend, 17–42. Cambridge: Cambridge University Press.

Klinteberg af, B. D. Schalling, and D. Magnusson. 1990. Childhood behaviour and adult personality in male and female subjects. *European Journal of Personality* 4: 57–71.

Latané, B. and J. M. Dabbs. 1975. Sex, group size, and helping in three cities. *Sociometry* 38(2): 180–194.

Latané, B. and J. M. Darley. Group inhibition of bystander intervention in emergencies. *Journal of Personality and Social Psychology* 10(3): 215–221.

Lefkowitz, M. M., L. D. Eron, L. O. Walder, and L. R. Huesmann. 1977. *Growing Up to Be Violent: A Longitudinal Study of Aggression.* Elmsford, N.Y.: Pergamon.

Levy, P., D. Lundgren, M. Ansel, D. Fell, B. Fink, and J. E. McGrath. 1972. Bystander effect in a demand-without-threat situation. *Journal of Personality and Social Psychology* 24(2, Nov.): 166–171.

Loeber, R. and M. Stouthamer-Loeber. 1986. Family factors as correlates and predictors of juvenile conduct problems and delinquency. In *Crime and Justice*, vol. 7, edited by M. Tonry and N. Morris, 29–149. Chicago: University of Chicago Press.

London, P. 1970. The rescuers: Motivational hypotheses about christians who saved Jews from the Nazis. In *Altruism and Helping Behavior*, edited by J. Macaulay and L. Berkowitz, 241–250. New York: Academic Press.

Maccoby, E. E. 1986. Social groupings in childhood: Their relationship to prosocial and antisocial behavior in boys and girls. In *Development of Antisocial and Prosocial Behavior*, edited by D. Olweus, J. Block, and M. R. Yarrow, 263–284. New York: Academic Press.

Magnusson, D. and L. R. Bergman. 1988. Individual and variable-based approaches to longitudinal-research on early risk factors. In *Studies of Psychosocial Risk: The Power of Longitudinal Data*, edited by M. Rutter, 45–61. Cambridge: Cambridge University Press.

Marcus, R. F. 1986. Naturalistic observation of cooperation, helping, and sharing and their associations with empathy and affect. In *Altruism and Aggression: Biological and Social Origins*, edited by C. Zahn-Waxler, E. M. Cummings, and R. Iannotti, 256–279. Cambridge: Cambridge University Press.

McCord, J. 1977. A comparative study of two generations of Native Americans. In *Theory in Criminology: Contemporary Views*, edited by R. F. Meier, 83–92. Beverly Hills: Sage.

McCord, J. 1983. A longitudinal study of aggression and antisocial behavior. In *Prospective Studies of Crime and Delinquency*, edited by K. T. Van Dusen and S. A. Mednick, 269–275. Boston: Kluwer-Nijhoff.

McCord, J. 1983. A forty-year perspective on effects of child abuse and neglect. *Child Abuse and Neglect* 7: 265–270.

McCord, J. 1984. A longitudinal study of personality development. In *Handbook of Longitudinal Research*, vol. 2, *Teenage and Adult Cohorts*, edited by S. A. Mednick, M. Harway, and K. M. Finello, 522–531. New York: Praeger.

McCord, J. 1991. Questioning the value of punishment. *Social Problems* 38(2): 167–179.

Milgram, S. 1963. Behavioral study of obedience. *Journal of Abnormal and Social Psychology* 67: 371–378.

Milgram, S. 1974. *Obedience to Authority: An Experimental View*. New York: Harper.

Moore, B. S., B. Underwood, and D. L. Rosenhan, 1973. Affect and altruism. *Developmental Psychology* 8(1): 99–104.

Nagin, D. 1978. General Deterrence: A review of the empirical evidence. In *Deterrence and Incapacitation: Estimating the Effects of Criminal Sanctions on Crime Rates*, edited by A. Blumstein, J. Cohen, and D. Nagin, 95–139. Washington, D.C.: National Academy of Sciences.

Olweus, D. 1979. Stability of aggressive patterns in males: A review. *Psychological Bulletin* 86(4): 852–875.

Pawelczynska, A. 1979. *Values and Violence in Auschwitz: A Sociological Analysis*, translated by C. S. Leach. Berkeley: University of California Press.

Plato. *The Republic*, translated by Paul Shorey.

Pulkkinen, L. 1984. The Inhibition and control of aggression. *Aggressive Behavior* 10(3): 221–225.

Pulkkinen, L. 1988. Delinquent development: Theoretical and empirical considerations. In *The Power of Longitudinal Data: Studies of Risk and Protective Factors for Psychosocial Disorders*, edited by M. Rutter, 184–199. Cambridge: Cambridge University Press.

Rheingold, H. and G. N. Emery. 1986. The nurturant acts of very young children. In *Development of Antisocial and Prosocial Behavior*, edited by D. Olweus, J. Block, and M. R. Yarrow, 75–96. New York: Academic Press.

Robins, L. N. and L. McEvoy. Conduct problems as predictors of substance abuse. In *Straight and Devious Pathways from Childhood to Adulthood*, edited by L. N. Robins and M. Rutter, 182–204. Cambridge: Cambridge University Press.

Rosenhan, D. L. 1978. Toward resolving the altruism paradox: Affect, self-reinforcement, and cognition. In *Altruism, Sympathy, and Helping: Psychological and Sociological Principles*, edited by L. Wispé, 101–113. New York: Academic Press.

Rosenhan, D. L., B. Underwood, and B. Moore. 1974. Affect moderates self-gratification and altruism. *Journal of Personality and Social Psychology* 30(4): 546–552.

Rosenhan, D. and G. M. White. 1967. Observation and rehearsal as determinants of prosocial behavior. *Journal of Personality and Social Psychology* 5: 424–431.

Rushton, J. P. 1979. Effects of prosocial television and film material on the behavior of viewers. In *Advances in Experimental Social Psychology, vol. 12*, edited by L. Berkowitz, 321–351. New York: Academic Press.

Staub, E. 1970. A child in distress: The influence of age and number of witnesses on children's attempts to help. *Journal of Personality and Social Psychology* 14(2): 130–140.

Staub, E. 1979. *Positive Social Behavior and Morality: Socialization and Development*, Vol. 2, New York: Academic Press.

Staub, E. 1986. A conception of the determinants and development of altruism and aggression: Motives, the self, and the environment. In *Altruism and Aggression: Biological and Social Origins*, edited by C. Zahn-Waxler, E. M. Cummings, and R. Iannotti, 135–164. Cambridge: Cambridge University Press.

Staub, E. 1989. *The Roots of Evil: The Origins of Genocide and Other Group Violence*. Cambridge: Cambridge University Press.

Sutherland, E. H. and D. R. Cressey. 1924/1974. *Criminology* (9th ed.). Philadelphia: Lippincott.

Sykes, G. and D. Matza. 1957. Techniques of neutralization: A theory of delinquency. *American Sociological Review* 22: 667–670.

Tremblay, R. E., L. Desmarais-Gervais, C. Gagnon, and P. Charlebois. 1987. The Preschool Behaviour Questionnaire: Stability of its factor structure between cultures, sexes, ages and socioeconomic classes. *International Journal of Behavioral Development* 10(4): 467–484.

White, G. M. 1972. Immediate and deferred effects of model observation and guided and unguided rehearsal on donating and stealing. *Journal of Personality and Social Psychology* 21(2): 139–148.

Whiting, B. B. and J. W. M. Whiting. 1975. *Children of Six Cultures: A Psycho-Cultural Analysis*. Cambridge: Harvard University Press.

Wicklund, R. A. 1975. Objective self-awareness. In *Advances in Experimental Social Psychology, vol. 8*, edited by L. Berkowitz, 233–275. New York: Academic Press.

Widom, C. S. 1989. Child abuse, neglect, and violent criminal behavior. *Criminology* 27(2): 251–271.

Wilkens, J. L., W. H. Scharff, and R. S. Schlottman. 1974. Personality type, reports of violence and aggressive behavior. *Journal of Personality and Social Psychology* 30(2): 243–247.

Zahn-Waxler, C. and M. Radke-Yarrow. 1982. The development of altruism: Alternative research strategies. In *The Development of Prosocial Behavior*, edited by N. Eisenberg, 109–137. New York: Academic Press.

Zahn-Waxler, C., M. Radke-Yarrow, and R. A. King. 1979. Child-rearing and children's prosocial initiations toward victims of distress. *Child Development* 50: 319–330.

Zahn-Waxler, C., M. Radke-Yarrow, E. Wagner, and C. Pyle. 1988. The Early Development of Prosocial Behavior. Presented at the ICIS meetings, Washington, D.C., April.

Zillman, D. 1979. *Hostility and Aggression*. Hillsdale, N.J.: Lawrence Erlbaum.

Zimbardo, P. G., C. Haney, W. C. Banks, and D. Jaffe. 1974. The psychology of imprisonment: Privation, power, and pathology. In *Doing Unto Others*, edited by Z. Rubin, 61–73. Englewood Cliffs, N.J.: Prentice Hall.

CHAPTER TWENTY-THREE

Ethnicity, Acculturation, and Opportunities

A Study of Two Generations*

THE NUMBER OF CITIES in the United States with populations of at least ten thousand people rose from five, in 1800, to 345, in 1890, marking the beginning of a transition from a rural to an urban society (Weber, 1899/1963; Thernstrom, 1964/1970). After a brief hiatus, brought about by water shortages and crop infestations at the end of the nineteenth century (Hicks, 1931/1961), another 14.5 million people arrived in the United States. Three quarters of them settled in cities (Axinn and Levin, 1975). For the first time, in 1920, census figures showed an urban population greater than the rural population.

Typically, immigrants lived in the poorest urban areas. Adding to Jeffersonian attitudes attributing virtue to farming and sin to urban life, settlement patterns of the newer immigrants contributed to anti-immigrant sentiments. Ethnic identities were sometimes forged and often maintained through newspapers written in native tongues of the immigrants (Gans, 1962/1982; Park et al., 1925/1967; Suttles, 1968; Warner, 1962). The crowded, demoralizing conditions in pockets of urban poverty where many immigrants settled also provided conditions for frequent drunkenness and persistent crime (Hawes, 1971; Hogan, 1985; Menninger, 1947; Shaw and McKay, 1942/1972; Tarde 1897/1969; Ward, 1989; Weber, 1899/1963).

Despite evidence showing that immigrants were not particularly prone to crime or drunkenness (Abbott, 1915; Powell, 1966; Taft, 1936; van Vechten, 1941), the long-standing belief that they were was fueled by arguments favoring prohibition and promoting restrictions on immigration (Board of State Charities of Massachusetts, 1872; Hofstadter, 1955; Panunzio, 1932; Sinclair, 1951; Ward, 1989).

*Reprinted from McCord, J. 1995. Ethnicity, acculturation, and opportunities: A study of two generations. Reprinted by permission from *Ethnicity, Race, and Crime: Perspectives Across Time and Place*, edited by Darnell F. Hawkins, 69–81. Albany: The State University of New York Press. Copyright © 1995 State University of New York. All rights reserved.

Congress established the forerunner of the Federal Bureau of Immigration in 1891 in a bill that excluded carriers of contagious diseases and "immoral" people. President Cleveland vetoed a law approved by Congress in 1893 that was designed to exclude most immigrants from eastern and southern Europe through a literacy test. The Emergency Quota Act of 1921 restricted the number of immigrants from any country to 3 percent of the United States population in 1910 who were from that country. The Johnson Immigration Act of 1924 squeezed even more tightly by limiting the number of immigrants from any country to 2 percent of the United States population in 1890 who were from that country.

Theories linking immigration to crime postulate that immigrants and their children turn to illegitimate activities when success through legitimate routes appears unattainable (Baltzell, 1964; Bell, 1960; Cloward and Ohlin, 1960; Glazer and Moynihan, 1963; Hartshorne, 1968; Hawkins, 1993; Nelli, 1969). The relation between mobility and crime, some believe, rests partly on the inability of immigrants to cope with the different environment they find in the cities where they settle (Park et al., 1925/1967). Under such circumstances parents may be unable to provide adequate control for their acculturating children (Gordon, 1964; Lukoff and Brook, 1974).

Theories that immigrants lack the ability to supervise and guide their children in a foreign culture complement those suggesting that living in unfamiliar environments blocks opportunities for success. Both associate crime with immigration.

Suggestions that frustrated desires for success lead to crime have been linked with assumptions that immigrants note their relative status. Yet whether immigrants feel deprived partially depends on the comparisons they make. If poor immigrants compare their conditions to those of middle-class Americans, they might be expected to feel deprived. If, on the other hand, immigrants compare their conditions to those they left behind, they might feel less deprived than the similarly situated native-born. Children of immigrants may be more likely than their parents to compare themselves with native-born Americans.

Despite perceived links between crime and immigration, the data are ambiguous. For example, comparative data show that although immigrants accounted for a disproportionate amount of crime in Boston for the year 1914, in Chicago native-born residents were more likely to be criminal (Gault, 1932). Crime rates in Philadelphia did not increase during periods of high immigration (Hobbs, 1943), and with the exception of Italians, homicide rates among immigrants were *lower* than those among native-born Americans (Lane, 1979). Additionally, a United States Immigration Commission report showed highest criminal rates among Americans of native parentage and higher criminal rates among children of immigrants than among immigrants (Park et al., 1925/1967).

Unfortunately, much of the information about how crime is related to ethnicity and nativity has depended on police records. These records as sources of evidence about ethnicity and immigration are likely to embody the prejudices of police and the self-interest of arrested individuals. To discern how immigration is related to crime, sources of information about crime should be independent of those for immigration and ethnicity.

TABLE 23.1   Fathers' Immigration and Fathers' Education (percent)

	Immigrant		Native-born	
	Catholic (N=117)	Protestant (N=29)	Catholic (N=97)	Protestant (N=51)
Through 8th grade	25.6	55.2	66.0	74.5
Less than grammar school graduate	74.4	44.8	34.0	25.5
	100.0	100.0	100.0	100.0

Note: Numbers do not total 336 because information on education was not available for 42 fathers.

The purpose of the present study is to investigate the relationship of crime to ethnicity, nativity, and religion. Information about ethnicity, nativity, and religion was gathered as part of an elaborate procedure for identifying families that would become part of an intervention program designed to help youths at risk for becoming delinquents. The background information is completely independent of data regarding crime.

Description of a Study of Immigrants

The study focuses on two generations of men residing in Cambridge and Somerville between 1935 and 1945. The sample was selected because the families lived in overcrowded, rundown neighborhoods. High-crime rates, poverty, and obvious property deterioration had been grounds for selecting neighborhoods. Criminal records for the men of both generations were traced until the men died or reached at least the age of forty.

The project originally included 506 boys from 466 families. To avoid duplication of families, only one son per family was included. To assure correct ethnic identification of the sons, only families in which the natural parents had been described were included (N=409). Because information was lacking regarding the religion of thirty fathers, these families too were omitted from analyses. The twenty-eight blacks (only seven of whom were born in the United States), five agnostics, four Jews, three Protestant Italians, and three Protestant Portuguese were also dropped because there were too few for separate analyses and they did not fit criteria for typical ethnicity. The remaining 366 pairs of fathers and sons provided data for analyses.

The sample included 76 Italian Catholics, 33 Portuguese Catholics, and a mixture of 94 pairs from such places as Greece (N=6), Ireland (N=18), French Canada (N=11), and eastern Europe (N=14). Among the mixed group, 58 pairs were Catholic and 36 pairs were Protestant. There were 133 father-son pairs in which the fathers were born in the United States of apparently Yankee heritage. Among them were 74 pairs of Catholics and 59 pairs of Protestants.

Fathers were born between 1872 and 1908, with a mean in 1896. The 173 immigrant fathers had been born an average of 4.5 years before the 163 native-born fathers ($t=5.9$, $p=.0000$). Sons were born between 1926 and 1934. The sons

TABLE 23.2   Fathers' Immigration and Fathers' Occupations (percent)

	Immigrant		Native-born	
	Catholic (N=113)	Protestant (N=27)	Catholic (N=88)	Protestant (N=49)
White-collar	14.2	7.4	10.2	32.7
Skilled or semi-skilled	51.3	81.5	67.0	55.1
Unskilled	34.5	11.1	22.7	12.2
	100.0	100.0	99.9[a]	100.0

Note: Numbers do not total 336 because information on occupation was not available for 59 fathers.
[a]Column does not sum to 100 due to rounding.

of immigrants had been born an average of five months before the sons of native-born men ($t=2.5$, $p=.0130$).

Few of the fathers had graduated from high school. Therefore, those who had graduated from eighth grade (grammar school) were considered to have had a relatively good education. The fathers' educations were related both to immigration ($F=20.15$, $p=.0000$) and religion ($F=8.5$, $p=.003$), but not to the interaction between immigration and religion. Catholic immigrants were the least educated and native-born Protestants were the most educated. The proportions who graduated from grammar school are shown in Table 23.1.

Fathers were classified in terms of the highest status occupation reported on any record available through 1948. Having been selected because of residence in congested urban areas, the sample was skewed toward blue-collar occupations. Nevertheless, differences in the fathers' occupations reflected both religion ($F=6.3$, $p=.04$) and the interaction between religion and immigration status ($F=8.17$, $p=.02$). Catholic immigrants were most likely to be unskilled laborers. Protestant immigrants were most likely to be skilled or semiskilled workers. Protestants born in the United States were most likely to hold white-collar positions. Table 23.2 shows the relation of fathers' occupations to these dimensions of ethnicity.

Information about the sons' occupations was collected in 1980. As can be seen in Table 23.3, the sons had risen in occupational status compared with that of their fathers, with a higher proportion holding white-collar jobs regardless of the nativity of their fathers. The father's religion ($F=7.3$, $p=.03$), but not his immigration status or the interaction between religion and immigration, was significantly related to the son's occupational status. As found for their fathers, Catholics were less likely than Protestants to have white-collar occupations. Conversely, Catholics were more likely to be unskilled workers.

Overall, then, the immigrant families seemed to be at a slight (though statistically reliable) disadvantage in terms of education and occupational status. Cross-generational improvements in occupation were slower among Catholics than among Protestants. Although few Irish Catholics appeared in the sample, the pattern of advancement in the suburbs was similar to that found in Boston (Thernstrom, 1973).

TABLE 23.3   Fathers' Immigration and Sons' Occupations (percent)

	Immigrant		Native-born	
	Catholic (N=135)	Protestant (N=35)	Catholic (N=100)	Protestant (N=55)
White-collar	31.9	48.6	28.0	38.2
Skilled or semi-skilled	45.2	45.7	56.0	50.9
Unskilled	23.0	5.7	16.0	10.9
	100.1[a]	100.0	100.0	100.0

Note: Numbers do not total 336 because information on occupation was not available for 11 sons.

[a]Column does not sum to 100 due to rounding.

Crimes, Nativity, Religion, and Generation

Analyses focused on four types of crimes. Personal crimes of violence included those crimes against persons listed in the Federal Bureau of Investigations Index— for example, assault, attempted assault, kidnapping, robbery, rape, murder, and attempted murder. Property crimes included such crimes on the FBI index as larceny, arson, larceny of auto, breaking and entering, attempted larceny, receiving stolen property, and theft. Crimes of drunkenness included public drunkenness and driving under the influence of alcohol. Misdemeanors consisted in nuisance crimes of business (for example, unlicensed hack, unlicensed sale of liquor), victimless sex crimes, trespass, gambling, contributing to the delinquency of a minor, and other misdemeanors against order or ordinances.

The first two, violent crimes and property crimes, are typically considered to be serious crimes. Theories explain their occurrence in relation to poverty, relative deprivation, anomie, frustration, differential association, and inappropriate home management. Each of these dimensions had been used to explain putatively higher crime rates among immigrants than among native-born.

Because of the impoverished conditions under which the families were living, the present analyses control effects of economic conditions. Without such controls, one might easily confuse effects of poverty with effects of immigration, ethnicity, or religion.

Drunkenness was part of the stereotype attributed to the newer immigrants in arguments favoring prohibition. Convictions for crimes of drunkenness and for misdemeanors could be expected to reflect both cultural differences and concurrent police policies.

Measures of prevalence were based on the CATMOD procedure provided in SAS 6.0 (1990). Because of redundancy, a saturated model could not be tested. Instead, for each crime, predictions were made by a model in which main effects of father's nativity, culture, religion, and generation were introduced together with three interactions: father's nativity by father's religion, culture by generation, and father's nativity by generation. Relations were considered to be significant if the probability for obtaining them by chance was less than .05.

No significant differences were found for any of the main effects or interactions in relation to the prevalence of criminals convicted for violent crimes. It is clear, however, that neither the immigrant fathers nor their sons were more likely to have been convicted for these violent crimes than were the native-born fathers and their sons. Among the immigrant fathers, 10.9 percent had been convicted for violent crimes as had 14.7 percent of the native-born fathers; 11.6 percent of the sons of immigrants and 13.5 percent of the sons of native-born fathers had been convicted for violent crimes.

Nativity ($\chi^2_{(1)}$=8.08, p=.0045), generation ($\chi^2_{(1)}$=5.89, p=.0152), and their interaction ($\chi^2_{(1)}$=4.63, p=.0314) were related to property crimes. Immigrant fathers were least likely to be convicted for property crimes, with 4 percent convicted as compared with 18 percent of their sons, 15 percent of the native-born fathers, and 23 percent of the sons of native-born fathers.

The prevalence of drunkenness crimes reflected ethnicity (as the term has been defined in this research). In ascending order, the rates of conviction were 14.5 percent of the Italians, 28.8 percent of the Portuguese, 33.5 percent of the *other* ethnics, and 34.6 percent of the Yankees were convicted for at least one drunkenness crime ($\chi^2_{(3)}$=15.35, p=.0015).

Prevalence of misdemeanors reflected generational differences, with sons more likely than their fathers to be convicted for these crimes against order and ordinances ($\chi^2_{(1)}$=4.27, p=.0387). Within the immigrant families, 22.5 percent of the fathers and 35.8 percent of the sons had been convicted for misdemeanors. Within the native-born families, 27.6 percent of the fathers and 33.7 percent of the sons had been convicted for misdemeanors.

None of the comparisons showed that immigrants or their sons were more likely to be convicted for crimes than were native-born men and their sons. The distributions are shown in Figure 23.1.

The prevalence of different types of crimes across ethnic groups is shown in Figure 23.2.

Although crime was not more prevalent among immigrant families than among native-born families, differential frequencies in convictions could account for a perception that immigrants were prone to crime. The general linear models procedure, SAS 6.0 (1990), was used to test this possibility for each of the four types of crime. Due to the redundancy of classes, a fully saturated model could not be used, so three sequential models were used instead. The first tested main, two-way, and three-way interacting effects of father's nativity, culture, and generation. The second tested main, two-way, and three-way interacting effects of father's nativity, father's religion, and generation. The third tested main effects of father's nativity, culture, and father's religion, and generation together with the interacting effects of father's nativity by father's religion, culture by generation, and father's nativity by generation. Relations were considered to be significant if the probability for obtaining them by chance was less than .05.

The first model showed no significant relations with violent crimes. The second indicated that father's religion by generation was related to violent crimes (F=5.87, df=1, p=.0156), with Catholic fathers and Protestant sons convicted more frequently. The third model suggested an additional interaction between

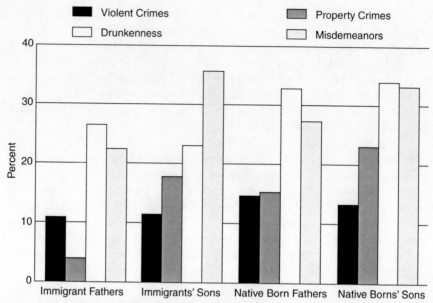

FIGURE 23.1   Immigration and crime (percent).

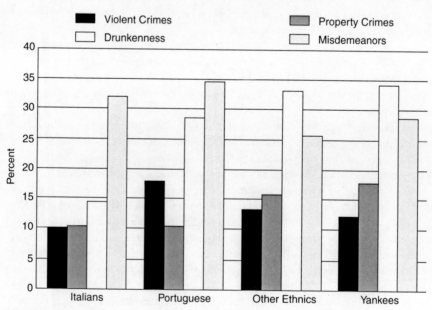

FIGURE 23.2   Cultures and crime (percent).

TABLE 23.4   Fathers' Immigration and Religion: Mean Number of Convictions for Violent Crimes

	Immigrant		Native-born	
	Catholic (N=137)	Protestant (N=36)	Catholic (N=104)	Protestant (N=59)
Fathers	0.20	0.08	0.40	0.10
Sons	0.15	0.31	0.17	0.14

TABLE 23.5   Fathers' Immigration and Culture: Mean Number of Convictions for Property Crimes

	Immigrant fathers			Native-born fathers		
	N	Fathers	Sons	N	Fathers	Sons
Italians	69	0.03	0.25	7	0.57	0.57
Portuguese	27	0.15	0.15	6	0.33	0.17
Other ethnics	77	0.04	0.87	17	0.18	0.47
Yankees	—	—	—	133	0.23	0.58

father's nativity and generation ($F=4.68$, $df=1$, $p=.0308$). Catholic native-born fathers and Protestant sons of immigrants had the highest crime rates for violence. These complex relations are shown in Table 23.4.

A somewhat different picture emerged in relation to property crimes. The first model revealed a main effect for generation ($F=19.18$, $p=.0001$) and an interaction effect for culture by generation ($F=2.82$, $df=3$, $p=.0382$). The second and third models showed significant effects only for generation. As can be seen in Table 23.5, the sons of Italian and *other* ethnic immigrants were likely to commit more property crimes than their fathers. Except for the sons of *other* ethnics, sons of immigrants were not likely to be convicted for more property crimes than were other similarly situated members of their generation. Immigrants had exceptionally low conviction rates.

Crimes of drunkenness had complex relationships involving the father's nativity, generation, and the father's religion. Statistics for the third model showed father's nativity ($F=12.21$, $df=1$, $p=.0005$), father's religion ($F=12.78$, $df=1$, $p=.0004$), and generation ($F=5.99$, $df=1$; $p=.0146$) to be significant predictors of rates for drunkenness crimes. As shown in Table 23.6, Catholic native-born fathers had the highest rates of conviction for drunkenness and sons of native-born Protestants had the lowest conviction rates.

Crime rates for misdemeanors reflected only a three-way interaction among father's nativity, culture, and generation ($F=3.17$, $df=2$, $p=.0428$). Among immigrants, Portuguese fathers had the highest rates; but their sons had no higher rates than did sons of Italian or other ethnic immigrants. Conviction rates for misdemeanors are shown in Table 23.7.

Table 23.6 Fathers' Immigration and Religion: Mean Number of Convictions for Drunkenness Crimes

	Immigrant		Native-born	
	Catholic (N=137)	Protestant (N=36)	Catholic (N=104)	Protestant (N=59)
Fathers	0.94	0.97	4.05	1.02
Sons	0.67	1.00	1.69	0.64

TABLE 23.7 Fathers' Immigration and Culture: Mean Number of Convictions for Misdemeanors

	Immigrant fathers			Native-born fathers		
	N	Fathers	Sons	N	Fathers	Sons
Italians	69	0.33	0.62	7	1.57	0.42
Portuguese	27	1.18	0.62	6	0.00	0.83
Other ethnics	77	0.35	0.69	17	0.59	0.59
Yankees	—	—	—	133	0.62	0.71

Summary and Discussion

A broad range of theories draws support from the belief that, historically, immigrants contributed disproportionately to crime in America. Evidentiary support has seemed to come from some studies that confounded socioeconomic conditions with nativity. Some theorists argue that immigrant groups lived in poverty when they came to America and that they were therefore temporary members of the *dangerous class*. As time passed and they became assimilated (the story goes), their conditions improved and they began to practice more socialized behavior. Variations of the theory have turned on whether the benefits of assimilation occur through decreased anomie accompanying increasing acceptance of middle-class norms or through successful participation in the competition for what is commonly believed to be the American style of achieving success. The present study raises questions about the fundamental claim on which these theories rest.

The study used official court records to ascertain criminality. Classifications of nativity, ethnicity, and religion came from independent records. Generation was controlled in the analyses. All the families had resided in impoverished areas of Cambridge and Somerville, Massachusetts.

The analyses showed that immigrants were *not* more likely than similarly situated native-borns to commit crimes of violence or property crimes. Nor were they more likely to be convicted for crimes related to drunkenness. The proportion of sons of immigrants who were convicted for misdemeanors was only slightly, and not reliably, greater than that of the same generation in native-born families. Among the fathers, immigrants were slightly, and not reliably, less likely to be convicted.

These results suggest that there has been misspecification of how crime is related to immigration, ethnicity, and religion. Differences in the frequencies of offending could provide a reasonable basis for the misspecification. Sons of Protestant immigrants had relatively high frequencies for crimes of violence; such was not the case for sons of Catholic immigrants. Sons of *other* ethnic immigrants had relatively high frequencies for crimes against property; such was not the case for sons of Italian or Portuguese immigrants. Immigrants themselves were less frequently convicted for both types of crime than were fathers born in the United States.

Of course what was true for Cambridge and Somerville may not be true for other locations. Nevertheless, correct identification of the causes relating phenomena turn upon finding those descriptions under which the relationships can be considered invariant across conditions. At least among those living in disordered, crowded, rundown areas considered in this study, neither immigrants nor their offspring were particularly likely to commit crimes.

Parallels have been drawn between the experiences of immigrants from Europe and the experiences of blacks who have migrated to northern cities. Arguments resting on such parallels have claimed that time will heal the wounds now festering in urban areas. The analogy on which this argument is based appears to rest on mistaken assumptions, so the conclusions should carry little weight.

It seems plausible that attributions of crime to immigrants has been a result of confusion and prejudice. The fact that immigrants lived in crowded, run-down, impoverished areas and that crime was rampant in such areas could lead to an assumption that immigrants were responsible for the crime. The ecological fallacy represented by such errors has been documented for other phenomena. Another form of confusion could occur because the immigrant criminals might be more memorable, thus seeming to account for a higher proportion of the disorders reported by contemporary observers. And finally, of course, the belief that immigrants were responsible for many of the ills of the city would be a not unexpected outcome of the widespread prejudices found with incoming foreigners seen as "babbling in alien tongues and framed by freakish clothes" (Barth, 1980, p. 15).

Unfortunately, what appears to be a false premise lies at the foundation of many *strong* theories. It remains to be seen whether a reexamination of the premises will lead to greater tolerance of differences or more accurate assessments of the current problems besetting American cities.

References

Abbott, G. 1915. Immigration and crime. *Journal of Criminal Law and Criminology* 6(4): 522–532.

Axinn, J. and H. Levin. 1975. *Social Welfare: A History of the American Response to Need.* New York: Dodd, Mead.

Baltzell, E. D. 1964. *The Protestant Establishment: Aristocracy and Caste in America.* New York: Vintage Books.

Barth, G. 1980. *City People.* New York: Oxford University Press.

Bell, D. 1960. *The End of Idealogy.* Glencoe, Ill.: Free Press.

Board of State Charities of Massachusetts. 1872. *Eighth Annual Report.* Boston: Board of State Charities of Massachusetts.

Cloward, R. A. and L. E. Ohlin. 1960. *Delinquency and Opportunity.* New York: Free Press.

Gans, H. T. 1962/1982. *The Urban Villagers*. New York: Free Press.

Gault, R. H. 1932. *Criminology*. Boston: D. C. Health.

Glazer, N. and D. P. Moynihan. 1963. *Beyond the Melting Pot*. Cambridge: M.I.T. Press.

Gordon, M. M. 1964. *Assimilation in American Life: The Role of Race, Religion, and National Origin*. New York: Oxford University Press.

Hartshorne, T. L. 1968. *The Distorted Image: Changing Conceptions of the American Character since Turner*. Cleveland: Press of Case Western Reserve University.

Hawes, J. M. 1971. *Children in Urban Society: Juvenile Delinquency in Nineteenth-Century America*. New York: Oxford University Press.

Hawkins, D. 1993. Crime and Ethnicity. In *The Socio-Economics of Crime and Justice*, edited by Brian Forst, 89–120. New York: M. E. Sharpe.

Hicks, J. D. 1931/1961. *The Populist Revolt: A History of the Farmers' Alliance and the People's Party*. Lincoln: University of Nebraska Press.

Hobbs, A. H. 1943. Criminality in Philadelphia: 1790–1810 compared with 1937. *American Sociological Review* 8: 198–202.

Hofstadter, R. 1955. *The Age of Reform: From Bryan to F.D.R.* New York: Alfred A. Knopf.

Hogan, D. J. 1985. *Class and Reform: School and Society in Chicago, 1880–1930*. Philadelphia: University of Pennsylvania Press.

Lane, R. 1979. *Violent Death in the City*. Cambridge: Harvard University Press.

Lukoff, I. F. and J. S. Brook. 1974. A sociocultural exploration of reported heroin use. In *Sociological Aspects of Drug Dependence*, edited by C. Winick, 35–59. Cleveland: CRC.

Menninger, W. C. 1947. The role of psychiatry in the world today. *American Journal of Psychiatry* 104(Sept.): 155–163.

Nelli, H. S. 1969. Italians and crime in Chicago: The formative years, 1890–1920. *American Journal of Sociology* 74(4): 373–391.

Panunzio, C. 1932. The foreign born and prohibition. *Annals of the American Academy of Political and Social Science* 163: 147–154.

Park, R. E., E. W. Burgess, and R. D. McKenzie. 1925/1967. *The City*. Chicago: University of Chicago Press.

Powell, E. H. 1966. Crime as a function of anomie. *Journal of Criminal Law, Criminology, and Police Science* 57: 161–171.

SAS Institute. 1990. Cary, North Carolina: Author.

Shaw, C. R. and H. D. McKay. 1942/1972. *Juvenile Delinquency and Urban Areas*. Chicago: University of Chicago Press.

Sinclair, A. 1951/1962. *Prohibition, the Era of Excess*. Boston: Little, Brown.

Suttles, G. D. 1968. *The Social Order of the Slum: Ethnicity and Territory in the Inner City*. Chicago: University of Chicago Press.

Taft, D. R. 1936. Nationality and crime. *American Sociological Review* 1: 724–736.

Tarde, G. 1897/1969. Criminal youth. In *On Communication and Social Influence: Selected Papers*, edited by T. N. Clarke. Chicago: University of Chicago Press.

Thernstrom, S. 1964/1970. *Poverty and Progress: Social Mobility in a Nineteenth Century City*. New York: Atheneum.

———. 1973. *The Other Bostonians: Poverty and Progress in the American Metropolis, 1880–1970*. Cambridge, Mass.: Harvard University Press.

van Vechten, C. C. 1941. Criminality of the foreign-born. *Journal of Criminal Law and Criminology* 32: 139–147.

Ward, D. 1989. *Poverty, Ethnicity, and the American City, 1840–1925*. New York: Cambridge University Press.

Warner, S. B., Jr. 1962. *Streetcar Suburbs: The Process of Growth in Boston, 1870–1900*. Cambridge: Harvard University Press.

Weber, A. F. 1899/1963. *The Growth of Cities in the Nineteenth Century: A Study in Statistics*. Ithaca: Cornell University Press.

CHAPTER TWENTY-FOUR

Learning How to Learn and
Its Sequelae*

HIGH SCHOOL IN TUCSON, ARIZONA, left me thinking that education was a matter of learning how to repeat what others wrote. Fortunately, at Stanford, I had two lucky breaks that taught me otherwise. The first was in a philosophy course that challenged me to think critically about what I read. The professor assigned a series of incompatible theories. When we realized that, being incompatible, they couldn't all be right, we were forced to rethink our earlier conviction concerning each. What a lesson that was. Thirty years later, I returned to Stanford and let Professor John Mothershead know that his course had made a tremendous difference in my life; it had turned me from an acceptor of received opinions into an independent and skeptical thinker.

The second lucky break came in the form of an extraordinary professor who agreed to give me a tutorial course. He agreed on condition that I would read Spinoza, a notoriously difficult project. Having practically no background, but loaded with enthusiasm, I agreed. The reading was dense; the weekly sessions downright painful. Each week, I reported on the sections I had read and what they seemed to mean. Professor Davidson asked for more. Why had Spinoza made that specific argument? What issues were relevant to the questions it addressed? Had the argument been made by others? He conveyed the clear impression that reading the text, even carefully reading the text, was not enough. I remember no compliments, no recognition of effort spent, nothing but a careful exposure of what it means to master a topic. His teaching, I believe, put me on track to become a researcher in a broad and multi-disciplined field that investigates justice.

William ("Bud") McCord and I had been friends since high school. We went to Stanford together and were married as undergraduates. We decided on academic

*Reprinted from McCord, J. 2002. Learning how to learn and sequelae. In *Lessons of Criminology*, edited by G. Geis and M. Dodge, 95–108. Cincinnati, Ohio: Anderson Publishing Co.; with permission from Matthew Bender & Company, Inc., a member of the LexisNexis Group, Copyright 2002. All rights reserved.

careers together. That decision was easy once we had been given the sensible advice to talk with people who occupied positions we envisioned ourselves as having in about 10 years. "Don't ask their advice," Professor Cowley said, "but talk with them about their daily routines. Ask them what they enjoy about their jobs. Then decide which lifestyle best fits you." We talked with business leaders in a variety of specialties, with lawyers who had become partners in firms, and with well-established bankers. These people were successful and most of them enjoyed what they were doing, but we found—hands down—that what the professors did was what we wanted to do. We also agreed that I would support Bud while he got his credentials before going on for my own.

After graduation from Stanford, Bud enrolled at Harvard to study with Sheldon and Eleanor Glueck and I got a position teaching children in Concord, Massachusetts. Classroom teaching provided an important opportunity for me to learn more about children. Occasionally, I used my sixth graders to experiment with theories about learning. The experiment I remember best involved teaching children what to value. At the beginning of the year, I asked the class to list their subjects in order of preference. Almost all the 30 children ranked arithmetic at the bottom. So arithmetic became my target. I instituted an Arithmetic Club. It would be open only to those who got 100 percent correct on an assigned paper. (Because I gave individualized assignments, everybody had a chance to join.) Members of the Arithmetic Club were given a special privilege: They were allowed to do weekly arithmetic homework which I would grade. At the end of the term, the class reevaluated their subjects. Confirming a theory about using rewards to shape preferences (based on my interpretation of some work done by Leon Festinger), arithmetic had moved upward for all the students and it had become a favorite for most. This classroom experiment exposed the folly of common practice in using homework as punishment, a practice that sends the message that learning is painful, rather than a privilege.

The classes also proved useful for pretesting the measurement instruments Bud and I intended to use in our work for *Psychopathy and Delinquency* (1956). One of the tests, designed to measure aggression, involved a dog. The children were to identify the dog's preferred solution in a variety of problem situations, one solution being aggressive, one ameliorating, and one withdrawing from the situation. Because we knew some of the delinquent children to be tested would be illiterate, we used pictures showing the situations and each of the choices. Before giving the test the first time, in my Concord classroom, I had rated the children for their aggression. To honor our own dog, we referred to the one in the test we had designed as "Chumley," asking for each situation, "What would Chumley want to do?" An example is a picture showing Chumley's family displaying a new baby to an unhappy dog. The attached choices asked: "Does he want to bite the baby (picture)? Does he want to go off in a corner to show how badly he feels (picture)? Or does he want to make friends with the baby (picture)?" Almost all the children picked the friendly choices for just about all the situations, with no differences between the most aggressive and the least. Two months later, I reintroduced the test, giving the dog a different name. Same situations and same pictures. This time the children were asked, "What would Rover want to do?" It was

Rover's family bringing home a new baby, having his bone stolen by another dog, seeing a birthday cake on the kitchen table, etc. Although the children had not differed in their perspectives of Chumley, with all finding him to be friendly, they differed in their assignment of preferences for Rover. The more aggressive ones indicated that Rover would want to bite the baby, fight the dog who took his bone, and take the birthday cake. We learned the importance of a name for attributing personality. We also had constructed a test that could be used for differentiating more aggressive from less aggressive children.

One of my aunts introduced us to Ernst Papanek, director of the reform school in upper New York State that took seriously delinquent boys from New York City. With Papanek's permission, Bud and I spent one summer working with and studying delinquents at Wiltwyck. In a reform school without bars, milieu therapy sought to change children by altering their environments. Papanek believed that using punishments would teach the children to use force to gain what they wanted. As an alternative, he manipulated the environment so that the children could learn the consequences of what they did without being punished. They were taught to repair damage. Their classrooms were models of compassion, as the specially trained teachers learned to cope with high degrees of maladaptation.

The whole day for each child was a part of his therapy. Cooks, for example, helped by teaching the children how to make pastries. Each child at Wiltwyck had a small plot of ground on which to grow flowers or vegetables. The boys were also taught to fight with gloves rather than fists. Floyd Patterson, the heavyweight boxing champion, was a graduate and returned annually to coach the boys. In the evenings, counselors retired to their quarters to read and play ping pong. I acquired a lifetime passion for ping pong. Much more important: I learned not to use punishments (i.e., the intentional giving of pain to control behavior).

Harvard had summer scholarships in Education. I was able to "test out" of most of the education courses and use the scholarships to take courses in philosophy. Once Bud received his Ph.D., I quit teaching in Concord and obtained a research assistantship at Harvard, working for a group of social scientists at the cutting edge of their fields. Eleanor Maccoby and Harry Levin were studying child development, using interviews with mothers and doll play with the children. I "coded" the doll interactions, which involved marking on a sheet of paper what the child did with dolls that represented a boy, a girl, a mother, and a father. John and Beatrice Whiting were developing codes to check theories of child development against a broader diversity of customs than can be found in the United States. I coded reports on discipline for the Human Relations Area Files housed at Yale. Wesley Allensmith set up experiments to identify and then study children easily led by temptation. In one, children were told they could get prizes by hitting a hidden target with a beanbag. They were also told that it was against the rules to look behind the cloth to see the target. Through a one-way mirror we could identify which children nonetheless peeked, and the studies then explored how those children differed from others who obeyed the rules. Although I didn't work for him, Roger Brown was also at the Laboratory of Human Development. Brown was studying the influence of language on children's thought. Every noon, John Whiting stirred up a pot of soup in the kitchen, where faculty and students ate together.

Whiting, director of the laboratory, had one clear rule: lunch conversation was to be about research. Students generally listened while the faculty talked. Listening to the discussion provided the most intense tutorial I have ever attended.

Most of the work for Sears, Maccoby, and Levin's *Patterns of Child Rearing* was done at the Laboratory of Human Development. They had used a questionnaire that involved detailed reporting by the mother about how parents treated their children and each other and how the children behaved. I still recall—and this was in 1955—the lunch in which Eleanor Maccoby described what they had learned about the relation between a mother's discipline and her child's misbehavior. I asked my first question: "How do you know that the mother's report is accurate?"

I had my doubts. Perhaps these came from having overheard my mother's frequent criticisms of me to her friends, criticisms that seemed to me unfair and inaccurate. Subsequent studies, by me and others, supported the skepticism.

My first son was born in December 1956. The pleasures, for me, of parenthood are beyond description. Though I hated being pregnant, I loved caring for Geoffrey. A fellow teacher at Concord had a baby the year before, and because both of us were convinced that punishments were unnecessary, we discussed alternative ways to teach our infants how to act. My work at Wiltwyck, too, contributed to a commitment to rear my children without using punishment.

Years later, I wrote about the theoretical grounds for that commitment in two articles: "Unintended Consequences of Punishment," published in *Pediatrics Supplement*, 1996, and "Discipline and the Use of Sanctions," published in *Aggression and Violent Behavior*, 1997. I hope the detailed explanations to be found in these articles will help many parents create comfortable nonpunitive environments in which to rear their children.

In the summer of 1957, I was offered a small sum of money to evaluate effects of the Cambridge-Somerville Youth Study on crime. Richard Clark Cabot, who had been one of Sheldon Glueck's professors, designed a randomized control study to test the idea that providing assistance to families of young boys in distressed neighborhoods would reduce delinquency. Each boy was matched to another with similar backgrounds, family structures, and parental behaviors. They also were matched in terms of such characteristics as early aggressiveness, intelligence, and physical strength. One boy in each pair was placed in the treatment group while the other was simply left to his community. The treatment program included tutoring, counseling, coaching in social skills, medical help, and leisure activities. Because of the matching, aggressive and nonaggressive kids were in both the treatment and the control groups.

Evaluation of the program back in 1948 had failed to find the anticipated benefits, and Gordon Allport believed that was because the evaluation had been carried out too soon. We tracked the records of the randomly assigned treatment and control boys and coded their case records on a variety of measures. *Origins of Crime* (1959) reported the results, which again failed to find anticipated benefits from the treatment. We did not even consider the possibility that the treatment might have been harmful!

The case records for the Cambridge-Somerville Youth Study were written with exquisite detail. Cabot, who had been president of the National Conference on Social Work in 1931, wanted to improve the practice of recording information so that case records would be more useful for designing treatments. He hired recorders to transcribe information about contacts between social workers and their clients within hours of the encounters. The case records included information about conversations and other interactions among family members. Such encounters typically took place about twice a month for more than five years, filling several hundred pages of narrative reports. I wanted to use the case records as a source of information about socialization and especially as a way of exploring the impact of child-rearing techniques.

Bud and I successfully applied for funds to code the case records for evaluations against independent information found in records of alcoholism and of crime. The result was *Origins of Alcoholism* (1960). This was the first longitudinal study of alcoholics and, because we learned about characteristics that preceded alcoholism, it enabled us to test which of them might be causal. The work benefited hugely from my training with Eleanor Maccoby. She had taught me to define variables carefully and avoid building evaluations into the coding scheme. The earlier codes, those used in *Origins of Crime*, reflected the categories used by the Gluecks. After 1957, all work based on the Cambridge-Somerville Youth Study case records used the redesigned coding scheme. Eleanor had also taught me to worry about reliability, so we tested reliability of ratings by having more than one person code a randomly selected group of case records and used only codes that attained a reasonable degree of reliability.

By autumn of 1957, I was a full-fledged student in philosophy, with a Josiah Royce Fellowship at Harvard. Concerned to bolster my knowledge, I convinced the teaching assistant in Quantitative Logic to tutor me in exchange for my doing his grading. I was reading Descartes and Hobbes, Hume, and Locke while struggling with Hilbert and Ackermann. A. I. Meldon, J. L. Austin, and W. V. O. Quine were lecturing, and Wittgenstein's *Philosophical Investigations* excited us all. H. L.A. Hart gave a seminar to which all our professors came to argue. It was a wonderful time and place to be learning.

Around that time, my husband was offered a position as Assistant Dean of Humanities and Sciences at Stanford. He loved teaching at Harvard, but he was enticed by the opportunities at Stanford. Although I had been offered, and wanted to accept, a Teaching Assistantship with Roderick Firth in Ethics, we went to California, and I returned to empirical studies as a Research Associate at Stanford.

We rented, for 99 years, a plot of land on Stanford grounds. My cousin Ellen designed our new house, checking the blueprints with her architect father, and I supervised the building. Ellen later became a Senior Editor at *Architectural Forum* and wrote pioneer articles about the relationships between buildings and their occupants. The house was a perfect environment for us, with Bud's study off a private patio and away from noise, and mine within sight and hearing of the play area for our children. Shortly after we moved in, our second son, Robert, was born.

In 1961, we joined 80 Stanford students to spend almost a year in France. Stanford owned a building in Tours that included dormitories and classrooms. We had a small apartment, and I struggled to learn French, attempting to imitate the accents I heard from kids in the parks as I supervised my children playing. In the summer, we lived in a beautiful village, Croix-de-Vie, on the Atlantic coast. With only outdoor plumbing and two young children, living was complicated. But daily shopping brought me into contact with friendly merchants who were willing to listen to my dimly comprehensible French. Their willingness to converse helped me to understand a culture in which relaxation and discussion took precedence over earning money and being successful.

When we came back to California, I received a Stanford Wilson Fellowship to study philosophy. I returned to a field that continues to be the foundation for my thinking. Donald Davidson, Patrick Suppes, Jaegwon Kim, and Richard Jeffrey were the faculty from whom I learned a great deal. Davidson was working on problems linking reasons to actions and puzzling over issues in the philosophy of language. Suppes was in the process of converting set theory to methods for teaching arithmetic to young children, so that his course in logic included a clear exposition of Peano arithmetic as well as first order predicate logic and the axioms of set theory. Kim brought out the relevance of Plato and Aristotle to contemporary issues in philosophy. And Jeffrey conveyed the thrill of discovering Russell's Paradox at the foundation of mathematics, the Lobatchevski interpretation of one of the axioms in Euclidean geometry, and the role of transformations for understanding physics. The department had a "pro-seminar" in which first-year graduate students were required to produce a paper in order to exhibit what they knew. The faculty took the opportunity to show how little we knew by asking tough questions. Although the process was difficult, it helped teach us high standards.

I write about my education hoping it communicates the sense of adventure and the pleasures and challenges of learning. Some of this, it seems to me, is denied students when courses are too easy and are designed primarily to help students "feel good about themselves." But back to the autobiographical story.

I was combining being a student with raising my sons, though I had stopped doing research in sociology. I loved my studies and I was doing well. Soon, I began to think about having an independent career that would grow out of my love of philosophy. Yet shortly after the second semester began, Bud began drinking heavily and became abusive. Bud and I had written extensively about alcoholism, in part because both of his parents had been alcoholics. We had noted, in *Origins of Alcoholism*, that our work would be justified if it contributed to prevention of alcoholism. And both of us believed for a while that our work had indeed saved him. I hoped that Bud's attacks might end when he saw that my independence would not reduce my love for him. To this day, I do not know whether to consider alcoholism as a disease for which one should not be held responsible. I do know that Bud objected to me taking on an independent career. He convinced my family and some of our friends (who were his colleagues) to urge me to drop out of school. Not wanting to be in the middle of a domestic argument, the Stanford philosophy department withdrew its financial support for me. This was 1963. I sometimes wonder whether women today realize how different it is both to have support from other women and to have a legal system that allows for their independence. (I grew up at a time when women could be fired from teaching positions if they became pregnant, when airline hostesses could be fired if they got married, and when it was legal to tell women that they need not apply for a position because a company or university was interested only in hiring males.)

There is little worth writing about here except to say that sometimes divorce is the best option. Years later, I mentioned feeling guilty because I had deprived my sons of living with their father. Both of them assured me that it had been the right decision. Interestingly, recent research has shown, contrary to popular opinion, that single-parent families are less likely to be damaging to children than are two-parent families in which the parents do not get along well.

Yet the period immediately following the divorce was difficult for me. Needing to support myself and two sons, I could not continue my studies. After a lean year of renting out a spare room in our house, tutoring kids, coaching tennis, and part-time consulting to put food on the table, I obtained a generous fellowship from the National Institute of Mental Health to finish graduate work. The fellowship gave me three years. My original plan had been to continue with philosophy. But I had a good publishing record in the social sciences, having co-authored four books and published 18 articles (some of which had been republished and had therefore reached a wide audience). Several professors counseled that it would be easier for me to find a position in the social sciences, so I decided to take courses in sociology. My sons often accompanied me to class, drawing quietly in the back of the room. I had jumped from being a Research Associate to becoming a student, from being a faculty wife to being a single mother. The shifts made dramatic differences in the way people interacted with me. Prompted by this sad experience, for my thesis, I ran an experiment to study the impact of status.

The experiment had me seen as acting in one of two roles simultaneously. So they would not see one another, a screen separated the two subjects in the experiment at the same time. One believed I was a professor (with "Professor McCord" on the door); the secretary I hired used the title three times as she spoke about me while leading the subject to the experimental room. The other believed I was a student, with "practice room" on the door and the secretary referring to "Joan, one of the students here" and using just "Joan" to refer to me. I described the study to both at once, so whatever differences were uncovered could not be attributed to differences in my behavior. (In my mid-thirties, I could pass for either a professor or a student.) The subjects were of the same sex and had been randomly assigned to each status. I knew neither the order of entry nor which had been led to believe I was a professor and which believed I was a student.

I was testing a central tenet of sociologists at Stanford: the belief that status mattered a great deal to everyone. I designed a measure of influence that allowed me to use only the subtle pressure of expressing my preference. The task was to select the best sentence from among sets in which one used an adjective, one an adverb before the verb, and one an adverb after the verb. Pretests had shown that without influence, students were equally likely to pick each of the sentence forms in a set. In the experiment, I expressed a preference to both high- and low-status subjects simultaneously. That preference was rotated so that each type of sentence was chosen, though for different pairs. Other people had shown that women were more easily influenced than were men, so I evaluated the task to be sure there was room for influence, that is, that there would not be a ceiling effect. My study demonstrated that status descriptions—in the absence of any behavioral differences—made a difference in terms of influence for males. Yet, contrary to the universal assumption about status, status mattered little in terms of influence to the females. I received a Ph.D. in sociology in 1968.

June 1968 was before there were any legal barriers to discriminating against women, so it was particularly difficult for me to find employment. I wanted to move East, where theater and classical music beckoned, but my few offers came from western schools. Luckily, I had a friend from Harvard days teaching at Drexel University in Philadelphia. He remembered that I loved philosophy and thought that at Drexel I could teach philosophy as well as sociology. After a successful interview, the boys, two dogs, two cats, and I moved to a house just outside of Philadelphia. For a few years, I taught four courses per quarter and barely kept my head above water. Even so, my schedule was flexible enough to allow me to cheer my sons through baseball and soccer seasons. I married my second husband, Carl Silver, in 1970. A specialist in human factors, he delighted in classical music, opera, and fine food. He had courted all three of us, wisely, for my sons and I were good friends and I listened to their counsel.

My earlier work on the causes of alcoholism and crime had been carried out with a sample then in their early thirties. I knew that alcoholism may not develop until later in life and also wanted to use the same sample to learn more about criminal careers. But longitudinal research, research that requires tracing individuals, was expensive and decidedly not in style. It was difficult to convince agencies that the expenses involved would produce enough benefits to make them worthwhile. Since 1970, partly as a consequence of my work, several federal agencies as well as many researchers have come to recognize that if we are to understand behavior, we must come to understand how it develops. That involves learning the sequence of events, which in turn, requires longitudinal studies. Although some knowledge of sequencing can be gained retrospectively, studies of memory have shown the hazards in assuming one should believe what people claim to remember.

After several attempts to get financial support for the study, the National Institute of Mental Health again came to my rescue; this time, with a three-year grant to retrace the former clients of the Cambridge-Somerville Youth Study. As a result of the design, the Cambridge-Somerville Youth Study offered an opportunity for a strong test of the possibility that providing families with multiple forms of assistance would be beneficial to their sons. Feedback from the participants indicated that they remembered the program and most believed it to have been helpful. I collected evidence from the courts, mental health facilities, alcoholism treatment centers, and death records.

Drexel, largely an engineering school, was not accustomed to social science research. There were no graduate students in sociology or any of the social sciences. Nevertheless, I managed to pull together a team of enthusiastic and capable researchers, and Drexel personnel included some exceedingly competent support staff. Michael Wadsworth, Jack Block, Jerry Bachman, and Glen Elder, among others, came to my advisory conferences, so I had colleagues with whom to discuss the project. The idea of having such annual conferences came from my

Program Officer at NIMH, Tom Lalley, who realized that research thrives on discussions and was kind enough to provide funds to make such discussions possible for me.

My team managed to find 98 percent of the former members of the Cambridge-Somerville Youth Study despite there having been no contact for 30 years. That took some fine detective work by a staff of amateur sleuths. Moreover, we managed to get approximately 75 percent of the men, who were in their late forties and early fifties, to respond either to questionnaires or to interviews. Richard Parente did the interviewing. He traveled throughout the country, tirelessly adjusting his schedule to accommodate others, but unwilling to accept a refusal. Rich was able to put people at ease, and convince almost everyone to let him talk with them. To assure equivalence of treatment, Rich was not informed about which of the men had been in the treatment group and which had been in the control group.

The men who had been in the treatment program were compared with others reared in similar families up to the age when treatment began. Had there been no treatment program, they could be expected to have similar lives. As it turned out, those in treatment died an average of five years younger, were more likely to be recidivist criminals, and more likely to have become alcoholics, manic-depressives, or schizophrenics. The treatment had been harmful! Results of this provocative study have been well scrutinized. They have been published in *American Psychologist* and by the National Academy of Sciences. The most recent report appears in "The Cambridge-Somerville Study: A Pioneering Longitudinal Experimental Study of Delinquency Prevention," published in *Preventing Antisocial Behavior: Interventions from Birth through Adolescence* (1992).

Because the evidence cast doubt on so many social assistance programs, it was initially difficult to get the results published. Yet subsequently, many other researchers have reported similarly negative results from treatment programs that give the appearance of being beneficial. This line of research brought me invitations to speak in Canada, France, England, Sweden, and Switzerland. Recently, Tom Dishion and I pulled together evidence on effects of intervention programs to argue that the problem is related to mutual support among misbehaving young adolescents. The resulting article appeared in the September 1999 issue of *American Psychologist*.

A second major thrust of my research focused on the powerful impact of parental socialization. The studies showed that family interactions, rather than the presence or absence of parental figures, accounted for major differences between criminals and noncriminals (McCord, 1982). Parental conflict and aggressiveness (e.g., using harsh punishments or throwing things when angry) appeared to produce the more serious types of violent crimes (McCord, 1991a). Because the records included information about the parents, I was also able to show that some of the continuity of crime across generations was due to the tendency of criminal fathers to behave in criminogenic ways (McCord, 1991b).

In 1987, I accepted an offer to move from Drexel to Temple University. Shortly after, I became President of the American Society of Criminology—the first woman to have the honor. The presidency was particularly pleasing because my son, Geoff (who is a philosophy professor at the University of North Carolina, Chapel Hill) came to Reno to introduce my Presidential Address (McCord, 1990). It has also been my good fortune to win recognition for my research, the Prix Emile Durkheim in 1993 from the International Society of Criminology and the Sutherland Award in 1994 from the American Society of Criminology.

Many of my newest projects focus on theory (McCord, 1997) or on methodology (McCord, 2000). Yet just about every topic related to criminology intrigues me. In recent years, thanks to Mark Haller, a colleague who is a historian, I have been reading social history and discovering the degree to which that history enlightens current issues in criminal justice. Effects of that reading appear in "Placing American Urban Violence in Context" (McCord, 1997).

For many years, my interests in criminology have been nourished through reviewing activities. Felice Levine (now Executive Secretary of the American Sociological Association) ran stimulating semiannual seminars to review applications sent to the National Science Foundation's Program in Law and Social Sciences on which I served from 1987 to 1991. I've also regularly been a reviewer for the Office of Juvenile Justice and Delinquency Prevention, the National Institute of Justice, the Center for Disease Control, the Department of Education, and several foreign granting agencies (as well as numerous journals and book publishers). Rarely, in my experience, are there sharp differences in evaluations at the top and bottom of the application piles. The interesting discussions occur in the middle ranges, as reviewing panels try to estimate the contributions an unseasoned applicant might make or the centrality of an issue being addressed by a well-qualified applicant. Rarely, too, have any of the reviewing panels expressed preferences that were not scientifically supported.

At Drexel, most of my students were the first in their families to go to college. The students spent half the year in jobs, through a "Co-op" program. It was a challenge to help them see the value of learning from books. In teaching sociology, I selected books that I found interesting, and then designed activities that they could use to help them see the relevance to everyday life of what they read. One of the more fruitful assignments was tied to Goffman's *Stigma*. Students were asked to talk with a stranger for 10 minutes, then introduce a stigma about themselves and try to continue the same topic of conversation. The students were wonderfully imaginative. One was fixing his car with a stranger watching, commenting, and praising his work. After 10 minutes, the student mentioned that he had learned to be a mechanic "at Holmesburg" (a local reform school). The stranger slammed down the hood of his car and almost broke my student's hand. Another applied for a job and was clearly about to be hired when she handed in the health portion of her application: She had listed "epilepsy in remission." She was pushed out the door amidst much yelling and anger. Another was talking with a stranger while waiting for the train. Her friend stopped by, by design, and said how glad she was to see my student well and out of Byberry (the local mental hospital). Although the stranger had offered to show my student around New York City, she left as soon as she heard the word "Byberry." Another, while changing a tire on the highway, confessed that he was just out of reform school and looking for a job. He was given advice by, as it turned out, a parole officer (a member of the "wise" as Goffman described them) who counseled him not to mention his incarceration when applying for the job. It pleased me particularly to win the University's Lindback Award for Distinguished Teaching.

At Temple, I periodically teach in the Intellectual Heritage program, where first- and second-year students are introduced to classic texts. In addition, I have had the pleasure of teaching graduate students as well as undergraduates. I have particularly enjoyed the handful of graduate students who, as my students, have shared with me the adventures of discovery.

One of the benefits of an academic life is the opportunity to travel. Editing for the Harry Frank Guggenheim Foundation took me to a small town in the mountains north of Rome. A project on the impact of developing democracies took me to Budapest and Prague. My research on psychopathy brought me to Valencia. My work on alcoholism resulted in trips to Tel Aviv and to Moscow just before the Soviet Union collapsed. As Vice President of the International Society of Criminology, I regularly visit Paris for meetings of the Board, and joined those who went to Rio de Janeiro to provide one of the courses sponsored by the ISC. My focus on longitudinal methodology has, over the years, resulted in invitations to Bristol and Cambridge (UK), Voss, Stockholm, Warsaw, Poland; Vienna, Taipei, Groningen, Freudenstadt, and Rhodes. There have been other trips as well, but these stand out. Carl liked to travel and often joined me after my work was finished. Together, we ventured into Egypt and Turkey, Korea and Japan, and drove throughout France and Ireland. Even after Carl was wheelchair bound, we went to Bayreuth, Germany, for the Wagner festival. Carl died in 1998. My son Rob (now President and CEO of the Eastern Technology Council and a venture capitalist) accompanied me for a week in China, where I was giving a couple of talks before going on to Canberra, Australia. In Canberra, I was assigned an office down the hall from the philosophy department, where son Geoff was on a research fellowship.

Writing about my life has forced me to recall events I had not thought about for years. Of course I have regrets, but on major choices, I lucked out. As a career skeptic, I am reluctant to give advice. Yet because the editors of this book requested each author to include advice for the readers, let me draw to a close by complying with that request.

I would urge women to obtain credentials so they can find interesting things to do, activities that will not be heavily dependent on events over which they will have little control. I would not trade being a mother for any opportunity at all, though I recognize that a taste for being a parent is far from universal. I would suggest to anyone considering academe, male or female, that it is better to work on projects you believe to be important than to select with an eye to winning praise or prizes. And I would encourage friends at any time to find fields of inquiry that intrigue them so that they can always experience the satisfactions of learning.

Note

I thank my son Geoffrey Sayre McCord for his careful editing of this manuscript.

Recommended Readings

The list is highly idiosyncratic, but I've identified four (maybe five, depending on how they are counted) that ought not be overlooked.

Plato. *Euthyphro* and *Meno* (various editions are available.)

Shaw, C. R. and McKay, H. D. *Juvenile Delinquency and Urban Areas.* The University of Chicago Press, 1942, revised edition, 1969.

Douglass, Frederick. *Narrative of the Life of An American Slave Written by Himself.* (Various editions are available.)

Jackson, K. T. *Crabgrass Frontier: The Suburbanization of the United States.* Oxford: Oxford University Press, 1985.

A Dozen of My Best

McCord, J. 2000. Developmental trajectories and intentional actions. *Journal of Quantitative Criminology* 16(2): 237–253.

McCord, J. 1997. Placing American urban violence in context. In *Violence and Childhood in the Inner City*, edited by J. McCord, 78–115. New York, NY: Cambridge Press.

McCord, J. 1997. He did it because he wanted to… In *Motivation and Delinquency, vol. 44* in Nebraska Symposium on Motivation, edited by W. Osgood, vol. 44, 1–43. Lincoln, NE: University of Nebraska Press.

McCord, J. 1997. Discipline and the use of sanctions. *Aggression and Violent Behavior* 2(4): 313–319.

McCord, J. 1996. Unintended consequences of punishment. *Pediatrics Supplement* 98(4): 832–834.

McCord, J. 1995. Crime in the shadow of history. In *Current Perspectives on Aging and the Life Cycle: Delinquency and Disrepute in the Life Course*, edited by J. Hagan, 105–118. Greenwich, CT: JAI Press.

McCord, J. 1992. The Cambridge-Somerville Study: A pioneering longitudinal experimental study of delinquency prevention. In *Preventing Antisocial Behavior: Interventions from Birth through Adolescence*, edited by J. McCord and R. E. Tremblay, 196–206. New York, NY: Guilford Press.

McCord, J. 1991a. Family relationships, juvenile delinquency, and adult criminality. *Criminology* 29(3): 397–417. Republished in *Crime and Criminals: Contemporary and Classic Readings in Criminology*, edited by F. R. Scarpitti and A. L. Nielsen. Los Angeles, CA: Roxbury Publishing.

McCord, J. 1991b. The cycle of crime and socialization practices. *Journal of Criminal Law and Criminology* 82(1 Spring): 211–228.

McCord, J. 1990. Crime in moral and social contexts. *Criminology* 28(1): 1–26. Republished in *Contemporary Masters of Criminology*, edited by J. McCord and J. H. Laub, 251–276. New York, NY: Plenum Press.

McCord, J. 1989. Theory, pseudotheory, and metatheory. In *Advances in Criminological Theory*, edited by W. S. Laufer and F. Adler, vol. 1, 127–145. New Brunswick, NJ: Transaction.

McCord, J. 1982. A longitudinal view of the relationship between paternal absence and crime. In *Abnormal Offenders, Delinquency and the Criminal Justice System*, edited by J. Gunn and D. P. Farrington, 113–128. Chichester, England: Wiley.

JOAN McCORD'S PUBLICATIONS

Books Authored or Edited

McCord, J., ed. 2004. *Beyond Empiricism: Institutions and Intentions in the Study of Crime. Advances in Criminological Theory, Volume 13*. Picataway, NJ: Transaction Publishers.

McCord, J., C. S. Widom, and N. A. Crowell, eds. 2001. *Juvenile Crime, Juvenile Justice*. Washington, DC: National Academy Press.

McCord, J., ed. 1997. *Violence and Childhood in the Inner City*. New York: Cambridge University Press.

McCord, J., ed. 1995/1998. *Coercion and Punishment in Long-term Perspectives*. New York: Cambridge University Press.

Wikstrom, P-O. H., R. V. Clarke, and J. McCord, eds. 1995. *Integrating Crime Prevention Strategies: Propensity and Opportunity*. Stockholm, Sweden: National Council for Crime Prevention.

McCord, J. and J. H. Laub, eds. 1995. *Contemporary Masters of Criminology*. New York: Plenum Press.

McCord, J. and R. E. Tremblay, eds. 1992. *Preventing Antisocial Behavior: Interventions from Birth through Adolescence*. New York: Guilford Press.

McCord, J., ed. 1992. *Facts, Frameworks, and Forecasts: Advances in Criminological Theory, Volume 3*. New Brunswick, N.J.: Transaction.

McCord, W. and J. McCord. 1964. *The Psychopath*. Princeton: Van Nostrand.

McCord, W. and J. McCord. 1960. *Origins of Alcoholism*. Stanford, Calif.: Stanford University Press.

McCord, W., J. McCord., and I. K. Zola. 1959. *Origins of Crime*. New York: Columbia University Press. Reprinted as No. 49: Patterson Smith Reprint Series in Criminology, Law Enforcement, and Social Problems. Montclair, N.J.: Patterson Smith, 1969. Paperback edition, 1972.

McCord, W. and J. McCord. 1956. *Psychopathy and Delinquency*. New York: Grune and Stratton.

Pamphlets Authored or Edited

McCord, J., C. S. Widom, M. I. Bamba, and N. A. Crowell, eds. 2000. *Education and Delinquency: Summary of a Workshop*. Washington, D.C.: National Academy Press.

Elliott, D., J. Hagan, and J. McCord. 1998. *Youth Violence: Children at Risk*. Washington, D.C.: American Sociological Association.

Forewords to Books

McCord, J. 1985. Causality and social theory. In *Stress and Stigma: Explanation and Evidence in the Sociology of Crime and Illness*, edited by U. E. Gerhardt and M. E. J. Wadsworth, 9–14. New York: St. Martin's Press.

McCord, J. 1979. Foreword to *Roots of Delinquency*, by M. E. J. Wadsworth, vii–ix. New York: Barnes and Noble.

Journal Articles and Chapters in Edited Books

McCord, J. 2005. Commentary: Aggression among females. In *The Development and Treatment of Girlhood Aggression*, edited by D. J. Pepler and K. Madsen, 285–288. Mahwah, N.J.: Lawrence Erlbaum Associates, Inc., Publishers.

McCord, J. 2004. Toward a theory of criminal responsibility. In *Beyond Empiricism: Institutions and Intentions in the Study of Crime*, edited by J. McCord, 147–176. Advances in Criminological Theory, Volume 13. Picataway, NJ: Transaction Publishers.

McCord, J. 2003 Cures that harm: unanticipated outcomes of crime prevention programs. *Annals of the American Academy of Political and Social Sciences* 587(May): 16–30.

McCord, J. and P. Ensminger. 2003. Racial discrimination and violence: a longitudinal perspective. In *Violent Crime: Assessing Race and Ethnic Differences*, edited by Darnell Hawkins, 319–330. New York: Cambridge University Press.

McCord, J. 2003. Juvenile Delinquency. In *The International Encyclopedia of Marriage and Family Relationships*, edited by J. J. Ponzetti, Jr., vol. II, 983–989. New York: Macmillan Reference USA.

McCord J. 2002. Forjar criminosos na família. In *Comportamento Anti-social e Família: Uma abordagem científica*, edited by A. C. Fonseca, 15–36. Coimbra: Livraria Almedina.

McCord, J. 2002. Counterproductive juvenile justice. *The Australian and New Zealand Journal of Criminology* 35(2): 230–237.

McCord, J. 2002. Learning how to learn and sequelae. In *Lessons of Criminology*, edited by G. Geis and M. Dodge, 95–108. Cincinnati, Ohio: Anderson Publishing Co.

Conway, K. P. and J. McCord. 2002. A longitudinal examination of the relation between co-offending with violent accomplices and violent crime. *Aggressive Behavior* 28(2): 97–108.

McCord, J. and K. P. Conway. 2002. Patterns of juvenile delinquency and co-offending. In *Crime and Social Organization: Advances in Criminological Theory*, edited by E. Waring and D. Weisburd, Vol. 10, 15–30. New Brunswick, N.J.: Transaction Publishers.

McCord, J. 2002. Family relationships and crime. In *Encyclopedia of Crime and Justice, Revised Edition*, Vol. 2, 677–684. New York: Macmillan Reference USA.

McCord, J. 2001. Psychosocial contributions to psychopathy and violence. In *Violence and Psychopathy*, edited by A. Raine and J. Sanmartin, 141–169. New York: Kluwer Academic/ Plenum Publishers.

McCord, J. 2001. Forging criminals in the family. In *Handbook of Law and Social Science: Youth and Justice*, edited by S. White, 223–235. New York: Plenum.

McCord, J. 2001. Alcohol and dangerousness. In *Clinical Assessment of Dangerousness: Empirical Contributions*, edited by G. F. Pinard and L. Pagani, 195–215. Cambridge, England: Cambridge University Press.

McCord, J. 2000. Contribuciones psicosociales a la violencia y la psicopatía, translated by Teresa Farnós. In *Violencia y psicopatía*, edited by Adrian Raine and José Sanmartín, 207–233. Barcelona, Spain: Ariel.

McCord, J. 2000. A theory of motivation and the life course. In *Social Dynamics of Crime and Control: New Theories for a World in Transition*, edited by Susanne Karstedt and Kai-D Bussmann, 229–241. Portland, Ore.: Hart Publishing.

McCord, J. 2000. Developmental trajectories and intentional actions. *Journal of Quantitative Criminology* 16(2): 237–253.

McCord, J. 2000. Longitudinal analysis: an introduction to the special issue. *Journal of Quantitative Criminology* 16(2): 113–115.

McCord, J. 1999. Intergenerational transmission of violence. In *Violence in America: An Encyclopedia,* edited by R. Gottesman, vol. 2, 174–177. Old Tappan, NJ: Scribner.

Dishion, T. J., J. McCord, and F. Poulin. 1999. When interventions harm: peer groups and problem behavior. *American Psychologist* 54(9): 1–10.

McCord, J. 1999. Understanding childhood and subsequent crime. *Aggressive Behavior* 25(4): 241–253.

McCord, J. 1999. Alcoholism and crime across generations. *Criminal Behaviour and Mental Health* 9: 107–117.

McCord, J. 1999. Crime: taking an historical perspective. In *Where and When: Historical and geographical aspects of psychopathology,* edited by P. Cohen, C. Slomkowski, and L. N. Robins, 17–35. Mahwah, NJ: Lawrence Erlbaum Associates.

McCord, J. 1999. Interventions: punishment, diversion, and alternative routes to crime prevention. In *The Handbook of Forensic Psychology, second edition,* edited by A. K. Hess and I. B. Weiner, 559–579. New York: Wiley.

McCord, J. 1998. Confounding factors and fictions of counting. *Colorado Law Review* 69(4): 927–944.

Crum, R. M., M. E. Ensminger, M. J. Ro, and J. McCord, J. 1998. The association of educational achievement and school dropout with risk of alcoholism: A 25-year prospective study of inner city children. *Journal of Studies on Alcohol* 59: 318–326.

McCord, J. 1998. Criminal behavior. In *Encyclopedia of Mental Health,* vol. 1, 635–642. San Diego, CA: Academic Press.

McCord, J. and M. E. Ensminger. 1997. Multiple risks and comorbidity in an African-American population. *Criminal Behaviour and Mental Health* 7: 339–354.

Ensminger, M. E., J. C. Anthony, and J. McCord. 1997. The inner city and drug use: initial findings from an epidemiologic study. *Drug and Alcohol Dependence* 48: 175–184.

McCord, J. 1997. He did it because he wanted to . . . In *Motivation and Delinquency,* edited by W. Osgood, vol. 44 in Nebraska Symposium on Motivation, 1–43. Lincoln, NE: University of Nebraska Press.

McCord, J. 1997. Discipline and the use of sanctions. *Aggression and Violent Behavior* 2(4): 313–319.

McCord, J. 1997. Placing American urban violence in context. In *Violence and Childhood in the Inner City,* edited by J. McCord, 78–115. New York: Cambridge Press.

McCord, J. 1997. On discipline. *Psychological Inquiry* 8(3): 215–217.

McCord, J. 1996 Considerations regarding biosocial foundations of personality and aggression. In *Understanding Aggressive Behavior in Children,* edited by C. F. Ferris and T. Grisso, vol. 794, Annals of the New York Academy of Sciences, Sept. 20, 253–256.

McCord, J. 1996. Unintended consequences of punishment. *Pediatrics Supplement* 98(4): 832–834.

McCord, J. 1996. Family as crucible for violence. *Journal of Family Psychology* 10(2): 147–152.

McCord, J. 1995. Juvenile delinquency. In *Encyclopedia of Marriage and the Family,* edited by D. Levinson, 413–416. New York: Macmillan.

Durning, P. J. and McCord. 1995. Attentes de rôles et représentations de la vie familiale des enfants et de leurs parents. Mise au point d'une série d'histoires à compléter. In *Education familiale, image de soi et compétences sociales,* edited by Y. Prêteur and M. de Léonardis, 151–165. Brussels: De Boeck Université.

McCord, J. 1995. Motivational crime prevention strategies and the role of opportunity. In *Integrating Crime Prevention Strategies: Propensity and Opportunity,* edited by P.-O. H. Wikstrom, R. V. Clarke, and J. McCord, 39–53. Stockholm: National Council for Crime Prevention.

McCord, J. 1995. Relationship between alcoholism and crime over the life course. In *Longitudinal Studies of Drugs, Crime and Other Deviant Adaptations*, edited by H. Kaplan 129–141. New York: Plenum.

McCord, J. 1995. Crime in the shadow of history. In *Current Perspectives on Aging and the Life Cycle: Delinquency and Disrepute in the Life Course*, edited by Hagan, 105–118. Greenwich, CT: JAI Press.

McCord, J. 1995. Ethnicity, acculturation, and opportunities: a study of two generations. In *Ethnicity, Race, and Crime: Perspectives Across Time and Place*, edited by D. F. Hawkins, 69–81. Albany: SUNY Press.

McCord, J., R. E. Tremblay, F. Vitaro, and L. Desmarais-Gervais. 1997. Boys' disruptive behavior, school adjustment, and delinquency: the montreal prevention experiment. *International Journal of Behavioral Development* 17(4): 739–752, 1994. Republished in *Offender Rehabilitation: Effective Correctional Intervention*, edited by F. T. Cullen and B. K. Applegate. Aldershot, UK.

McCord, J. 1994. Aggression in two generations. In *Aggressive Behavior: Current Perspectives*, edited by L. Rowell Huesmann, 241–251. New York: Plenum.

McCord, J. 1994. Inner city life: contributions to violence. In *Violence in Urban America: Mobilizing a Response*, edited by National Research Council and J.F. Kennedy School of Government, Harvard University, 100–104. Washington, D.C.: National Academy Press.

McCord, J. 1994. Resilience as a dispositional quality: some methodological points. In *Educational Resilience in Inner-City America: Challenges and Prospects*, edited by M. Wang and E. Gordon, 109–118. Hillsdale, NJ: Lawrence Erlbaum Associates.

McCord, J. 1994. Family socialization and antisocial behavior: searching for causal relationships in longitudinal research. In *Cross-National Longitudinal Research on Human Development and Criminal Behavior*, edited by E. G. M. Weitekamp and H-J Kerner, 177–188. Dordrecht, Netherlands: Kluwer.

McCord, J. 1994. Les rôles parentaux et leurs effets. In *Education et famille*, edited by P. Durning and J.-P. Pourtois, 81–89. Brussels: De Boeck-Wesmael.

McCord, J. 1993. Considerations of causes in alcohol-related violence. In *Research Monograph No. 24. Alcohol and Interpersonal Violence: Fostering Multidisciplinary Perspectives*, edited by S. Martin, 71–79. Rockville, MD: U.S. Department of Health and Human Services, NIH Publication No. 931-3496.

McCord, J. 1993. Crime, conscience, and family. In *The Socioeconomics of Crime and Justice*, edited by B. Forst, 65–87. New York: M.E. Sharpe.

McCord, J. 1993. Descriptions and predictions: three problems for the future of criminological research. *Journal of Research in Crime and Delinquency* 30(4): 413–426.

McCord, J. 1993. Conduct disorder and antisocial behavior: some thoughts about processes. *Development and Psychopathology* 5: 321–329.

McCord, J. 1993. Gender issues. In *Female Criminality: The State of the Art*, edited by C. Culliver, 105–118. New York: Garland Press.

McCord, J. 1992. Les effets d'un programme de prévention — Trente ans plus tard. In *Récidive et Réhabilitation*, edited by M. Killias, 107–112. Chur/Zürich, Switzerland: Verlag Rüegger AG.

McCord, J. 1992. Freedom of the press in a democracy. *International Annals of Criminology* 30(1, 2): 55–64.

McCord, J. 1992. The Cambridge-Somerville Study: a pioneering longitudinal experimental study of delinquency prevention. In *Preventing Antisocial Behavior: Interventions from Birth through Adolescence*, edited by J. McCord and R. E. Tremblay, 196–206. New York: Guilford Press.

McCord, J. 1992. Deterrence of domestic violence: a critical view of research. *Journal of Crime and Delinquency* 29(2): 229–239.

McCord, J. 1992. Another time, another drug. In *Vulnerability to Drug Abuse*, edited by M. Glantz and R. Pickens, 473–489. Washington, D.C.: American Psychological Association Press.

McCord, J. 1992. Understanding motivations: considering altruism and aggression. In *Facts, Frameworks, and Forecasts: Advances in Criminological Theory*, 3, edited by J. McCord, 115–135. New Brunswick, N.J.: Transaction.

McCord, J. and M. Jacobs. 1991. Response to Jim Hackler. In *Official Responses to Problem Juveniles: Some International Reflections*, edited by J. Hackler, 59–62. Oñati, Spain: International Institute for the Sociology of Law.

McCord, J. 1991. The long reach of childhood. *International Annals of Criminology* 29(1–2): 89–96.

McCord, J. 1991. Family relationships, juvenile delinquency, and adult criminality. *Criminology*, 29(3): 397–417. Republished in *Crime and Criminals: Contemporary and Classic Readings in Criminology*, edited by F. R. Scarpitti and A. L. Nielsen. Los Angeles, Calif.: Roxbury Publishing, 1999.

McCord, J. 1991. Competence in long-term perspective. *Psychiatry* 54(3): 227–237.

McCord, J. 1991. Questioning the value of punishment. *Social Problems* 38(2): 167–179. Republished in *Readings in General Psychology*, edited by L. Fernandez. Dubuque, Iowa: Kendall/Hunt, 2000.

McCord, J. 1991. The cycle of crime and socialization practices. *Journal of Criminal Law and Criminology* 82(1, Spring): 211–228.

Tremblay, R. E., J. McCord, H. Boileau, P. Charlebois, C. Gagnon, M. LeBlanc, and S. Larivée. 1991. Can disruptive boys be helped to become competent? *Psychiatry* 54(2): 148–161. Republished in *Canadian Delinquency*, edited by J. H. Creechan and R. A. Silverman. Scarborough, Ontario: Prentice Hall Canada Inc., 1995.

McCord, J. 1990. Problem behaviors. In *At the Threshold: The Developing Adolescent*, edited by S. S. Feldman and G. R. Elliott, 414–430, 602–614. Cambridge, MA: Harvard University Press.

McCord, J. 1990. Comments on 'Something that works in juvenile justice.' *Evaluation Review* 14(6, Dec.): 612–615.

Farrington, D. P., R. Loeber, D. S. Elliott, J. D. Hawkins, D. B. Kandel, M. W. Klein, J. McCord, D. C. Rowe, and R. E. Tremblay. 1990. Advancing knowledge about the onset of delinquency and crime. In *Advances in Clinical Child Psychology*, edited by B. B. Lahey and A. E. Kazdin, vol. 13, 283–342. New York: Plenum.

McCord, J. 1990. One perspective on the state of criminology. In *Advances in Criminological Theory*, edited by W. S. Laufer and F. Adler, vol. 2, 167–174. New Brunswick: Transaction.

McCord, J. 1990. Long-term perspectives on parental absence. In *Straight and Devious Pathways from Childhood to Adulthood*, edited by L. N. Robins and M. Rutter, 116–134. Cambridge: Cambridge University Press.

McCord, J. 1990. Crime in moral and social contexts. *Criminology* 28(1): 1–26. Republished in *Contemporary Masters of Criminology*, edited by J. McCord and J. H. Laub, 251–276. New York: Plenum Press, 1995.

McCord, J. 1989. Behandlingsforskning kräver utvärderingar ("A Plea for Experimental Designs"). *Apropa* 15(5): 9–15.

McCord, J. 1989. Theory, pseudotheory, and metatheory. In *Advances in Criminological Theory*, edited by W. S. Laufer and F. Adler, vol. 1, 127–145. New Brunswick N.J.: Transaction.

McCord, J. 1988. L'evaluation des Interventions: en Premier Lieu, Ne Pas Nuire. In *Education Familiale: Un panorama des recherches internationals*, edited and translated by P. Durning, 211–224. Vigneux: Matrice.

McCord, J. 1988. Parental aggressiveness and physical punishment in long-term perspective. In *Family Abuse and Its Consequences: New Directions in Research*, edited by G. T. Hotaling, D. Finkelhor, J. T. Kirkpatrick, and M. A. Straus, 91–98. Beverly Hills, Calif.: Sage.

McCord, J. 1988. Identifying developmental paradigms leading to alcoholism. *Journal of Studies on Alcohol* 49(4): 357–362. Republished in *Society, Culture, and Drinking Patterns Reexamined*, edited by D. J. Pittman and H. R. White, 480–491. Piscataway, N.J.: Center of Alcohol Studies, 1991.

McCord, J. 1988. Alcoholism: toward understanding genetic and social factors. *Psychiatry* 51(2): 131–141.

McCord, J. 1988. Changing times. *The Criminologist*, 13(1), 2(5–7). Republished in *Sociology: Fourth Edition*, edited by J. E. Farley, 30-31, 1998. Revised and republished in *Sociology: Fifth Edition*, edited by J. E. Farley, 30–31, 2003.

McCord, J. 1988. Parental behavior in the cycle of aggression. *Psychiatry* 51(1): 14–23. Translated and republished as *Le Comportement des parents dans le cycle de l'agression* in *Famille: Inadaptation et intervention*, edited by M. A. Provost and R. E. Tremblay, 87–105. Ottowa: Agence d'Arc, 1991.

McCord, J. 1987. Intervention as prevention. In *Handbook of Forensic Psychology*, edited by A. K. Hess and I. B. Weiner, 584–601. New York: Wiley.

McCord, J. 1986. Review essay: understanding and controlling crime: toward a new research strategy by D. P. Farrington, L. E. Ohlin, and J. Q. Wilson. *Criminology* 24(4): 799–808.

McCord, J. 1986. Instigation and insulation: family and later criminal behavior. In *Development of Antisocial and Prosocial Behavior*, edited by J. Block, D. Olweus, and M. R. Yarrow, 343–357. New York: Academic Press.

McCord, J. 1986. Computing: is it a better mousetrap? *Behavior Research Methods, Instruments and Computers* 18(2): 210–213.

McCord, J. 1985. Deterrence and the light touch of the law. In *Reactions to Crime: the Public, the Police, Courts, and Prisons*, edited by D. P. Farrington and J. Gunn, 73–85. Chichester, England: Wiley.

McCord, J. 1985. Faculty responses to the computerization of a university. *Computers and the Social Sciences* 1(3/4): 173–179.

McCord, J. and M. E. J. Wadsworth. 1985. The importance of time in stress and stigma paradigms. In *Stress and Stigma: Explanation and Evidence in the Sociology of Crime and Illness*, edited by U. E. Gerhardt and M. E. J. Wadsworth, 53–64. New York: St. Martin's Press.

McCord, J. 1984. Early stress and future personality. In *Stress and Disability in Childhood*, edited by N. R. Butler and B. D. Corner, 105–112. Bristol, England: John Wright.

McCord, J. 1984. A longitudinal study of personality development. In *Handbook of Longitudinal Research, vol. 2, Teenage and Adult Cohorts*, edited by S. A. Mednick, M. Harway, and K. M. Finello, 522–531. New York: Praeger.

McCord, J. 1984. Drunken drivers in longitudinal perspective. *Journal of Studies on Alcohol* 45(4): 316–320.

McCord, J. 1983. Family relationships and crime. In *Encyclopedia of Crime and Justice*, edited by S. H. Kadish, vol. 2, 759–764. New York: The Free Press.

McCord, J. 1983. A forty year perspective on effects of child abuse and neglect. *Child Abuse and Neglect* 7: 265–270.

McCord, J. 1983. A longitudinal study of aggression and antisocial behavior. In *Prospective Studies of Crime and Delinquency*, edited by K. T. Van Dusen and S. A. Mednick, 269–275. Boston: Kluwer-Nijhoff.

McCord, J. 1983. Alcohol in the service of aggression. In *Alcohol, Drug Abuse, and Aggression*, edited by E. Gottheil, K. E. Druley, T. E. Skolada, and H. M. Waxman, 270–279. Springfield, Ill.: Charles C. Thomas.

McCord, J. 1983. The psychopath and moral development. In *Personality Theory, Moral Development, and Criminal Behavior*, edited by W. S. Laufer and J. M. Day, 357–372. Lexington, Mass.: D.C. Heath.

McCord, J. and L. Otten. 1983. A consideration of sex roles and motivations for crime. *Criminal Justice and Behavior* 10(1): 3–12.

McCord, J. 1982. The Cambridge-Somerville Youth Study: a sobering lesson on treatment, prevention, and evaluation. In *Practical Program Evaluation for Youth Treatment*, edited by A. J. McSweeny, W. J. Fremouw, and R. P. Hawkins, 11–23. Springfield, Ill.: Charles C. Thomas.

McCord, J. 1982. A longitudinal view of the relationship between paternal absence and crime. In *Abnormal Offenders, Delinquency and the Criminal Justice System*, edited by J. Gunn and D. P. Farrington, 113–128. Chichester, England: Wiley.

McCord, J. 1981. A longitudinal perspective on alcoholism. In *Matching Patient Needs and Treatment Methods in Alcoholism and Drug Abuse*, edited by E. Gottheil, A. T. McLellan, and K. A. Druley, 105–113. Springfield, Ill.: Charles C. Thomas.

McCord, J. 1981. Alcoholism and criminality: Confounding and differentiating factors. *Journal of Studies on Alcohol* 42(9): 739–748.

McCord, J. 1981. A longitudinal perspective on patterns of crime. *Criminology* 19(2): 211–218.

McCord, J. 1981. Consideration of some effects of a counseling program. In *New Directions in the Rehabilitation of Criminal Offenders*, edited by S. E. Martin, L. B. Sechrest, and R. Redner, 394–405. Washington, D. C.: The National Academy of Sciences.

McCord, J. 1980. Patterns of deviance. In *Human Functioning in Longitudinal Perspective: Studies of Normal and Psychopathological Populations*, edited by S. B. Sells, R. Crandall, M. Roff, J. Strauss, and W. Pollin, 157–167. Baltimore: Williams and Wilkins.

McCord, J. 1980. The treatment that did not help. *Social Action and the Law* 5(6): 85–87.

McCord, J. 1979. Some child-rearing antecedents of criminal behavior in adult men. *Journal of Personality and Social Psychology* 37(9): 1477–1486. Reprinted in *Criminology Review Yearbook*, edited by S. Messinger and E. Bittner, vol. 2. Beverly Hills, California: Sage, 1980. Reprinted in *Psychological Explanations of Crime*, edited by D. P. Farrington. Aldershot, England: Dartmouth. 1994.

McCord, J. 1978. A thirty-year follow-up of treatment effects. *American Psychologist* 33(3): 284–289. Reprinted in *Evaluation Studies Review Annual*, edited by L. Sechrest, S. G. West, M. Phillips, R. Redner, and W. Yeaton, vol. 4. Beverly Hills, Calif.: Sage, 1979. In *Criminology Review Yearbook*, edited by S. Messinger and E. Bittner, vol. 1. Beverly Hills, Calif.: Sage, 1979. In *Juvenile Delinquency Readings*, edited by J. G. Weis, R. D. Crutchfield, and G. S. Bridges. Boston, Mass., Pine Forge Press, 2001.

McCord, J. 1977. A comparative study of two generations of native Americans. In *Theoretical Concerns in Criminology*, edited by R. F. Meier, 83–92. Beverly Hills, Calif.: Sage.

McCord, J. 1972. Etiological factors in alcoholism: Family and personal characteristics. *Quarterly Journal of Studies on Alcohol* 33(4): 1020–1027.

McCord, J. 1972. Some differences in backgrounds of alcoholics and criminals. In *Nature and Nurture in Alcoholism*, edited by F. A. Seixas, G. S. Omenn, E. D. Burk, and S. Eggleston, 183–187. New York: New York Academy of Science, vol. 197, May.

McCord, J. and S. Clemens. 1964. Conscience orientation and dimensions of personality. *Behavioral Science* 9(1): 18–29.

McCord, J., W. McCord, and A. Howard. 1963. Family interaction as antecedent to the direction of male aggressiveness. *Journal of Abnormal and Social Psychology* 67(1): 239–242. Reprinted in *Contemporary Research in Social Psychology*, Edited by H. C. Lindgren. New York: Wiley, 1973.

McCord, J., W. McCord, and E. Thurber. 1963. The effects of maternal employment on lower class boys. *Journal of Abnormal and Social Psychology* 67(1): 177–182. Reprinted in *Bobbs-Merrill Reprint Series in the Social Sciences*, P-510. Reprinted in *VIP Readings in Psychology*. Lexington, Mass.: Xerox Publishing Co., 1975.

McCord, W. and J. McCord. 1963. A longitudinal study of the personality of alcoholics." In *Society, Culture, and Drinking Patterns*, edited by D. Pittman and C. Snyder, 413–430. New York: Wiley, 1963.

McCord, W., J. McCord, and P. Verden. 1962. Family relationships and sexual deviance in lower-class adolescents. *The International Journal of Social Psychiatry* 8(3): 165–179.

McCord, W., J. Porta, and J. McCord. 1962. The family genesis of psychosis: A study of the childhood backgrounds of twelve psychotics. *Psychiatry* 25(1): 60–71.

McCord, J., W. McCord, and E. Thurber. 1962. Some effects of paternal absence on male children. *Journal of Abnormal and Social Psychology* 64(5): 361–369. Republished in *Studies in Adolescence*, edited by R. Grinder. New York: Macmillan, 1963. Republished in *Educational Psychological Reprint Series*, edited by R. Youtz. Bergenfield, N.J.: Beaver Island Publishing Co., 1968.

McCord, J. and W. McCord. 1962. Cultural stereotypes and the validity of interviews for research in child development. *Child Development* 32(2): 171–185.

McCord, W., J. McCord, and A. Howard. 1961. Familial correlates of aggression in nondelinquent male children. *Journal of Abnormal and Social Psychology* 62(1): 79–93. Reprinted in *Bobbs-Merrill Reprint Series in the Social Sciences*, P–511.

McCord, W. and J. McCord. 1960. A tentative theory of the structure of conscience. In *Decisions, Values, and Groups*, edited by D. Willner. New York: Pergamon, 1960.

McCord, J., W. McCord, and E. Thurber. 1960. The effects of foster home placement in the prevention of adult anti-social behavior. *Social Service Review* 34(4): 415–420. Reprinted in *Cases and Material on Family Law*, edited by R. J. Levy. Boston: Little, Brown, 1975.

McCord, W. and J. McCord. 1960. Some contemporary theories of alcoholism. *Quarterly Journal of Studies in Alcohol* 20(4): 727–749.

McCord, W., J. McCord, and P. Verden. 1960. Familial correlates of 'psychosomatic' symptoms in male children. *Journal of Health and Human Behavior* 1(Fall): 192–199.

McCord, W., J. McCord, and A. Howard. 1960. Early familial experiences and bigotry. *American Sociological Review* 25(5): 717–722. Reprinted in *Race and Ethnicity*, edited by P. L. van den Berghe. New York: Basic Books, 1970.

McCord, W. and J. McCord. 1959. The intellectual in American society. *Educational Horizons* 37(4): 127–134.

McCord, J. and W. McCord. 1959. A follow-up report on the Cambridge-Somerville Youth Study. *Annals of the American Academy of Political and Social Science* 32(2): 89–96. Reprinted in *Delinquency*, edited by J. W. Barth. Boston: Allyn and Bacon, 1974.

McCord, J. and W. McCord. 1958. The effects of parental role model on criminality. *Journal of Social Issues* 14(3): 66–75. Reprinted in *Perspectives in Crime and Delinquency: A Sociological Reader*, edited by D. R. Cressey and D. Ward. New York: Harper and Row, 1967. Reprinted in *Personality and Social Systems*, edited by N. J. Smelser and W. T. Smelser. New York: Wiley, 1970. Reprinted in *Readings in Juvenile Delinquency*, edited by R. Caven. Philadelphia: Lippincott, 1975. Reprinted in *Wege der Forshung*, edited by P. Kornadt. Darmstadt: Wissenschafliche Buchgesellschaft, 1975.

McCord, W. and J. McCord. 1953. Two approaches to the cure of delinquents. *Journal of Criminal Law, Criminology and Police Science* 44(4): 442–467.

Book Reviews and Miscellaneous Publications

McCord, J. Crime prevention: a cautionary tale. *Evidence-Based Policies and Indicator Systems* (pp. 186–192). Conference Proceedings, University of Durham, England, July, 2001 (published Autumn, 2002).

Boruch, R., M. Bullock, D. Cheek, H. Cooper, P. Davies, J. McCord, H. Soydan, H. Thomas, and D. de Moya, C2 Steering Group and Secretariat. The Campbell Collaboration: Concept, Status, and Plans. *Evidence-Based Policies and Indicator Systems* (pp. 45–72). Conference Proceedings, University of Durham, England, July, 2001 (published Autumn, 2002).

McCord, J. and C. S. Widom. May 25, 2001. A Better Way to Handle Juvenile Offenders. *National Academies Op-Ed Service Archive*.

McCord, J. 1998. Review of *Race in the Hood*, by H. Pinderhughes. *Social Forces* 77: 385–386.

McCord, J. 1998. Review of *The APSAC Handbook on Child Maltreatment*, edited by J. N. Briere, L. Berliner, J. A. Bulkley, C. Jenny, and T. Reid. *Criminal Behavior and Mental Health* 8(2): 159–160.

McCord, J. 1997. Review of *Witnessing for Sociology*, edited by P. J. Jenkins and S. Kroll-Smith. *American Journal of Sociology* 102(5): 1506–1507.

McCord, J. 1994. Crimes through time. Review of *Crime in the Making: Pathways and Turning Points through Life*, by R. J. Samson and J. H. Laub. *Contemporary Sociology* 23(3): 414–415.

McCord, J. Review of *Policing Domestic Violence: Experiments and Dilemmas*, by L. W. Sherman. *The Criminologist* 18(5): 15.

McCord, J. 1991. Review of *Parent-Adolescent Relationships*, edited by B. K. Barber and B. C. Rollins. *Contemporary Sociology* 20(2): 305–306.

McCord, J. 1989. Courts as crucible. Review of *From Children to Citizens: The Role of the Juvenile Court*, edited by F. X. Hartmann. *Contemporary Psychology* 34(2): 117–118.

McCord, J. 1987. Review of *Institutional Settings in Children's Lives*, by L. G. Rivlin and M. Wolfe. *Child Development Review* 61(1): 105–106.

McCord, J. 1983. No wine in new bottles. Review of *Drinking and Crime: Perspectives on the Relationship between Alcohol Consumption and Criminal Behavior*, edited by J. J. Collins, Jr. *Contemporary Psychology* 28(2): 148–149.

McCord, J. 1983. Review of *Women Who Embezzle or Defraud: A Study of Convicted Felons*, by D. Zeitz. *Contemporary Sociology* 12(1): 58.

McCord, J. 1982. Review of *Deviant Behavior in Defense of Self*, by H. B. Kaplan. *American Journal of Sociology* 87(5): 1236–1237.

McCord, J. 1980. Fibber McGee's closet. Review of *The Psychological World of the Delinquent*, by D. Offer, R. Marohn, and E. Ostrov. *Contemporary Psychology* 25(1): 58–59.

McCord, J. 1978. Review of *The Delinquent Way of Life*, by D. J. West and D. P. Farrington. *Journal of Criminal Law and Criminology* 69 (2): 261–263.

INDEX